Thomas Aquinas and Karl Barth

Thomas Aquinas and Karl Barth

An Unofficial Catholic-Protestant Dialogue

Edited by

Bruce L. McCormack and Thomas Joseph White, O.P.

WILLIAM B. EERDMANS PUBLISHING COMPANY
GRAND RAPIDS, MICHIGAN / CAMBRIDGE, U.K.

Wm. B. Eerdmans Publishing Co.
2140 Oak Industrial Drive N.E., Grand Rapids, Michigan 49505 /
P.O. Box 163, Cambridge CB3 9PU U.K.

Printed in the United States of America

19 18 17 16 15 14 13   7 6 5 4 3 2 1

Library of Congress Cataloging-in-Publication Data

Thomas Aquinas and Karl Barth: an unofficial Catholic-Protestant dialogue /
    edited by Bruce L. McCormack and Thomas Joseph White, O.P.
        pages   cm
    Includes bibliographical references and index.
    ISBN 978-0-8028-6976-0 (pbk.: alk. paper)
    1. Thomas, Aquinas, Saint, 1225?-1274.   2. Barth, Karl, 1886-1968.
    3. Catholic Church — Doctrines.   4. Protestant churches — Doctrines.
    5. Catholic Church — Relations — Protestant churches.
    6. Protestant churches — Relations — Catholic Church.
    I. McCormack, Bruce L., editor of compilation.

    BX891.3T46   2013
    230'.044092 — dc23

                                                          2013009747

www.eerdmans.com

Contents

Contents

Preface

The essays in this book stem originally from a conference at Princeton Theological Seminary June 19-22, 2011. The editors would like to thank that institution for its hospitality and generosity in hosting this event. A special word of thanks is in order to the Center for Barth Studies. In addition, the event was co-sponsored by the Pontifical Faculty of the Immaculate Conception in Washington, D.C., with the support of Fr. Steven Boguslawski, O.P., and Fr. Gabriel O'Donnell, O.P.

Special thanks for this project should go to Adam Eitel and Matthew Bruce, both doctoral candidates at Princeton Theological Seminary. It was in large part due to their initiative that this project was conceived and carried out. Adam contributed greatly to the concrete planning of the original conference. Matthew helped immensely in the editing of the text of this volume, and in the preparation of the Bibliography. The love of theology that inspires both of them is palpable, and it has helped give rise to the discussions in this volume.

We would like to thank also the many people at Eerdmans who have made this project possible, not least Bill Eerdmans Jr. himself, Linda Bieze, and their editing staff. It has been a privilege to work with them.

This collection of essays represents the efforts of theologians to compare and contrast two auspicious theological thinkers. Comparative reflection on the thought of Aquinas and Barth is no mean task. We would be remiss if we did not thank above all the contributors to this volume. Their great efforts have produced a book that contributes in an important way to deeper understanding of the thought of Aquinas and Barth. Their essays also make a genuine contribution to the work of contemporary theology and they are a model of honest, profound, and charitable ecumenical dialogue among Christians. We hope these essays, then, can serve as an example of the exercise of seeking of truth in theological discussion, wherever it is to be found. May they also help to indicate the irreplaceable resources that exist in the work of traditional Christian thinkers such as Aquinas and Barth. They are sources of true intellectual life and help even now, and especially now, to illumine the world with the light of Christ.

Bruce L. McCormack
Thomas Joseph White, O.P.
Easter, 2012

Introduction: Thomas Aquinas and Karl Barth — An Unofficial Catholic-Protestant Dialogue

Thomas Joseph White, O.P.

Why compare Aquinas and Barth theologically?

In a 1929 essay, T. S. Eliot wrote that "Dante and Shakespeare divide the modern world between them, there is no third."[1] This statement, while inherently controversial, is intelligible. It suggests there is to the literature of these two authors a scope, depth, and brilliance that exceeds the work of all others. They alone each realize in a unique way the plenitude of the art of poetic literature. Is Dante a greater writer than Tolstoy? Perhaps. But is he more modern? There are reasons one might argue in the affirmative. Dante wrote in the vernacular and his fascination with Greco-Roman antiquity prefigures the humanism of the Renaissance. He addressed his culture not with the authority of a cleric, or by writing theology, but as a layman writing poetry. Most especially, he tried to articulate in synthetic presentation a beautiful "narrative of the whole." This narrative aspires to a study of the objective meaning of all things, but unfolds from within the vantage point of a given human subjectivity. The protagonist's own narrative opens up to the stories of other human beings and their developmental becoming, portraying the unfolding of reality as a divine and human drama ultimately composed by God. So while Dante treats in earnest the subjects

---

1. T. S. Eliot, "Dante," in *Selected Essays, 1917-1932* (Boston: Houghton Mifflin, 1950), p. 225.

Bruce L. McCormack, the coeditor of this volume, has kindly read this introduction carefully and made comments. The argument is ultimately my own, but I would like to thank him for his critical and helpful contribution to its formulation.

I

of heaven, purgatory, and hell, he is simultaneously exploring a vision of the theological resolution of the tensions inherent in historical human existence, tensions that haunt modern human beings, and that are otherwise illustrated by the work of the English Bard: those between philosophy and faith, virtue and vice, artistic and physical beauty, politics and justice, and the sorrows of this life in relation to hope in the life to come. Indeed, Dante might even rival Shakespeare as a typically modern interpreter of the sense of human existence, as no one can say lightly that his Virgil or Beatrice teaches us less about what it means to be human than does Hamlet or Cordelia. On this reading, however, that which is most modern is that which is also perennially insightful and profound, but timeless in a way that is accessible also to our epoch.

How does such an excursus help us to answer our opening question? We are suggesting a transposition by analogy, of course, from literature to the domain of theology, from Dante and Shakespeare to Aquinas and Barth. For these latter two are, arguably, the greatest proponents of Christian theology of a traditional form that might viably thrive in a modern context. In that sense, each one is indicative of a certain kind of orthodox Christianity that can speak to the heart of the contemporary world. One might argue that this is just as true of Aquinas as of Barth, just as Barth can arguably be presented, for all his modern influences, as a traditional thinker who is attempting to uncover anew the essential, perennially viable principles of Christian doctrine.

Evidently, one can present other Christian thinkers as candidates for orthodox *ressourcement* in a contemporary context: Maximus the Confessor, Calvin, Bonaventure, Augustine, just to name a few. Why privilege the use of these two thinkers, then, in an ecumenical context, and for the purposes of Catholic-Protestant dialogue? In his book *Three Rival Versions of Moral Enquiry,* Alasdair MacIntyre notes rightfully that intellectual arguments are maintained down through time within living traditions of thought, as in the case of, say, Platonism, Thomism, Utilitarianism, or Kantian liberalism.[2] Of course, such traditions present viable explanations of reality because they offer principles for the interpretation of our common experience. But they also do so because they develop their own explanations in competition with alternative historical rivals, through a gradual process of dialectical interaction. To de-

---

2. Alasdair MacIntyre, *Three Rival Versions of Moral Enquiry: Encyclopaedia, Genealogy, and Tradition* (Notre Dame: Notre Dame University Press, 1991).

velop organically, an intellectual tradition must dialectically "out-explain" the truths and falsehoods of rival understandings of reality, while continually presenting anew the truth of its own inner principles, making them perennially plausible in new and challenging contexts.

By these standards, Aquinas and Barth both present us with formidable examples of intellectual achievement. Aquinas, for instance, managed to rethink the patrimony of medieval Augustinianism in dialogue with Aristotelian philosophy and epistemology. He did so as a commentator on Scripture and a biblical theologian, even while assimilating insights from Dionysius, Seneca, Proclus, and the Church fathers. The principles of theology and philosophy he articulated have been elaborated down through time by the Thomist tradition, in complex and enduring ways, including in dialogue with the development of the modern sciences, modern philosophy, and historical-critical exegesis.[3] Thomism as a living form of thought continues to develop, then, even at the heart of modernity. For all its modest effect on the culture at large, it is in truth a formidable intellectual tradition.

Barth, meanwhile, clearly understood himself as a kind of re-founder of the Protestant confessional tradition in the modern world. His interpretations of Luther and Calvin are based on an attempt to discern what is at the core of the Reformed doctrinal tradition, transposing these principles into a new key. Most notably, Barth was concerned to respond dialogically and critically to the heritage of liberal Protestantism, even as he was ever aware of the strident challenges of secular modernity, in its philosophical, scientific, and political-economic forms. Nor did he remain content simply to engage critically the post-Reformation intellectual traditions, but was susceptible to a catholic range of ancient influences as well, from the Greek and Latin patristic traditions to a limited but real engagement with the medieval scholastic heritage. There can be no controversy in saying that Barth is one of the greatest, if not the greatest, of Protestant thinkers, and that his vision of theology remains a privileged, if not the privileged, intellectual paradigm of this tradition in a contemporary context. When we see Barth's great influence upon thinkers such as Eberhard Jüngel, Wolfhart Pannenberg, and Robert Jenson, but also Hans Urs von Bal-

---

3. Consider as a single example the work of Benedict Ashley, *The Way toward Wisdom: An Interdisciplinary and Intercultural Introduction to Metaphysics* (Notre Dame: University of Notre Dame Press, 2006).

3

thasar and Walter Kasper, it is not unreasonable to speak (in broad terms at least) about a Barthian tradition.

One can rightfully set Thomism and Barthianism in fruitful ecumenical conversation, then, because each offers us a profound vision of reality understood theologically in light of Jesus Christ. The principles of each have attained an intense degree of intellectual universality through conversation with a complex flux of competing voices and explanations. And at the same time, each of these traditions is rooted firmly in a confessional tradition. For Aquinas sees himself no less as a biblical theologian than Barth, but he also thinks that the Catholic tradition and official doctrinal heritage are essential to an understanding of the faithful and ecclesiastical interpretation of Scripture. Speaking of the Creed, he writes:

> . . . a new edition of the symbol becomes necessary in order to set aside the errors that may arise. Consequently to publish a new edition of the symbol belongs to that authority which is empowered to decide matters of faith finally, so that they may be held by all with unshaken faith. Now this belongs to the authority of the Sovereign Pontiff, "to whom the more important and more difficult questions that arise in the Church are referred," as stated in the Decretals [Dist. xvii, Can. 5]. Hence our Lord said to Peter whom he made Sovereign Pontiff (Luke 22:32): "I have prayed for thee," Peter, "that thy faith fail not, and thou, being once converted, confirm thy brethren." The reason of this is that there should be but one faith of the whole Church, according to 1 Corinthians 1:10: "That you all speak the same thing, and that there be no schisms among you"; and this could not be secured unless any question of faith that may arise be decided by him who presides over the whole Church, so that the whole Church may hold firmly to his decision. Consequently it belongs to the sole authority of the Sovereign Pontiff to publish a new edition of the symbol, as do all other matters which concern the whole Church, such as to convoke a general council and so forth.[4]

Barth does not dismiss this scriptural claim of Catholic Christians by way of a modern liberal or glibly latitudinarian distrust of religious au-

---

4. *ST* II-II, q. 1, a. 10. (All citations of the *ST,* unless otherwise noted, are taken from the 1920 translation by the English Dominican Province, *Summa Theologica* [New York: Benziger, 1947].)

thority, one that would refuse claims to divine revelation more generally. On the contrary, he shows great intellectual respect and interest in the challenge and promise of such Catholic doctrine.[5] He thus engages such claims critically but seriously, and believes that he has reasons to demur from the authority of the Catholic tradition on grounds that are themselves strictly theological. Revelation is grounded in the event of Jesus Christ. It is mediated in a unique way by Scripture alone, and it is appropriated by the Church in ways that are ever open to eschatological correction.

> As a Church authority the authority of the confession [of creedal statements] cannot be an absolute but only a relative one. The infallible and therefore final and unalterable confession is the praise which the Church as the body eternally united to its Head will offer to its Lord in this its own eternal consummation. . . . Here the ways of Roman Catholic and Evangelical doctrine obviously diverge. . . . Dogma in the Evangelical sense is the Church counter-witness to this witness of revelation. This means there can never be a final word, but only a word which is imperative and binding and authoritative until it is succeeded by something else. The Church confesses, and it also appropriates earlier and other confessions. But even as it does so, it remains open to the possibility that it may be better instructed by the Word of God, that it may know it better and therefore confess it better. In its confessing it has always before it the *eschaton* of the praise of God in its consummation. . . . Indirectly even the Roman Catholic Church has recognized this. It does not admit any perfectibility of dogma, but it does admit a perfectibility of the Church proclamation of dogma. And this is confirmed in its history and practice in which there are obviously dated and antiquated and corrected dogmas and also those which are new and obviously clearer and more definite.[6]

5. See most notably his discussion of the Catholic magisterium and his comments on the Vatican I declaration of papal infallibility in *CD* I/2, pp. 546-72, especially pp. 567-59. (All citations of the *CD* are from the translation edited by Bromiley and Torrance, *Church Dogmatics*, 4 vols. in 13 parts [Edinburgh: T. & T. Clark, 2000 (1936-75)].) Barth is critically aware that he is writing as a Reformed theologian, whose views on this subject matter touch intimately also upon the relations of the Reformed and Lutheran traditions, which differ on the relative weight that might be given to conciliar decrees.

6. *CD* I/2, pp. 657, 659.

In choosing to place the traditions of Aquinas and Barth in dialogue, then, we are not choosing an overly complacent or irenic form of ecumenism! The first principles that each adopts are in part truly representative of longstanding points of dispute between Catholics and Protestants. Precisely for that reason, however, these two traditions which are quite cosmopolitan in themselves can profit from interaction with the doctrinal alterity of one another. The point is not to create a new synthesis (though some have tried, as we shall note below). Rather, the idea is to challenge ourselves to think about our confessional commitments at a more profound level theologically, and to think about our theology in a truly confessional way, so that tradition is not set aside too lightly. The presupposition of this form of ecumenical dialogue is at once simultaneously "convergent" and "relational." That is to say, the goal is to underscore both the real places of ongoing difference between the Roman and Reformed traditions, even while identifying points of agreement, or at least areas of potential doctrinal confluence. The attempt to overcome mutual misunderstanding or to rearticulate doctrines in ways that allow both parties to find common agreement must pass through the honest exposition of integral doctrinal concerns and commitments, and even places of outlying intellectual conflict. What binds such an enterprise together in unity? A common faith in Jesus Christ, a common aspiration to true Christian charity, and a common desire to discover honestly the fullness of the truth. That is enough to create a dialogue!

In what follows below, we will introduce the comparison of the theology of Aquinas and Barth (as well as their contemporary disciples) by considering briefly three distinct topics: (1) How do Aquinas and Barth each approach theology considered as a science of divine revelation? (2) Why is Christology the core organizing principle of Barthian theology, while Trinitarian monotheism is central to Thomism? (3) How might Thomists and Barthians discuss the status of theology in modernity? Does modern Christian theology rightly aspire to be postmetaphysical, or is it the discipline *par excellence* that calls forth the recovery of ontological thinking, subordinate to and in the service of Scripture? A consideration of these questions serves as a helpful initiation to the aspirations of this volume.

The Primacy of Revelation and the Unity of Knowledge: Thomist and Barthian Versions of This Claim

Aquinas and Barth both construe theology as a science, and each is concerned with the unifying role theology plays with regard to all other forms of discourse. Each, however, pursues this task in a different context and in differing ways. Aquinas composed theology, of course, just as the institution of the medieval university was coming to maturity, and in the midst of the epistemological crisis generated by the Latin translation of the Aristotelian corpus. A central concern in this context was raised by the *Posterior Analytics,* with its definition of science based on the subject studied.[7] A science is defined by the knowledge of a given topic and that topic is considered according to its causes.[8] What, then, is the status of sacred theology as a science? What is its subject matter? How does it compare to the natural forms of study promoted within philosophy, mathematics, and logic, as well as the observational sciences and the practical arts? At the heart of this question is also the issue of the unity of the university as a culture, both academic and ecclesial. What is it that binds all of the distinct disciplines of the university together? Can theology give architectonic unity to the multiplicity of secular and philosophical disciplines?

Aquinas famously offers original and powerful answers to these questions. He characterizes theology first and foremost as *sacra doctrina:* divine teaching. That is to say, the science of revelation takes its starting points from the divine revelation, which has God the Holy Trinity as its subject of knowledge. God reveals himself in Holy Scripture as understood and explicated within ecclesial tradition, and this forms the basis of our science about God.[9] Christian theology is rooted in divine revelation and seeks to understand who God is in himself.[10]

However, Aquinas simultaneously makes two crucial qualifications. First, the "divine teaching" given to the Church is not one that

7. On the way this problem was raised in the medieval university, see Ulrich G. Leinsle, *Introduction to Scholastic Theology,* trans. M. J. Miller (Washington, DC: Catholic University of America Press, 2010), pp. 120-81.

8. Aristotle, *Posterior Analytics* I, 27-28 (87a31-87b5).

9. *ST* I, q. 1, aa. 2-3. See James Weisheipl, "The Meaning of *Sacra Doctrina* in *Summa theologiae* I, q. 1," *The Thomist* 38 (1974): 49-80; Adriano Oliva, *Les débuts de l'enseignement de Thomas d'Aquin et sa conception de la Sacra Doctrina* (Paris: Vrin, 2006).

10. *ST* I, q. 1, a. 7; II-II, q. 1, a. 1.

allows us to grasp God immediately by way of vision, but is itself received in faith. Just in that respect then it is a knowledge *in via,* on the way toward the final end of faith, the beatific vision of God. Because of the continuity between revelation-in-the-faith now and the vision of God that is to come, *sacra doctrina* is a true science of God, but it is a subalternate science, a foreshadowing in faith of the knowledge *(scientia)* that God has of himself, and that the blessed possess in heaven.[11] Just as Aristotle claims that the scientific precision of music theory (the science of harmonics) is subalternate to principles derived from mathematics, so by proportionate analogy, the science of *sacra doctrina* in this life is subalternate to the science of God in the next. Thus theology is inherently open to eschatological fulfillment.

Second, though, *sacra doctrina,* for all its imperfection, is still able to subordinate other lesser sciences to itself. This "subordination" should not be confused with subalternation. A subalternate science receives its principles from another: there is not a distinctly musical form of mathematics and there is not true Christian theology derived from something other than the knowledge God has of himself. Subordination, meanwhile, presumes a relative autonomy or distinction of principles proper to distinct sciences. Mathematics cannot be equated with logic, nor metaphysical philosophy with biology. Some of these irreducibly distinct sciences can, however, subordinate others to themselves, not by imperial domination, but by respectful examination "from a higher plane." So metaphysics (the study of being) can examine the ontological status of biological realities, or mathematic numbers. This does not mean it imposes its procedures onto them, but on the contrary, requires that it respect their distinctive principles and conclusions. One can ask, for example, do numbers exist in reality apart from matter as Plato thought, or are they grasped in separation from concrete quantities only by abstraction, as Aristotle thought? This is a distinctly metaphysical question. Biology, likewise, can examine a living body in such a way as to take account of the truths of physics and chemistry, while still looking at that which is specific to the *living* organic body as such.

Aquinas argues that theology is subalternate to the knowledge God has of himself and that he reveals to us, but that theology subordi-

---

11. *ST* I, q. 1, a. 2. The notion of a subalternate science is taken from *Post. Analytics* I, 7 (75a38-b20).

nates the other, lesser forms of analysis to itself.[12] That is to say, it respects the proper principles and conclusions of logic, mathematics, observational sciences, metaphysics, and so on, but it also is able to bring a higher and deeper causal explanation to bear on all that is found within the realm of creation, and therefore within this realm of natural learning.

This project of Aquinas is sometimes seen as one that gives overly assertive status to philosophy (Aristotle's philosophy in particular) and that subdivides or even separates the realms of theology and philosophy artificially. This is a possible interpretation of Aquinas, but it is on many fronts also a very dubious one. For if there is one guiding concern that becomes manifest in works like the *Summa contra gentiles* and especially the *Summa theologiae,* it is that of the unity of all things seen in light of God's revealed wisdom. The assimilative power of theology to natural learning is respectful, but is also real. The first question of the *Summa theologiae,* then, seeks to pose the basis for a thoroughgoing Trinitarian interpretation of all of reality, and of all that the human mind might come to understand naturally, seeing this natural knowledge "always, already" theologically, in the light of the missions of Christ and the Holy Spirit. Integration is a primary concern of the grace-nature unity envisioned by Aquinas, and not merely distinctness. This concern is also shown in the very way Aquinas reinterprets Aristotelian and neo-Platonic doctrine on a number of fronts so as to make the very philosophical vision of reality he receives from these philosophies open to the higher lights of faith and biblical understanding. One can perceive clear evidence of this in Aquinas's rereading of the metaphysical tradition in light of the "real distinction" between *esse* and essence in all created entities, which opens up metaphysics *from within the purview of its own principles* to a profoundly scriptural interpretation of created ontology.[13] Likewise, one finds in the analysis of the human soul a dual insistence: the soul is the form of the body, and so the human being is only intelligible as an ontological unity of body

---

12. *ST* I, q. 1, a. 5, co. and ad 1-2.

13. See the famous argument to this effect by Étienne Gilson in *Elements of Christian Philosophy* (Garden City, NY: Doubleday, 1960), pp. 164-83. Ralph McInerny has argued in turn that Gilson overstates the effects of revelation upon philosophy in Aquinas, and thereby overlooks Aquinas's originality and insight as a philosopher and interpreter of Aristotle. *Praeambula Fidei: Thomism and the God of the Philosophers* (Washington, DC: Catholic University of America Press, 2006).

and soul.[14] But also, the soul is spiritually subsistent and incorruptible, even separated from the body.[15] Philosophical reason can be employed to defend these viewpoints from within the purview of a Christian vision of reality, but it cannot say what happens to the soul after death. Christian revelation, meanwhile, affirms the "interim state" of the separated soul (judged immediately after death for either eternal salvation or damnation) as well as the centrality of the resurrection, as the reunification of body and soul.[16] Knowledge of such truths transcends the competence of natural reason, but is harmonious with our limited philosophical understanding of the human person. In a procedure such as this, then, theology is not simply sequestering itself off from philosophy to give the latter free rein, nor importing the conclusions of the latter into itself uncritically. Rather it is assimilating the subordinate sciences critically, scrutinizing them from within, not to destroy them, but so that they, by opening themselves up to divine revelation, *might become more deeply themselves.*

No doubt one reason that Barth's thought has been so important not only to Protestants but also to Catholics is because of his rearticulation of the centrality and primacy of divine revelation even in the midst of a post-Enlightenment, modern intellectual context. Like Aquinas, Barth also believes in the unity of all sciences and discourses within or in a sense in subordination to the science of theology. That is to say, divine revelation can be understood as the object of the science of theology, and the study of theology offers the ultimate forum for the interpretation of the meaning of reality.[17] Yet Barth also sets out to articulate his vision of the superiority or ultimacy of revealed knowledge and theological science quite differently from Aquinas on a number of points.

The most famous of these, if not the most important, concerns

14. *ST* I, q. 76, a. 1; *SCG* II, c. 56. All citations of the *SCG,* unless otherwise noted, refer to *Summa Contra Gentiles,* 4 vols. (Notre Dame and London: University of Notre Dame Press, 1975 [1955-57]).

15. *SCG* II, cc. 49-51, 79-81; *ST* I, q. 75, aa. 2 and 6. See the helpful recent discussion of some of these arguments by Edward Feser, *Aquinas* (Oxford: Oneworld, 2009), pp. 151-62.

16. *SCG* IV, cc. 79 and 91.

17. *CD* I/1, pp. 5-11, 275-87. Barth approvingly cites *ST* I, q. 1, a. 5 on p. 5 regarding the subordination of all sciences to the truth of theology, but goes on to express his ambivalence about the very notion of theology as a science.

Barth's controversial rejection of the contributions of philosophical knowledge of God (so-called natural theology) to the work of any truly scientific theological discourse.[18] Theological knowledge is built upon the foundation of uniquely Christological criteria. For that very reason, it cannot be considered a "science" in the generic way other forms of learning typically may be, but it must be redefined dialectically in light of the Scriptures, over against such conceptions.[19] Theology is a science uniquely at the service of the dogmatic proclamation of the Church. It is initiated only through the action of divine revelation given to the human subject by the Word of God, through the medium of Scripture, and not through any self-initiated project of human understanding of God.[20] There is more at stake in this assertion than merely the refutation of Roman Catholic theological methods, or even those of liberal Protestantism.[21] Barth is on one level trying to recover the epistemological premises that he thinks were implicitly uncovered in the Reformation and which are proper to true Christian understanding. On another level, he is seeking to reassess the integrity of theology as a science even despite modern, secular university life, where it is already dismissed as a form of premodern learning. To the extent that theology depends for its cultural justification upon an apologetic derived from philosophy, ethics, or historical religious studies, it will inevitably cease to have any sufficient credibility as a science in itself.[22] This is the case precisely because the credibility of theology as a science is established not from without, but from the Word of God communicating itself in faith.[23] To the extent that they are tempted to justify the study of this subject by appeal to the canons of extrinsic forms of learning, theology's practitioners are in fact tempted to betray the true object of the science (God and his revelation). Such intellectual utilitarianism, whether modernizing and liberal or archaic, Catholicizing, and intellectually defensive, is something alien to the study of God as

18. *CD* I/1, pp. 41-42, 280.

19. *CD* I/1, p. 279.

20. *CD* I/1, pp. 283-84.

21. On the context of Barth's rejection of the *analogia entis,* see Bruce L. McCormack, "Karl Barth's Version of an 'Analogy of Being': A Dialectical No and Yes to Roman Catholicism," in *The Analogy of Being: Invention of the Antichrist or the Wisdom of God?* ed. Thomas Joseph White, O.P. (Grand Rapids: Eerdmans, 2011), pp. 92-108.

22. *CD* I/1, pp. 8-10.

23. *CD* I/1, pp. 12-13, 223-27.

such.[24] Theology should be free to explore the glory of its object independently, without being instrumentalized in the defense of a romanticized past intellectual history, or in defense of a contemporary secular intellectual tradition alien to the gospel.

Theology has its grounding, then, in a sphere that transcends all ordinary forms of human learning, and it inevitably stands apart from them as an alternative, more final arbiter for the explanation of reality. It does so because it seeks to reflect upon God's own Word and the proclamation of that Word by the Church.[25] Theology thus originates with an explanation of reality given by God in Jesus Christ, and it is only by being attentive to this object that it can speak about anything else. Such a stance safeguards theology as an independent "science" in a very unique sense. Does it also imply, however, that theological reflection is wholly alien to other modes of explanation, or that those explanations are alien to theology? Barth does not think so. It is true that Christian theology possesses a dialectical and critical relationship to human learning: it is permitted and even required to underscore the limits and provisionality of alternative forms of human discourse in the presence of the more fundamental and determinative discourse that is the Word of God. This claim is not made, however, by way of a denigration or denial of any particular form of non-Christian learning, modern or ancient.[26] On the contrary, theology can in a sense assimilate critically the real but imperfect truths of human knowledge, both old and new. It does so for the sake of the exploration of its proper subject matter, however: God revealed in Jesus.

A philosophical likeness to this theological claim is to be sought, perhaps, in Barth's own intellectual proclivity toward Kantian epistemology.[27] The Kantian tradition asserts philosophically that the historical human subject can never finally construct more than a merely provisional and hypothetical account of the ultimate meaning of reality. For Barth, this is the imperfect, philosophical grasp of what revelation gives us to understand more profoundly: that there is a nonviability in all attempts to understand comprehensively the human being apart

24. *CD* I/1, pp. 285-86.
25. *CD* I/1, pp. 71-87.
26. See the forceful affirmations to the contrary: *CD* I/1, pp. 5-8, 283-84.
27. On Barth's Kantian influences, see Bruce L. McCormack, *Karl Barth's Critically Realistic Dialectical Theology: Its Genesis and Development, 1909-1936* (New York: Oxford University Press, 1995).

from the grace given in Jesus Christ.[28] In saying this, Barth was speaking in a sense to the heart of the twentieth-century European crisis of meaning. His thought — like that of the later Heidegger — predicts aspects of postmodernism.[29] Not because nontheological disciplines lack their own starting points and integrity (Barth is not antifoundationalist in this sense), but because total explanation is not accorded by grounds stemming from reason alone. With Kant we can say that such total explanations are either inaccessible, or they are uniquely theological in kind. Stated positively, it is the revelation given in Jesus Christ that reveals to us the true identity of God, as well as the ultimate meaning of the creation and the nature of the human person. God elects us to reconciliation with himself in Christ, thereby manifesting his own identity as triune and our identity as human beings. The human being thus comes to understand himself or herself as a *creature* and as a being called by grace to stand in relation to God. The narrative meaning of the whole of creation, then, takes on its inward form in light of the covenant of grace, and this covenant has at the heart of its scientific intelligibility the mystery of God himself as triune.[30]

One can readily see the attraction of Barth's scientific theology. It allows a relative respect for the modern academy and its plethora of disciplines, but also shows a circumspect mistrust of importing too ambitiously other domains of learning into theology per se. The inward content of theology is provided by Scripture itself. Still, there is in Barth a cosmopolitan discourse about everything. Does he not engage freely and in creative fashion a striking variety of topics, seeking to illumine them theologically from within the purview of Scripture and tradition? These topics include Protestant scholastic understandings of nature, modern exegetical arguments for the historicity of the resurrection, the notion of creation and its philosophical history, the conception of the human person as body and soul in patristic thought, the Cartesian problematic of certitude, Sartrean conceptions of nothingness, Nietzsche on freedom, and so forth. And in doing so, Barth also purposefully and critically accepts a wide range of influences into his thought, not least from both classical and modern philosophical

28. See, for example, the reflections of *CD* III/2, pp. 20-26.

29. On the simultaneously postmodern and religious elements of Heidegger's later work, see Julian Young, *Heidegger's Later Philosophy* (Cambridge: Cambridge University Press, 2002).

30. We are alluding here to several major themes in *CD* III/1.

sources. After all, with and against Aquinas, Barth can speak about God as pure act; and with and against Hegel, he can speak of God as the event in which God elects humanity.[31] Analogous things occur in his treatment of the human being, wherein he takes up and reiterates Christologically a host of modern philosophical concepts of human nature.[32] Barth can be read as a precursor to the post-Enlightenment desire for "holism" in religious thought, a holism that is distinctly theological and Christological in kind. However different from Aquinas, he rejoins him on his own terms in the "catholic" effort to understand all things created within a unified theological vision.

Can Barth and Aquinas be read in their respective forms of scientific enterprise in convergent fashion? A preeminent interpretive tradition of English-speaking Barthian thought has argued that this is the case. George Lindbeck in his landmark book *The Nature of Doctrine* suggests that both thinkers can be understood as articulating a unified theological vision of the world, one that assimilates other forms of critical inquiry into itself, offering comprehensive religious languages for reality, or "cultural-linguistic systems."[33] This influential claim has had a diversity of echoes in thinkers as diverse as Augustine Di Noia, Bruce Marshall, and George Hunsinger.[34] Meanwhile, Thomas Torrance has argued that Barth is to be read as standing in the lineage of classical, premodern Christology (Athanasius and Cyril) with its ambitious assimilation of the classical ontology of the West.[35] A reading of Barth that would combine these two trends could argue that he is fundamentally a classical, tradition-based Christian thinker, someone seeking to rearticulate the longstanding truths of the patristic and medieval traditions creatively and critically, in a post-Reformation, but also post-Kantian, post-Hegelian context.

From the other side of the ecumenical divide, one can find ways

31. *CD* II/1, pp. 257-72; *CD* II/2, pp. 155-75.

32. *CD* III/2, pp. 325-436.

33. George Lindbeck, *The Nature of Doctrine: Religion and Theology in a Postliberal Age* (Louisville and London: Westminster John Knox, 1984).

34. J. A. Di Noia, O.P., *The Diversity of Religion: A Christian Perspective* (Washington, DC: Catholic University of America Press, 1992); Bruce Marshall, *Trinity and Truth* (Cambridge: Cambridge University Press, 1999); George Hunsinger, *Disruptive Grace: Studies in the Theology of Karl Barth* (Grand Rapids: Eerdmans, 1992).

35. See, for example, Thomas Torrance, *The Christian Doctrine of God: One Being Three Persons* (Edinburgh: T. & T. Clark, 1996).

to read Aquinas in a more predominantly Barthian fashion, so as to minimize or even reenvisage a supposed distinction of philosophy and theology in Aquinas himself. Thomism is then understood in "post-liberal" terms as "theology all the way down." Here Aquinas's Christian neo-Platonic influences from Augustine and Dionysius might be emphasized, as a form of thought not immediately subject to Aristotelian philosophical explanation.[36] Aquinas is even sometimes envisaged as a quasi-eclectic thinker who is seeking to widen the scope of theological vision to include all the predominant strands of philosophy in his time. This theological "holism" is found in various ways in the thought of David Burrell, John Milbank, and Fergus Kerr.[37] One arguably finds something analogous in the vast project of Hans Urs von Balthasar. The latter, in his trilogy of the *Theo-Logic, Theological Aesthetics,* and *Theo-Drama,* sets out to interpret the transcendentals of truth, beauty, and goodness in the light of Christology, and so also to reenvisage key themes of Barth's Christology in harmony with Aquinas's metaphysics. Our point here is not to attempt any kind of basic sketch of the broad array of these positions, but simply to note that there are available to contemporary theology a rich variety of theological projects arguing for potential forms of convergence between Aquinas and Barth.

Nevertheless, there are reasons to consider challenges and objections to these multi-sided projects of convergence. The point here is not to deemphasize the ecumenical enterprise, but to think more deeply about the confessional and methodological commitments of these two great thinkers and the traditions they represent. The hope thereby is to consider alternative possibilities to contemporary theology, but also thereby to rejoin the ecumenical effort in such a way as to give voice to what may be important outstanding and unresolved questions.

Contemporary Barthian thought, for instance, can be seen developing in some quarters toward a more distinctly confessional stance, understanding Barth as a great interpreter of and advocate for the

---

36. See, for example, John Milbank and Catherine Pickstock, *Truth in Aquinas* (London: Routledge, 2000), who appeal in particular to Fran O'Rourke, *Pseudo-Dionysius and the Metaphysics of Aquinas* (Leiden and New York: E. J. Brill, 1992).

37. David Burrell, *Aquinas: God and Action* (Notre Dame: University of Notre Dame Press/London: Routledge and Kegan Paul, 1979); John Milbank, *The Word Made Strange: Theology, Language, Culture* (Oxford: Blackwell, 1997); Fergus Kerr, *After Aquinas: Versions of Thomism* (Oxford: Blackwell, 2002).

confessional tradition of the Reformed ecclesial communities.[38] This is more in keeping with the prevalent German-speaking Barth tradition, which has consistently acknowledged his confessional allegiances, but also the ontologically experimental aspects of his thinking that cause him to differ from premodern Protestant orthodoxy. A line of thinking descending from Eberhard Jüngel pays special attention to the ways in which Barth's theology can be read in tandem with Heideggerian concerns about metaphysics, and interpreted as a theological critique of classical metaphysics and pre-Kantian Christian theology.[39] The values enumerated in this approach stand in marked contrast with the direction Thomism has taken in recent years. A number of scholars in that field have sought to defend and reappropriate philosophical or metaphysical dimensions of Aquinas's thinking, as distinct from and complementary to his theology.[40] One can also note a prevalence of sublime historical studies of Aquinas that seek implicitly to illustrate the perennial intelligibility of his Trinitarian and Christological thought, even in its "premodern" form.[41] Such theological efforts would suggest that in some real sense the wisdom inherent in Aquinas's theology and philosophy remains of enduring value and requires a recovery of the ontological and philosophical dimensions of the scholastic tradition.

Concerns such as these open us up to a less convergent, more "relational" version of ecumenical dialogue, one that also invites us to consider again and in greater depth the relations between revelation, theology, modernity, and the philosophical heritage of classical Chris-

---

38. In recent years, see the work of John Webster, *Word and Church: Essays in Church Dogmatics* (London: T. & T. Clark, 2006); Bruce L. McCormack, *Orthodox and Modern: Studies in the Theology of Karl Barth* (Grand Rapids: Baker Academic, 2008); Paul Nimmo, *Being in Action: The Theological Shape of Barth's Ethical Vision* (London: T. & T. Clark, 2011); Keith L. Johnson, *Karl Barth and the Analogia Entis* (London: T. & T. Clark, 2011).

39. Eberhard Jüngel, *God as the Mystery of the World*, trans. Darrell L. Guder (Grand Rapids: Eerdmans, 1983); *God's Being Is in Becoming: The Trinitarian Being of God in the Theology of Karl Barth*, trans. John Webster (London: T. & T. Clark, 2004).

40. See Matthew Levering, *Scripture and Metaphysics: Aquinas and the Renewal of Trinitarian Theology* (Oxford: Blackwell, 2004); Lawrence Feingold, *The Natural Desire to See God according to St. Thomas Aquinas and His Interpreters* (Naples, FL: Sapientia, 2010); Reinhard Hütter, *Dust Bound for Glory: Explorations in the Theology of Thomas Aquinas* (Grand Rapids: Eerdmans, 2012).

41. See Gilles Emery, O.P., *The Trinitarian Theology of St. Thomas Aquinas,* trans. Francesca Aran Murphy (Oxford: Oxford University Press, 2010).

tianity. What does it mean to be "modern and orthodox," and how do the respective projects of Aquinas and Barth contribute to the discussion of this question? The essays in this volume are not meant to sublimate the distinctive ideas of Barth and Aquinas, nor do they seek to establish a realm of premature irenicism. They are meant, however, to voice the concerns of two distinctive traditions that speak profoundly to one another, in the midst of questions that are modern and ancient, theological and philosophical, Catholic and Protestant. What is theology as a science? The essays in this book present different but also partially convergent and mutually enriching answers to that question.

What Is the Core of Theology?
Christocentricity vs. Trinitarian Theocentricity

Although it is overly simplistic, one can in fact characterize Barthian thought as grounded or centered in Christology, and as tending from that starting point toward a study of the Holy Trinity. Knowledge of God is given historically in Christ, who is the crux of the divine economy, but knowledge of God in history also leads us into an understanding of who God is as Trinity in God's own inner life. Aquinas's theology, meanwhile, is ordered in virtually the contrary direction. His is a Theo-centric Trinitarian theology that begins with a consideration of the immanent life of God in himself, and moves out into an analysis of the divine economy, culminating (in the *Summa theologiae,* at least) in a study of the history of the Word made flesh. Are these approaches opposed or are they in some ways convergent? What is at stake theologically in the consideration of the question? To answer these questions, let us consider briefly Barth as a Christological thinker in his given historical context, before in turn considering the theology of Aquinas in his respective intellectual environment.

Standard accounts of twentieth-century theology portray that century as the age of a great renewal of Trinitarian theology, and it is indisputable that there was an important emergence of major doctrinal treatments of the Trinity in this epoch, above all in the works of Barth, Rahner, and Balthasar. Yet in another sense, one might qualify this first statement so as to say that modern theology has approached the renewal of Trinitarian theology primarily through the lens of Christocentricism. In this respect, Barth has had a major influence upon modern dogmatic theology, both Protestant and Catholic. How and why has this been the case?

To answer this question, one must consider the challenges that philosophical historicism has posed to the consideration of God in modern theology. A first consideration is epistemological, and has to do with the effects of Kantian philosophy upon the exercise of the post-Kantian philosophical disciplines. It is a given of Kantian theory that the human knower, as a subject of experience, is unable by the work of analysis of sensible objects to acquire demonstrable knowledge of "causes" that transcend the realm of the senses as such (nonsensible causality).[42] In fact, "causality" itself is a heuristic concept of the knowing subject that is useful for the explanation and ordering of our sensate experience, but the notion does not allow us to attain even to the "noumena" or inner essences of realities themselves.[43] In other words, by way of simple experience the human mind cannot attain to stable metaphysical knowledge of the structures of things in themselves, nor can it attain to inferential or indirect demonstrative knowledge of the existence of God.[44] After Kant, the old age of metaphysics is placed radically in question. Posed positively, this means that the human mind always knows what it knows under the constraints of a given time and space, construing meaning and order for itself under the influences of a given human culture, in a given historical context with its limited perspectives and intellectual horizons. If this is the case, how can there be a revelation given in Jesus Christ that is of universal import, particularly if this revelation occurs in a given time and place, and if our understanding of that revelation is situated in yet another, very different historical context? The epistemological stance of Kant opens up to us the hermeneutical problems posited by Wilhelm Dilthey and Hans-Georg Gadamer. How does the historical setting of any given text or its subsequent interpreters affect the possibility of claims to persistent truth down through time?

To this we can add an ontological perspective: being is not known primarily in what transcends history, according to Hegel and Schelling, but in and through the becoming and narrative of history.[45] The reduc-

---

42. Immanuel Kant, *Critique of Pure Reason,* trans. N. K. Smith (New York: Macmillan, 1965), A609/B637.

43. Kant, *Critique of Pure Reason,* A84-92/B117-24.

44. Immanuel Kant, *Prolegomena to Any Future Metaphysics,* trans. P. Carus and J. Ellington (Indianapolis and Cambridge, MA: Hackett, 1977), §§56-57.

45. G. W. F. Hegel, *Phenomenology of Mind,* trans. J. B. Baillie (New York: Harper,

tion of human existence to the immanent sphere of history without recourse to knowledge of the transcendent God might seem like a philosophical deficit after Kant. However, it is interpreted as an opportunity by Hegel. The historical process of the world itself is identified as the immanent sphere of the manifestation and development of pure spirit, God. The history of human beings, then, is the locus of the historical becoming of the deity.[46] Ontology and theology do not depend for their existence as sciences, then, upon our capacity by thought to transcend history. Rather, historical becoming itself can ultimately only be understood ontologically and even theologically.[47] We find God not above but within the historical becoming of the world. How, if at all, might this idea be of positive import to modern Christian dogmatics?

Third, and last, historical biblical studies insist that Jesus of Nazareth be interpreted from the point of view of his historical consciousness as a person of his epoch. According to Johannes Weiss and Albert Schweitzer, he was an eschatological preacher whose message was elaborated within the context of Second Temple Judaism.[48] Is this a historically plausible hypothesis, and if so, how does it relate to traditional Christological claims? There emerges in modern theology the problem of how to respond doctrinally to the trends in modern historical-Jesus studies. What should one make of the historical situatedness of Christ's human consciousness? It would seem that Christianity must hold that God the Son truly became a subject of history, and yet expressed his relationship to his Father and to the Holy Spirit by way of a particular human self-understanding, in a given historically contingent context.

Karl Barth's treatment of these questions in the early volumes of the *Dogmatics* came to serve as an important referent for discussions of theology that took place in the twentieth century. For on the one hand, Barth adopted the full force of the Kantian prohibitions on natural knowledge of God, accepting that this implied a reassessment of the re-

1967), pp. 767, 780-81; *Lectures on the Philosophy of Religion,* vol. 3, ed. Peter C. Hodgson, trans. R. F. Brown, P. C. Hodgson, and J. M. Steward (Berkeley: University of California Press, 1985), pp. 86, 194; F. W. J. Schelling, *Philosophie der Offenbarung,* ed. Manfred Frank (Frankfurt am Main: Suhrkamp Verlag, 1977), pp. 197-98.

46. Hegel, *Phenomenology of Mind,* p. 772.

47. Hegel, *Phenomenology of Mind,* pp. 801-8.

48. Albert Schweitzer, *The Quest of the Historical Jesus: A Critical Study of Its Progress from Reimarus to Wrede* (first German edition 1906), trans. William Montgomery (London: A. & C. Black, 1910), pp. 330-403.

lationship between Christian doctrine and the classical metaphysical ontology of antiquity and the scholastic age. Furthermore, he was not wholly unsympathetic to Hegel and Schelling in their attempts to articulate the meaning of "deity" in historical terms and by way of the processes of human history. One can speak not only of the event of God's self-unveiling to man, but also of God's own life and essence as an event of God's being with man.

What is crucial to note, however, is that while Barth did interact intellectually with these authors, he also attempted to rearticulate these intellectual traditions in what he saw to be uniquely and holistically theological senses, based on Scripture. The perspective by which we judge the impotence of human knowledge of God and the historically bound frame in which human beings attempt to derive meaning from the universe is a Christocentric epistemological perspective. It is in light of Christ that we can see truly what we can and cannot know of God, and it is in light of Christ that we come to know what our history is and who God is with us in history. On this view of things, our time-bound historical way of being is not an obstacle to knowing the true God who transcends history, simply because God has elected to make our human history the locus of his own self-disclosure to us, as God. The Trinitarian God willingly reveals himself to us in the event of the Incarnation, life, death, and resurrection of Jesus. There is, then, an "analogy of faith" or a likeness between God and human beings, given uniquely in the history of Jesus Christ. The ontological and epistemological limitations of our historical manner of existing are the conditions in which God in his eternal "event" of being Father, Son, and Holy Spirit discloses himself to us in Christ.

> If we are to maintain the *analogia fidei* and not fall into untheological thinking, we must be guided by the Christological consideration of the incarnation of the Word as the *assumptio carnis*. The unity of God and man in Jesus Christ is the unity of a completed event. Similarly the unity of divine revelation and human religion is that of an event. . . . As God is the subject of the one event, so, too, he is of the other. The man Jesus has no prior or abstract existence in the one event but exists only in the unity of that event, whose subject is the Word of God and therefore God himself: very God and very man. Similarly in the other, man and his religion is to be considered only as the one who follows God because God has pre-

ceded the man who hears Him, because he is addressed by God. Man enters, therefore, only as the counterpart of God.[49]

This analogical use of "event" language is important. Ironically, Barth takes up the modern categories of ontology as a series of historical events, and transposes them Christologically into a consideration of the inner life of God. God not only reveals himself to us in history, but also reveals to us his own inner history as God.[50] One might think that this would exclude any positive evaluation of classical categories of thought about divine being (pure actuality, infinity, goodness, immutability, eternity, etc.). However, Barth seeks instead to reevaluate these categories Christologically, and to place them under reconsideration with those inherited from the modern German idealist tradition, seeking to ground both sets of categories in new ways in the consideration of the God of the New Testament.[51] In other words, the event of the Lord in time gives us objective knowledge of who God always, already is. This allows us to evaluate the whole of the classical and modern intellectual traditions under the rubric of a Christological form of thinking.

This all has implications for theology's treatment of the historical life of Jesus. In the Incarnation of the Word, God has made himself a true subject of the events of history, and so one might expect Barth to insist upon the importance of historical study of the Gospels. However, he argues instead by appeal to the doctrine of revelation. Insight into the historical identity of Jesus is given to us uniquely through the activity of God who alone can reveal himself in Christ in the power of the Holy Spirit. Modern historical study of Jesus, therefore, cannot supplant the saving knowledge given by revelation, and therefore is neither to be feared nor particularly depended upon, either to tell us who God is or to decry our beliefs about God. The history of Jesus is given to us instead primarily by the theological portrait of Christ presented in the Gospels. Its inner core is found in Jesus' relation to the Father and the Holy Spirit, expressed particularly in the obedience of Christ. In the obedience of Christ crucified, God unveils to us his own kenotic self-emptying in time. There, the relations of Jesus to the Father and the Spirit are manifest in his historical life. They thus show us who God is

49. *CD* I/2, p. 297.
50. *CD* II/2, pp. 161-65.
51. *CD* IV/1, pp. 180-204, 375-76.

eternally. The human historical life of the Word made flesh is an expression of who the triune God is, in God's eternal reciprocity of relations, as Father, Son, and Holy Spirit.

How should we sum up the points briefly enumerated above? Barth took up the challenge of modernity regarding the historical conditions of our thought and of our very being, and he rearticulated theological doctrine Christologically so as to respond to these challenges. In doing so he made the historical event of Christ the locus of the objective knowledge and presence of God given to human beings. He also creatively and freely made use of historical analogies to articulate what God has revealed to us of himself in the event of God's being human. Simultaneously, however, he argued that in Christ true knowledge of who God is *eternally* is given to us in time. Therefore, the historical life of God with us invites us into the transcendent life of God beyond us. The Trinity becomes the ultimate ground for the interpretation of human history, and appears as the condition of possibility for all our knowledge of God given in Christ.

This pattern of theological interpretation has been highly influential in modern German-speaking theology, both Protestant and Catholic. Following Barth, thinkers like Rahner and Balthasar, Moltmann and Kasper, Pannenberg and Ratzinger all sought in differing but related ways to recover an emphasis on Trinitarian theology grounded in the history of revelation.[52] This history transpires in and through the divine economy, culminating in the event of the cross and the resurrection wherein the Trinitarian life of God is ultimately unveiled. Even in the midst of our confusing, fragmented history, then, and even in the midst of human suffering and tragedy, God reveals to us who God is. Through a Christocentric attention to the core of revelation, we travel back into the ground of revelation, and that ground is the eternal life of the Trinity itself. Modern theology tends after Barth

52. Hans Urs von Balthasar, *Theo-drama*, vol. 4, trans. Graham Harrison (San Francisco: Ignatius Press, 1994); Walter Kasper, *Jesus the Christ*, trans. V. Green (London: Burns & Oates, 1976), pp. 181-85; Kasper, *The God of Jesus Christ*, trans. Matthew J. O'Connell (New York: Crossroad, 1989), pp. 189-97; Jürgen Moltmann, *The Crucified God*, trans. R. A. Wilson and John Bowden (New York: Harper & Row, 1974); Wolfhart Pannenberg, *Systematic Theology*, vol. 2, trans. Geoffrey W. Bromiley (Grand Rapids: Eerdmans, 1994), pp. 375-79, 317-51; Karl Rahner, *The Trinity*, trans. Joseph Donceel (London: Herder & Herder, 1970); Joseph Ratzinger, *The God of Jesus Christ: Meditations on the Triune God*, trans. Brian McNeil (San Francisco: Ignatius Press, 2008), pp. 81-84.

to begin in Christology and to terminate in Trinitarian theology as its ultimate goal.

Aquinas's procedure follows virtually the inverse route. The *Summa theologiae* begins with the doctrine of God, and proceeds to examine the production of creatures, especially angels and men. It then considers the return of spiritual creatures back to God. This return occurs through grace, by way of the call given to rational creatures to attain to beatitude, to true and lasting happiness. This happiness consists in the vision of the essence of God. Aquinas's exploration of the science of theology occurs, then, in three parts. The first part of the *Summa* examines the mystery of God one and three, the meaning of creation, and the natures of angels and human beings. The second part of the *Summa* looks at the moral life of the human person: the calling to eternal life, the structure of the moral act, the virtues and their development under the effects of grace. The third part considers Christ, who is our way back to God: the Incarnation, the historical life of Jesus, his saving death, resurrection, and ascension, and the theological meaning of the final judgment. Aquinas died before completing his treatment of the sacraments and the last things (death, judgment, heaven, hell, purgatory, the final resurrection). Nevertheless, his treatise clearly lays the groundwork for a treatment of these subjects that is Christological, portraying the sacraments as the effects of redemption, sacred means by which we return to God in Christ, in view of eternal life.

Marie-Dominique Chenu famously characterized this architectonic vision by employing the notion of an *exitus-reditus* schema: Aquinas portrays creatures as proceeding from God and returning to God, by a movement first of initial emanation proceeding to gradual teleological perfection.[53] The historical economy is duly acknowledged, but is also taken up into a larger contemplative vision of eternity: all things are from God and for God, attaining their true meaning and end in Christ. In this vision of things, Christ is the way in which human beings come back to God, and he restores the promise of beatitude after it is threatened by human sinfulness. Consequently, for Chenu, Christology remains relative, in a certain sense, to the human vocation to eternal life. God has become man so that we might be saved.

53. Marie-Dominique Chenu, O.P., *Toward Understanding Saint Thomas,* trans. A.-M. Landry, O.P., and D. Hughes, O.P. (Chicago: Henry Regnery, 1964), pp. 304-14.

There is much to be said in favor of Chenu's interpretation of the *Summa* on this point. For one thing, it allows us to read Aquinas as a theologian of the divine economy and as a theologian of history, so to speak. Scholasticism is not opposed to a scriptural, linear view of time, but accepts fully a biblical vision of history, while acceding simultaneously to a yet deeper dimension of Scripture: the theocentric perspective. What occurs in time is, after all, a reflection of the goodness of God and of God's own inner mystery. Consequently, attention is given to the historical economy in view of a deeper understanding of God in himself. Aquinas underscores this truth in the first question of the *Summa,* which is concerned with the true nature of theology as *sacra doctrina.* For there he states that theology as a science has as its subject the study of God, and that faith orders the human mind toward the immediate knowledge of God as he is in himself. Simultaneously, however, theology is not only a science, but also a wisdom precisely because it considers God as the first principle of all other things, and all things in light of God.

> This doctrine is wisdom above all human wisdom; not merely in any one order, but absolutely. For since it is the part of a wise man to arrange and to judge, and since lesser matters should be judged in the light of some higher principle, he is said to be wise in any one order who considers the highest principle in that order: thus in the order of building, he who plans the form of the house is called wise and architect, in opposition to the inferior laborers who trim the wood and make ready the stones: "As a wise architect, I have laid the foundation" (1 Cor. 3:10). Again, in the order of all human life, the prudent man is called wise, inasmuch as he directs his acts to a fitting end: "Wisdom is prudence to a man" (Prov. 10:23). Therefore he who considers absolutely the highest cause of the whole universe, namely God, is most of all called wise. Hence wisdom is said to be the knowledge of divine things, as Augustine says (*De Trin.* xii, 14). But sacred doctrine essentially treats of God viewed as the highest cause — not only so far as He can be known through creatures just as philosophers knew Him — "That which is known of God is manifest in them" (Rom. 1:19) — but also as far as He is known to Himself alone and revealed to others. Hence sacred doctrine is especially called wisdom.[54]

54. *ST* I, q. 1, a. 6.

This sapiential understanding of theology is contemplative and theocentric: it seeks perspective on all that exists in light of what is ultimate and eternal, not so as to capture the eternal within the inscape of human understanding, not so as to ignore the complexity of human history, but so as to lead human understanding out from creatures into the pursuit of the mystery of God.

Does this understanding of theology displace the focus from Christ onto the human vocation to beatitude? To say so would constitute a serious misunderstanding of Thomistic theology.[55] For the core focus throughout Aquinas's work remains the mystery of the Holy Trinity. Theology is about learning to see the Trinitarian God as the ultimate principle of reality, and about learning to see all things other than God in light of the Trinity and for the Trinity. This must be the case also as regards Christology. After all, one can hijack Christocentricism in order to displace the center of theology's attention away from God in himself and toward the historical development of creation and human beings in Christ.[56] Christology without theocentricism can become itself a pronounced form of anthropocentricism!

The Christology of Aquinas, however, avoids this danger, as it has its origin in a theology of the "missions" of the Son and the Holy Spirit.[57] The missions, meanwhile, are explained by the eternal processions.[58] Consequently, the Christology of Aquinas is rooted in a theology of the Trinity. On the one hand, the processions of the most Holy Trinity simply are what God is: the Father eternally begets the Son as his intelligible Word and Wisdom.[59] The Father and the Son eternally spirate the person of the Spirit as their shared, mutual love.[60] The missions of the Son and Spirit, meanwhile, are the processions themselves rendered present to spiritual creatures by sanctify-

---

55. See, in this respect, the Christological reflections on Chenu's schema offered by Jean-Pierre Torrell, O.P., *Initiation à saint Thomas d'Aquin* (Paris: Cerf, 1993), pp. 226-27.

56. See, in this respect, the Thomistic concerns raised regarding Scotism by François Daguet, O.P., *Finis Omnium Ecclesia. Théologie du dessein divin chez Thomas d'Aquin* (Paris: Vrin, 2003).

57. *ST* I, q. 43, aa. 1 and 5; III, prologue, q. 1, aa. 1-3.

58. *ST* I, q. 43, a. 1: "The mission of a divine person [denotes] . . . (1) the procession of origin from the sender, and . . . (2) a new way of existing in another. Thus the Son is said to be sent by the Father into the world, inasmuch as He began to exist visibly in the world by taking our nature." See also *ST* I, q. 43, a. 8.

59. *ST* I, q. 27, aa. 1-2.

60. *ST* I, q. 27, a. 5; q. 36, aa. 2-4; q. 37, a. 2.

ing grace.[61] God sends the Holy Spirit into the world to reveal the Son. God sends the Son into the world to reveal the Father. The mission of the Holy Spirit thus leads us to Christ and Christ leads us to the Father.[62] The Father sends the Son and the Spirit into the world by grace so that we may participate in the divine life, through acts of faith, hope, and love, inward graces that allow us to commune with the living God.[63]

Given this understanding, the visible missions of the Son and the Spirit are ordered toward our inward communion with God by grace. The Word becomes flesh, and his mission is accompanied by the visible mission of the Spirit at Pentecost. These mysteries occur so that we might be led back into communion with the Holy Trinity, with the life of God in himself. Christology, therefore, is not relative to anthropology. Nor is the study of human nature and history resolved into a kind of Christological monism. From a Thomist perspective, such ideas are inevitably anthropocentric and focus excessively upon the creature rather than the Creator. Instead, both the study of the human person and the study of the Incarnation and the Paschal mystery send us back to an ever-deeper understanding of the most Holy Trinity, the inner mystery of God himself.

Does this mean that Aquinas ignores the scriptural history in and through which Christ makes himself known to us, and in and through which the Spirit instructs the Church? Does he pretend artificially and pretentiously to go back behind the process of history (to which we are inextricably bound) in order to try (in vain!) to perceive God's own way of thinking? Luther and Barth were famously critical of what they label a *theologia gloriae* as opposed to a *theologiae crucis,* a theology based on the ascent of human speculation rather than the descent of God upon the cross.[64]

It would be errant to think that Aquinas was insensitive to the scriptural starting points of all theology. On the contrary, he is explicit in stating that he believes all foundations of Catholic teaching to reside

---

61. *ST* I, q. 43, aa. 2-3.

62. *ST* I, q. 43, a. 7, co. and ad 6; a. 4, ad 2.

63. *ST* I, q. 43, aa. 5-6.

64. On the distinction between a *theologia gloriae* and a *theologia crucis* as applied to the possibility of philosophical theology, see Luther's *Heidelberg Disputation,* §§20-22 (in *Luther's Works,* American Edition, vol. 31, ed. Harold J. Grim [Philadelphia: Fortress Press, 1957], pp. 52-54), and Barth's *CD* I/1, pp. 178-79.

in the givens of Scripture itself.[65] Tradition in the Church remains authoritative, but only because it is a reading out of what is implicitly and really contained in Scripture, however proximately or remotely.[66] The Church and the pope can read Scripture without error, but in doing so, they remain relative to the Word of God given through Christ and the Apostles, with revelation having closed in the Apostolic age.[67] Furthermore, St. Thomas wrote commentaries on two Gospels and all the letters of Paul (as well as Hebrews). As Gilles Emery has shown, Aquinas in his scriptural commentaries is concerned consistently to demonstrate exegetically the well-founded character of classical orthodox claims about Jesus, while also making use of his exegetical readings as the basis for the arguments he gives in the *Summa theologiae* regarding the very nature and identity of God.[68] The arguments of the *Summa* always begin from the premises of authority precisely because theology is a science that takes its starting points from revealed truths.[69] Consequently, in the case of Christology, Aquinas shows repeatedly the scriptural well-foundedness of his portrait of Christ, his Incarnation, public life, passion, and resurrection.[70]

It is equally important to underscore that Aquinas makes an overt distinction between the order in which a reality is made manifest to us (and in which we come to know that reality) as distinguished from the order in which a reality exists in itself. The first is the order of knowledge and leads us to the *via inventionis,* the way of discovery, while the second is the order of being, and leads us to the *via judicii:* judgments about the natures of things in themselves.[71] This distinction is based on a fundamental realism about the way we learn in general. We walk into a magnificent building, and from within discover only progressively the architect's grand design for the whole structure. We see flowers bloom and can study biologically the causes for the time and manner of this blossoming. We see people suffer physically or express joy on the exte-

65. *ST* I, q. 1, a. 8, ad 2.
66. In IV *Sent.,* d. 17, q. 3, a. 1, sol. 5; d. 27, q. 3, a. 3. ad 2; *ST* III, q. 64, a. 2, ad 3.
67. *ST* II-II, q. 1, aa. 9-10.
68. See Emery, *The Trinitarian Theology of Saint Thomas Aquinas,* pp. 15-35.
69. *ST* I, q. 1, a. 8, co.
70. For typical examples of Aquinas's Christological exegesis of Scripture, see *ST* III, q. 1, a. 2; q. 36, a. 1; q. 39, a. 1; q. 40, a. 3; q. 41, a. 6; q. 42, a. 3; q. 45, a. 1; q. 47, a. 2; q. 48, a. 3; q. 53, a. 1.
71. *ST* I, q. 79, a. 8.

rior and infer from this their inner states of body or soul. In all these cases, the human mind moves from peripheral effects to the cause of those effects and subsequently comes to understand these effects in light of their initially hidden inner causes. So it is with Trinitarian theology: we move initially from the mystery of Christ into the mystery of the Trinity, but once we come to understand the ultimate principle of explanation, we can order our vision of the whole architectonically so as to see all that is second in light of what is truly first. This is why Aquinas will say that the two central mysteries of Christianity are that of the most Holy Trinity and that of the Incarnation.[72] The Incarnation is our way into the discovery of the Trinity, and the Trinity is that which gives us to understand the deepest meaning of the Incarnation.

If we understand Aquinas in this light, then the old Lutheran adage of scholastic theology as *theologia gloriae* may be inherently unhelpful for understanding what is really going on. It is true that in the first part of the *Summa* Aquinas makes extensive use of philosophical or metaphysical reflections on God's simplicity, perfection, goodness, infinity, eternity, and so on.[73] Furthermore, in contrast with certain postmodern readings of Aquinas, it would seem that Aquinas himself is clear that he thinks that philosophical arguments employed *within* theology can also stand on their own as demonstrative, natural forms of reasoning.[74] However, it is also the case that when St. Thomas makes use of metaphysical thinking within the context of his scriptural and doctrinal reflections on God, he is also "always, already" working within faith, in view of a deeper knowledge of the Holy Trinity. Such reflection entails (among other things) making use of natural reason at the service of the monotheistic confession of faith in the biblical God of Israel, the one God who is Father, Son, and Holy Spirit. Consequently, what Aquinas is exacting from human intellectual life in his theology is a submission or subordination of reason to faith, one that does not destroy but heals and restores human rationality. The mind turns back toward God as the central preoccupation of human thought and human love, and this occurs both supernaturally and nat-

---

72. *Compendium theologiae,* I, c. 2.

73. In particular *ST* I, qq. 2-11.

74. See the arguments from Aquinas's text to this effect in Anna Bonta Moreland, *Known by Nature: Thomas Aquinas on Natural Knowledge of God* (New York: Crossroad, 2010); Thomas Joseph White, O.P., *Wisdom in the Face of Modernity: A Study in Thomistic Natural Theology* (Naples, FL: Sapientia, 2009).

urally. Thus, the theocentric character of Aquinas's Trinitarian theology brings with it a spiritual itinerary and an inward conversion under grace through which the human intellect and will attain a new rectitude in Christ.[75]

Ultimately, of course, the final end of the human person for Aquinas is the beatific vision, the immediate vision of God the Holy Trinity. This is given by the final grace of the *lumen gloriae,* a vision of intellectual intuition that succeeds faith, and that occurs in the world to come.[76] If this is the case, then, theology is itself always a subalternated science, a study conducted *in via,* on our earthly pilgrimage toward beatitude. Consequently, the notion of theology as a *theologia gloriae* is not wholly wrong, if one considers the final end or teleology of the act of faith: faith is ordered toward the glory of vision. However, it is problematic to claim that Aquinas would see this orientation as a *natural* dimension of theology, one stemming from metaphysical knowledge of God. In fact, Aquinas affirms categorically the contrary: we cannot incline ourselves by our own natural powers toward the beatific vision.[77] Correspondingly, reflection on the simplicity of God by way of philosophical reflection, even within sacred theology, serves to underscore the incomprehensibility and transcendence of God, who cannot be grasped in himself by the powers of reason alone. In the famous words of Aquinas, by the best efforts of human inquiry, we can come to know not what God is, but only that he is and what he is not.[78] This apophatic tendency in Aquinas's thought is meant to help us recognize the gratuity of the gift of faith in God as Trinity, a gift that is given without merit and by God's free decision to manifest and reveal himself.[79]

---

75. See Gilles Emery, O.P., "Trinitarian Theology as Spiritual Exercise in Augustine and Aquinas," in *Trinity, Church, and the Human Person: Thomistic Essays* (Naples, FL: Sapientia, 2007), pp. 33-72.

76. In *ST* I, q. 12, a. 1, Aquinas grounds his theological claims regarding the beatific vision in the promise of 1 John 3:2: "We shall see him as he is." In q. 12, a. 2, he argues from 1 Corinthians 13:12 ("for now we see as through a glass darkly . . .") to the need for the particular grace of the light of glory in order that the created intellect might enjoy immediate knowledge of God.

77. *ST* I-II, q. 62, a. 3; *ST* I-II, q. 114, a. 2. See, likewise, *De veritate.* q. 14, a. 2; q. 22, a. 5; *ST* I-II, q. 15, a. 4; q. 25, a. 2.

78. *ST* I, q. 3, prologue.

79. *ST* I-II, q. 114, aa. 2 and 5. See the study of Joseph Wawrykow, *God's Grace and Human Action: "Merit" in the Theology of Thomas Aquinas* (Notre Dame: University of Notre Dame Press, 1996).

Furthermore, this apophatic character of Aquinas's thinking about God carries over even into his Trinitarian theology as a helpful reminder about dogmatic theology as it is conducted in this life *under the regime of faith*. For even when we come to know *by the unmerited grace of faith* who God is as Trinity in God's own inner life, this is not a knowledge by way of an immediate sight or perfect rest. The life of faith remains unpossessive of the greatest and highest form of knowledge. Faith invites us to live in hope for what we do not yet possess perfectly, and it calls us by this very measure into a Christian life of discipleship, one that aims to persevere in obedience to the gospel unto death, by grace.[80] It is important, especially for our own spiritual health, then, to maintain a realistic sense that the mystery which we already know still evades us in some ultimate sense, and has yet to be comprehensively possessed. "We see now in a mirror darkly, but then face to face" (1 Cor. 13:12). Aquinas's theology is not a *theologia gloriae,* but is in some respects its contrary: a theology ordered toward eschatological realization and a higher form of mystical life. Doctrinal theology, then, is noble and necessary but it is conducted in a temporal and human mode that is inherently imperfect. To be true, it must take full stock not only of its wonderful nobility, but also of its inherent limitations.

Barth and Aquinas each in differing ways lead us into a profound reflection on the mystery of God and God's relation to the divine economy. What is the normative role that Christ plays in our knowledge of God? How are Christology and Trinitarian theology interrelated in keeping with the economic revelation of the identity of God? What role if any should metaphysical thinking about God play in what we say about what God is, and about what God is not? On these points, a comparison of the ideas of Aquinas and Barth on topics related to the doctrines of God, Trinity, and Christ underscores multiple points of likeness and difference. Their respective teachings can enrich and nuance our constructive disagreements, while inviting us to pursue important points of convergence.

---

80. *ST* I-II, q. 114, a. 9; II-II, q. 17, aa. 2, 5, 7.

Theology in Modernity: Postmetaphysical, or the Discipline That Calls for the Recovery of the Metaphysical?

One of the key differences that exists between Aquinas and Barth concerns the question of the role of metaphysics in the thought of each. This topic is deeply interrelated to the question of the modern viability or plausibility of either as a thinker in a post-Kantian context. Is the age of grand metaphysical schemas not finished, and do we not live in what Jürgen Habermas has termed a "postmetaphysical age"?

Here, however, ambiguities abound. Consider, for example, the denomination of Aquinas as a "metaphysician." Do we mean by this that his ontology can be treated similarly to those that were criticized overtly by Immanuel Kant, that is to say, on the model of the thought of Wolff or Baumgarten? A number of contemporary studies have suggested that such conceptual characterizations are in fact implausible.[81] Furthermore, such a schematization ignores the tendencies of modern Thomism. As Joseph Ratzinger observed in an essay in 1967, Aquinas was read in the mid-twentieth century (by theologians like Congar, Chenu, and Schillebeeckx) largely as a theologian of the divine economy, that is to say, as a theologian of history.[82] This occurred, he notes, while his philosophy was being read in tandem with Heidegger (by Gilson, Fabro, Siewerth, and others).[83] Heidegger claimed that there was a forgetfulness of Being *(Sein)* in the traditions of Enlightenment ontology, and countenanced a recovery of doctrines of Parmenides. Thomists, meanwhile, claimed analogously that there was a modern

---

81. See, for example, Olivier Boulnois, *Être et représentation. Une généalogie de la métaphysique modern à l'èpoche de Duns Scot (XIIIe-XIVe siècle)* (Paris: Presses Universitaires de France, 1999), especially pp. 457-515; Boulnois, "Quand commence l'ontothéologie? Aristote, Thomas d'Aquin et Duns Scot," *Revue Thomiste* 95 (1995): 85-105; Jean-Luc Marion, "Saint Thomas d'Aquin et l'onto-théo-logie," *Revue Thomiste* 95 (1995): 31-66; and Jean-François Courtine, "Métaphysique et ontothéologie," in *La Métaphysique,* ed. J. M. Narbonne and L. Langlois (Paris and Quebec: J. Vrin and Les Presses de l'Université de Laval, 1999), pp. 137-58.

82. Joseph Ratzinger, "Salvation History, Metaphysics and Eschatology," in *Principles of Catholic Theology: Building Stones for a Fundamental Theology,* trans. Mary Frances McCarthy, S.N.D. (San Francisco: Ignatius Press, 1987), pp. 171-90.

83. Gustav Siewerth, *Der Thomismus als Identitätssystem* (Frankfurt: Verlag Schulte-Bulmke, 1939); Étienne Gilson, *Being and Some Philosophers* (Toronto: Pontifical Institute of Mediaeval Studies, 1952); Cornelio Fabro, *Participation et causalité selon saint Thomas d'Aquin* (Paris and Louvain: Publications Universitaires de Louvain, 1961).

Enlightenment forgetfulness of Aquinas's doctrine of *esse*. It is the doctrine of existence as distinct from essence that allows us to consider with sufficient realism the ontological facticity and singularity of human beings in history, while also acknowledging the transcendence and ineffability of God as *ipsum esse subsistens,* one who is wholly other to all our rationalist, "essentialist" constructs.[84]

At the time of the Second Vatican Council, then, Aquinas was increasingly being read in tandem with modern existentialist and historicist concerns, against the perceived ahistorical naïveté of Enlightenment rationalism. In the post-Conciliar age, however, historicizing forms of ontological thinking led to acute internal tensions within Catholic theology. This occurred as classical dogmas were reinterpreted systematically so as seemingly to translate Christianity into a modern, postmetaphysical setting. Doctrines submitted to radical revision by influential thinkers like Edward Schillebeeckx and Hans Küng included the following: the divinity of Christ; the existence and perennial necessity of the seven sacraments; the ontological status of the "character" of baptism, confirmation, and ordination; the capacity of the Church to proclaim Christian truths in an infallible and permanent way.[85] For these thinkers, the vehicle for expressing the gospel in modernity is above all that of political narrative (including an intensive dialogue with other religions and with modern secular political movements), not dogma or ontology.[86] Arguably, modern Catholicism when rearticulated in this hermeneutical light began to resemble nineteenth-century liberal Protestantism in significant ways.

Unsurprisingly, then, there arose against these trends a counter-critique. Theologians such as Balthasar, Ratzinger, and Daniélou questioned whether theology was now marked by an uncritical rejection of

84. See, for example, Gilson, *Being and Some Philosophers,* pp. 70-72.

85. See Edward Schillebeeckx, O.P., *God and the Future of Man,* trans. N. Smith (New York: Sheed & Ward, 1968), pp. 1-50; Schillebeeckx, *Jesus: An Experiment in Christology,* trans. H. Hoskins (New York: Crossroad, 1979), pp. 140-271, 652-69; Schillebeeckx, *Ministry: Leadership in the Community of Jesus Christ,* trans. J. Bowden (New York: Crossroad, 1981); Hans Küng, *The Church,* trans. Ray and Rosaleen Ockenden (New York: Sheed & Ward, 1968), pp. 354-59, 388-480; Küng, *Infallible? An Inquiry,* trans. E. Quinn (Garden City, NY: Doubleday, 1971). Also instructive is the later work of Küng, *Christianity: Essence, History and Future,* trans. J. Bowden (New York: Continuum, 1995), pp. 28-60, 162-96.

86. See, for example, the principles articulated by Schillebeeckx in *Christ: The Experience of Jesus as Lord,* trans. J. Bowden (New York: Crossroad, 1981), pp. 30-64.

essential norms in dogma, traditional moral teachings, and the very notion of perennial philosophical truths.[87] Ratzinger, for example, began to argue by 1977 for the recovery of an essential role of metaphysics in theology, and sought to advance a more metaphysical reading of Aquinas on human personhood and eschatology.[88] Such a line of thinking suggests that precisely in order to affirm a permanence for the true teachings of the Scriptures, it is necessary to appeal intelligently to our capacity to make permanent truth claims about God, creation, physical and living beings, the human person and moral actions.[89] Cosmology and metaphysics are not opposed, then, to a scriptural theology of sacred history because that history transpires *within* the ontological order of creation, under the providential governance of God.[90] God realizes in time his revelation of himself, and his corresponding desire to restore all things in Christ, beatifying human beings by grace. But this means that human beings in their historical existence are called out of the sphere of historical becoming as such, into an encounter with the eternal life of God. As in Aquinas's *exitus-reditus* schema, history is "deciphered" intellectually against the backdrop of eternity.[91]

On this view, the future of modern Christian theology is not

87. For Hans Urs von Balthasar, see in particular *The Moment of Christian Witness,* trans. R. Beckley (San Francisco: Ignatius Press, 1994), originally published in German as *Cordula oder der Ernstfall* (Einsiedeln and Trier: Johannes Verlag, 1966); Jean Daniélou emphasized the importance of traditional dogmas as well as philosophical metaphysics in his post-Conciliar writings. See, for example, *Why the Church?* trans. M. de Lange (Chicago: Franciscan Herald Press, 1975).

88. See in particular the 1979 article of Joseph Ratzinger, "What Is Theology?" in *Principles of Catholic Theology,* pp. 315-21, and the monograph originally published in 1977: *Eschatology, Death and Eternal Life,* trans. Michael Waldstein and Aiden Nichols, O.P. (Washington, DC: Catholic University of America Press, 1988).

89. Ratzinger, "What Is Theology?" p. 316: "I am convinced . . . that the crisis we are experiencing in the Church and in humanity is closely allied to the exclusion of God as a topic with which reason can properly be concerned — an exclusion that has led to the degeneration of theology first into historicism, then into sociologism, and, at the same time, to the impoverishment of philosophy. . . . If theology has to do primarily with God, if its ultimate and proper theme is not salvation history or Church or community but simply God, then it must think [of God] in philosophical terms."

90. See the profound exploration of this theme by M.-J. Le Guillou, O.P., in his *Le mystère du Père. Foi des apôtres, Gnoses actuelles* (Paris: Fayard, 1973), especially pp. 201-85.

91. See the reflections to this effect by M.-J. Le Guillou, O.P., *Christ and Church: A Theology of the Mystery,* trans. C. Schaldenbrand (New York: Desclée, 1966), pp. 161-84, 327-67.

postmetaphysical, and in fact, no historically viable form of thought can be postmetaphysical. For thought itself is concerned with what is true and real, and therefore with whatsoever exists. It cannot forsake a consideration of that which exists any more than it can forsake itself. All that exists, however, is given to us to consider within a larger order of creation, one that need not be, but which is. The mystery of our being, therefore, necessarily stands in relation to the eternal mystery of God and evokes that mystery. There is no opposition, then, between historical thinking versus ontological thinking. Rather, theology that has an overt concern with ontology (including the being and natures of God the Son) must also be thoroughly concerned with the realities of our historicity in its cosmological, biological, and human forms.

Barth is of course a very important dialogue partner for anyone interested in the question of the eventual fate of metaphysics or the future of theology in a distinctively modern context. In the famous *analogia entis* controversy with Erich Przywara, Barth began to articulate what might be characterized as a distinctively theological ontology, one that is both post-Kantian and Christological. Here the recourse to the so-called *analogia fidei,* or "analogy of faith," is of capital importance. That term has first and foremost an epistemological meaning for Barth. It is only in light of the action of God revealing himself in Christ that we come to perceive a likeness between human beings and God.[92] Nevertheless, this likeness is also ontological and is one that we find in the person of Christ himself and in human beings. The likeness between God and man is one established by God's election of humanity in Christ, and realized most perfectly in the event of the Son being human.[93]

An influential interpretation of Barth on this matter is offered by Jüngel, who portrays Barth's theological ontology as a theologically fitting response to Heidegger's criticisms of the western metaphysical tradition, and in particular, his critique of natural theology as "onto-theology."[94] Where metaphysics and natural theology fail to attain to true knowledge of God, and even lead to a problematic idea of God (one that atheism in turn rejects), the revelation of God in Christ unveils to us an ontology of love. God the Trinity is manifest in Christ

---

92. *CD* I/1, pp. 12, 243-47, 437; I/2, pp. 270, 297, 471.
93. *CD* IV/1, pp. 203-7.
94. Jüngel, *God as the Mystery of the World,* pp. 277-80.

crucified as the hidden ground of the world, even in a postmetaphysical age.[95]

On this view, then, one could argue that Barth's Christology diagnoses philosophical metaphysics as something inherently problematic *for theological reasons.* In light of Christ, we see the pretence and limitation of all human striving for knowledge of God, just as we also see the graciousness of the true knowledge of God that is given in Christ alone. If it is possible to construct a theological ontology without resorting to philosophical metaphysics, then clearly "metaphysics" and "ontology" are not synonyms and ought not to be spoken of as if they were. Instead, we should say that any attempt to speak of the reality of God and the reality of human beings which adopts a starting point other than the narrated history of Jesus of Nazareth as attested in Holy Scripture is "metaphysical"; any attempt to do so that remains consistently tied to that history and to it alone is "postmetaphysical." Or rather, the modern crisis of metaphysical thinking about the nature and existence of reality is not resolved "from below" through human reflection on natural experience, but "from above" through the history of God's being human with us.

It might seem at this juncture that differences between Barth and Aquinas simply lead to an irresolvable impasse. That may be. However, while Barth was clearly ambivalent about classical metaphysics *if it was taken as a project of philosophy,* he was also an avid opponent of the "historicism" of modernism and a critic of the deontologized theology of liberal Protestantism.[96] Another way of saying this is: Barth was deeply interested in ontological structures in reality, read theologically. His treatment of divine attributes in *Church Dogmatics* II/1 is intended in some respects as a thoroughly scriptural and Christological rereading of the classical heritage of western metaphysics. Yet in another respect, it is the most forceful restatement and reconsideration of traditional "divine names" ontology enunciated by any Protestant thinker in modernity. Barth does, for example, have his own well-developed

95. A contemporary continuation of this theme is found in Kevin Hector, *Theology without Metaphysics: God, Language, and the Spirit of Recognition* (Cambridge: Cambridge University Press, 2011).

96. See, for example, *CD* II/1, pp. 337-41, regarding the divine attributes as reinterpreted by Biedermann and Schleiermacher in terms of human interiority and religious feeling. See, likewise, in *CD* IV/2, pp. 49-69, the discussion of the Son's existence as God and man, one hypostatic subject having both a divine and a human essence.

doctrine of God as *actus purus,* even if that term is understood by him differently than it is by Aquinas.[97] Each of them would claim that the notion has a grounding in Scripture, even if it is not literally employed there. Each of them would claim that the term is deeply ontological in signification, denoting fundamental differences that obtain between the actual existence of creatures and the pure actuality of the Trinitarian God on whom they depend for their being.

We may conclude from these brief reflections that we stand before two irremediably different ways to approach the epistemological and philosophical crises of modernity and postmodernity. There is the Barthian, which aspires to a holistic, Christological discourse, and the Thomist, which retains the distinction of the philosophical analysis of reality, but within and at the service of theological interpretation of revelation. These two approaches offer each other interesting challenges and raise reasonable mutual concerns about the approach employed by the other. Nevertheless, despite the differences, we can also note potential points of convergence or confluence between the two. Consider three brief ideas.

First, Thomism is just as concerned as Barthianism to invest in the theological scrutiny of philosophical ideas and arguments, analyzing the latter not only in terms of their own natural premises and conclusions, but also in terms of their harmony with revelation and their suitability for employment in the articulation of sacred truths. The Thomistic philosophical tradition, then, is one deeply affected and informed from the beginning by the influences of Scripture and theology. There is a kind of scriptural, theological holism to this form of thinking that is arguably as or more unified than that offered by Barth, since it has its roots in the patristic age and has continued in dialogue with diverse philosophical theories up into the contemporary era.

Second, Barth himself is deeply influenced by the conversation with both ancient and modern philosophical thinkers. He underscores the homogenously theological character of his work even in his assessment of philosophies and non-Christian religious traditions. In all this, however, he is doing something *like* Aquinas, despite their differences: he is seeking to speak in a theologically unified way *even through*

---

97. CD II/1, p. 264: "*Actus purus* is not sufficient as a description of God. To it there must be added at least *'et singularis.'* . . . God is in Himself free event, free act and free life."

and in the philosophical and conceptual idioms of his age. He seeks to rethink these idioms dialectically from within a distinctly theological science, so as to assimilate them into a Christological and scriptural vision of reality. This is not wholly unlike Aquinas's approach. Perhaps Barthians might suggest to Thomists ways to interact *philosophically* with modern intellectual traditions, while Thomists might suggest to Barthians ways to critique *theologically* these same traditions.

Consider finally that both Aquinas and Barth acknowledge that the process of interaction between theology and intellectual culture occurs down through time. As such it must be a discipline bound both by norms of reference to tradition and by events of progress and ever-new discernment. There is something to the life of theological science that is "ever ancient, ever new." The procedure of critical reflection on human intellectual culture, then, cannot ignore the contributions of the ancients and medievals, nor can it fail to engage modern and contemporary philosophical and scientific understandings of reality. Thomists may argue that the tradition of perennial philosophy to which they appeal can help engage with the modern challenges of theology as well or better than any rival tradition. They can question whether Barth at times renounces on some profound level the permanent contributions of the patristic and medieval ages. Barthians, meanwhile, see themselves as taking seriously the weight of the past while moving with evangelical discernment and theological creativity into the future. This entails a decisive acceptance of the truth of the critical moment in which we inhabit, a time of thought that is indelibly marked by the challenges of modernity, including the Kantian critique and post-Hegelian historical ontology, as well as the thought-world of the modern scientific age. On this view, Barth has given us discernments of who we should seek to be as modern, orthodox theologians, and we should give heed to his insights.

Ultimately, whether one is Thomist or Barthian (or neither at all), it remains the case that these two powerful thinkers and the traditions that stem from them have much to contribute to theological discussion, and they can do so especially by way of mutual examination, encouragement, and profound speculative interaction. Both Aquinas and Barth invite us to think vigorously about the future of theology as a science of God.

Conclusion: Five Topics in View of an Ecumenical Goal

This edited volume seeks to promote a comparison of Thomist and Barthian reflections on major theological themes. The idea is to take topics of comparison that are sufficiently important as to permit a profound comparison of Aquinas and Barth. Consequently, the essays in this volume are divided into five headings, each treated by a Catholic Thomist and a Protestant Barthian, respectively. The topics considered are: (1) divine being, (2) the Trinity, (3) Christology, (4) grace and justification, and (5) covenant and law.

What, in the end, does a realistic ecumenism hope to achieve? What can be obtained in the dialogue between doctrinally divided Christians by an examination of their respective theological traditions? At base, we are seeking in Christian friendship to see the other Christian analogically: to try to understand better how that person sees the world, and to appreciate the Christian identity of the person in that seeing and its outward expression. We are also above all trying to find points of intellectual unity or convergence. This must be undertaken, however, in a way that is respectful of the conscience and tradition of each one. This entails that we have the respect and trust to disagree and to argue. Ecumenical conversation should seek yet unseen grounds for reconciliation and not seek immediate agreements that depend too readily on the premature capitulation of one side or the other.

Christian ecumenism is a Christ-centered task. The Second Vatican Council document on the unity of Christians, *Unitatis Redintegratio,* states in its opening paragraph the following: "many Christian communions present themselves to men as the true inheritors of Jesus Christ; all indeed profess to be followers of the Lord, but they differ in mind and go their different ways, as if Christ himself were divided. Certainly such division openly contradicts the will of Christ, scandalizes the world, and damages that most holy cause, the preaching of the gospel to every creature."[98] This means that Christians have a certain kind of obligation to seek unity among themselves for the love of the truth, in the name of fraternal unity, and for the sake of the spreading of the gospel.

This obligation is not a Pelagian exercise, however. No one who

---

98. Translation from *Vatican Council II,* vol. 1: *The Conciliar and Post Conciliar Documents,* rev. ed., ed. A. Flannery, O.P. (Northport, NY: Costello Publishing, 2004).

conducts a genuinely Christian ecumenical dialogue hopes to do so only by his or her own powers, and without due reference to God's grace and an abandonment to divine providence. We are meant to try our best to obey Christ's commandment: that Christians might be one, as he and the Father are one (John 17:21). But we are meant to do so only ever in recourse to the unique saving work of the grace of God, in the Holy Spirit. *Sola gratia:* for it is only the grace of Christ that can save us and guide us. If we confide ourselves in earnest to the Holy Spirit, a genuine dialogue regarding the truth of Christianity can be conducted between Catholics and Protestants, one that occurs in a spirit of friendship. Such friendship cannot fail to bring spiritual fruits into the lives of Christians, graces that will build up in both seen and unseen ways the ecclesial body of Christ.

I. The Being of God

Karl Barth on the Being of God

Robert W. Jenson

Philipp Melanchthon, a founder of my theological tradition, notoriously recommended eschewing the theme of God's being and sticking to his *beneficia,* his works on our behalf. Barth rebukes him pretty sharply for this, but Melanchthon had a point: discoursing of God's "being" is indeed a perilous exercise, whether it is ventured by those whose speculative style Melanchthon deplored or by Karl Barth or Thomas Aquinas or by someone giving a lecture on them.

To be sure, for Barth it all begins with the simple affirmation that *God is.* Which does not mean that the attempt to *unpack* the simple "God is" has no pitfalls.

Nevertheless, I cheerfully accepted Professor McCormack's invitation. I thought I more or less knew what Barth thought about *das Sein Gottes* — he pronounced it *Sain* to show he was Swiss, which may not be entirely beside the point — and I thought I more or less knew what I might say on the subject. But, considering some of the scholars before whom I would be saying it, and my long furlough from hands-on Barth scholarship, I did think I should probably brush up some text. And that too seemed a straightforward task: there is after all a big piece of *Kirchliche Dogmatik* II/1 directly on the matter.[1]

So I took the volume off the shelf where it had long been resting from earlier labors and reread the passage. And then I went back to read some bits again. And then I studied my old annotations. And then

---

1. Karl Barth, *Kirchliche Dogmatik,* 4 vols. in 13 parts (München: C. Kaiser; Zürich: Theologischer Verlag Zürich, 1932-67) (henceforth *KD*), II/1, §28.

43

I spent a lot of time in a chair with my eyes closed — prompting Blanche Jenson to ask if I really had nothing to do. And the more I pondered, the less sure I was about what I was reading.

Gottes Sein, Barth defines, to begin the part of the *KD*[2] I thought would be my text, is *das was Gott zu Gott macht,* "that which makes God to be God." Then he provides a Latin label from the tradition: our question is about God's *essentia,* his essence — in epexegetical German, his *Wesen.*

I hadn't remembered him setting things up quite *that* way. For this is of course the language of standard substance-metaphysics: for every independent constituent of reality there is an *essentia,* a subsisting definition, which determines it to be what it is — in our case, which "makes God to be God" — and by possessing which the substance exists. With respect to God, western theology has generally agreed with Thomas that in this life we do not know God's essence, but we have also supposed that there is a divine essence to be known. With this opening definition Barth seems to share at least the second supposition.

But can *Karl Barth* really think in these terms? So straightforwardly that he defines his task in them? That was what threw me. Can he be at home in an ontology of substances and their determining essences? He proceeds immediately from this opening definition to three characterizations of God's being: God is *Ereignis, ich,* and *Entscheidung,* "event, first-person person, and decision." Surely setting up an event, or a sheer *ich,* or a decision, as anything like what the tradition has thought of as an essence is a wildly implausible proceeding?

And it must be remembered that Barth is not offering event or person or decision as metaphors or slogans for something else. He is *recruiting* them for use in formal ontological propositions.

After a while I decided I must over time have gotten out of synch with the general discourse of the passage, and I turned for help to the chapter in which it appears.[3] The chapter has the title *Die Wirklichkeit Gottes,* "the reality of God" — or perhaps "the reallyness of God." Staring at that, a dialogue with *wirklich* formed unbidden in my head — perhaps shaped by the style of German students of fifty years ago. It's got to be in German to start: "Wirklich?" "Ja, wirklich," "Seltsam!" As in: "Really?" "Yes, really." "She's married *him?*" "She has indeed." "Strange."

I imagined an exchange with that sort of intonation and that gen-

---

2. *KD* II/1, §28.1.
3. *KD* II/1, chapter VI.

eral pattern, as an exchange internal to faith: "In dem Christus-geschehen offenbart sich Gott als Gott." "Wirklich?" "Ja wirklich," "Wie so?" Perhaps, I thought, it is conversation of this sort to which my passage belongs. "In what happens with Christ, God reveals himself as God." "Really?" "Really." "How is that?" "How it is, is as an event that simply occurs, as a person who persists in his self-introduction to us, as a decision that brooks no reasons or challenge." "Remarkable." I think these dreamings made some progress. But there was still that initial specification of God's being as an *essentia,* for which I could think of no Barthian use.

Perhaps, I proposed to myself, one should think of a retroactive qualification of Barth's initial language. We are later instructed to take other big-ticket words, like "act" or "love," when used of God, as words ripped from our language by the event of revelation, deprived of con-text by the underivable *facticity* of the revelation, its utter contingency amid all other acts or loves or whatever, and made to apply properly only to the reality revealed. At every dialectical turn Barth commands us promptly to turn our attention from the language we are using to the encounter sheerly as such. Thus we are in effect told that "God acts" is to be understood as "an act occurs," which differs from other acts in that it is not the act *of* anything other than the act himself — and that "act himself" is not a slip.

Perhaps we are to experience "being" and "essence" in the same way. And perhaps Barth was after all thinking primarily in German. I was at this point tempted to think of Barth's revealed divine "essence," *das Wesen Gottes,* as a *Wesen,* which like Heidegger's is simply *west an,* which *is* in that it sheerly *comes on* to us. I am still tempted.

Now — in my chapter on God's reality, Barth says that its matter had in principle been dealt with in the previous chapter on the knowl-edge of God.[4] So I beat a further retreat, to that chapter. And there I got some decisive help.

On the very first page, Barth insists on something to which he will return again and again: that in the event of revelation God is our *Gegenstand,* our object, an *other* which is simply and unavoidably *there* for us and which we therefore can actually *know.*

That goes decidedly against the grain of much modern theology — which is probably why Barth harps on it. Any doctrine that begins

---

4. *KD* II/1, chapter V.

with God's *non*objectivity is by this rule just so about some other God than the one revealed in Christ. God is indeed hidden, but this is not by metaphysical distance, not by not being our object, but rather by the opposite, by being altogether in our face.[5] Anything like the metaphor-theology of not too long ago is disqualified at the start — as may be some traditional apophaticism.

The puzzle of Barth's use of traditional substance/essence language resolves itself a little. For the ontology of substances and their essences was created by Aristotle in part to present the fundamental constituents of reality as at once independently given and knowable. And that is what Barth's *Gegenstand* is.

Barth of course hastens to insist that God as our object is utterly unlike any other of our objects. He attacks this from a spider's web of angles. Let me devise something that perhaps captures their common spirit: in the *Gegenstand* which confronts us in revelation, which there *stands* over *against* us, we confront the only one of our objects that is *irreducibly Gegenstand,* the one that *stands* fast *against* the imperialism of our subjectivity. God in his revelation is an object that repels and reverses modernity's rule of the knower over his object — a dominance that perhaps goes back to the very origin of western thinking.[6] In revelation we are confronted by our Lord, who precisely when he stands with us stands most unavoidably over against us.

And then there is one particular specificity of this object that must be considered separately. God according to Barth can be an object for us because as Father, Son, and Spirit he is object for and in himself. For the Father and the Son, each has the other as his object, and so on around the triune relations.

Now that *did* help. For one thing, it reminded me that all this discussion of God's being comes in the dogmatics after the doctrine of the Trinity. And if Barth in a way starts over again with each new volume, he does sometimes expect us to remember what he has earlier laid down. Perhaps some of my unease came from forgetting a final context, forgetting where I was in the dogmatics, forgetting that Barth does not first develop the doctrine of God's being and then specify this God's triunity; that it goes the other way around. He expects us to know that it is a triune God of whose essence he speaks.

---

5. Like the God of Luther's theses for the *Heidelberg Disputation.*
6. Heidegger's *Seinsvergessenheit.*

If the essence that confronts us in revelation is a unique essence in that he persists in *Gegenständlichkeit* — persists in intruding as our object — and if he so persists because he is triune and therefore is comprehensively object for himself, then what it means that God is *essentially* our object is that he is *antecedently* object in the complex of the triune relations. God's "essence" obtains in that — to choose one possible statement of the relations — the Father commands the Son, the Son obeys the Father, and the Spirit opens them to be thus object — *Gegenstand* — for each other. And so on.

Back to my text. After the opening definition that discombobulated me, Barth proceeds to what he will — after the fact — call "formal" descriptions of God's being.[7] We have already noted them. God's being is *Ereignis, ich,* and *Entscheidung,* event, first-person person, and decision.

God's being is *Ereignis,* event. For God to be is to *happen,* full stop. Barth lays it down: "event," used of God, is a last word; we are not to ask why this event happens or who is responsible for it or what its context of other events might be, or any of the other questions that would be suggested by our previous use of the word. The German *ereignen* allows one to devise a neat formula: *Gott ereignet sich* — maybe "God behappens himself." It seems to me that someone who wished to say what Barth says, might simply say that and fall silent.

Or rather, given what we have now been reminded of, one at this point might expect Barth to lay this out on the reality of the Trinity. Since he did not, let me devise something for him. God is event in the revelation because as Father, Son, and Spirit he is event in himself. A Trinitarian "person," to borrow from Thomas, is a subsistent relation, a relation that is its own term. Since the classically posited relations in God are active, as terms they will be events. The Father begets the Son, and thus both happen. The Son responds to the Father, and thus both happen. Etc.

This event that God is, is *God* in that doer and act are the same. And now I have shifted language as Barth does, from "event" to "act": for the God-event is not impersonal, not if it is Father, Son, and Spirit. There is after all a doer in the picture so that the event is an action. What is special about this event is not that it *lacks* a doer but rather that doer and act are one. Something analogous is sometimes said about us: who and what I am is what I in fact do and suffer through my

7. *KD* II/1, §28.1.

life. But with us there is always a residue of reference to a personhood not yet and perhaps never determined by act; not so with God.

The event of the *Lord* must be free, that is, an act, that is, *personal.* So we come to the second characterization of God's being: for God to be is to be an *ich,* a first-person person. "God's being is act" is to mean that for God to *be* the event that he is, is for God to *do* the event that he is.

Is such a proposition intelligible? I seem to understand it, but there will be scoffers. It seems to me that it is intelligible if it too is laid out in Trinitarian fashion: God the Father begets the Son and breathes the Spirit; and Son and Spirit, the act of the Father, are the same God as he. And so on.

To repeat: God is an *ich,* a first-person person. Which within Barth's whole thinking is to say that the reality encountered in the revelation *addresses* us, to introduce himself. "I am [the name], your God, who brought you out of the house of bondage." And the speaker is *God* in that he *never relents* from addressing us. He addresses us, and we indeed respond; but we always and only respond. We are even allowed to speak of him in the third person, but this speech is true only as it is recruited to converse with one who remains its first-person speaker.

Lurking behind this is surely the famous *Herrschaft und Knechtschaft* passage of Hegel's *Phenomenology of Spirit* — an observation that I do not intend as a criticism. A finite I/Thou pair must always contest which will dominate, which will seize and hold the first person, which will be the lord and which the slave. The I who in the revelation addresses us is *God* in that in this case there is no such contest, not because he perfectly enslaves us but because he perfectly enables us.

God's being is, finally, *Entscheidung,* decision. To be irreducibly first-personal, an *ich* that also as our object remains always subject, this *ich* must — and here in the transitional passage comes a pileup of rhetoric — be his own knowledge of himself, be his own will for himself, must *sich selbst setzen* and *unterscheiden,* must posit and distinguish his own reality. That is to say, he must essentially be a sheer *decision,* a decision not made by anyone except the person that is the decision. A decision eternally occurs, that is God.

And here the Trinitarian substance of all this discourse is allowed to peep out a bit. In the fine print, we are told that the *Sein* we can specify as *Entscheidung* is the one named Father, Son, and Spirit, that in the total revelation that is how he introduces himself.

Let me drag that a bit further out of hiding — for we are verging on a point of some difficulty in interpreting Barth, a difficulty that occasions some controversy. Does Barth mean that a decision occurs in the life lived between antecedently given triune hypostases? Or is the threefold being of God itself given in the event that is a decision? Barth can, it seems, be read either way. And I will trespass on other lectures no further.

We have come to the end of the "formal" specifications of God's being. Barth moves to specification of, as he puts it, the "content" of this essence. The following segment[8] has the title *Gott als der Liebende,* "God as the loving One."

Barth begins by noting that all the formal specifications could easily collapse to an empty tautology "God is God" — probably you have noticed that yourselves. What keeps the tautology from collapse to nullity, he now says, is that God's address to us *introduces* himself, and so tells us his name. "I am 'Father, Son, and Holy Spirit.'"

The name prevents the tautology from collapse in that it at once tells of God as an agent in created time, as Creator, Redeemer, and Sanctifier of us creatures, *and* is the personal proper name of God himself. It tells of God as one who works loving involvement with us *and* is personally named by that work. God seeks community with us, and does so in that he as Father, Son, and Spirit has community in himself.

This statement of God's essence must again be specified. God is the one who loves *in Freiheit,* in freedom.[9] To speak of God's freedom is, according to Barth, to attempt speech of the deepest secret of God's being: that God is free is *das göttliche,* the godliness, of the event or *ich* or decision that is God. Through the whole preceding discourse, Barth has barraged us with rhetoric and dialectically tortured concepts, in a mighty effort to say how the event or the personhood or the decision that is God differs from other events or persons or decisions we encounter, to say what it is that makes the divine being divine. He concludes the passage on God's being by facing that task directly.

The being of God, however described, is the being of *God* in that it is freely whatever it is. That is: always and in all connections God "begins with himself"; he needs nothing to be and to be what he is, not even possession of his own essence, not even an antecedent "himself" with which to begin.

8. *KD* II/1, §28.2.
9. *KD* II/1, §28.3.

Since Barth concluded his formal descriptions of God's essence with "decision," *Entscheidung,* we might expect him to rely on this notion to speak of God's freedom; he has already laid it down that God is irreducibly person in that he is his own decision. He does not: the notion of decision almost vanishes, to reappear in the next part-volume, subsumed under the notion of "choice." We will come to that.

And then, in my pilgrimage, I saw that I would have to turn also to the following chapter on God's perfections, a.k.a. his attributes, or at least to its introductory portion.[10] And here I for once found what I expected: a polemic against the way in which the notion of God's *simplicity* has often — according to Barth — been used. For better or worse, all the determinants of recent objections to the conceptual hegemony of the notion of divine simplicity are there in the small print.

Whether as event or *ich* or decision, God is the *living* God, and a life has a *way;* it cannot be pictured as a geometrical point, whether on a line or as the center of a wheel. God's essence, says Barth, is indeed not divided, but its simplicity is precisely the richness of one utterly coherent *life.* Therefore, even as God's attributes are each identical with his essence, and therefore identical with each other — as the standard maxim has it — this is not to be taken as the tradition, in Barth's judgment, too often has. For each divine perfection is identical with each other perfection *and* with all the others taken not identically but *together,* precisely in their distinction from one another. Thus in himself, and not merely in his relation to us, God is, for example, *both* merciful and just, and both of these things must individually be said to be speaking of the one godly essence.

And here one perhaps discovers why "decision" had to disappear, to reappear in the next part-volume reconstructed as "choice." For a decision can be punctual, a choice cannot; a choice anticipates something and leaves something behind.

And so I have to add, from II/2,[11] yet another determinant of God's being, which must cast its light back over everything that has gone before and over the whole previous course also of this talk: God is the event that he is and the person that he is; he lives the life that he does, in that he *chooses* himself. And the event of this choice is the same event as the triune choice of Christ to be our savior.

10. *KD* II/1, §29.
11. *KD* II/2, §§32-33.

This is an even more drastic doctrine than might at first appear. For Jesus Christ, as the *God-man,* is in person the salvific bond — the covenant — between God and man. And since when God chooses this bond, he determines himself, also as he is the eternal Son, the eternal choice is not merely that the Son *will* be the man, it is the eternal fact of the Son's reality as God-man. Before all creation, the God-man Jesus Christ is actual in the being of God; God is never God except as in the Son he is Jesus Christ. In this context, *das was Gott zu Gott macht* is that there is Jesus Christ.

One thing that appears when the implications of this are cast back is that what is decided in the being of God as decision is the whole of God's history with us; that what God as an indomitable speaker says is indeed comprehensive, the great metanarrative of creation, reconciliation, and redemption; that what happens as God is God *for* the rest of reality.

This is confirmed by what turns up in the section[12] on God's perfections. For the discussions under that title amount to an entire theology. Vice versa, we may say that the whole of the *Church Dogmatics* is a doctrine of God's perfections.

Can we pull all this together?

Concerning the language-aspect of the matter, authorized speech about God's being shrinks to the tautology "God is God." *And* it expands to a universal discourse. In Barth's thought, what joins the contraction and the expansion is the triune name, as "Father Son and Spirit" at once tells God's whole history with his creation and names his one richly simple essence.

This character of faithful speech precisely mirrors the fact of God, which brings us to another pair of propositions. God's being is an *im*plosion of freedom, so sheerly contingent that it is not contingent *on* anything and so is the one necessity. *And* it is an *ex*plosion of love, so sheerly a commitment to the other that it is freedom. In Barth's thought, what joins these is his doctrine of election.

As for what joins these two sets of propositions, I will not propose an answer to that question, for fear I would intrude too badly on another essay.

---

12. *KD* II/1, §§30-31.

Theology, Metaphysics, and Discipleship

Richard Schenk, O.P.

Ergo in Christo crucifixo est vera Theologia et cognitio Dei.

M. Luther[1]

The Question in Its Ecumenical Context and Goal

Robert Jenson's preface to his *Systematic Theology*[2] points a light toward a water channel deep enough to keep the five paired themes of this book from floundering in the rocky shallows of seemingly familiar, ecumenical harbors. What we are seeking to do is to inscribe the conversation of Thomas Aquinas and Karl Barth into a broader Roman/Reformed dialogue, indeed to seek a renewal of this dialogue by a confrontation of two, but just two, of its most treasured authors. What Jenson's preface adds is the requisite initial insight that this inscription into an ecumenical context is not an arbitrary, but a somehow necessary beginning. All systematic theology must begin from the realization that its proponents speak from separated, often even fragmented, standpoints that need to be marked, as if by buoys. The wonders and the wounds of our speaking with and of God are not segregated from

---

1. Martin Luther, *Die Heidelberger Disputation* 1518, Probationes Conclusionum, XX, cited here according to Otto Clemen, *Luthers Werke, Studienausgabe,* vol. 5, 3rd ed. (Berlin: De Gruyter, 1963), pp. 375-404, here, p. 388, ll. 29-30.

2. Cf. Robert W. Jenson, *Systematic Theology,* vol. 1: *The Triune God* (Oxford: Oxford University Press, 1997), pp. vii-x.

one another into separate harbors. Ecumenism is in this sense not one theological topic among many, but a dimension of every theological discussion of which we are capable at present, precisely in our limited ways.

By way of my own preface, I would like to complement Jenson's crucial insight by two observations that will guide me toward what I should be looking for when I look back at what Thomas Aquinas has written about our looking toward God. For the most divisive moment in ecumenical conversation hinges arguably more on the context of hermeneutical intentions than on the literal comparison of conflicting texts.

The first observation is drawn directly from those "critical reflections" on the Second Vatican Council's Decree on Ecumenism that Karl Barth formulated in preparation for his 1966 trip to Rome to discuss the final documents of the council. As recorded in *Ad Limina Apostolorum,* in regard to the Decree on Ecumenism, Barth asked himself: "Why is the most grievous, the fundamental schism — the opposition of Church and Synagogue (Rom. 9-11, Eph. 2) — not dealt with here, but only spoken of as the relation of the Church to 'Abraham's stock' in the Declaration on the Relationship of the Church to Non-Christian Religions?"[3]

As a standard for the adjudication of inner-Christian differences, a Roman-Reformed dialogue viewed in the context of Jewish-Christian dialogue will therefore need to show its preservation of the "type" and its continuity in the "principles" of First Covenant faith and the thoroughgoing rejection of Marcionist temptations.[4] The overcoming of Marcionist temptations is accomplished by a twofold distancing, characteristic of most forms of ecumenism: distance from the condemnation or even the ignoring of the other; and distance from the claim to have ingested and transformed into oneself the shape and strength of the other. It involves positively what Rémi Brague has called the nondigestive inclusion of the *relatum,*[5] which acknowledges the origin

3. The translation used here will be that of Keith R. Crim: Karl Barth, *Ad Limina Apostolorum: An Appraisal of Vatican II* (Richmond, VA: John Knox, 1968), p. 30.

4. For an opposing view, cf. Adolf von Harnack, *Das Evangelium vom fremden Gott. Eine Monographie zur Geschichte der Grundlegung der katholischen Kirche. Neue Studien zu Marcion* (Darmstadt: Wissenschaftliche Buchgesellschaft, 1985), and Harnack, *Marcion. Der moderne Gläubige des 2. Jahrhunderts, der erste Reformator* (Berlin: W. de Gruyter, 2003).

5. Cf. Rémi Brague, "Inklusion und Verdauung. Zwei Modelle kultureller Aneig-

and initial development of a strength in foreign context, even as it strives to replicate much of that strength for its own form, vitality, and context. This refers not only to the principle of monotheism. Reformed and Roman forms of Christianity must demonstrate what John Henry Newman called the "preservation of type." In reference to the First Covenant, that will mean the kind of religion capable of "theodicy," of questioning the continuing facticity of what even God cannot want simply and absolutely. It is a feature of the First Covenant that has continued to be embodied by Judaism and its members *post Christum,* the "living letters of the law," to cite a term coined by St. Bernard.[6] It is a feature of our faith, the centrality of which has been underscored by the events of the last century. Whereas "theodicy-capability" is demonstrated by Christianity in such documents as the second and third petitions of the Our Father, it is a type of religiosity least obfuscated in the Jewish preservation of the First Covenant, documented, for example, in the Chassidic saying of Rabbi Chanoch of Alexander (d. 1859): "The real exile of Israel in Egypt was that they had learned to bear it."[7] The attempt to retrieve from Thomas Aquinas something of value for today's discourse on God will seek to stress the non-normativity, the ungodly dimension of human suffering as a hallmark of this type of theodicy-capability. The basic question will be: What form must theology take today in order to keep the theodicy question open and free from artificial "solutions"? If Thomas Aquinas still belonged to an epoch when the impassibility of God commonly was argued "for God's sake," if the nineteenth and twentieth centuries saw manifold attempts on both sides of the major western confessional divide to argue the possibility of God "for the sake of humanity," then a discussion after the catastrophes of the twentieth century will need to ask what a rereading of Thomas could tell us about the impassibility of God argued "for the sake of humanity."

A second observation on the ecumenical context of our discussions follows from Brague's distinction. In avoiding the extremes of ex-

nung," in *Hermeneutische Wege. Hans-Georg Gadamer zum Hundertsten,* ed. G. Figal et al. (Tübingen: Mohr, 2000), pp. 293-306; translated into English in the collection Rémi Brague, *The Legend of the Middle Ages: Philosophical Explorations of Medieval Christianity, Judaism, and Islam* (Chicago: University of Chicago Press, 2011).

6. Cf. Jeremy Cohen, *Living Letters of the Law: Ideas of the Jew in Medieval Christianity* (Berkeley: University of California Press, 1999).

7. Cf. Martin Buber, *Die Erzählungen der Chassidim* (Zürich: Manesse, 1949), p. 838.

clusion and ingestion, genuine ecumenical methodology must be manifold, combining the contrary but not contradictory tools of both convergent and relational ecumenism. As regrettable as ecclesial division might be, it is not an evil that can be overcome by encouraging at this point in time the renunciation of confessional identity. Ecumenical *"Burgfrieden"* is at times necessary, but it can come at a high price. From the *Formula concordiae* of 1577 to the Leuenberg Agreement of 1973, from the decrees of Paul V in 1607 to the main body of texts in the Joint Declaration on the Doctrine of Justification in 1999, the single-minded search for inter- and intraconfessional consensus has shown the danger of weakening first self-identity and then also relationality to the other as other. The recent slowing of ecumenical dialogue is arguably in good part the unintended consequence of the loss of confessional, even intraconfessional, identities. The discourse between Thomas Aquinas and Karl Barth can contribute to the flourishing of Christian existence not only by reaching a shared consensus, but also by defining identities as distinct in relation to one another.

Some twenty years ago, Paul Ricoeur identified "translation" as one of three models of qualified integration (alongside the "exchange of memories" and "forgiveness") as a basis for a new ethic in Europe after the fall of the wall.[8] All three models have ecumenical significance, but none is simply a model of convergence and seamless consensus. Ricoeur's analysis of "translation" as a bilingual ideal preferable to Esperanto, the coinage of a common language, can provide us a model. The challenge to translators, by listening to the foreign discourse from which they translate, is to develop not-yet-realized possibilities of their own language, into which, ideally, they are translating, as they seek to raise the "genius" of their own language to the level of the foreign one.[9] The Bible translations of Hrabanus Maurus and Martin Luther, like the translations of scholastic terminology by Eckhart and Zwingli, developed the German language, discovered in it new possibilities, and raised it to a level with the older languages. The ecumenically situated discussion of Thomas Aquinas challenges the Catholic partner to find historically well-founded dimensions in

---

8. Paul Ricoeur, "Welches neue Ethos für Europa?" in *Europa imaginieren,* ed. Peter Koslowski (Berlin: Springer, 1992), pp. 108-22.

9. Ricoeur names the goal of the translator as follows: "den Genius seiner eigenen Sprache auf die Niveau desjenigen der Fremdsprache zu heben."

Richard Schenk, O.P.

Thomas's thought that could not have been identified prior to their ecumenical critique.

As Barth's and Brague's remarks suggest, bilateral dialogue has always tended of itself to become multilateral dialogue. Not only will the Protestant partners run the spectrum from Luther's *theologia crucis* of the Heidelberg Disputation in 1518 to the more confidently epistemological implications of the *Extra Calvinisticum,* but the preunderstandings of Catholic theology in general and of something like Thomism in particular are anything but uniform. A direct comparison of Thomas (d. 1274) and Barth (d. 1968) is made more difficult not only by the 700 years that separate them, but by their belonging to discrete theological types that were in conflict with one another prior to the confessionalization of western Christianity. Among the options of the later thirteenth century, it was the covenantal development of Augustine (so-called neo-Augustinianism)[10] that most clearly anticipated Calvin[11] and perhaps even Barth. Thomas owed much to Augustine, but in questions of theodicy — the matrix of every theology of grace — he initially stayed closer to Augustine's neo-Platonist antipode, Dionysius the Areopagite. In steering a path between Augustine's sense that evil is permitted by God directly for the individual's good of justice or the individual's good of mercy, and Dionysius's sense that evil is permitted by God indirectly for the cosmic but not necessarily for the individual good, Thomas is able to keep open the theodicy question by saving it from specious solutions, individual or cosmic.[12] Whereas Calvin might well have tended to follow Augustine, the presence of both theological types within the subsequent Catholic tradition suggests that many questions, like theodicy or the topic of a suffering God, are arguably less ecumenical themes than ones of theological typology accentuated by diachronic distance.

10. Cf. Berndt Hamm, *Promissio, Pactum, Ordinatio. Freiheit und Selbstbindung Gottes in der scholastischen Gnadenlehre,* Beiträge zur historischen Theologie 54 (Tübingen: Mohr Siebeck, 1977); and William J. Courtenay, *Covenant and Causality in Medieval Thought* (London: Variorum Reprints, 1984).

11. Jan Marius and J. Lange van Ravenswaay, *Augustinus totus noster. Das Augustinverständnis bei Johannes Calvin,* Forschungen zur Kirchen- und Dogmengeschichte 45 (Göttingen: Vandenhoeck & Ruprecht, 1990).

12. Cf. Richard Schenk, O.P., "From Providence to Grace: Thomas Aquinas and the Platonisms of the Mid-Thirteenth Century," *Nova et Vetera,* English Edition, 3 (2005): 307-20.

Because of the memory of Luther's identification in the *Heidelberg Disputation* in 1518 of scholasticism with the *"theologia gloriae"* (explicitly in conclusions 21 and 24 together with their proofs), the challenge is heightened to find in Thomistic thought the often-hidden potential of a *"theologia crucis."* The argumentative goal of these present reflections is not to claim a potential consensus of Thomas's thought with any but a few of Luther's forty Heidelberg theses, not to establish for these two theologians a third language, an Esperanto, but to elicit from the "genius" of scholastic language its otherwise implicit theology of the cross. This discovery of new possibilities within Roman Catholic thought through its encounter with specific Protestant challenges must be a central Catholic goal of the present ecumenical dialogue. Taking both of these contextual observations together, the goal of the present essay is to identify in a historically credible manner within Thomas's writings the dimension of a theodicy-capable theology of the cross.

The Hermeneutical Place of Thomas's Doctrine of God in the Interpretation of Gerhard Ebeling

The Theological Locus of the Experienced Inability of Philosophy to Answer the Question of the Gracious God

Given the goal of looking back to Thomas for something anticipatory of a theology of the cross with its concomitant stress on the distinction of law and gospel (or of law and the grace of faith, as in the Heidelberg Disputation's conclusion 26), it will be helpful to recall a Protestant theologian whose thought can be situated between Thomas and Barth. In twin essays from 1964 and 1965, Gerhard Ebeling did much to correct the stereotypic preunderstanding, common even among many Catholic authors, of Thomas's sense of the relation of theology to philosophy. In a nearly fifty-page article "On the Hermeneutical Locus of the Doctrine of God in Peter Lombard and Thomas Aquinas,"[13] Ebeling restricts his

13. Gerhard Ebeling, "Über den hermeneutischen Ort der Gotteslehre bei Petrus Lombardus und Thomas von Aquin," first published in *Zeitschrift für Theologie und Kirche* 61 (1964): 283-326, cited here according to Ebeling, *Wort und Glaube,* vol. 2: *Beiträge zur Fundamentaltheologie und zur Lehre von Gott* (Tübingen: Mohr Siebeck, 1969), pp. 209-56; and Ebeling, "Existenz zwischen Gott und Gott. Ein Beitrag zur Frage nach der Existenz Gottes," first published in *Zeitschrift für Theologie und Kirche* 62 (1965): 86-113, cited here ac-

investigation to examining and comparing the opening articles in Peter Lombard's *Sentences* and especially Thomas Aquinas's *Summa theologiae* to explicate their doctrines of God. Thomas begins by asking, "Whether, besides philosophy, any further doctrine is required?" Proceeding from this small textual basis, Ebeling draws out with an uncanny insightfulness the significance that Thomas establishes the necessity and nature of theology as "sacra doctrina" not so much upon the strengths as upon the inadequacies of "philosophical disciplines," including all other experience-based forms of knowledge.[14] In an important development of structures of a futuristic eschatology still implicit in Peter Lombard, who simply starts with the de facto familiarity of the Christian theologian with the Scriptures and their tradition, Thomas by contrast "founds the necessity of the *sacra doctrina* in a limitation and deficiency of the *philosophicae disciplinae*."[15] This limitation is an important part of an answer raised by the relative strength and ability of the experiential disciplines to speak of God. "Philosophical discourse about God appears at first rather as a challenge and threat to *sacra doctrina,* by placing in question the need for and thus also the legitimacy of such a doctrine . . . so that we are surprised to see Thomas at the very beginning of his *Summa* wrestling with the objection and threat posed to *sacra theologia* by the philosophical disciplines, not because they claim that we can know nothing of God, but because they claim to know something of God and speak of Him validly."[16]

Ebeling recognizes an identification of the essential weakness of philosophy at the heart of its relative strength as the realization of the place where the *sacra doctrina* of the gracious God begins and remains an abiding principle. In words other than Ebeling's, the philosophical disciplines can tell us there is a God, but not the God of grace or salva-

---

cording to Ebeling, *Wort und Glaube,* vol. 2, pp. 257-86. Along the same lines, cf. Walter Mostert, *Menschwerdung. Eine historische und dogmatische Untersuchung über das Motiv der Inkarnation des Gottessohnes bei Thomas von Aquin* (Tübingen: Mohr, 1978); and Mostert, "Glaube und Trauer. Zur Frage der Wahrheitserkenntnis bei Thomas von Aquin und Martin Luther," in *Glaube und Hermeneutik. Gesammelte Aufsätze,* ed. Pierre Bühler and Gerhard Ebeling (Tübingen: Mohr Siebeck, 1998), pp. 69-79.

14. It is the insight that separates Ebeling from Barth's very different interpretation of Thomas; cf. Eugene F. Rogers, *Thomas Aquinas and Karl Barth: Sacred Doctrine and the Natural Knowledge of God* (Notre Dame: University of Notre Dame Press, 1995).

15. Ebeling, "Über den hermeneutischen Ort," p. 231.

16. Ebeling, "Über den hermeneutischen Ort," p. 233.

tion driving that first-level insight. Experience can confirm a natural desire for the resurrection, but not its realization. What Kant will call an antinomy, the necessity of posing and the impossibility of deciding an ultimate question due to plausible but merely partial evidence on opposing sides, applies not only to the famous issues of the thirteenth century, like the noneternity of the world, but to the beginning of theology in the question of the gracious, revealing, and saving God. It is precisely the strength of experience and reason to pose this question that also reveals their weakness to answer it. For Thomas, it is this experienced weakness of the philosophical disciplines that is also the very condition of the possibility of faith in the God of grace, revelation, and salvation.[17]

Ebeling's Sense of the Admitted Weakness in Argumentation of the Philosophy of God

In the year following the first publication of "On the Hermeneutical Locus . . . ," Ebeling published a continuation under the title, "Existence between God and God."[18] Here he mentions another form of the dialectic between philosophy's strengths and weaknesses. Ebeling identifies three steps, or better "leaps," in Thomas's philosophical doctrine of God.[19] After admitting that God's existence is not self-evident, Thomas adds that the ways we come to know the existence of God are first of all difficult, rare, and quite imperfect reflections on the lack of self-sufficiency in that realm of being of which we are a part. The second step is the denial that this insufficiency can ground itself. Not so much a positive concept of God, but a "protest," as Ebeling says, a denial that the non-self-sufficient of which we are a part can be all there is makes for that second leap. Thomas adds that this is also the beginning of metaphysics, that act of *"separatio,"* acknowledging that matter and motion cannot be all there is.[20] And, finally, there is the leap by

17. Cf. Thomas Aquinas, *De veritate,* q. 14, aa. 1-5.

18. Ebeling, "Existenz zwischen Gott und Gott."

19. Ebeling, "Existenz zwischen Gott und Gott," pp. 270-72, concentrating on *ST* I, q. 2, aa. 1-3.

20. Cf. the introduction by Armand Maurer to his translation of Thomas Aquinas, *The Division and Methods of the Sciences: Questions V and VI of his Commentary on the* De Trinitate *of Boethius* (Toronto: Pontifical Institute of Mediaeval Studies, 1963).

which what was negatively pointed to is then said to be what all consider as God. Ebeling's point is underlined elsewhere by Thomas's insistence that God is not the proper object of metaphysics but merely its principle.[21] Far from the sovereignty suggested in the scholastic handbooks, Catholic and Protestant, of early modernity, metaphysics of this kind is more an acknowledgment of finitude than an assertion of cognitive power. It is the realization of the limited outcome of this reflected experience of finitude, the experience of nonexperience, that Ebeling identifies as the hermeneutical locus of and point of departure for theology as *sacra doctrina*.

Other Textual References to the Abiding Limitation of Experience

Ebeling might have easily strengthened and expanded his case by referring to any number of texts that Thomas wrote, sometimes without great controversy in his own day, all of which refer to the same kind of "seam" between experience and faith in God which was visible in that opening article of the *Summa theologiae*, for example, Thomas's insistence that the believer does not acquire the kind of immediate knowledge or experience of God that could make faith certain, lucid, or superfluous. Among the topics that Thomas chose for his earliest series of university disputes (1257-59) was that concerning the very nature of faith, including the lack of insight at the beginning and end of faith's exercise; faith, we hear, is more restless than any science and cannot be pacified by it.[22] The presence of sanctifying grace eludes the reflection of every believer, whose question, how to find a gracious God (not so unlike Luther's question, "Wie kriege ich einen gnädigen Gott?"), remains without a tangible answer based solely on human nature and experience. The limits of analogy and the abiding conflict between the projected fullness of the signification of the best perfections found in the world of experience and that always less-than-divine mode of signification by which we conceive of them is yet another expression of the Dionysian rather than the Augustinian contours of Thomas's thought. To know the world perfectly would demand knowing God and the transcendental perfections perfectly; so that, instead, the mysterious-

21. Aquinas, *In Metaphysicam Aristotelis,* Prologue.
22. Aquinas, *De veritate,* q. 14, a. 9.

ness of God implies the mysteriousness of the world as well. The five questions that open the second part of Thomas's *Summa theologiae* and describe the universal desire for beatitude and our inability in this life to ever attain it, place the whole description of Christian existence and the life of grace under the *ratio* of an unrealized, a future eschatology. It is not until the third part of the *Summa* that some degree of that beatitude shines forth, like rays of the sun peeking out from a clouded sky, in Christ, his continued existence in the Church, and his presence to the still unperfected blessed souls awaiting resurrection.

Some of these topics reached the level of controversy. Despite recent memory of the censure of his Parisian confrère, Stephanus de Varnesia, in 1241, Thomas insisted on reaffirming the axiom, *gratia praesupponit naturam,* and its corollary, *fides praesupponit rationem.* But in a way that Ebeling has prepared us for, the "nature" that is presupposed and preserved by grace is the experience of finitude, the insight that what can fail, will fail; this is the prerequisite of grace. Where the neo-Platonic authors of the axiom in the context of the early theodicy works, *Unde malum?* had referred only to providence in general and to the cosmic hierarchy it had to maintain, Thomas inserts personal grace, revealing God's strength in human weakness to a doubting humanity. In another controversy, this principle of inevitable finitude is affirmed by Thomas over and against the Joachite enthusiasts, even among the mendicants. The Church, Thomas reminds his contemporaries, in all its ministers and religious, in its teaching and its worship, will remain an imperfect community until the end of time.

Ebeling could have easily fleshed out his insightful reading of Thomas's sense of the abiding limits of experience and reason by recalling one of Thomas's major and most self-defining conflicts with his neo-Augustinian opponents. Thomas's second Parisian regency (1268-72) was marked especially by the debates around whether, if not every human being, at least the Christian believer knows by reasoned reflection on experience that the world had a beginning. Famously, Thomas denied this; rather, on his account, even Christians must continue to believe what they cannot experience: that the world was not eternal. Reason and experience could at best identify as uncertain the arguments pointing to the world's eternity. Belief in the God of the Scriptures does not make for a completely new body of evidence; believers remain in the same common world of basic experience and reason as nonbelievers. The systematic intentionality of his position is attested to by the fact that Thomas was challenged on this position not only by his Franciscan colleagues, notably Bonaventure, John Pecham, and later William de la Mare, but also by his secular ones. The issue would be brought up by the episcopal censures of 1270 and 1277 — in the latter case, illustrating the condemnation with a citation from Thomas's apologia, *De aeternitate mundi*. On a scale of strong to weak reason, Thomas championed in this issue even for believers something in the middle, something quite close to Kant's sense of the antinomies.[23] In Thomas's view, God had the choice to create the world from all eternity; the faith that, in the context of salvific history, he did not do so, the faith that the world had a beginning, could never be made superfluous by evidence *a priori* or *a posteriori*.

The later handbook traditions of Catholic and then also Protestant theology taught us to expect the so-called treatise on God at the beginning of theology. Ebeling's reflections on the methodological introduction to the *Summa theologiae* and the foundational distinction between philosophy and faith — obviously, in human beings, not in God — comes as a surprise, then, when, in reading what had been billed as a treatise on God, it turns out in nearly every article to be a treatise on our human standing before God, affirming our difference from him in the hope of finding his grace, in the development of the theodicy question. Sometimes this interplay has been named by Thomas's edi-

---

23. Cf. Anton Antweiler, *Die Anfangslosigkeit der Welt nach Thomas von Aquin und Kant* (Trier: Paulinus-Verlag, 1961). Among the many historical publications on this debate, cf. Ignatius Brady, "John Pecham and the Background of Aquinas's *De Aeternitate Mundi*," in *St. Thomas Aquinas, 1274-1974: Commemorative Studies*, ed. Armand Maurer et al. (Toronto: Pontifical Institute of Mediaeval Studies, 1974), vol. 2, pp. 141-55 and 156-78, respectively; James A. Weisheipl, *Friar Thomas D'Aquino: His Life, Thought, and Work* (Garden City, NY: Doubleday, 1974), pp. 285-90, followed by the "Corrigenda and Addenda" of the second edition, p. 475; Weisheipl, "The Date and Context of Thomas's *De aeternitate mundi*," in *Graceful Reason: Essays Presented to Joseph Owens*, ed. Lloyd Gerson (Toronto: Pontifical Institute of Mediaeval Studies, 1983), pp. 239-71; Boethius of Dacia, *On the Supreme Good. On the Eternity of the World. On Dreams*, trans. John F. Wippel (Toronto: Pontifical Institute of Mediaeval Studies, 1987), pp. 9-19 and 36-67, respectively; Richard C. Dales, *Medieval Discussions of the Eternity of the World* (Leiden: Brill, 1990); J. M. B. Wissink, ed., *The Eternity of the World in the Thought of Thomas Aquinas and His Contemporaries* (Leiden: Brill, 1990); Richard C. Dales and Omar Argerami, eds., *Medieval Latin Texts on the Eternity of the World* (Leiden: Brill, 1991); Rolf Schönberger, "Der Disput über die Ewigkeit der Welt," in *Über die Ewigkeit der Welt. Bonaventura, Thomas von Aquin, Boethius von Dacien*, ed. Peter Nickl (Frankfurt am Main: Klostermann, 2000); as well as the extensive literature on the censures by the bishop of Paris in 1270 and 1277.

tors in the titles given to the articles: whether God's beatitude includes the beatitude of anyone who will ever be blessed; whether his goodness includes every nondivine goodness as well, or his truth all truth; how God exists in all things; how all is life in him; on the constant coexistence, despite occasional appearances to the contrary, of both mercy and justice; on providence, election, and predestination; on the creative ideas that God has of his creation; on whether God could have made this world better or why the best of all possible worlds is itself not a possibility at all. In all those titles God is only part of the question. But the presence of our acknowledging our difference to God, which is conceivable only on the basis of our standing before him, is found in articles where this is not expressed in the title. The articles on the perfections of God, such as the simplicity, perfection, infinity, immutability, eternity, and unity, are questions that make sense only in contrast with what is complex, imperfect, finite, etc. The questions as to his will quickly come to his indirect tolerance of evil and the difference of his consequent will on earth that is so different from his antecedent and unconditioned will in heaven.

Because, in all these questions about God-and-x, the x is most usually the human being who is questioning God about his own self and future, the treatise on God has the structure of theodicy. The theodicy question is never just about God, his knowledge, power, and goodness. These are put in question only when a nondivine but nevertheless precious being suffers in a way opposed to what its dignity seems to call for. Theodicy is therefore always and of necessity also anthropo-dicy, cosmo-dicy. The predominance of God and humanity prepares the reader for Christology and soteriology, where these issues recur, from mercy and justice to the importance of both God and humankind as well as the long lack of evidence about God's salvific will and to the difference of what he unconditionally wills from much that he merely permits. The repeated use of scriptural references reminds the reader that this is no philosophical tractate *De Deo uno*. The histories of Maimonides and Peter Comestor would have reminded Thomas of the long and dramatic struggle of the First Covenant people to come to a fully monotheistic faith. The proximate preparation of Trinitarian faith was not polytheism, but monotheism, just as the Trinity is not named by narratives of three persons but by their confession as one God.

Richard Schenk, O.P.

Thomas's Last Writing

The Affinity to the Goals of Jenson's Theology

The way in which metaphysics persists within theology as a part of the Christian's confession of the abiding need for grace from Another can be shown in Thomas's last known words, writing, and controversy. That text also shows a Thomas Aquinas who is closer to agreeing with Robert Jenson's notion of the goals of a genuine theology than might often be suspected, even by Jenson himself; their differences appear to be far more one of argumentative means than argumentative ends. That a theistic determinism must be rejected *inter alia* in the interests of safeguarding the logic of intercessory prayer is a shared thesis that not only names a central concern of Jenson's contribution but also of Thomas's own final testimony. Let me recall first Professor Jenson's reflections in his "Ipse Pater Non Est Impassibilis," from his essay in the volume *Divine Impassibility and the Mystery of Human Suffering*:

> As the general assignment of our conference supposes, our attempts to construe the fact of providence are indeed a chief place where difficulties with God's impassibility/passibility impede our efforts. According to Thomas — whom I should doubtless forebear to cite in this company — God's universal knowledge and universal will are such . . . that God's foreseeing determines what is seen. . . . It is apparent that this doctrine must provoke some questions. One is the so-called problem of theodicy. In my judgment this problem is in this life insoluble. . . . In my view, however, the really difficult question concerns the meaningfulness of petitionary prayer — which is, after all, the kind most recommended and practiced in Scripture. Suppose I pray for someone's recovery. If the Lord foresees from all eternity that my friend will/not recover, and if that foreseeing determines the event, and if he thus already knows what he ordains and ordains what he knows, what role does my petition have? . . . Prayer is involvement in Providence. If prayer is anything less, it is simply a pitiful delusion. Perhaps if we were more straightforwardly to consider the biblical necessity of the two sentences previous to this one [the basic implication of which is that we ought to regard prayer as "mattering to" and "affecting" God], dis-

cussion of God's relation to our time, and so of his passibility/
impassibility, would make more progress.[24]

After the episode of December 6, 1273, after which Thomas ceased
to write or dictate, saying that his previous work seemed like so much
straw in comparison to newer revelations, there was in fact one and
only final letter that scholars assume he wrote.[25] It was likely in late
January or February, just weeks before Thomas's death on March 7,
1274, and it was addressed to Bernard of Ayglier, a longtime friend, the
abbot of Monte Cassino. It seems that a faction of the monks was
moved to call into doubt the meaningfulness of intercessory prayer for
the very objections that Jenson recites: *If the Lord foresees from all eternity
that my friend will/not recover, and if that foreseeing determines the event, and
if he thus already knows what he ordains and ordains what he knows, what role
does my petition have?* Thomas agrees that, if these conditions were true,
prayer would be nonsensical; but he attempts to show, with the help of
Boethian neo-Platonic metaphysics, that foreseeing does not entail determination; but rather, that God allows contingent factors such as ill-
ness, accidents, and the fragile goodwill of friends to play a role, a fore-
seen role, in what happens to us. God does not ordain death, but he
permits it, and at times he postpones it. What this means is that we
cannot consider ourselves subject to fate, but must keep open the
theodicy question of why God might, or might not, grant our prayers.
Thomas's use of metaphysics allows him here to avoid determinism
and, joining Jenson and Barth, to remain a theologian and a disciple.

24. Robert Jenson, "Ipse Pater Non Est Impassibilis," in *Divine Impassibility and the
Mystery of Human Suffering,* ed. James F. Keating and Thomas Joseph White, O.P. (Grand
Rapids: Eerdmans, 2009), pp. 125-26.
25. Cf. David Berger, "Die letzte Schrift des heiligen Thomas von Aquin," *Forum
Katholische Theologie* 14 (1998): 221-30.

Richard Schenk, O.P.

APPENDIX

To the Reverend Father in Christ, Lord Bernard,
by the grace of God the venerable Abbot of Monte Cassino,

Brother Thomas de Aquino, his devoted son,
ready to obey him at every time and place.

Venerable Father, I would have preferred to meet in person with the brethren, convened for this purpose, to speak to those who find scandalous the words of the illustrious doctor, Gregory the Great. But the length of the divine office and the scope of the pre-Lenten practices make this impracticable,[26] and yet perhaps it is more fruitful this way, so that what is commended to writing might be able to be of use not only to those present now but also to others yet to come. I see in this occurrence also something of God's hand, that your letters should reach me here at Aquino just as I am on my way to France; for it was here that Blessed Maurus, the disciple of our holy Father Benedict, when sent by him to France, was deigned worthy to receive the letters and the precious gifts of so great a father.[27]

In order to more fully alleviate the doubts, lets us include in these present reflections the very words of St. Gregory (*Moralia* XIII), which engendered doubts and errors in those not understanding the matter: *It must be known,* he says, *that the generosity of God provides sinners with a space for penance, but because the times received are applied not to the fruit of penance but to the practice of iniquity, they lose what they were able to merit from divine mercy, although almighty God knows in advance the time of death for each human being, in which his/her life is ended, and although it is impossible that they should die at another time than precisely then. For if they remind us of the fifteen years added to Hezekiah's life, it is true that the time of his life grew in relation to when he ought to have died.[28] But the divine dispensation already then knew this time, at which it later removed him from this present life.[29]*

26. In 1274, Easter Sunday fell on April 1.

27. In a note from July 18, 2008, Prof. John Wickstrom confirmed the now probable identity of "Euchaeia" in the "Maurusvita und Aquino" in Thomas's letter.

28. Cf. 2 Kings 20:6.

29. In his commentary on the literal sense of Job, likely written in Orvieto between 1261 and 1265, Thomas concludes the preface with a note praising Gregory's inter-

With these words the luminous doctor lucidly identifies the two-fold consideration of every human being: one in relation to himself, the other in relation to divine foreknowledge. The human being, considered just in himself, that is, in those things that happen to him, is not subjected to necessity. But it is possible that something can happen to him that in turn brings about an effect that is then not just by chance, either, as Gregory expressly mentions regarding sinners, when he states: *but because the times received are applied not to the fruit of penance but to the practice of iniquity, they lose what they were able to merit from divine mercy,* even though that loss had not been necessary.

Whence those things that happen to a human being do not come about by necessity. This holds true for death, too, as well as for several other things which humans do or suffer; and yet all things are subject to divine providence.

If the human being is considered in relation to divine providence, what he does or suffers incurs a kind of necessity, not of an absolute sort such that, considered in itself, it is altogether impossible that it could have happened otherwise, but rather according to a "conditional necessity," because the following conditional sentence is necessary: "If God foreknows something, it will come about." For these two are not able to exist side by side: that God would foreknow something, and that then it would not be. Because then God's foreknowledge would be fallible. It is completely impossible that truth itself would suffer falsity. Which is what the immediately following words of St. Gregory mean, when he adds: *Although almighty God knows in advance the time of the death each human being, in which his/her life is ended, and although it is impossible that they should die at another time than precisely then,* that is, at a time other than the one foreknown by God. . . . For these two are not able to exist side by side: that God would foreknow that someone would die at a given time, and that he would in fact die at another time. For then the knowledge of God would be fallible.

Considered just in himself, a human being is able to die at another time. Who doubts, when threatened, that he really could be pierced by a sword, burnt by fire, or see his life end sooner by a fall or a trap? This is the distinction meant by the following words of Gregory's text, when he adds: *For if they remind us of the fifteen years added to Heze-*

---

pretation of the spiritual sense of the biblical book. The dispute among the monks was, however, about the literal sense of Gregory's text.

kiah's life, it is true that the time of his life grew in relation to when he ought to have died.

It would be nonsense to say that someone merited something that could never happen. Considered in himself, Hezekiah could have died at that earlier time. But considered in relation to divine knowledge, these two cannot stand side by side: that he would die at one time, and that God would foreknow him to die at another. And in order for us to induce in the minds of those doubting by a kind of eyewitness, by a faith that has come to see what the words of the Church doctor are expressing, it is necessary to consider the difference between divine and human knowing. For the human being is subject to change and time, in which prior and posterior have their place, and so we know things one after another, some before and others later. We recall what is past, we see what is present, we anticipate what will come about. But God is free of all change, according to a word in the book of the prophet Malachi: "I am God and I will not change." So He surpasses all succession of time. Past and future are not found in Him. But all that will happen or has happened is in Him as present. Just as He said to His servant, Moses: *I am Who am.* Therefore in that way He foreknows from all eternity that this one will die at this time, as we say in our manner. But if it were stated in His manner, He sees him die in the way I see Peter sitting when he is sitting. Now it is evident that merely from the fact that I see someone sitting, no necessity of his sitting was generated. For it is impossible that these two statements be true at one and the same time: that I should see someone sitting and that he should not be sitting. And it is similarly impossible for God to foreknow that something will happen that would not come about; and, yet, nevertheless, it is not the case that, due to this, what will happen will happen by necessity.

This is what I have written, dear Father, obeying your command, in order to lead back those who have strayed. If what is said here does not yet convince them, I would not hesitate to write again at your request.

Father, may you flourish for many years to come. Frater Reginald commends himself to you.[30]

---

30. A critical edition of the Latin text of this letter can be found in Antoine Dondaine, "La Lettre de Saint Thomas à l'Abbé du Montcassin," in *St. Thomas Aquinas 1274-1974: Commemorative Studies,* 2 vols. (Toronto: Pontifical Institute of Mediaeval Studies, 1974), vol. 1, pp. 87-108.

II. Trinity

Can Humility and Obedience Be Trinitarian Realities?

Guy Mansini, O.S.B.

In *Mere Christianity*, C. S. Lewis describes our condition as one in which, as sinners, we need to repent, and at the same time as one in which, as *sinners*, enemies of God, we cannot repent. The odd thing is that while only a bad man needs to repent, it is only a good man who can repent, and it takes the best man to repent perfectly. God, Lewis says, wants to teach us repentance, wants to train us in penance such that, just as our reasoning now is a share in his infinite Reason or Logos, so our repentance would be a share in a perfect, than which no greater can be conceived, divine penance. Alas, there is no such thing as divine penance. "We now need God's help," Lewis writes, "in order to do something which God, in His own nature, never does at all — to surrender, to suffer, to submit, to die." And again, "God can share only what He has: this thing, in His own nature, He has not."[1] In order to do what he needs to do for our salvation, but what he cannot do in his own nature, which is to surrender in obedience and to submit in humility, to repent in suffering and death, he takes our nature.

In this way, Lewis seems to arrive at a genuine insight into the logic of the Incarnation, an insight recognizably related to the great western soteriology of atonement, the "satisfaction theory" of St. Anselm. According to much modern, I mean, twentieth-century theology, however, Lewis is doing no such thing. Rather he has betrayed a great naïveté about the Godhead. He has produced a superficial and unsatisfactory account of how God saves man. On this view, there *is*

---

1. C. S. Lewis, *Mere Christianity* (San Francisco: Harper, 2001), pp. 57-58.

such a thing as divine repentance, a sort of perfect and infinite repentance prior to the penance enacted on our behalf by Christ on Calvary. There is, for some twentieth-century theologians, a divine suffering. This suffering is animated by a divine humility and proceeds from a divine obedience. The Incarnation manifests these divine things to us, and this is a part, at least, and perhaps we should rather say, the sum of the revelation of the Trinity of Persons. The suffering of Christ, including especially his humility and obedience unto death relative to his Father and as displayed preeminently in the garden, serves to manifest his identity as Son and so the distinction of Persons, and they could not do that unless in some way they constituted the Person of the Son.[2]

On this view, further, it would seem that the only point of the Incarnation could be so to manifest things to us. For Lewis, the point is that only if incarnate can the Son of God do certain things for us. But for this modern theological way, God does not need to become man in order to do something that, in his own nature, he cannot. For indeed, in his own nature, he can and does do all the suffering, and enacts all the required humility and obedience imaginable.

Is it true that the suffering and obedience and humility of the incarnate Son manifest his divine identity because it constitutes it? Bruce Marshall has called this assumption into question.[3] We must distinguish, he says, between the things that constitute the divine Persons, namely the eternal processions, and those things — properties, features, actions within the created order — that manifest the persons in the economy of salvation. The temporal missions of the Son and the Holy Spirit manifest their eternal processions, but are not identical

---

2. For an intradivine or immanent humility and obedience of the Son, see preeminently Karl Barth, *Church Dogmatics* IV/1 (Edinburgh: T. & T. Clark, 1956), §59, esp. pp. 192-93, 200-204, 209-10. Among the many beholden to Barth for this teaching, see Jürgen Moltmann, *The Crucified God* (New York: Harper & Row, 1973), pp. 202-7, 240-47; and Hans Urs von Balthasar, *Mysterium Paschale* (Edinburgh: T. & T. Clark, 1990), pp. 79-83, and *Theo-Drama: Theological Dramatic Theory*, vol. 5 (San Francisco: Ignatius Press, 1998), pp. 236-39. For contemporary discussion of Barth on this issue, see Bruce L. McCormack, "Divine Impassibility or Simply Divine Constancy? Implications of Karl Barth's Later Christology for Debates over Impassibility," in *Divine Impassibility and the Mystery of Human Suffering*, ed. James F. Keating and Thomas Joseph White, O.P. (Grand Rapids: Eerdmans, 2009), pp. 150-86; and Thomas Joseph White, O.P., "Intra-Trinitarian Obedience and Nicene-Chalcedonian Christology," *Nova et Vetera*, English Edition 6 (2008): 377-402.

3. Bruce Marshall, "The Dereliction of Christ and the Impassibility of God," in Keating and White, eds., *Divine Impassibility and the Mystery of Human Suffering*, pp. 246-98.

with them. According to St. Thomas, the missions add something to the processions in order both to declare them to us and to accomplish our salvation, but what is added — say, in the mission of Christ, his humanity, and, in the moment of the passion, his suffering and obedient humanity — is not the very modality of the procession and does not constitute the Person.[4] I think this is right. This insight is concordant with Lewis. It restores the intelligibility of Lewis's apologia for the Incarnation and passion of the Son of God.

Marshall's point can be explored in two ways (at least). First, we might move from the top down. From a consideration of the processions, relations, and persons in God, we might then consider the missions, and think what they might be in relation to the processions and Persons. This is how St. Thomas proceeds in the great *Summa*. Second, however, we might start with the missions, the *priora quoad nos,* and ascend to the Persons and processions. This last way is, in today's context, the most important, I think. Differences of Trinitarian theology are differences about how to take the Scriptures.[5]

Humility and Obedience

I would like to begin, then, with the humility and obedience of Christ.[6] It is perhaps the case, not only that we haven't thought enough about processions and missions, though I think that is certainly true, but also that we have not thought enough about humility and obedience. I would like to begin with them, moreover, as very definitely understood, as very particularly located within a form of life, within a tradition of Christian living, namely western monasticism. This will give us some assurance that we are not imagining what humility and obedience might

---

4. St. Thomas, *ST* I, q. 43, a. 1: "Missio . . . divinae Personae convenire potest, secundum quod importat ex una parte processionem originis a mittente; et secundum quod importat ex alia parte novum modum existendi in aliquo. Sicut Filius dicitur esse missus a Pater in mundum, secundum quod incoepit esse in mundo visibiliter per carnem assumptam: et tamen ante 'in mundo erat,' ut dicitur Ioan. 1."

5. They are also, doubtless, differences of metaphysics, though ideally this is so only secondarily, as governed once again by how one takes Scripture.

6. The humility of Christ is *coram Deo;* his attitude during his passion relative to his persecutors should be called not humility but meekness. For meekness, see St. Thomas, *ST* II-II, q. 157.

be, but are consulting a real experience of and acquaintance with these things. A mature expression of an already long monastic tradition can be found in the sixth-century *Regula Monachorum* or *Regula Sancti Benedicti,* as it is called — St. Benedict's *Rule* for monks. It is a tradition, moreover, that is scripturally inspired. We won't be looking outside of Scripture, but to a way of life informed by the constant meditation on Scripture, *lectio divina,* and to a way of prayer whose backbone is the recitation of the Psalms. Ansgar Kristensen has it that "the Rule is intended simply as an aid for monks to live by the Scriptures."[7] So to speak, it stands to Scripture taken practically, as directing us how to live, the way the Rule of Faith stands to Scripture taken speculatively, as informing us how to think about the Holy Trinity and the Incarnation.[8]

In guiding the monk how to read the Scriptures for the practical direction of his life, the *Rule* directs him to two dispositions especially, or what we might call two architectonic and related patterns of moral choice and action, obedience and humility. It does so, moreover, and for our purposes this is very significant, on the ground of the obedience and humility of Christ. The express teaching of the Lord about the excellence of humility is invoked (*RB* 7.1, quoting Luke 4:14, 18:14: "Whoever exalts himself shall be humbled, and whoever humbles himself shall be exalted"). More importantly, the example of Christ is invoked: Philippians 2:8, "he became obedient unto death" (at *RB* 7.34) and John 6:38, "I have come not to do my own will, but the will of him who sent me" (twice, at *RB* 5.13 and 7.31). It might well be said, in fact, that the very spring of monasticism is the desire to follow Christ precisely in the humility and obedience displayed on the cross, the humility and obedience St. Paul recommends to us in recommending that we have the mind of Christ (Phil. 2:5). The hymn in the second chapter of Philippians has evoked a tradition of speculative commentary, especially with regard to what a divine "emptying" of oneself might mean.[9] But it has also evoked a tradition of practical commentary by way of the practical cultivation of the humility and obedience expressly there attributed to Christ. This practical commentary is the tradition of the

7. Ansgar Kristensen, "The Role and Interpretation of Scripture in the Rule of Benedict," in *RB 1980: The Rule of St. Benedict in Latin and English with Notes,* ed. Timothy Fry, O.S.B. (Collegeville, MN: Liturgical Press, 1981), pp. 467-77, at p. 470.

8. This analogy is suggested if not stated by Kristensen, "The Role and Interpretation of Scripture in the Rule of Benedict," p. 468.

9. For a brief account of which, see Barth, *Church Dogmatics* IV/1, pp. 180-83.

monastic life.[10] As for Karl Barth, the humility and obedience of Christ are indeed a "unique locus of revelation," but for the monastic tradition, a unique locus for the revelation of a practical order of Christian life to be realized in the cenobium.[11]

Humility and Obedience in the Rule *of Benedict*

We begin with humility. According to the *Rule,* there are twelve steps or degrees of humility.

The first step is that a monk "keep the fear of God always before his eyes" (7.10; Ps. 35[36]:2).[12] He is to keep in mind at every moment "that all who despise God will burn in hell for their sins, and all who fear God have everlasting life" (7.11), remembering "that he is always seen by God in heaven, that his actions everywhere are in God's sight and are reported by angels at every hour" (7.13).

The second step is that a monk "loves not his own will nor takes pleasure in the satisfaction of his desires" (7.31), and the third "that a man submits to his superior in all obedience for the love of God" (7.34). The chapter on obedience, in fact, makes of it the first, not the third step of humility. They are evidently intimately connected, and have both to do with what we should cheerfully recognize as a breaking of the monk's will, a sort of smashing of the ego. It is understandable, therefore, that obedience under unjust circumstances, obedience unto

---

10. See, for example, John Cassian, Conference 19 of Abbot John on the end of monastic life, where in chapter 6 the excellence of the cenobitic life is grounded in the obedience the monk gives to his abbot, since in this way he imitates the obedience of Christ according to Philippians 2:8, in John Cassian, *The Conferences,* Ancient Christian Writers 57, trans. and annotated by Boniface Ramsey, O.P. (New York: Newman Press, 1997). See also the saying of Abba Hyperichius, chapter XIV.11 of the *Verba seniorum* in the *Vitae Patrum* (PL 73.950AB) on the work of the monk: "Dixit abbas Hyperichius: Quia ministerium monachi est obedientia, quam qui possidet, quod [col. 950B] poscit exaudietur, et cum fiducia Crucifixo astabit; etenim Dominus sic venit ad crucem, factus scilicet obediens usque ad mortem." I am grateful to my confrère, Fr. Harry Hagan, O.S.B., for these references and for this way of looking at monasticism. See also the suggestive remark of Barth on monasticism, *Church Dogmatics* IV/1, p. 190.

11. For Barth, see White, "Intra-Trinitarian Obedience," p. 379.

12. Quotations from the *Rule* are from the text and translation of *RB 1980: The Rule of St. Benedict in Latin and English with Notes,* ed. Timothy Fry, O.S.B., trans. Timothy Horner, Marian Larmann, et al. (Collegeville, MN: Liturgical Press, 1981).

suffering, makes up the fourth step of humility (7.35-36). Moreover, just as humility is expressly something *coram Deo,* so obedience to the superior is obedience given to God (5.15).

The mortification unto death of the old self is prominent in some of the later steps of humility. The sixth has it that the monk "is content with the lowest and most menial treatment *(omni vilitate vel extremitate)*" (7.49). The eighth is that a man "does only what is endorsed by the common rule of the monastery and the example set by his superiors" (7.55). A monk does not indulge the vanity of sticking out, of being egregious — *ex grege,* outside the flock. He doesn't make his ego, his self, shine with the light of his own exceptional views and choices. Likewise, the ninth step is "that a monk control his tongue and remain silent, not speaking unless he is asked a question" (7.56). He does not intrude himself, his *self,* into the conversation. He doesn't impose himself by imposing his views.

The most extraordinary expression of this smashing of the ego, however, is the seventh degree, "that a man not only admit with his tongue but is also convinced in his heart that he is inferior to all and of less value *(inferiorem et viliorem),* humbling himself" (7.51). Here the *Rule* would have us follow the advice of St. Paul, "in humility count others better than yourselves" (Phil. 2:3), which seems to be part of what it means to have the "mind of Christ" (2:5). Can one think of oneself as inferior to all and of less worth than any other and do so truly? With the realization that everything the monk has and is that is good is from God, a gift of either creation or grace, and that everything he has apart from God, everything left over that he owes purely and simply to himself, a self independent of God, is sin, the answer is yes.[13] His true self, however better endowed than another, is what he has received wholly from God and is not, in that sense, his own, his own self as made only by himself.

What is this true self? Its form is indicated at the end of the chapter on humility (7.67-69).

> Now, therefore, after ascending all these steps of humility, the monk will quickly arrive at that perfect love of God which casts out fear (1 John 4:18). Through this love, all that he once performed with dread, he will now begin to observe without effort, as though

13. See *RB* 4.42-43: "If you notice something good in yourself, give credit to God, not to yourself, but be certain that the evil you commit is always your own and yours to acknowledge."

naturally, from habit, no longer out of fear of hell, but out of love for Christ, good habit and delight in virtue. (7.67-69)[14]

This is important. The abasement of humility and the ignorance of the good that makes obedience necessary are in themselves negative things. Much more evil is the overweening love of one's own will, and it is salutary that humility and obedience react rightly to this evil. This means that humility and obedience are not chosen for themselves. They are chosen in view of something else. Humility and obedience are instrumental; they are chosen unto a good beyond them. The *Rule* does not inculcate some mystical attachment to dark things.[15]

Humility as presented according to the express teaching of the *Rule* seems evidently to be a virtue of a created will, considering that will as before God, as is clear from the first degree, and also as fallen and sinful, as is clear throughout the *Rule*'s discussion, but especially in the fifth degree, which is that a monk manifest his sinful thoughts to his abbot (it is taken for granted that he will have them) (7.44). Humility is something realized in relation to other persons, each with their own will: the will of the other monks of the cenobium; the will of the abbot, especially; and as mediated by the abbot and community, the will of God. Further, as already noted, humility is something instrumental.

There is something in addition to the express teaching of the *Rule*, however, and this is the enactment of humility according to the discipline that the *Rule* enjoins. Infractions of the Rule, together with such things as pride and outright disobedience to one's superiors, merit the punishment of excommunication (*RB* 23). As punishment, separation from the community, either the choir or the table, is a suffering or penalty imposed on the malefactor. However, it is to lead to "satisfaction," which the Rule understands as the malefactor's willing amendment of his fault. The malefactor "is punished" — passive voice

---

14. See also *RB* Prol. 49: "As we progress in this way of life and in faith, we shall run on the path of God's commandments, our hearts overflowing with the inexpressible delight of love." And see chapter 72, "The Good Zeal of Monks."

15. This denouement of humility in the *Rule* distinguishes it from the false humility that is the instrument of *ressentiment*, for which see Friedrich Nietzsche, *The Genealogy of Morals,* trans. W. Kaufmann (New York: Vintage, 1967), First Essay, sections 10, 11, 14, or from humility as an instrument of social control, for which see the interpretation given to Clement of Rome's recommendation of humility in Klaus Wengst, *Humility: Solidarity of the Humiliated* (Philadelphia: Fortress Press, 1988), pp. 54-57.

— according to the agency of the abbot. The malefactor "makes satisfaction" — active voice — according to his own agency. Now, the way to
make satisfaction is *humility* (27.3 and 45.2). And one humbles oneself in
the *Rule* by *prostration* (43.2-3, 7-8: probably also at 45.1 and 46.3). In
other words, the humility that satisfies for offense is enacted corpore-
ally by abasing oneself quite literally, making oneself low (perhaps the
first sense of *humilis*), getting close to the earth *(humus).*[16] Humility appears therefore as especially a virtue of the *embodied* rational creature.
Furthermore, it illuminates the sense of "satisfaction" as a transaction
between opposable wills; the offended community and abbot are "satis-
fied" by the humility and obedient will of the miscreant monk, the em-
bodiment of whose interior disposition is prostration.[17]

Humility has already introduced us to obedience, one of its signs
and enactments, and a brief word about chapter 5 will therefore suffice.
The duality of wills presupposed by humility is signified in the most
basic way by the evocation of the external voice of the superior that is
heard by the monk. At the voice of the superior, obedient monks "put
aside their own concerns, abandon their own will, and lay down whatever they have in hand" (5.7-8). "They follow the voice of authority"
(5:8). This insistence on the voice of authority picks up on the construction of the very word, *"ob-audire."* To obey is to hear very thoroughly and completely and with all one's faculties, as it were. Also, this
insistence on the voice recalls the opening exhortation of the Prologue:
Obsculta, "listen," "attend with the ear of your heart" and take up the
"labor of obedience" (Prol. 1 and 2). That is to say, listen, and take up
the labor of listening, of attending to a mind and a will that is not your
own. Obedience, and the salvation it brings, like faith, comes from
hearing (Rom. 10:17). The monk is not God, and the sign of this is that
he is not the abbot. Therefore, "the obedience shown to superiors is
shown to God" (5.15). Quite clearly, there is no obedience without two
wills, wills that can be opposed to one another (cf. 5.14). In this light,
and if God's will is one, as there is only one God, obedience does not
seem possible unless there is some created will. That is, the realm of
obedience, its first possibility, presupposes creation. And this would be
true of humility as well.

---

16. See Wengst, *Humility,* chapter 2.

17. It is the abbot who determines the extent of satisfaction according to *RB* 44.2-
10 ("usque dum [abbas] benedicat et dicat: Sufficit").

Would it be too abrupt and simpleminded at this juncture to ask what place such things, such attitudes and motions of the heart, could have *in divinis?* What place is there for the Son to think himself *inferiorem et viliorem* within the Trinity? Would not such thinking immediately generate a problem with the singleness of the divine mind and a second problem with either the truth of the divine understanding or the equality of Persons?

What sort of analogy can save these things, humility and obedience, and render them serviceable for speaking of God? What can make them divine properties, properties that can help us conceive the processions and the distinctions of Persons? The grades of humility are not like the grades of being, and we do not seem to have on our hands something that can be asserted formally, if only analogously, of God. It would not occur to anyone reading the *Rule* to suppose that "humble" and "obedient" are divine names, nor, to take a glance at eastern monasticism, do they appear in the *Divine Names* of the Areopagite.

St. Thomas on Humility and Obedience

There is a direct line from the monastic tradition to St. Thomas, whose early education, after all, was at Monte Cassino. He expressly takes up chapter 7 of the *Rule* in dealing with humility, and offers a systematization of the twelve degrees of humility. He cites especially the *Moralia* of Gregory the Great in treating of obedience. Gregory, it will be remembered, is the biographer of St. Benedict, and is himself a monk in the city of Rome. What St. Thomas achieves is to insert both humility and obedience without irony into a systematic context whose framework is Aristotle's analysis of the virtues in the *Nicomachean Ethics.*

St. Thomas treats humility at length in the *Secunda pars* (II-II, q. 161). Humility is a species of modesty (cf. q. 160), which is a part of temperance (cf. q. 141), the virtue by which our appetite for the pleasures especially of touch is moderated (q. 141, a. 3).[18] Modesty is merely a "potential part" of temperance, however, extending temperance to appetites less

---

18. To be sure, humility does not show up in Aristotle's *Ethics,* and one can wonder whether it could even be known as a virtue apart from revelation. Part of the genius of St. Thomas is to balance humility with (a rather overhauled) magnanimity in *ST* II-II, q. 161, a. 1, by which we are saved from spiritual despair.

difficult to moderate than the desire for the pleasures of touch (q. 143, a. un). One of these "appetites" is hope. Unmoderated by the virtue of humility, hope would incline us to what is above us in a disproportionate way (q. 161, a. 1). Humility makes hope just, as it were. Especially, humility regards our proper subjection to God, and reverence is its cause.

> . . . a special reason for restraining the presumption of hope is taken from reverence for God, from which it happens that a man not attribute to himself more than is fitting to him according to the grade which has been allotted him by God. Whence humility seems especially to regard the subjection of man to God. (q. 161, a. 2, ad 3; and see a. 1, ad 5; a. 3, c.; and a. 4, ad 1)

The concupiscible appetite is the subject of temperance, but it is not the subject of humility, which, like modesty, is a virtue annexed to temperance, one of its "potential parts" but not one of its species. Since it governs hope, which is an act of irascible appetite, humility too has its subject there (q. 161, a. 4, ad 2). The concupiscible and irascible appetites are verified in their proper sense in man, the rational animal, but not in angels or God. It immediately follows that whatever virtue has its subject in such appetites could not properly be found in them either.

It would be hard to overstate the importance for human beings of just this virtue, however. While it does not share in the formal perfection of charity by which most of all we are made holy and conformed to Christ, St. Thomas thinks of humility as a sort of foundation of a holy life, since it removes what gets in the way of such a life, which is pride.

> And in this way humility holds the first place [among the virtues]: insofar, that is, as it expels pride, which God resists, and renders a man subordinate and always open [*patulum*] to receiving the influx of divine grace, insofar as it takes away the inflation of pride; as it is said in James, that "God resists the proud but gives grace to the humble" (4:6). And in this way, humility is called the foundation of the spiritual edifice [*spiritualis aedificii fundamentum*]. (q. 161, a. 5, ad 2)

Humility turns out to be a sort of spiritual site preparation; it bulldozes away the brush and bramble of egoism.[19] It clears space for some-

---

19. St. Thomas endorses the comparison of what is proper to oneself to what is of God in others at *ST* II-II, q. 161, a. 3, ad 2, which we have seen in the seventh degree of hu-

thing to be built on a clean foundation.[20] In his commentary on St. Matthew's Gospel, he says more simply and boldly that humility orders one rightly to oneself and to God, and renders one *capax Dei*.[21] While humility is therefore an indispensable part of our relation to divine things, it is just as evidently not itself one of them.

> Something is said to be perfect in two ways. In one way, simply speaking: that is, a thing is perfect if there is no defect found in it, neither according to its own nature nor in regard to anything else. And in this way God alone is perfect, to whom humility does not belong according to the divine nature but only according to the assumed nature. (q. 161, a. 1, ad 4)

That is to say, God can be humble only if he first becomes man.

St. Thomas likewise devotes a question to obedience in the *Secunda pars*. Obedience, he says, is a part or species of *observantia*, which we might render "respectfulness" or even "reverence" (see q. 104, a. 3, ad 1), and "by which worship *(cultus)* and honor are shown to persons established in dignity" (q. 102, a. 1). *Observantia* is a virtue annexed to justice, one of its "potential parts" (q. 80, a. un), where justice is understood as the virtue by which "what is owed to another is given him according to equality" (q. 80, a. un; see q. 58, a. 11). *Observantia* is not a species of justice simply speaking, but a virtue annexed to it because it falls away from the *ratio* of justice in that, just as piety does not recompense parents according to equality, so neither does *observantia* render a wholly adequate respect to superiors (q. 80, a. un). Still, even as justice properly regards another person (q. 58, a. 2), just so does obedience regard another will, the will of some superior. It knits together the human community in the way that in the natural order the subordination of lower causes to superior causes makes for an ordinate and unified world.

---

mility, but when expressly referring to this degree, at q. 161, a. 6, ad 1, he defends its possibility on the basis of our ignorance of what is really in others, following the Gloss.

20. Cassian, *Conferences,* Conference 19, chapter 2, section 1, p. 670, also likens humility to a foundation; it is "the mother of all the virtues and the foundation of the entire spiritual structure" ("virtutum omnium mater, ac totius spiritualis structurae fundamentum solidissimum") (PL 49.1128A). St. Thomas is evidently paraphrasing Cassian in q. 161, a. 5.

21. *Super Evangelium S. Matthaei Lectura,* ed. Raphael Cai (Rome: Marietti, 1951), at 11:29, no. 970.

> Just as from the divinely instituted natural order, lower things of
> nature have necessarily to be subordinate to the motion of higher
> things, so also in human things, from the order of natural and di-
> vine law, inferiors are held to obey superiors. (q. 104, a. 1)

Christianized society imitates the Christianized neo-Platonist hierarchy of causes. "To obey," like "to be caused" or "to be moved," belongs
exclusively to the created order, the order of things that emanate from
the Creator. The order of nature, relative to God, requires distinction in
being and power. The order of human beings, relative to God, requires
in addition distinction of will. It is the will of the superior, human or
divine, that obedience regards, and its special object is the superior's
precept, tacit or expressed (q. 104, a. 2).

Dietrich von Hildebrand on Humility

What St. Thomas calls reverence *(reverentia),* or "openness" in discussing humility, Dietrich von Hildebrand calls "response to value." The
great phenomenologist of things Christian describes humility at great
length in *Transformation in Christ.* The humble man "grasps the objective meaning of values in its independence from the pursuits of the
subject, and honors them with an unhampered and adequate response."[22] The first step of von Hildebrand's axiology can be briefly
recalled. There are three categories of the "important," three ways in
which our interest is solicited, three springs of subsequent action.
First, there is the subjectively satisfying or pleasure. Second, there is
the objective good of the person, the pursuit and even the possession
of which may or may not be subjectively satisfying. Medicine for children is sugar-coated. And then, third, there is value — the important
in itself, the *bonum honestum.*[23] Values are both ontological or substantive and qualitative. Among the qualitative values are moral values.
The key to the moral life is responsiveness to all values in their majesty
and in their independence of whatever the moral subject thinks of

---

22. Dietrich von Hildebrand, *Transformation in Christ: On the Christian Attitude*
(Manchester, NH: Sophia Institute Press, 1990 [German, 1940]), p. 155.

23. Dietrich von Hildebrand, *Ethics* (Chicago: Franciscan Herald Press, 1953), chapter 3.

them. Such responsiveness plays a constitutive role in acquiring the moral virtues.

As it is for St. Thomas, therefore, humility, openness to value, is foundational for von Hildebrand. This character of humility, however, is merely generic, something that it shares with all the virtues.[24] In order to bring out its specific character and properties, von Hildebrand proceeds by way of contrasting humility to various sorts of pride. Its specific character emerges against the foil of the sense of self of the pantheist monistic idealist.

> By contrasting [humility] with this type of pride [that of the idealist or pantheist], we are better able to grasp the specific nature of humility. Humility involves the full knowledge of our status as creatures, a clear consciousness of having received everything from God.[25]

Humility is therefore the openness to God of the creature who is conscious of himself as such, and acknowledges the Creator as the giver of all good things. Von Hildebrand picks out three aspects of this that are specific to humility. There is "first, awareness of, and responsiveness to, the glory of God."[26] The response consists of "holy joy and loving adoration."[27] To be sure, responding to the glory of God we become aware of "our sinfulness and our weakness."[28] But humility, as is clear also for St. Thomas, would be what it is without sin. Second, there is "the confrontation of our own person with the infinite Person who is God."[29] In this confrontation, we are aware not only of the infinite distance between us and God, but also acknowledge that, across that distance, from the pure generosity and love of God, we have received all that we have, all that is good, of both nature and grace.[30] Third, there is "our awareness of God's personal appeal addressed to each of us as to *this* specified individual."[31] According to this aspect and not withstanding that we are dust and ashes, we are ready to let God make of us whatever

24. Von Hildebrand, *Transformation*, p. 156.
25. Von Hildebrand, *Transformation*, p. 157.
26. Von Hildebrand, *Transformation*, p. 159.
27. Von Hildebrand, *Transformation*, p. 159.
28. Von Hildebrand, *Transformation*, p. 160.
29. Von Hildebrand, *Transformation*, p. 160.
30. Von Hildebrand, *Transformation*, pp. 161, 163, 164 (mercy and grace).
31. Von Hildebrand, *Transformation*, p. 168.

he will, and especially, we are ready to let him make us holy. We can say succinctly, then, that humility is the acknowledgment of the glory of God, and of the generosity of God to us, from a position that knows itself to be infinitely beneath God. It is a properly *creaturely* response to God. It is a properly *creaturely* good. It depends for its shape on the fact that it is a grace draped over *created* shoulders.

Let us sum up. In itself humility is a disposition proper to the rational creature as such *coram Deo*. By it we recognize the infinite majesty of God, we acknowledge the comprehensive character of our debt to him as Creator and Redeemer, and we assent to whatever call he addresses to us, to whatever mission upon which he sends us. In this last aspect, humility prepares for and passes over into obedience,[32] the exercise of will by which we subordinate ourselves to the precepts of God, both those common to all men and whatever particular precept he enjoins on us. Obedience is the most immediate and natural expression and fruit of humility. More radically, humility makes us *capax Dei*, but is not itself "of God." Both humility and obedience are instrumental unto the possession of such unqualified goods as charity. Humility appears also as the soul of satisfaction for offense. Most importantly for our purposes, humility and obedience are human things. They do not belong only to sinful man, but to man, though doubtless the sinner's need for them is increased. To think there are humility and obedience in God is to think there are two wills in God. To think there is humility in God is additionally to think that there is irascible appetite in God, which is to say also corporeality.

Locating the Humility and Obedience of Christ

Have we gained anything by visiting a small part of the monastic literature of the sixth century? Yes. There is a certain freshness and clarity in the first appearance of things to us. The value of the age of the fathers is that they are those to whom Christian things first appeared. Their descriptions of Christian things have therefore a sort of authority that is not to be replaced by any subsequent analysis or categorization. On the other hand, St. Thomas's insertion of humility and obedience into a systematic context, while it certainly does not deform the monastic

---

32. Von Hildebrand, *Transformation*, p. 185, quoting the *Rule*.

apprehension of them, nonetheless adds a certain completion to it, by relating them to the other virtues, and all the virtues to the structure of the human soul, and also by explicitly asking the question about whether they can be found *in divinis.* Turning to von Hildebrand, finally, we pair the first appearance of these things with a modern phenomenologist's description of them.[33]

Humility, doubtless, is a very Christian thing, and indeed and in the first place, one of the things of Christ. The monk undertakes the labor of humility; he takes up "the weapons of obedience," the Prologue says (Prol. 3), "to do battle for the true King, Christ the Lord." St. Benedict's protreptic evokes Christ in his glory, the glory that he had before the foundation of the world. We are to serve him in the same way as he attained that glory, by sharing his sufferings (Prol. 50). But heaven itself is indeed glorious, a kingdom and the place of kings; the place of humility and obedience and suffering is here. What would cause us to mix things up?

As we have seen, humility and obedience (and satisfaction) require a duality of persons, a duality of wills, and indeed a hierarchy of persons and wills. This argues the location of these things exclusively in the created will of Christ. "In the days of his *flesh,*" Hebrews says, "He offered up prayers and supplications" (5:7). Within the Trinity, there seems to be given only the first requirement, a plurality of Persons or supposits. "A plurality of supposits . . . is required that someone be the lord of another simply speaking," St. Thomas says.[34] Can there also be thought to be a plurality of wills? And if so, why cannot there be supposed as well a hierarchy or at least an ordered relation of wills in the Trinity?

Plurality of Supposits, Unity of Will

This line of questioning is very difficult to deal with because it is basic, and is accompanied by the modern world's forgetfulness of and sometimes denial that "nature" names anything objective and real, some-

33. For a contrast of the scholastic "theology of Christian things" with the phenomenologist's "theology of disclosure," see Robert Sokolowski, *Eucharistic Presence: A Study in the Theology of Disclosure* (Washington, DC: Catholic University of America Press, 1994), chapter 1.

34. *ST* III, q. 20, a. 2, ad 2.

Guy Mansini, O.S.B.

thing that we do not construct according to some nominalist account of knowledge, but something we discover. This forgetfulness and denial is deep and inveterate, and so I do not know with what hope (moderated by humility, after all) I can do anything in short compass. The following can at least remind us of the traditional discourse that is needed here.[35]

Will is the appetite that follows on intellect.[36] It is the appetite that follows upon knowledge of the intelligible good and relates the one who wills to his own good, his end.[37] What the good is to which appetite orders some substance is determined by the nature of the substance. How this good is to be attained is likewise determined by the nature. A nature is a finality; it is "a principle of motion and rest in that to which it belongs essentially and not accidentally."[38] That is, it is the first principle of the "motions" or operations of the substance, operations by which the substance attains its end and finds "rest." "Nature" is "essence" spoken with reference to the operations of the substance.[39]

So it is the nature of animals for them to seek their good according as their senses present it to them. They flourish according as they successfully catch the scented and seen prey, according as they seek and find their mate, and according as they enjoy that *sensorium* of which their senses determine the scope. It is the nature of men to seek their good according as it is rationally known, which introduces them to the good as such and lifts them into the spiritual order.[40] Reason gives

35. For modern difficulties with nature, see Robert Sokolowski, *Phenomenology of the Human Person* (Cambridge: Cambridge University Press, 2008), pp. 112-16, and "Formal and Material Causality in Science," *American Catholic Philosophical Quarterly* 69 (1995): 57-67.

36. *ST* I, q. 19, a. 1; *In librum de Divinis Nominibus expositio*, no. 402; *In De Anima*, no. 288. See further references in Michael Sherwin, *By Knowledge and by Love: Charity and Knowledge in the Moral Theology of St. Thomas Aquinas* (Washington, DC: Catholic University of America Press, 2005), pp. 21-22.

37. *ST* I, q. 82, a. 1.

38. *Physics* II.1; 192b22-23, or, in the Latin St. Thomas worked with: "principium motus et quietis in eo in quo est primo et per se et non secundum accidens."

39. Lawrence Dewan, O.P., "Nature as a Metaphysical Object," in his *Form and Being: Studies in Thomistic Metaphysics* (Washington, DC: Catholic University of America Press, 2006), pp. 205-28, at p. 212.

40. *ST* I, q. 59, a. 1. Wherever there is mind, there is ordination to the *bonum universale*. How that good is to be possessed differs according to nature; men do not possess it as do the angels, nor, strictly, does one angel possess it in specifically the same way as another.

them dominion over their own inclinations to their end, and how it is to be attained. The inclination over which we have dominion because of mind — that is the will.[41] Men flourish as men according as they speak the truth that displays all things, do the good for its own sake, and realize that there is a Truth and a Goodness beyond the world to whom they are beholden.

The nature determines the way to the good of the substance, which is to say it specifies the ensemble of powers to be deployed in attaining the end of the substance. If the end is the possession in knowledge and love of the intelligible good, then the principal power that unfolds from the nature or essence of the thing is the intellect. Here is St. Thomas in the *De unitate intellectus:*

> It is manifest . . . that the intellect is the principal thing in man, and that it uses all the powers of the soul and members of the body as its instruments; and on this account Aristotle very acutely said that the intellect is man or "most of all" is man.[42]

And the appetite that follows upon intellect, as has been said, is the will. Just as little as one existing nature can have two intellects, therefore, can it have two wills. The one intellect — numerically one faculty or power — is the way this nature is related to the intelligibility of the real. Following upon intellect, the one will — numerically one faculty or power — is the way this nature is related to its end.[43] Two wills would require two intellects. If it is correct to describe the intellect as the "principal" faculty in man, however, that which uses all the other powers of the soul and members of the body as its instruments, as St. Thomas does, then two intellects would make for two rulers of the one nature. Two wills and two intellects in numerically one nature would be

41. See Sherwin, *By Knowledge and by Love,* p. 27.

42. *Sancti Thomae Aquinatis Tractatus de unitate intellectus contra Averorroistas,* ed. Leo Keeler, S.J. (Rome: Pontifical Gregorian University, 1946) c. 4, para. 89: "Manifestum est autem quod intellectus est id quod est principale in homine, et quod utitur omnibus potentiis animae et membris corporis tamquam organis; et propter hoc Aristoteles subtiliter dixit, quod homo est intellectus 'vel maxime.'" For a contemporary presentation of this work, see Ralph McInerny, *Aquinas Against the Averroists: On There Being Only One Intellect* (West Lafayette, IN: Purdue University Press, 1993).

43. The inclination of a nature where the nature is rational or intellectual is will. See *ST* I, q. 60, a. 1. Where there is one nature there is one inclination of nature, and one will — by which *one* will many things can be willed.

a sort of psychic equivalent to having two heads for one body. When that happens and there are two individuals that, somatically, are inadequately distinct, we think we see something *monstrum*. Again, if the nature of a substance is ordered to the sensorium of the visible, then one power of sight unfolds. There may be two eyes, but binocularity does not ordinarily make for two sights, and when it does there is breakdown and the condition is pathological.

Now, the divine nature is one. There is one and only one instance of divinity, which is to say that the God of Abraham, Isaac, and Jacob is the only God, and that there are no other gods with him. This God is also triune, Father, Son, and Spirit. There are three Persons; are there also three wills? Will follows intellect, and if there are three wills, then there are three intellects. Will relates the one who wills to his good. Can will be pluralized by a relation to three different ends, three different goods? If the difference is more than numerical, then there are three divine natures, that differ intrinsically and whose difference must be according to some principle of better and worse, higher and lower, and the equality of persons is destroyed. This is conveniently called Arianism.

Alternatively, can three wills following upon three minds be differentiated in the way three men are differentiated, where the good to which the will orders the men is the same end according to a specifically identical nature? But this has not been thought to be distinct from tritheism. Nor is it easy to see how one infinitely perfect and immaterial mind is to be distinguished from another infinitely perfect mind, nor how one infinitely perfect will is to be distinguished from another infinitely perfect will.

In the *De unitate intellectus,* St. Thomas says that "if there be one intellect for all men, it follows necessarily that there would be one who understands, and consequently one who wills," from whence "it would further follow that there would be no difference among men as to the free choice of the will."[44] That one intellect makes for only one who understands is true for human beings, true for human nature. In God, on the other hand, we want to say that, though there be only one divine in-

---

44. *De unitate intellectus,* c. 4, para. 89: "Si igitur sit unus intellectus omnium, ex necessitate sequitur quod sit unus intelligens, et per consequens unus volens . . . et ex hoc ulterius sequitur quod nulla differentia sit inter homines, quantum ad liberam voluntatis electionem. . . ."

tellect and only one divine will, there are nevertheless three who understand and three who will. Nonetheless, it still holds, even *in divinis,* that if there are *differences* as to choice, *differences* as to what is willed and so different and many acts of willing, then there are many intellects and many who understand, many wills and many who will. And these many would be individuals, individual realizations of a nature that is only specifically and not numerically the same. If the *Rule* of Athanasius is the correct interpretation of Nicea, on the other hand, then we are required to confess one numerically identical nature.[45]

St. Thomas deploys the principles of this argument also in an expressly Trinitarian context. "Since the proper action of anything follows its nature, the proper action of something does not belong to anything unless it belongs to the nature of the thing." However, Scripture imputes "the proper actions of God" to the Son, such things as to create, to conserve, to cleanse from sin. Therefore, "the Son of God is of the divine nature." Moreover, St. Thomas says, it follows from John 5:19 ("Whatever the Father does, these things also the Son does likewise") that the divine nature of Father and Son is numerically one nature. For from the "likewise" it follows that the Son operates, not as an instrument, but properly. Each Person does the same work, wholly and entirely, and not as three men rowing a boat, each contributing part of the work. Therefore, "the power of the Father and of the Son is the same in number," and "since power follows the nature of a thing, it is necessary that the nature and essence of Father and Son be the same in number."[46]

This argument is not bound to the peculiarities of the Aristotelian-Platonist metaphysics of St. Thomas. Everyone will recognize it as a redeployment of one of St. Gregory of Nyssa's arguments in his *Ad Ablabium* for the impropriety of speaking of three Christian Gods.[47] The point of

---

45. From the *Rule* it follows that we should say that the Father is the one God, and also that the Son is the one God. Therefore, each is the one numerically same deity, and "deity" just means "divine nature" as "humanity" means "human nature."

46. *Summa contra gentiles,* Editio Leonina Manualis (Rome: Marietti, 1934), IV, c. 7. For this argument in St. Thomas, see Gilles Emery, O.P., *The Trinitarian Theology of St. Thomas Aquinas,* trans. Francesca Murphy (Oxford: Oxford University Press, 2007), pp. 308-11, 349-55.

47. The other argument, by contrast, rests on manifestly Platonic grounds. For an analysis of the *Ad Ablabium,* see Lewis Ayres, *Nicaea and Its Legacy: An Approach to Fourth-Century Trinitarian Theology* (Oxford: Oxford University Press, 2004), pp. 244-363, and

Guy Mansini, O.S.B.

departure of his argument is the unity of the operation of the three Persons from which he concludes to the oneness of deity. To suppose the Father commands and the Son obeys within the Trinity is to suppose that there are operations proper to the Father that are not the operations of the Son and vice versa. It is just such a supposition that gives us "three Gods," according to Gregory. He lists such divine operations *(energeiai)* as providentially beholding and guiding the course of the entire universe, giving life to men, judging, and saving believers. Such operations, he says, are common to Father, Son, and Spirit. That they are is the teaching of sacred Scripture. He does not argue this at length, but illustrates it for the activity of judging, which is the Father's according to Genesis 18:25 and Romans 3:6, the Son's according to John 5:22, and the Holy Spirit's according to Isaiah 4:4 and Matthew 12:28. These activities are common to the three, not the way that three speeches of three orators are one and the same activity. Rather, the divine activity of provident rule or of judging is one and numerically only one distinct operation.

> We do not learn that the Father does something on his own, in which the Son does not co-operate. Or again, that the Son acts on his own without the Spirit. Rather does every operation that extends from God to creation and is designated according to our differing conceptions of it have its origin in the Father, proceed through the Son, and reach its completion by the Holy Spirit. It is for this reason that the word for the operation is not divided among the Persons involved. For the action of each in any matter is not separate and individualized. But whatever occurs, whatever in reference to God's providence for us or to the government and constitution of the universe, occurs through the three Persons, and is not three separate things.[48]

Three things can be noted here. First, it is a question of one and the same operation, not three operations of the same sort. There is one divine judgment, not three, even as there is one divine providence. Second, no Person operates separately from the others; "the action of each

Giulio Maspero, *Trinity and Man: Gregory of Nyssa's* Ad Ablabium (Leiden: E. J. Brill, 2007), esp. pp. 53-60.

48. Gregory of Nyssa, *An Answer to Ablabius: That We Should Not Think of Saying There Are Three Gods,* trans. Cyril Richardson, in *Christology of the Later Fathers,* ed. Edward R. Hardy (Philadelphia: Westminster, 1954), pp. 261-62.

in any matter is not separate." Last, each Person does the one operation wholly and completely, for "the word for the operation is not divided among the Persons."[49] It is not, in St. Thomas's words, as if each Person performs part of the activity, as three men rowing the same boat. In that case we have three powers. Operation, to be sure, is correlated with power, and three parts can be correlated with three powers. Where the operation is one and whole, however, it can be correlated with only one power. So the three, each performing the one and whole operation, do so by one and the same power. That there be one power and so one essence is the only premise upon which it can be said that three individuals perform numerically one and the same operation. On the other hand, if there really is an operation of the Son — say, an obedience and humility — that is not that of the Father, whose own proper operation relative to the Son is to command, then there are two powers, two wills. For Gregory, according to this scenario there are also two natures or essences, and two Gods.[50]

According to Gregory, the distinction of the Persons is not to be sought in finding distinct operations for them, but is accounted for by the circumstances of their origin, "with respect to causality."[51] It is the unity of their operation, however, that saves Trinitarian doctrine from tipping over into tritheism. This unity does not preclude that each Person works as the Person he is.[52]

If humility and obedience are realized between two distinct wills,

49. Gregory of Nyssa, *An Answer to Ablabius*, p. 262.

50. The argument is common to the fathers; see Lewis Ayres, *Nicaea*, p. 280; he gives the versions of Hilary, Ambrose, and Augustine in chapter 15. Perhaps its earliest deployment is in St. Irenaeus, *Adversus Haereses* IV.20.6: "Thus, therefore, was God revealed; for God the Father is shown forth in all these, the Spirit indeed working [*operante*], and the Son ministering [*administrante*], while the Father was approving [*comprobante*], and man's salvation [was] being accomplished" (*Ante-Nicene Fathers*, vol. 1, ed. A. Roberts and J. Donaldson [Grand Rapids: Eerdmans, 1975], p. 489). St. Irenaeus emphasizes the distinction of personal characteristics that remain in the one operation of the Three, and evidently thinks he is doing nothing but reporting 1 Corinthians 12:4-6, where the gifts *(charismata),* the services *(diakoniai),* and the works *(energemata)* are the same thing, and the Three thus work the same work and so are the one God. Barth, in the very section where he introduces obedience into the Trinitarian relations (*Church Dogmatics* IV/1, pp. 201-2), also expressly excludes tritheism (p. 205).

51. Gregory, *An Answer to Ablabius*, p. 266.

52. For which same doctrine in St. Thomas, see Gilles Emery, O.P., "The Personal Mode of Trinitarian Action in St. Thomas Aquinas," in his *Trinity, Church, and the Human Person: Thomistic Essays* (Naples, FL: Ave Maria Press, 2007), pp. 115-53.

therefore, if it takes two wills, two rationally or intellectually operating appetites, to make the space in which they can appear, then humility and obedience have no place in the Trinity. They are created things. Christ, who is the Second Person of the Blessed Trinity, is humble and obedient. Therefore, he acts humbly before his Father and obeys him in virtue of the assumed human nature, not in virtue of the one single divine nature that he shares with Father and Spirit. He shares in humility and obedience, created things, in virtue of his created, assumed nature.[53]

St. Thomas recognizes a triple subjection of Christ to his Father, but all three are in virtue of the assumed human nature. The first is according to the "degree of goodness, insofar as the divine nature is the very essence of goodness," while human nature is not. The second is according to power, according as the assumed human nature, like all creatures, is subject to the divine operation. And in a third way, "human nature is especially subjected to God by its own proper act, that is, insofar as by its own will it obeys God's commands."[54] Further, "it is not to be understood simply speaking that Christ is subject to the Father but only according to his human nature."[55]

The humility and obedience of Christ do not, then, manifest a deeper, Trinitarian humility and obedience. They manifest the distinction of Persons, as Christ obeys his Father in the garden of Gethsemane. Further, insofar as they are the humility and obedience as of a son, they manifest the very manner of the procession, namely, generation.[56]

Emptying Himself and Taking the Form of a Servant

Perhaps the argument from unity of operation will have seemed to ignore the most salient point where the question of humility and obedience must be taken up relative to the Trinity, and that is the Incarnation itself. It may well be that the humility and obedience of Philippians 2:8 are certainly the human humility and human obedience of Christ ("being found in *human* form he humbled himself"). But there

53. St. Thomas has a succinct statement of this in the *Summa contra gentiles* IV, c. 8.9-10.

54. *ST* III, q. 20, a. 1.

55. *ST* III, q. 20, a. 1, ad 1.

56. This is White's point in "Intra-Trinitarian Obedience." See also Sokolowski, *Eucharistic Presence,* p. 126.

remains what seems the prior event of the Son's emptying himself, taking flesh, becoming man, putting on the form of a servant (2:7). How can that not be construed as an act of humility and obedience? The argument from identity of operation notwithstanding, there are some things that are true of one Person and not another, most obviously, the Incarnation. The Son and only the Son becomes incarnate and lives a human life. Incarnation is not in that sense an act common to the three, and so the argument from unity of operation, where the operation is such a thing as divine judgment or divine providence, is irrelevant. Does not the fact that it is the Son and only the Son that becomes incarnate require some distinction of understandings and willings within God and prior to the Incarnation of the Son? And, a second objection, if the Son proceeds as Word from the Father who speaks, does not the very force of the diction — *ob-audire,* obedience — ineluctably lead us to think of the Person of the Son as constituted by a wholly divine obedience?

Even St. Thomas seems to recognize some opening for a subjection of the Son prior to the Incarnation, commenting on Philippians:

> When he says, "but he [emptied] himself" [taking the form of a servant], etc., Paul commends the humility of Christ, first as to the mystery of the Incarnation, and second as to the mystery of the passion, where we have "he humbled himself," etc.[57]

"First as to the mystery of the Incarnation." So, there is humility and by implication obedience in the very event of the Incarnation itself.

Let us once more return to these things as given in monastic tradition. In the practices of humility and obedience, the distinct personal realities of monk and abbot come to manifestation, and do so in virtue of distinct understandings and willings. Robert Sokolowski happily characterizes obedience as one of what Peter Strawson calls the "reactive attitudes," a response to someone's personal agency when it is directed precisely to me as also a personal agent.[58] The idea is that the personal agency of the one who commands me deploys an understanding not originally my own, a will not originally rooted in my own incli-

---

57. *Super Epistolam ad Philippenses Lectura,* in *Super Epistolas S. Pauli Lectura* II, ed. Raphael Cai, O.P. (Rome: Marietti, 1953), c. 2, lect. 2, no. 56.

58. Sokolowski, *Eucharistic Presence,* p. 126; see Peter Strawson, *Freedom and Resentment and Other Essays* (London and New York: Routledge, 2008), pp. 6-7, 10-11.

nation, and one not necessarily in accord with it. The one who orders "acts"; I "react" to his action directed precisely at me. This is the situation envisaged by the *Rule*. When he commands, the abbot is understanding that it is a good thing for him by his command to help this or that monk to live according to the *Rule*. For his part, the monk is understanding that it is good for him to obey the abbot's command and so live according to the *Rule*. The "I think" and "I will" of the abbot are not the "I think" and "I will" of the obedient monk, albeit both thinkings and willings have as their object one and the same thing, namely that this monk fulfill this command, conform to such and such a provision of the *Rule*. Moreover, the practices of humility and obedience seem to require such distinct thinkings and willings. Distinct thinkings and willings, in turn, require distinct intellects and wills. It is precisely as not his will that the abbot's will comes to the monk. It is precisely as not his practical intellect but the abbot's that the command lights up some course of action as "good to be done." Distinct intellects and wills, in turn, flow from distinct natures or essences. The abbot and monk are distinct persons in instantiating distinct and distinctly operating natures.

Therefore, if it is true to speak of the humility and obedience of the Son relative to the Father, and this prior to the Incarnation, then the divine essence is verified in the Father, and also distinctly in the Son, and they are more fittingly to be spoken of as two Gods, not one and the same God, one and the same deity.

And this must hold good also in thinking about the Incarnation.

How then shall we read Philippians, as also such things as John 6:38, "I have come down from heaven not to do my own will," if this is not a motion of humility and subjection in the divine will just as such? Such passages induce a sort of optical illusion, where we envisage a time in eternity before the angel is sent to Mary. The Son humbles himself, however, not prior to becoming man, but in becoming man, in taking unto himself the assumed nature: that is the emptying, according to St. Thomas:

> He very beautifully says that "he emptied himself." For the empty is opposed to the full. The divine nature, however, is full enough, because there is the perfection of every good. Exodus 33:19 says: "I will show you every good." Human nature, on the other hand, and the human soul, are not full, but in potency to fulfillment, because the

soul has been made as a blank slate. Human nature is therefore empty. Therefore he says, "he emptied himself," because he assumed a human nature.[59]

The divine nature is full; the human nature is empty: the only way he can be empty, can empty himself, is to assume the empty nature. The emptying and the humbling are not something before the Incarnation but are coincident with the assumption of the human nature of Christ. As to the divine will of the Son itself, it is one with the nature, one with the infinite act of divine being. There is no diremption in it. It does not change in the Incarnation. And there is no obedience as of one Person to another: the "decision" for the Incarnation is common to the three, as is the efficient work of creating the human nature of Christ.

The abbot commanding understands the same thing as does the monk who should obediently do. Contrariwise, the three Persons understand different things about the Persons (for instance, that the Father is not the Son), but in the same understanding. They understand what they do about the divine nature, themselves, and creatures in one act of understanding. In one act of understanding, furthermore, they understand that the Second Person is incarnate. And in one act of will, they will his Incarnation, which is to say in one act of will they will the creation of the humanity of Jesus, and will it to be in virtue of the divine act of being, and will it to be the humanity of the Son exclusively.

Once incarnate, the Son can then have an understanding and a willing distinct from the one understanding and willing common to the three. So Sokolowski:

> It seems that the Incarnation allowed a kind of response by God to God himself to take place, a response that could not have occurred in any other way. . . . When it did occur as an action, it opened the possibility of a response, a reaction of another will: the obedient choice of the man Jesus. In becoming obedient to death, even to death on the cross, Jesus allowed an exchange to take place between God's choice and a created counterchoice.[60]

And again:

---

59. *Super Epistolam ad Philippenses Lectura*, c. 2, lect. 2, no. 57.
60. Sokolowski, *Eucharistic Presence*, p. 75.

> The splendor of the Redemption lies not simply in our liberation from sin, but primarily in the admirable exchange of choices between the creature and God. The Son as eternal could not have done this, because his will as eternal is not different from that of the Father.[61]

The obedience of Christ, like the humility, is strictly true of him in virtue of the assumed nature.

Is Not the Word a Sort of Subsistent Hearing and So "Obedience"?

If what we are saying is true, then what we might call the "indexicalization" of the Persons of the Trinity requires the Incarnation. Von Balthasar imagines the Son "offering" to become incarnate and the Father being "touched" at this offering, which is very much to think of the Trinitarian Persons speaking to one another.[62] Bernard Lonergan asks whether the divine Persons say "I" or "You" to one another, and his response can be taken as a commentary on such a way of speaking as Balthasar's.

> What is said . . . can be taken in two senses. In one way, according to its relation to the one speaking, and thus the Word is spoken [by the Father]. In another way, it can be taken according to the relation of what is spoken to the objects known. And in this way, just as the Father speaks from the understanding of God and of the Father and of the Son and of the Holy Spirit and of all creatures and of all things possible, so through the Word are spoken God and the Father and the Son and the Spirit and all creatures and all possible things. Wherefore, all that can be signified by the pronouns "I" and "You" is spoken by the Father through the Word; but within the Godhead, there are not to be heard material sounds, nor are there many distinct conceptions of things, but only one who is Word.[63]

61. Sokolowski, *Eucharistic Presence*, p. 75.

62. Hans Urs von Balthasar and Adrienne von Speyr, *To the Heart of the Mystery of Redemption* (San Francisco: Ignatius Press, 2010), p. 37.

63. Bernard Lonergan, S.J., *De Deo Trino*, vol. 2: *Pars Systematica* (Rome: Pontifical Gregorian University, 1964), p. 196. See *ST* I, q. 34, a. 1, ad 3.

The Father does not speak to the Word; he speaks the Word. The Word does not listen to the Father; he is spoken by the Father. My word does not obey me, but the one to whom I address the word obeys me. Being spoken, as is the Word, is not the same as hearing. Commenting on John 15:15, St. Thomas says:

> Since . . . to hear is to receive knowledge from another, the Son's hearing of the Father is nothing else than to receive knowledge from him. The knowledge of the Son, however, is his essence. Therefore, for the Son to hear the Father is to receive his essence from him.[64]

Which is to say, it is to proceed from him. We return to the first procession, which does not require two minds and so is not ground for two wills.

Conclusion

In this way, should we speak of "confining" suffering and humility and obedience to the humanity of Christ and to the created order, and is this confinement an implied limitation of things divine? But we do not need either for our example or our salvation a divine suffering, a divine humility, or a divine obedience. We need to learn to obey humanly; we need to humble ourselves and obey in our humanity. This was our point of departure in C. S. Lewis. Even if there were some divine humility and obedience, some doubtless different and higher form of these *in divinis*, they could be nothing to us. Rather, the obedience Christ gives to his Father is precisely the obedience we need to see and need ourselves to give: the obedience of a created, human will.

On the other hand, if there is a Trinitarian humility and obedience much the same as ours, then another problem arises, and that is, paradoxically, that the Incarnation itself, the assumption of humanity, can in itself establish no new thing for the Son, and specifically, no newly experienced humility. The Son already knows humility and obedience vis-à-vis his Father. There is no abasement in taking the form of a servant, the form of humanity, because he is already and eternally in

---

64. *Super Evangelium S. Ioannis Lectura*, ed. Raphael Cai, O.P. (Rome: Marietti, 1952), no. 2017.

the form of a servant. The Incarnation is a motion from one servitude to another. The Son does not empty himself in becoming man if he is taking up a manner of being he already possesses eternally. Whether or not the processions make for a divine humility and obedience just in themselves or in dependence on a prior divine decision that they have such a form matters not. The Incarnation — the one St. Paul refers to in Philippians — is no longer itself something unheard of from the foundation of the world.

We might say, in other words, that for those who want an intra-Trinitarian obedience and humility, the Word has already taken our humanity in his very manner of proceeding from the Father; he has become human eternally so that he can become human in time. There is an Incarnation before there is an Incarnation.[65] Surely, something must be wrong? The procession of the Son takes place according to what we human beings need in order that our operation be healed, according to what we need to exercise our humanity in a properly human and excellently human way. But in this way, there seems to be a confusion of natures as great as any ever imagined by Eutyches or Apollinaris, albeit one that takes place eternally, prior to the Incarnation.

It is time to conclude. There are four possible locations for humility and obedience in thinking about God: (a) in the relation of the Persons just in themselves; (b) in the relation of the Persons in themselves but in view of the economy; (c) in the event of becoming incarnate; (d) in the passion and death. The first and the second imply tritheism, and the second implies that God is other than he would be apart from the economy of salvation, and that therefore he is no longer the transcendent Creator. The third is a sort of illusion. The fourth is verified, and moreover, as *the only one that is attested by Scripture as read by the fathers.* Christ learned obedience, Hebrews says, by what he suffered, and the suffering is the suffering of the cross (5:8). This is introduced by the clause, "although he was Son." So, notwithstanding the fact that he is the divine Son and so could be expected to know no obedience, he nonetheless learned it in the days of his flesh. What is learned is something not previously known or experienced or possessed.

---

65. See White, "Intra-Trinitarian Obedience," p. 397, and the "inversion of the Son's mission into the life of God."

Processions and Missions: A Point of Convergence between Thomas Aquinas and Karl Barth

Bruce L. McCormack

Introduction

In the winter semester 1928-29, Karl Barth devoted his seminar in Münster to the first book of Thomas's *Summa theologiae*. He reported his findings to his good friend, Eduard Thurneysen, in the following words:

> The problem of Catholicism absorbs my attention, now as before, in the most lively way. This has been occasioned, most recently, by my reading of Thomas whom I am treating in my seminar. Every page I have read has been strangely instructive; strangely, because the man has gone to work with a meticulous precision which has not allowed us, up to now, to raise a single objection. He knew everything, but everything, leaving aside the one thing that he didn't know, viz. that man is a liar. But without really knowing it, he knew this truth too and took it everywhere into consideration, displayed it to its best advantage and, as a consequence, knew everything else so brilliantly and comprehensively that one feels blown away and would have to become Catholic if one were not held fast by that one point. On the basis of that one point, one must — even while being continually instructed, grateful, and full of admiration — one must understand everything else differently, even in those cases in which one finds nothing to oppose.[1]

1. Karl Barth to Eduard Thurneysen, December 23, 1928, in *Karl Barth–Eduard Thurneysen Briefwechsel*, vol. 2: *1921-1930*, ed. Eduard Thurneysen (Zürich: Theologischer Verlag Zürich, 1974), p. 638.

Now it must be remembered that Barth is writing all of this privately to his dearest friend and closest comrade in all matters theological. He feels no need to explain what he means by "that one point." But it is really not that hard to guess, given the things he did say in print about Roman Catholic theology. The "one thing" would have to be the *analogia entis* — the use made of natural theology. And here, in this context, he is suggesting that the use of natural theology doesn't take the sinfulness of sin seriously enough. Thomas, he says, doesn't fully grasp the fact that "man is a liar." It is the knowledge gained by "the light of natural reason" — being "led from God's effects to the knowledge of 'what must necessarily belong to God as the first cause of all things'"[2] in the first of the three divisions that make up Thomas's treatise on God — which is the sticking point, the one point in whose light everything else is understood differently. In spite of this difference, however — a difference that, in my view, is truly fundamental — it is astonishing how much convergence can be achieved on particular questions. A case in point is the question of the relation of the Trinitarian processions to the Trinitarian missions.

To highlight the convergence between Thomas and Barth on processions and missions (as I will be doing in this essay) requires that I begin with a retraction — at least where Thomas is concerned. In an article first published in 2007, I made the assertion that it was common in "traditional" Trinitarian theology to understand the self-constitution of God as necessary and the election of God as free.[3] And given that those to whom I was responding at the time — specifically Edwin van Driel and Paul Molnar — understood God to be "free" to create and redeem or not to do so as he pleased, it seemed to me that the only account of "freedom" adequate to this conception was that of a deliberative choice made among options in the absence of a determinate end, a "voluntaristic" account in other words. Moreover, since voluntaristic freedom is the very opposite of "necessity" in the sphere of human action (the two are in fact deliberately defined in opposition to each another), it then also seemed right to conclude that what was envisioned was a two-act play in pretemporal eternity: the first consisting in a "necessary" act and

---

2. Gilles Emery, O.P., "*Theologia* and *Dispensatio*: The Centrality of the Divine Missions in Teaching St. Thomas's Trinitarian Theology," *The Thomist* 74 (2010): 551; here citing Thomas, *ST* I, q. 12, a. 12.

3. Bruce L. McCormack, "Seek God Where He May Be Found: A Response to Edwin Chr. van Driel," *Scottish Journal of Theology* 60 (2007): 66-67.

the second consisting in a "free" act. I continue to believe that I was right with respect to the implications of the views of my critics, but recently a forceful challenge has emerged with respect to the question of whether Thomas may adequately be characterized in this way.

In a recently published essay, Matthew Levering argues that the supposition that all classical orthodoxy understood the processions and the missions as two acts is wrongheaded. And his chief witness for the tradition is Thomas Aquinas. For Thomas, as Levering reads him, there is only *one act* in pretemporal eternity with two "terms" — one eternal (God's being) and one temporal (the effect on creatures). "In this one act, which is necessary with respect to God's being and free with respect to creaturely being, God 'wills both himself to be, and other things to be. . . .'"[4] The formulation may seem paradoxical but the significance of the affirmation of a single act is clear enough. It means that the creature is already contained in the divine processions: "the creature is not absent from divine procession, although it is secondary because of the twofold 'term' of the procession, in which the eternal 'term' has priority. The temporal 'term' is the election of adopted sons in the Son, Jesus Christ."[5] What Levering is saying is that Thomas understood the missions of God to be contained in the processions, which is then the explanation for how the missions can manifest the processions.

Now I am going to leave aside here the question of whether Levering is right to say that Thomas is faithfully expounding the tradition in uniting the processions and the missions in this way; that would require another essay. But I do find his reading of Thomas himself compelling — and a good corrective to a misunderstanding I have entertained for far too long — again, where Thomas is concerned. Certainly, Levering's reading of Thomas comports very nicely with the groundbreaking work of Gilles Emery on Thomas's Trinitarian theology, even as it takes up a question that (to my knowledge) Emery has left untouched thus far. But the decisive point for my purposes is this: if Levering is right, then it becomes possible to read Thomas on the relationship of the processions and the missions so as to back him "down" into

---

4. Matthew Levering, "Christ, the Trinity, and Predestination: McCormack and Aquinas," in *Trinity and Election in Contemporary Theology*, ed. Michael Dempsey (Grand Rapids: Eerdmans, 2011), p. 264 (here citing Thomas, *ST* I, q. 19, a. 2).

5. Levering, "Christ, the Trinity, and Predestination," p. 263.

Barth. And it is possible to read Barth on the same question so as to back him "up" into Thomas. I deliberately choose these spatial metaphors because they give expression to the differing starting points of the two theologians. The later Barth, at least, is a strictly "Christocentric" theologian; he wishes to say nothing of God that finds no firm ground in the narrated *history* of Jesus of Nazareth as attested in Holy Scripture. Thomas, on the other hand, knows of two paths for acquiring knowledge of the triune God: the divine self-revelation *and* metaphysics. For this reason, Barth always starts with Christ whereas Thomas is willing — at least in the first division of his treatise on God (on the divine "essence") — to start with creation as the effects of a First Cause. Again: this is the "fundamental difference"[6] between Barth and Thomas. But it does not prevent an astonishing degree of convergence on a very important question in Trinitarian theology.

In what follows, I will begin with Thomas's view of the relationship of processions and missions. And given that this subject matter has decisive implications for current debates over the logical relationship of Trinity and election, I will also touch upon Thomas's understanding of election in relation to both processions and missions. Throughout, I will allow myself to be instructed by Levering and Emery.

In a second section, I will take up Karl Barth's view of the same topic. Here I will be much more brief. I have already written a great deal pertinent to this problem and will simply lay out the position on the question that is required by the later Barth's doctrines of election and Christology.

In a final section, I am going to discuss the relevance of what we have learned in the first two sections for current debates over Trinity and election. I might as well tell you now: even though I am convinced by Levering's reading of Thomas, it does not mean that a defense of Thomas constitutes, at the same time, a defense of my critics in this debate. In my view, Levering's Thomas stands much, much closer to me

---

6. It seems to me that faith and order dialogue has gone just about as far as it can go toward establishing visible unity by focusing on convergences. This strategy has achieved much that is good and salutary but it has a built-in tendency to set to one side the truly "fundamental differences" that cause each side to understand even convergent doctrinal comments differently. As Charles Morerod has wisely said, "the real threat to ecumenism today is the failure to identify differences properly." See Morerod, *Ecumenism and Philosophy: Philosophical Questions for a Renewal of Dialogue,* trans. T. C. Scarpelli (Ann Arbor, MI: Sapientia Press, 2006), p. xix.

than he does to my critics. And because of this, I cannot see any reason to believe that the work Levering has done offers any reason to think that a bridge might be built between Thomas and my critics in the Trinity and election debate, to say nothing of Thomas and Reformed orthodoxy. The old Reformed dogmaticians did not affirm that processions and missions are rightly understood as a single divine act with two terms. And they certainly could not affirm the reason Thomas offers for their unity — reasons having to do with the nature of divine goodness and a conclusion he drew from the pure actuality of divine being. We will return to both of these points in due course. I now turn then directly to Thomas.

The Divine Son Is Never Unrelated to Creatures: A Reading of Thomas

For the sake of those unfamiliar with the vocabulary used by theologians when reflecting on the doctrine of the Trinity, it would perhaps be best if we began with some basic Thomistic definitions. Trinitarian "processions" are "relations of origin." The Son is "begotten" from the Father; the Spirit "proceeds" from the Father and the Son. Each of these terms has a biblical root — the first in John 1:14 and the second in John 15:26.

For Thomas, it is the differing modes of origination that give rise to "personal properties." The two processions give rise, logically, to four relations: paternity, filiation, spiration, and procession. And it is finally the relations (as the consequence of the processions) that constitute the Persons. As Thomas puts it, "a divine person signifies a relation as subsisting."[7] So "Persons" are subsisting relations.

Now to speak of something as "subsisting" means basically that it has concrete reality; it has been made real. Moreover, the divine "essence," defined as that which is common to the Three, subsists in the subsistence of the Persons. It has no reality when considered independently of the Persons as though it were a fourth something standing behind or beneath the Persons.

---

7. *ST* I, q. 29, a. 4. All citations of the *ST* are to the translation by the Fathers of the English Dominican Province, *Summa Theologica*, 5 vols. (Westminster, MD: Christian Classics, 1981).

To put it this way is also to suggest that the Persons do not "derive" from the essence. It is not the divine essence which "begets" the Son or breathes forth the Spirit. It is the Father who does these things. So even if Thomas treats the essence before he treats the Persons, this does not mean that the essence is ontologically prior to the Persons. It is not even the case that the Father is *ontologically* prior to the act of begetting if by that were meant that the Father is the Father "before" begetting the Son. To be sure, the Father is *logically* presupposed in the begetting. But a Father abstracted from the act of begetting is a Father without a Son and therefore no Father at all. The Father is the Father only in relation to the Son. To speak of the Father as "logically" presupposed in the act of begetting, then, has to do only with the way we necessarily order our concepts (in accordance with the mode of our understanding). Emery explains it this way. "What Thomas rejects . . . is that the supposit to whom belongs the notional act [of begetting] could be thought in a pre-relational or essential manner (as subsisting essence), independently of his constitution as a person, that is to say independently of his personal relation."[8] And he continues, "The Father is thought of as subject of a personal act because *he is a person.* It is also for this reason that, in the case of the personal property of the Father, insomuch as this property constitutes the person of the Father, it ought to be thought as a precondition (it is 'pre-understood') to the notional act of begetting: Here, the relative property of the first person precedes the act *in the order of concepts,* 'as the person who acts is *pre-understood* to his action.'"[9] In accordance with our human mode of understanding, we invariably think that there can be no act without a preexisting subject of that act. And that is true on the level of finite creatures to whom being must be given "before" they can act. But God the Father does not preexist the act of begetting the Son. He is what he is (a "Person") *in* that eternal act. We make a mistake, therefore, if we understand the logical priority of the Father as an ontological priority in the sense of a preexisting subject.

It might well seem that the case would be otherwise with the spiration of the Spirit, given that it is the Father *and the Son* who breathe

---

8. Gilles Emery, O.P., "Essentialism or Personalism in the Treatise on God in St. Thomas Aquinas?" in Emery, *Trinity in Aquinas* (Ann Arbor, MI: Sapientia Press, 2003), p. 192.

9. Emery, "Essentialism or Personalism?" p. 193 (emphases mine).

forth the Spirit.[10] But again, this is conceptual only. The begetting of the Son has a conceptual priority over the spiration of the Spirit. But that does not change the fact that the processions are simultaneous.

Thus far, the eternal processions. We come now to the divine "missions." The "missions" have to do with the redemptive work of the triune God in this world. The "Father" sends his Son into this world to be united with human flesh. And Father and Son send the Holy Spirit into human souls to reorder them after the image of the Son and to enable them to participate in the divine processions. Thus, only the Son and the Spirit have missions. The Father, as the One who only sends, has no mission.

Examined more closely, the "missions" have an integral relation to the processions. Emery says, "A divine person's mission has two constitutive features: (1) this person's eternal procession; (2) the divine person's relation to the creature to whom this person is made present in a new way."[11] Notice that the mission is not said here to be new to or even in God. But it does achieve a new kind of presence *to the creature* (as over against the presence of the triune God to and in creation). Notice too that the eternal processions are "present in" the missions.[12] Expressed from the other side, "the mission bears *within* itself the eternal procession of the person sent."[13] The reason for this is twofold. First, the missions of the Son and the Spirit in this world are in accordance with the personal properties that constitute them as Persons.[14] The Son is properly Word. As the One through whom all things were made, it is "fitting" that all things should be "remade" through his redemptive activity. The personal property of the Holy Spirit is that of Love, the Love that unites Father and Son eternally. It is "fitting" then that the Spirit should be "shed abroad" in human hearts in order to engender love for God in them. But, secondly, the missions bear the processions in themselves because, as Emery puts it, "mission does not comprise a 'movement' properly speaking, since the divine persons are unchanging."[15] For Thomas, God's being is pure act; there is, in him, no unrealized potentiality. That being the case, God does not do anything truly new. All

---

10. Emery, "Essentialism or Personalism?" p. 193.
11. Emery, *"Theologia* and *Dispensatio,"* p. 521.
12. Emery, *"Theologia* and *Dispensatio,"* p. 522.
13. Emery, *"Theologia* and *Dispensatio,"* p. 527.
14. Emery, *"Theologia* and *Dispensatio,"* p. 530.
15. Emery, "Essentialism or Personalism?" p. 160.

that God does is somehow contained in the eternal processions. I will return to this point in a moment.

What then about creation? Where does it fit? At this point, the language of "economy" becomes a bit too imprecise. Certainly, both creation and redemption are works of God directed toward objects other than himself. God's relation to these other objects is transitive in nature (as opposed to the immanent relations constituted by the divine processions). As such, both creation and redemption belong to the divine economy. But now, does creation belong to the divine processions or the divine missions? The answer is more complex than those armed with a typically Protestant understanding of the *ad intra* — *ad extra* distinction might expect. If we say with Matthew Levering that "[e]lection (new creation) constitutes the purpose of creation, and both should be seen in terms of the Word Christ Jesus,"[16] then it might well seem that creation belongs with the missions. If, on the other hand, we say that creation has a significance in its own right (as, perhaps, a source of revelation), which can be understood without reference to the Incarnation (and, therefore, to Christology), then we would find ourselves far less certain whether to assign creation to the processions or the missions. The situation is rendered even more complex by the fact that Thomas treats creation as the third division of his doctrine of God, something the later Protestant orthodox did not do. So does creation belong to the processions or the missions — *or does it somehow belong to both?*

According to Thomas, "the processions of the divine persons are the cause of creation."[17] To understand what this means, it would help to return for a moment to the relation of essence and Persons. The divine essence, we have said, subsists in the subsisting relations that are the Persons. Thus, the relations that constitute the divine Persons are the divine essence. And that means that whatever belongs to God essentially cannot be abstracted from the event in which God has his being, the event of the divine processions. But it belongs to the divine goodness to overflow. As Levering says, "God does not 'act for the acquisition of some end; he intends only to communicate His perfection, which is His goodness.' We might imagine that God is such because in the fullness of his eternal processions, God has all he needs and does

---

16. Levering, "Christ, the Trinity, and Predestination," p. 268.
17. *ST* I, q. 45, a. 6, ad 1.

not mind sharing; but such a view distorts the reality of God. It is because God is so good that he is supremely self-diffusive both in himself
(in the divine processions) and 'for us.'"[18] Therefore, the divine Persons
are "naturally" causative and not just as a consequence of willing.

We can give this conclusion even greater precision by means of
what might seem to be a brief detour (in truth, it is not) through
Thomas's understanding of the divine knowing and willing. For
Thomas, knowing and willing are immanent operations, as opposed to
the exercise of power, "which proceeds to an exterior effect."[19] Where
knowledge is concerned, the first thing to observe is that God has perfect knowledge of himself. As we have said, God is pure act and one way
of viewing this act is as an act of understanding. To put it this way is already to say that God's "act of understanding must be His essence and
His being."[20] Now in knowing himself perfectly, God also knows all
things perfectly: "if anything is perfectly known, it follows of necessity
that its power is perfectly known. But the power of anything can be perfectly known only by knowing to what that power extends. Since, therefore, the divine power extends to other things by the very fact that it is
the first effective cause of all things . . . God must necessarily know
things other than Himself."[21] For Thomas, it is true of all knowing that
the form of a thing known is in the knower. And given that God's
knowledge is perfect, the forms of things known are in him perfectly.
God knows all things not simply "in general" — which would be to say
that he knows the being of all things but not the things themselves; he
knows all things in their distinction from one another, individually.[22]

From the observations made thus far, it is but a short step to say
that God's self-knowledge is causative. "The knowledge of God is the
cause of all things. For the knowledge of God is to all creatures what
the knowledge of the artificer is to things made by his art. Now the
knowledge of the artificer is the cause of the things made by his art
from the fact that the artificer works through His intellect. Hence, the
form of the intellect must be the principle of action."[23] But, "the intel-

18. Levering, "Christ, the Trinity, and Predestination," pp. 263-64 (here citing *ST* I,
q. 43, a. 4).
19. *ST* I, q. 14, introduction.
20. *ST* I, q. 14, a. 4.
21. *ST* I, q. 14, a. 5.
22. *ST* I, q. 14, a. 6.
23. *ST* I, q. 14, a. 8.

Bruce L. McCormack

ligible form does not denote a principle of action in so far as it resides in the one who understands unless there is added to it the inclination to an effect, which inclination is through the will. . . . Now it is manifest that God causes all things by His intellect, since His being is His act of understanding; and hence His knowledge must be the cause of things, in so far as His will is joined to it."[24]

Now when Thomas speaks here of "joining" the will to knowledge, he is not referring to a distinct act *subsequent to* the act of self-knowing. It is important to remember here that there is in God, as Levering insists, but *one* act. God's knowing of all things that will ever exist and his willing of them belong to one and the same eternal event, the event of his own being. We might rightly say, the divine predestination (in which the will of God directed toward external effects is contained) stands in the closest possible proximity to the event of God's being. Election cannot be a second act, as Levering rightly insists, because that would put God in the position of knowing what he is going to will (in election) "before" he has willed it (which Thomas would rightly regard as sheer nonsense). For Thomas, there can no such "before." God's knowledge is never not already joined to his will. And so, election is *logically* subsequent to God's self-knowledge and his willing of himself, but it is not a separate act.

Where then does creation belong? Well, it might seem that creation, at least, would have to be a "separate" act in God. After all, Thomas does think that God not only knows all things that will ever be in knowing himself, but all things to which his power could have been extended — counterfactuals in other words.[25] And given that this is so, it might then also seem that God must select among the options available to him in this world (as opposed to others) or "decide" not to create at all. But such a conception would require that God deliberate "before" deciding what he will do, and do so as if he were indeterminate, that is, as if he did not have a final end that conditioned his decision making — which would reintroduce the problem of two acts.

We arrive at the same conclusion when we consider "will" in God more directly. For Thomas, just as "knowing is His [God's] own being, so is His willing."[26] What ties the two together is once again the diffu-

24. *ST* I, q. 14, a. 8.
25. *ST* I, q. 14, a. 9.
26. *ST* I, q. 19, a. 1.

sive nature of the divine goodness. The divine goodness contains in itself an inclination that others might obtain a share in it. And so, Thomas says, God "wills both Himself to be, and other things to be; but Himself as the end, and other things as ordained to that end, inasmuch as it befits the divine goodness that other things should be partakers therein."[27] And so, God "wills things other than Himself by willing His own goodness."[28] Does this mean that God wills things other than himself "necessarily"? The answer depends on what is meant by "necessarily." Thomas holds that God wills himself — and, therefore, his goodness — absolutely; he wills other things "by supposition." That is to say, "since the goodness of God is perfect and can exist without other things, inasmuch as no perfection can accrue to Him from them, it follows that for Him to will things other than Himself is not absolutely necessary. Yet it can be necessary by supposition, for supposing that He wills a thing, then He is unable not to will it, as His will cannot change."[29] The Reformed orthodox of the seventeenth century could say this much — but with a significant difference. If hypothetical necessity were grounded in an act of will that is *separated* from God's willing of his own goodness — which is what takes place when we introduce deliberation and a choice among options into the concept of divine willing — then we would have to say that God is what God is with absolute necessity and that God creates and redeems with an absolute freedom. But Thomas does not think in this way. For him, the willing of the divine goodness contains in itself the willing that others will partake of that goodness. Or, to put it another way, God's willing of other things is absolute with regard to its origin (i.e., the willing by God of the being of his own goodness) but "free" with respect to its end in creatures. But again, we have to understand that the divine freedom is not understood here voluntaristically. Moreover, when Thomas says that the divine goodness could exist without creatures, he says this not because he is trying to secure a voluntaristic conception of freedom but only because he is trying to ward off the mistaken notion that anything could be added to the perfection of the divine goodness through creaturely participation in it.[30] And so, I

27. *ST* I, q. 19, a. 2.
28. *ST* I, q. 19, a. 2, ad 2.
29. *ST* I, q. 19, a. 2, ad 2.
30. *ST* I, q. 19, a. 2, ad 2.

think it is right to conclude that creation is logically subsequent to election just as election is logically subsequent to the divine self-knowledge. But election and the creation to which it gives rise are contained in the divine self-knowledge and self-willing.

A final question: What does all of this have to do with processions and missions? How are the divine self-knowing and self-willing related to processions and missions? The short answer to this question is this: To say that "God causes things to be by knowledge and will"[31] and to say that "the generation of the Son and the spiration of the Holy Spirit cause created effects"[32] is really to say the same thing from two different standpoints; first, from the standpoint of what must be said under the heading of that which pertains to the divine essence and, second, from the standpoint of what must be said under the heading of that which pertains to the differentiation of Persons. That this should be so testifies to the very tight integration of Thomas's treatments of the one God and of the Trinity. God knows himself in his eternal Word; knowledge occurs *in* the eternal begetting of the Son. And God wills himself in the eternal Spirit; the love of the Father for the Son and of the Son for the Father occur in their mutual spiration of the Spirit. And it goes without saying that this is one eternal event, without "before" and "after" — so that we can only speak of a logical priority of the begetting over spiration.

It remains only to add that because "the Word expresses all that is in the Father, the Word also expresses the creatures that preexist in the Father. And since the knowledge of God is the cause of creatures, the Word is not only the exemplary expression of creatures, but he is also the efficient cause that produces creatures."[33] Matthew Levering draws the inevitable conclusion for the question of the "subject" of election insofar as the question applies specifically to the Son (and not just to the Trinity as a whole). "Does Aquinas conceive of a divine Son who *then* has a relationship with creatures as 'Jesus Christ'? No. For Aquinas . . . the divine Son is never unrelated to creatures."[34] For Levering, as for Barth, Jesus Christ is the subject of election. That the two theologians mean something different by this is no secret to Levering; that is what

---

31. Levering, "Christ, the Trinity, and Predestination," p. 254.

32. Levering, "Christ, the Trinity, and Predestination," p. 254.

33. Gilles Emery, O.P., "The Treatise on the Trinity in the *Summa Theologiae*," in Emery, *Trinity in Aquinas*, p. 152.

34. Levering, "Christ, the Trinity, and Predestination," p. 261 (emphasis mine).

he too wishes to establish. The question is: How are we to understand the root cause(s) of these differences? I will turn to that question in the next section of my essay.

Before leaving Thomas, I should make mention of a provocative suggestion made recently by Gilles Emery. Emery believes that the time may have come to dispense altogether with the distinction between the immanent Trinity and the economic Trinity.[35] He observes that the distinction all too easily suggests the existence of two Trinities, rather than simply two perspectives from which the one and only Trinity is rightly conceived. What Emery proposes that we do is to replace this distinction with Thomas's understanding of the relation of processions and missions: "I would suggest that St. Thomas's doctrine of divine missions and processions offers a powerful alternative to the scheme of the 'economic Trinity' and the 'immanent Trinity.' In Aquinas, the missions are in no way separated from the processions. There is no need to reunite the economic Trinity and the immanent Trinity (after having started by distinguishing them), because, for Aquinas, *the missions bear in themselves the eternal mystery of the divine persons.*"[36] For my own part, I agree completely with Emery's worries over the uses made of the modern distinction between the immanent and the economic Trinities. And I agree that a better solution would be found in a well-ordered understanding of the relation of the processions and the missions. The stage is set for a consideration of Karl Barth.

The Missions as the End of the Processions: A Reading of Karl Barth

What is typically thought of as Karl Barth's "doctrine" of the Trinity is found in *Church Dogmatics* I/1. In truth, the treatment of the Trinity there is designed to ground the concept of revelation, which is the subject matter under consideration in the Prolegomena volumes (*CD* I/1

35. Emery, *"Theologia* and *Dispensatio,"* pp. 516, 557-61. A similar point is made by Bruce D. Marshall, who finds the root of the shortcomings of modern doctrines of the Trinity generally to lie in "widespread eclipse . . . of the carefully worked-out distinction between procession and mission [in Thomas] by the much more malleable and imprecise distinction between the immanent and the economic Trinity." See Marshall, "The Unity of the Triune God: Reviving an Ancient Question," *The Thomist* 74 (2010): 29.

36. Emery, *"Theologia* and *Dispensatio,"* p. 560.

and I/2).[37] Barth expressed the point of view that would govern his treatment of the Trinity throughout the phase stretching from 1924 through (roughly) 1940 in the following words: "The problem of the Trinity is the problem of the knowledge of the inexhaustible living-ness or the unsublate-able [*unaufhebaren*] subjectivity of God in His revelation."[38] Notice that it is the *knowledge* of God that is at stake for Barth; theological epistemology stands at the center of his interests in this phase of his development. Moreover, the phrase "unsublate-able subjectivity" points to the problem that then occupied Barth intensively. How does it come about that God remains God precisely in his self-revelation? How can revelation occur, in other words, without God placing himself under the epistemic control of the human knower? If you do not understand these questions against the background of Kant's epistemology, then you will not have understood them at all. In any event, the doctrine of the Trinity is here treated in I/1 as foundational to the answer Barth would give to these questions. God remains God in that he reveals himself through the veil of creaturely flesh and creaturely words. In that the media of his self-revelation are never more than "veils," in that God remains hidden in the "veils," God remains *subject* of the knowledge of God before, during, and after revelation.[39] That is the meaning of "unsublate-able subjectivity." God is indissolubly Subject — even when and as he makes himself "objective" — that is, gives himself to us in an object.

Given that Barth has a revelational (or epistemological) rather than Christological (or ontological) concentration at this time, it is not surprising that he should have given little or no attention to some rather important questions — among them, the question of the relation of the processions to the missions. He does treat the processions, however. And, from what he says about them, a clear picture of the distinction of the processions from the missions can be formed that also allows us to deduce his understanding of their relation.

37. All citations of the *CD* are to the translation edited by Bromiley and Torrance, *Church Dogmatics,* 4 vols. in 13 parts (Edinburgh: T. & T. Clark, 2000 [1936-75]).

38. Karl Barth, *Unterricht in der christlichen Religion,* vol. 1: *Prolegomena, 1924,* ed. Hannelotte Reiffen (Zürich: Theologischer Verlag Zürich, 1985), p. 120; cf. *CD* I/1, p. 348, *Leitsatz.* And see also Karl Barth to Eduard Thurneysen, May 28, 1924, in *Barth-Thurneysen Briefwechsel,* vol. 2, p. 254.

39. See on this point, Eberhard Busch, *Karl Barth und die Pietisten. Die Pietismuskritik des jungen Karl Barth und ihre Erwiderung* (München: Chr. Kaiser Verlag, 1978), p. 93.

At this point in time, Barth held that "the only possible thing we can say of this begetting is how it did not take place. . . . Taken strictly, even the concept of *communicatio essentiae* says something which cannot be said without denying the unity of God's essence. . . ."[40] Barth's concern here is, in part at least, that the divine essence not be divided. But beyond that, he is far more concerned to say that human language fails to reach divine reality; the two fall apart. "Even though we reproduce the [Nicene-Constantinopolitan] dogma or indeed the very statements of Holy Scripture, it is only by God's grace and not intrinsically that the content of knowledge can be proper to what we think and say. Regarded immanently, what we think and say will always be in itself inadequate and broken thought and utterance."[41] And so, even the language of "very God of very God" is fraught with peril. "The difficulty in even this very simple formula consists in the fact that as soon as we try to explain the *ek* [i.e., God *of* God] . . . it unavoidably gives rise to the idea of two autonomous beings in a specific relation of dependence to one another, or, if this concept is avoided, it becomes meaningless, so that there is no longer any reference to a distinction in the *Deus verus.* *Deus verus* and *Deus verus* do not confront each other as autonomous beings but are twofold in one and the same autonomous being. This is what no language can render adequately; even the language of dogma can render it only very inadequately."[42] What we catch sight of here, I think, is the fact that the "wholly otherness" of God is still a rather formal concept for Barth, much as it had been in his Romans commentary. It has yet to be given a material (i.e., Christological) specification such as would allow for a real relation of God to the creaturely veil of his self-revelation and (most importantly) *of the creaturely veil to him.*

To the extent that Barth thought about the relation of proces-

40. *CD* I/1, p. 431.
41. *CD* I/1, p. 428.
42. *CD* I/1, p. 429; cf. p. 433: "We do not know what we are saying when we call God Father and Son. We can say it only in such a way that on our lips and in our concepts it is untruth." Cf. p. 436 where, after citing Thomas to the effect that the begetting of the Word is by intelligible emanation, Barth writes: "We do not know what we are saying when we call Jesus Christ the eternal Word of God. We know no word which, though distinct from a speaker, still contains and reproduces the whole essence of the speaker." And, finally, on the *homoousios,* p. 440: "it is plainly referring to an essence of which we have no idea at all; it thus becomes a concept of the type philosophy usually calls 'empty concepts.'"

sions to missions at all, he seems to have understood them as two distinct activities. In treating, for example, the creedal phrase "begotten, not made," he writes, "He is not from God in the way that creatures from the highest angel to the smallest particular of sun-dust are from God, namely, by creation.... This can, of course, be said of the human nature of Christ.... But it cannot be said of Him who here assumes human nature, of Him who here exists as man ... but does not allow His being and essence to be exhausted or imprisoned in His humanity, [of Him] who is also in the full sense *not* man in this humanity."[43] That last clause especially seems to suggest that the eternal Son has an identity distinct from that which he possesses as united to creaturely flesh (i.e., as "Jesus Christ"). And if that were the case, then the relation of the processions and missions could only be analogical at best.

I mention this in order to make an important point. It really isn't possible to build a bridge from the assumed distinction of processions and missions in I/1 to Thomas's integration of them. A bridge to Thomas could only be built at the point at which Barth's focus on his dialectical conception of revelation gave way to a more strict "Christocentrism" in his theologizing — which is to say, at the point at which he tried to comprehend all Christian doctrines (creation, providence, anthropology, etc.) through the lens of his mature Christology. And that only happened with his revision of election in *CD* II/2 — for reasons I will explain. When that took place a bridge could indeed be built to Thomas. But here in I/1, the only bridge that could be built was to Reformed orthodoxy and to the manual Thomism of late nineteenth- and early twentieth-century Catholicism (whose influence can be found throughout his treatise on the Trinity).[44]

To make a long story short, the turning point came with Barth's thesis in *CD* II/2 that "Jesus Christ" is not only the object but also the subject of election.[45] To say that Jesus Christ is the subject of election

43. *CD* I/1, p. 430.

44. On this point, see Bruce L. McCormack, "The Lord and Giver of Life: A 'Barthian' Defense of the *Filioque*," in *Rethinking Trinitarian Theology: Disputed Questions and Contemporary Issues in Trinitarian Theology*, ed. Giulio Maspero and Robert J. Wozniak (London: T. & T. Clark, 2012), pp. 231-53.

45. See Barth, *CD* II/2, p. 102. I have treated the relation of Trinity and election numerous times and at great length. It is not necessary to repeat all of that here. Those interested in further reading might wish to consult the following: Bruce L. McCormack, "Trinity and Election: A Progress Report," in *Ontmoetingen — Tijdgenoten en Getuigen.*

and to mean it as Barth means it requires, at a minimum, that the event of God's self-constitution as triune (i.e., the processions) and the event of his turning toward the human race in the covenant of grace (i.e., the missions) be one and the same event — albeit *one event with two terms.* Matthew Levering's formulation of Thomas's understanding of the relation of processions and missions is equally apt for Barth — with the following difference. Barth attains to it by means of a strictly "Christocentric" approach that works exclusively from the economy to the so-called "immanent Trinity," whereas Thomas is willing both to work in that way and to supplement it with metaphysical speculation (as touching upon the divine essence).[46] *That,* I would submit, is the root of all the remaining differences between the two theologians. But this fundamental difference cannot be allowed to conceal from us the very real convergence. To the extent that Thomas *also* works "from above" (from a metaphysically generated conception of the divine "essence") and not just from the economy, the convergence arises as a result of reading him "down" into Barth (from the processions to the missions). And even though the later Barth refuses this option (so that even his conception of the divine essence has been, in a sense, "historicized"), it still remains possible to read him "up" into Thomas (from the missions to the processions). The point of convergence (after *CD* II/2) is the shared affirmation of a single eternal act in which both the processions and the missions take place.

What do I mean by a "historicizing" of the divine "essence"? Election is an eternal act of self-determination. In it, a "determination" is given, according to Barth, to the divine "essence," which makes its content to be "essential." And since its content is seen by him to consist in God's eternal decision to be a God who suffers and dies in time, then the humility and obedience leading to that suffering and dying are not

---

Studies aangeboden aan Gerrit Neven, ed. Akke van der Kooi, Volker Küster, and Rinse Reeling Brouwer (Kampen: Kok, 2009), pp. 14-35; McCormack, "God *Is* His Decision: The Jüngel-Gollwitzer 'Debate' Revisited," in *Theology as Conversation: The Significance of Dialogue in Historical and Contemporary Theology (A Festschrift for Daniel L. Migliore),* ed. Bruce L. McCormack and Kimlyn J. Bender (Grand Rapids: Eerdmans, 2009), pp. 48-66.

46. Already in I/1, Barth announces a principle that would attain greater self-consistency and ontological significance once he had revised his doctrine of election: "we have consistently followed the rule, which we regard as basic, that statements about the divine modes of being antecedently in themselves *cannot be different in content* from those that are to be made about their reality in revelation" (*CD* I/1, p. 479; emphasis added).

"accidents" (i.e., something added to a divine "essence" conceived as complete "in itself") but are, in fact, made essential to him. "It is only the pride of man, making a god in its own image, that will not hear of a determination of divine essence in Jesus Christ."[47] On this basis, the later Barth makes humility and obedience to be "personal properties" of God in his second mode of being.[48]

To his thesis on election then ("Jesus Christ is the Subject of election"), Barth has added a Christological thesis. The Subject who suffers humanly in time is the Son of God, the second "Person" of the Trinity. And Barth means this to be taken with strict seriousness. When he says that God suffers, he does not mean this merely in the sense that human suffering "belongs" to the Word (in the possessive sense) as a consequence of the hypostatic union. He does not even mean to say it in the sense that, in the "Person" of the Word incarnate, an impassible divine nature "encounters" the suffering that takes place in the human nature in such a way that the impassible divine nature remains untouched by that encounter.[49] No, he means that God makes himself passible — and that he can do this without introducing change into his being because passibility is made "essential" to him by the eternal divine election.

Now please understand that when I say all of this, I do not say it as a challenge to Thomas — at least not as Matthew Levering reads him. For as we have seen, Levering too says that "the divine Son is never unrelated to creatures."[50] But I do say it as a challenge to those interpreters of Barth who read into him a two-act drama in pretemporal eternity in order to secure conceptions of "necessity" and "freedom" that Thomas too would have to reject. For the later Barth, the processions contain the missions and cannot be rightly construed apart from them.

---

47. *CD* IV/2, p. 84.

48. See on this point, Barth, *CD* IV/1, pp. 193, 200-201. See also Bruce L. McCormack, "The Doctrine of the Trinity after Barth: An Attempt to Reconstruct Barth's Doctrine in the Light of His Later Christology," in *Trinitarian Theology After Barth*, ed. Myk Habets and Phillip Tolliday (Eugene, OR: Pickwick, 2011), pp. 87-118.

49. Cf. Bruce D. Marshall, "The Dereliction of Christ and the Impassibility of God," in *Divine Impassibility and the Mystery of Human Suffering*, ed. James F. Keating and Thomas Joseph White, O.P. (Grand Rapids: Eerdmans, 2009), pp. 257-58: "just because he is impassible he destroys death by 'tasting' it — destroys death, as it were, on contact." We might say of Marshall's view: God touches human suffering without himself being touched by it. His nonaffectivity (which is what "impassibility" finally means) remains intact.

50. Levering, "Christ, the Trinity, and Predestination," p. 254.

In sum, the later Barth begins with a conception of the divine missions and asks: What must God be if the missions are what they are? This is a quasi-transcendental move that does not find in God anything more than is necessary to explain the missions. Thomas, too, would like to move from the missions to the processions. As Levering puts it, "we know the processions only through the missions."[51] As a description of what is said within the confines of Thomas's treatment of the Trinity, I think this is true. But we must remember that the relations to which the processions give rise are, for Thomas, the *Christian* description of the divine *essence*. And Thomas knows of another path for gaining knowledge of the divine essence — so that an integration of the knowledge from the one source and the knowledge from the other source becomes necessary.[52] Given that this is so, I don't think there can be any question but that knowledge of the divine essence conditions *to some degree at least* Thomas's understanding of the processions even as he seeks to understand the processions from a starting point in the missions.[53] Certainly, the knowledge of God acquired from his cre-

---

51. Levering, "Christ, the Trinity, and Predestination," p. 257.

52. Levering concludes his magnificent essay with a gentle rejoinder to me, a rejoinder that confirms the difference I have here been trying to explain. "As McCormack says, then, let us 'seek God where he may be found' [i.e., in the missions] — but not without the help of metaphysics." See Levering, "Christ, the Trinity, and Predestination," p. 273.

53. Nicholas Healy has suggested that, in a way similar to Barth, Thomas too uses a quasi-transcendental argument through the whole of his doctrine of God. His argument in support of this conclusion points to the importance of the concepts of "Word" and "Love" for Thomas's elaboration of the immanent Trinity in the second division. And so, he concludes that "we know these things of God's immanent life simply because Scripture tells us so." See Healy, "Karl Barth, German-Language Theology, and the Catholic Tradition," in Dempsey, ed., *Trinity and Election*, p. 241. This is much too brief and unguarded to be convincing. Certainly, it leaves out of account the fact that Thomas's essentialism finds its roots in inferences drawn from created effects with respect to the nature of their cause. By contrast, the great strength of the work of a specialist like Thomas Joseph White, O.P., is that he is willing to acknowledge and defend Thomas's natural theology without detriment to the latter's exposition of the Trinity and the high degree of integration between the first two parts of Thomas' treatise on God. See White, *Wisdom in the Face of Modernity: A Study in Thomistic Natural Theology* (Naples, FL: Sapientia Press, 2009). The odd thing is that Healy grants, in passing, that "knowledge of God comes in two forms" (p. 239) or has two sources, but then suppresses the significance of it by insisting that Thomas has scriptural warrant for doing natural theology. That might well be (it is debatable, of course). But a scriptural warrant for doing natural theology

ative activity constitutes the basis of Thomas's "essentialism" — which in turn conditions what he is able to say about the "processions," how they preserve and protect the divine simplicity, etc. And I would go so far as to suggest that, to the extent that words like "necessity" and "freedom" fall apart in the writings of even the very best readers of Thomas (and Levering is certainly one of them), this happens because the "necessity" in question is a function of a metaphysically based understanding of the divine essence, of what it means to say that something is "essential" to God, while "freedom" alone is defined strictly on the basis of a self-revelation in Christ which might not have been.[54] Barth, on the other hand, does not have the problem of integrating knowledge derived from one source and knowledge from another source. That is the fundamental difference. For the later Barth, the missions *fully* express the processions; the missions are not merely analogically related to the processions. And yet, in spite of this truly funda-

---

doesn't make natural theology anything other than "natural"; it is hardly an exercise in exegesis. I think what we see in the clash between the perspectives of a Healy and a White is a collision between a Yale-trained Catholic theologian who tends to read Thomas through the lens provided by Barth, and a Dominican who is willing to acknowledge the fundamental difference between the two that I have identified in this essay. Before leaving Healy, I might add that he also suggests that "McCormack's" doctrine of election is "speculative and uncritical." The explanation for this rather astonishing conclusion is to be found in an unsupported assertion, viz. that my "proposed doctrine of election is grounded not on Scripture but on a transcendental deduction, and thus on logic rather than revelation" (p. 242). Normally, I would not mind being accused of employing a "rigorous logic" (p. 242); there are surely worse things. But the truth is that the transcendental move I make is one already made by Barth himself. That I follow his leading in making it presupposes that the exegesis offered by him in support of his starting point in the narrated history of Jesus of Nazareth is convincing and that his exegesis of passages touching upon the divine election is equally so. Thus, the transcendental move is not a standalone argument, divorced from exegetical considerations. Since my doctrine of election differs not at all from Barth's, I would have thought that to be rather obvious.

54. Things fall apart for Levering when he writes, "a distinction must be made between this intra-divine communication [i.e., of the divine goodness in the processions] — which *pace* McCormack is not 'free,' because it belongs to who God is by nature rather than to who God has willed to be — and the free extra-divine communication of divine goodness that reaches its height in the incarnation of the Son Jesus Christ" (Levering, "Christ, the Trinity, and Predestination," pp. 256-57). It is my conviction that this asseveration is much too strong, even and especially on Levering's own reading of Thomas. If it is true that there is one eternal act with two terms, then the meanings of words like "necessity" and "freedom" must condition each other because both are defined by the one act.

mental difference in theological method, the two great theologians meet in the middle.[55]

The Debate over Trinity and Election Revisited

Twelve years ago, I published an essay that has been the subject of a good bit of discussion and criticism among specialists in Barth's theology. In it, I made the suggestion that the predominant strand of Barth's thinking subsequent to revising his doctrine of election invites us to think of the divine election as constitutive of God's being. My way of formulating this was, admittedly, provocative. I suggested that we might think of triunity in God as a "function" of the divine election.[56]

---

55. Thomas clearly holds, at the very least, that the missions include the processions. Barth holds that the missions include the processions because the processions include the missions. Is this a substantive difference? On the face of it, Bruce Marshall seems to think it is. He writes, "Mission includes procession, but procession does not include mission; procession is necessary for mission, but mission is not necessary for procession." See Marshall, "The Unity of the Triune God," p. 20; cf. p. 29. But Marshall too says, much like Levering, that "the temporal coming forth of sent from sender in which the missions consist must be the very same coming forth as the eternal procession by which that person originates from the Father (and, as the case may be, from the Son). The temporal procession or coming forth must, in other words, be numerically identical with the eternal procession" (p. 22). But if the temporal coming forth is the "very same coming forth as the eternal procession" and indeed, numerically identical with it, it is hard to avoid the conclusion that the processions contain the missions.

56. Bruce L. McCormack, "Grace and Being: The Role of God's Gracious Election in Karl Barth's Theological Ontology," in *The Cambridge Companion to Karl Barth*, ed. John Webster (Cambridge: Cambridge University Press, 2000), p. 103: "The denial of the existence of a *Logos asarkos* in any other sense than the concrete one of a being of the Logos as *incarnandus*, the affirmation that Jesus Christ is the second 'person' of the Trinity and the concomitant rejection of free-floating talk of the 'eternal Son' as a mythological abstraction — these commitments require that we see the triunity of God logically as a function of divine election." There was, in this formulation, no rejection of the concept of a *Logos asarkos* but an affirmation that the *Logos asarkos* is, as such, the *Logos incarnandus*. But the claim that triunity is a function of election must remain one-sided where it is not made clear that the event in which God constitutes himself as triune is also the event in which God turns toward us in electing grace. Given that it was a set of logical relationships I had in mind, one could begin with either end of the relation (with either election or triunity); and so long as one is willing to grant that there is but one act with two terms, no substantive difference would be introduced by the decision made. See on this point, Bruce L. McCormack, "God *Is* His Decision: The Jüngel-Gollwitzer 'Debate' Revisited."

In doing so, I had no intention of suggesting that election has an "on-tological priority" over Trinity. I spoke only of a logical priority. But this was enough to make my proposal controversial.[57]

Since then, the strategy of my critics (considered collectively) has been to put me on the horns of a dilemma.[58] Either I say that a decision

---

57. It is perhaps worth noting that "Grace and Being" proved to be a provocation for two theologians from whom I had not anticipated a negative reaction. George Hunsinger and John Webster were both present in 1994 when I gave a lecture in St. Paul, Minnesota, in which I spelled out in some detail the significance of Barth's doctrine of election for his understanding of divine and human being. It is true that I did not con-nect the dots to triunity on that occasion — *because I had not myself connected them at that point in time.* I did not do so until I read Thies Gundlach's fine book in 1996 — and, there-fore, *after* the publication of my book on Barth's development. See Gundlach, *Selbst-begrenzung Gottes und die Autonomie des Menschen* (Frankfurt am Main: Peter Lang, 1992). But I thought that the step from the ontological significance of election to triunity was a small and natural one to take and did not think it would surprise or cause offense to either friend. After all, neither offered any objection whatsoever to the account given in that 1994 lecture in the discussion that followed but seemed approving. The lecture it-self remains unpublished and bore the title "Radical Autonomy or Communicative Freedom: Divine Election and Human Freedom in the Theology of Karl Barth." Do I need to add that I did not have any of this in mind when writing the final chapter of my book on Barth's development (as Michael Dempsey seems to think)? See Dempsey, "In-troduction," *Trinity and Election,* p. 3.

58. The best and clearest expression of this can be found in Bruce D. Marshall, "The Dereliction of Christ and the Impassibility of God," pp. 286-87: "Making the iden-tity of the divine persons, and thus of the one God, depend on temporal actions, events, or states of affairs evidently requires accepting one of two alternatives: (1) The identity of each person is itself contingent, since it includes or depends on that which is contingent — so that, for example, 'God is the Father' is only contingently true, and God is only con-tingently the Father. (2) The temporal actions, events, or states of affairs on which the identity of each divine person depends are themselves necessary, since the identities of these divine persons are not contingent — so that, for example, 'God the Father com-mands Jesus to suffer and die' is true necessarily, and it is impossible for God the Father not to command (or to have commanded) Jesus to die." Leaving aside the fact that I do not make the identity of the divine persons to "depend" on temporal actions or events, there can be no question but that Marshall's either-or follows rather neatly from his premise, viz. that we are right to distinguish in God a necessary act of self-constitution and contingent act of entering into a covenant of grace with human beings. But the fact that he can simply take the validity of this premise for granted and proceed to draw con-clusions from it shows that (1) he thinks acceptance of it is unavoidable and that (2) my rejection of it cannot be taken seriously. But the two-act drama is *not even* necessitated by the metaphysical speculation by means of which he (with Thomas) grounds the divine unity. For Thomas, as we have seen, does not affirm two divine acts but only one act with two terms. What then *is* the source of the two-act drama? Its source lies, I would suggest,

(even an eternal divine decision) requires the (prior) existence of a subject who makes that decision — in which case I am guilty of making the preexisting subject an unknown x (an absolutely hidden God). Or I say that there is nothing "behind" the decision (i.e., no preexisting subject), that God is what he is "in" the decision — in which case, I seem to empty the talk of "decision" of any real content. And in doing that, I make creation and redemption to be "necessary" for God, thereby setting aside the divine freedom.

In truth, I do not think this dilemma to be real at all. For only the second of the two issues named is a real one for me. The first is a bit of a nonstarter. Just as Thomas says that the Father does not *preexist* the act of begetting the Son (so that there is no Father without the Son), so I also say that the Father does not *preexist* the decision in which he both constitutes himself as triune and turns toward the human race in the Son and the Spirit. For both Thomas and me, the precedence of the Father is strictly logical, belonging to the question of the right ordering of concepts. Thomas resists saying that the Father is "before" the begetting just as I resist saying the Father is "before" the decision that takes place in and with the begetting. What I have done, however, is to bind knowing and willing together in God in a slightly different way than he does. On my proposal, God's self-knowing takes place in the event of his generation of the Son to be the Redeemer of the world. But Thomas, too, joins knowing and willing — and does so precisely in the divine processions. For he says that while the Son proceeds by intelligible emanation (as Word), the Holy Spirit (as Love) proceeds from both by "will" (under-

---

in the univocal application to God of definitions of "necessity" and "contingency" that have been acquired through an analysis of temporal events. A "necessary" event, for Marshall, is one that could *not* have turned out otherwise, being causally dependent on an event or events that precede it. A "contingent" event is one that *could* have turned out differently (one, that is, that is brought about by free rational creatures). Such definitions certainly have their applicability as applied to temporal events. Applied to God, however, such definitions have a built-in tendency to "separate" into two events what is, in fact, a single event. So if we are to use such terms at all, we cannot and must not define them in opposition to each other. God, we might say, is contingently necessary and necessarily contingent. He is contingently necessary in that the one act in which he gives to himself the kind of freedom he enjoys (a freedom "for us") is an act that makes necessary (essential) to him all that it contains. He is necessarily contingent in that he has and exercises no "freedom" prior to this act which makes necessary, so that all his freedom in relation to us is an expression of who and what he "necessarily" is. In any event, Marshall and I are like ships passing in the night. He is trying to hold me to a premise I reject.

stood in terms of inclination).[59] Thomas, too, is feeling his way toward joining divine knowledge and will but he does so on the basis of a metaphysical conception of the divine essence that gives the processions a logical priority over the missions. I join knowledge and will on the basis of a conception of election that gives the missions a certain logical priority over the processions as their end. But the two conceptions are quite close one to the other. In fact, I think it is fair to say that the divine goodness performs the same function in Thomas's theology that the divine self-determination does in mine. Each of these conceptions, in their differing ways, gives us a reason to include the missions in the processions and the processions in the missions. And they can do this because both are, at the end of the day, descriptions of the divine essence. In any event, I do not need to posit the existence of an unknown subject behind the act of self-determination; that is not a necessary consequence of my description of the eternal electing activity in which God has his being. God's being is a being in the act of electing that constitutes him as triune — and that is all that can be said. Would God have been the triune God had he not created the world? The question is, as Robert Jenson has recently observed, nonsense[60] — apart from the embrace of metaphysics and, with that, the embrace of natural theology.[61]

Of course, a decision that has always taken place doesn't look anything like the decisions made by finite rational creatures like ourselves; that goes without saying. So the "freedom" of God is the only real issue here. But it is God's decision making that defines what it means to make a decision, not our own. What makes a decision truly "decisive" is the fact

59. *ST* I, q. 27, a. 3.
60. Robert W. Jenson, "Once More the Logos *asarkos*," *International Journal of Systematic Theology* 13 (2011): 131.
61. The first half of Marshall's either-or, discussed above (in n. 58), understands the divine election as a strictly contingent act, stripped of any hint of necessity. Defined in this way, he notes that God's being cannot be "dependent" upon a "decision which might not have been made" without making God's being as Father, Son, and Holy Spirit equally contingent. In other words, God might not have been triune. See Marshall, "The Dereliction of Christ and the Impassibility of God," p. 287. That the divine decision is contingent *in Marshall's sense* is something I once believed; I do so no longer. But that doesn't mean I am now ready to say the opposite: that God could *not* have decided otherwise. What I do think is simply that the form of the question is wrongheaded. It asks us to think about an *eternal* divine decision on the basis of terms derived from an analysis of the temporally structured decision making of humans — a sheer anthropomorphizing of the divine, then.

that it perfectly achieves the ends contained in it. A choice among options is not required and is, in fact, true only of finite creatures. God does not weigh "possible outcomes" of a decision made before deciding. God knows himself, as Thomas rightly says, with complete comprehension. And if God knows himself perfectly, then he also knows — in the same act of immediate intuition — what he will do in relation to things outside of himself. Moreover, God also wills himself precisely in knowing himself; self-knowledge and self-willing are identical in him. And if in knowing and willing himself God knows and wills others things, then aseity and decision making are inextricably intertwined in him. They can be "separated" for analysis only at great risk. And so Barth is right to say, "The fact that God's being is event, the event of God's act, necessarily means that it is His own conscious, willed, and executed decision. . . . No other being is *absolutely* its own conscious, willed and executed decision."[62] In any event, there is no subject somewhere "behind" the decision. God's being is a being-in-act, a being in the act of electing.

Now all of this might seem to make creatures "necessary" to the being of God; certainly critics of my proposal have repeatedly suggested as much. And I will grant immediately that I do not see necessity and freedom as oppositional terms when defined by God's being-in-act — which means that the attempt to define divine "freedom" *over against* "necessity" is a mistake. But that then suggests that the real issue is the meaning of freedom in God.

Let's start, then, with what my critics and I agree upon. We agree that freedom in God means that God is not conditioned by anything outside of himself in electing (his election is, after all, unconditional). And we agree that God never acts out of need or want.[63] But that is as

---

62. *CD* II/1, p. 271 (emphasis mine).

63. Marshall's second alternative as set forth above (in n. 58) would make me guilty both of making God dependent upon the world and of making God need the world. If the divine identity is constituted by temporal events and God could not be God without them, then God needs those events in order to be the God he is. See Marshall, "The Dereliction of Christ and the Impassibility of God," p. 290. But God's identity is not constituted by temporal events on my view; it is constituted by the eternal and sovereign (i.e., unconditioned) act of self-determination for Incarnation, etc., which makes the identity of the second person of the Trinity to be "Jesus Christ." And the obedience of Jesus Christ to the command of his Father is not something that takes place first in time (which would, perhaps, make the divine identity to be "dependent" on temporal events); it is something that takes place already in pretemporal eternity. It is true that the man Jesus must *also* will to do the will of his Father in time in order for this eternal

far as our agreement goes. In my view, freedom in God must be defined by the life-act in which God eternally *is*. We must not abstract from this act in order to define words like "freedom" and "necessity" on some other basis, seeking then to apply the definitions we have acquired to God. Nor may we seek the meaning of divine "freedom" in some sort of ontic space "behind" the eternal decision in which God elects and is triune. There is in God no unrealized potentiality. On this point, at least, I agree with Thomas. But I would add that, for me, this means that God's freedom is founded in the one eternal act and is, therefore, a freedom "for" creation and redemption. To ascribe freedom to God for other possibilities would seem to me to require a rejection of the one-act model upon which Levering too insists. No, God is free in the one act of self-constituting electing grace. And that means that his freedom is a freedom for that to which he gives to himself, a freedom to realize his electing purposes.

This also has implications for how we understand divine power. Power in God is not the freedom to do this or that; it is the power to realize perfectly that which he has chosen to do. There is, in God, no *potentia absoluta;* the only power there is in God is "ordained" power.[64]

Conclusion: A Word to the Situation

Gilles Emery argues, rightly I think, that Thomas achieved a finely tuned balance between "essentialism" and "personalism."[65] It is the doctrine of the Trinity (the differentiation of divine persons) that constitutes Thomas's "personalism." His "essentialism" is a function of his willingness to employ a bit of metaphysical speculation in treating the divine "essence" in the first division of his treatise on God. But Emery

---

obedience to be made concretely real in time. Marshall, too, is a dyothelite, so he will understand my reasoning on that point. But a God who has exhaustive foreknowledge will know what the man Jesus will do. Therefore, there is no "dependence" in God on temporal events and if no "dependence," then no "need" (in the customary sense of that word).

64. God's power is his ability "to do what He wills." As such, it is "victoriously opposed to 'power in itself.'" See Karl Barth, *Dogmatics in Outline* (New York: Harper & Row, 1959), p. 47.

65. This is the burden of the whole of Emery's very fine essay "Essentialism or Personalism in the Treatise on God in St. Thomas Aquinas?" The answer given to the rhetorical question posed by the title is that it is not necessary to choose between them.

also believes that it is the "personalism" that is decisive in establishing the unity of the first two sections of the treatise. And, most importantly, "in the order of our access to the knowledge of the Trinity, the *dispensatio* [or 'economy'] comes first."[66] So, where the Trinity is concerned, the order of knowing begins with the missions, a point also made by Levering.[67] The order of teaching (or "exposition"), on the other hand, which is founded upon the knowledge acquired in this way, admits of a certain flexibility. One can either start with Christ's "divinity" (which is to say, with the "essence" common to the three members of the Trinity) or one can begin with the Word of God incarnate. Either order of teaching is acceptable. Thomas used the first in his *Summa theologiae* but he used both in his commentaries on Scripture. What that tells us is that he could just as easily have started with the Trinity in the *Summa* and treated the divine essence in the second place.

I mention this because of an interesting development from within the camp of the "Barthians." In a recent essay on ecclesiology, John Webster wrote, "I propose to begin from a conception of God's perfection. The prevailing voices in ecclesiology would bid us begin elsewhere, most often in a doctrine of the economic Trinity; that they are mistaken in doing so . . . will, I hope, become evident as the argument proceeds."[68] Webster explains his uneasiness with an economically grounded doctrine of the Trinity in another essay. "Theologians in the Reformed tradition," he says, have rightly maintained "an asymmetry between 'immanent' and 'economic' in teaching about God's triune being."[69] Where this asymmetry is neglected, there is a great danger that "the entire being of the Son" will be "collapsed into the event of the incarnation."[70] Whether this worry is justified in relation to Barth is not at issue here. Webster does not think it is and I agree — though for quite different reasons than his. What is clear, though, is that Webster himself has become more and more clearly Thomistic in his thinking of late — and, indeed,

66. Emery, *"Theologia* and *Dispensatio,"* p. 518.
67. Levering, "Christ, the Trinity, and Predestination," p. 261.
68. John Webster, "The Church and the Perfection of God," in *The Community of the Word: Toward an Evangelical Ecclesiology,* ed. Mark Husbands and Daniel J. Treier (Downers Grove, IL: InterVarsity, 2005), p. 79.
69. John Webster, "Article Review: Webster's Response to Alyssa Lyra Pitstick, *Light in Darkness," Scottish Journal of Theology* 62 (2009): 204.
70. Webster, "Article Review: Webster's Response to Alyssa Lyra Pitstick, *Light in Darkness,"* p. 206.

in one respect at least, hyper-Thomistic. Like Thomas, he too would concede that the economy is first in the order of knowing but that the immanent Trinity (the divine "perfection") is first in the order of being.[71] But his unwillingness to make room for the possibility that one might just as well proceed in the order of exposition from the missions to the processions rather than solely from the processions to the missions suggests a break with Thomas's more dialectical strategy. Whether this unwillingness rests on an allergic reaction to developments internal to Protestant theology or is more principled remains to be seen.

For now, I will simply point out that Webster seems quite definitely committed to Thomas's delicate balancing of "essentialism" and "personalism." And given that you cannot have Thomas's "essentialism" at all (however you adjust it to "personalism") without accepting the metaphysical speculation that made it possible in the first place, I wonder how long it can be until Webster is also defending natural theology. After all, a commitment to natural theology is entailed in Thomas's metaphysics. Even more: acceptance of the *analogia entis,* which is embedded in all talk of an asymmetry between the immanent and the economic, will need to become principled.[72]

In one respect, I am glad for this development. For it does have the potential for bringing clarity into the debate described in the preceding section — which up to now has generated more heat than light. What is true for Webster is true for all "Barthians" who wish to uphold an analogical interval in the relation of the immanent Trinity to the economic Trinity. You cannot have such an interval without a principled commitment to natural theology and the *analogia entis.* As Webster continues further along the path he has now charted, I suspect that he will make that clear to all — and the future of Barth's theology in the English-speaking world will then depend on how many "Barthians" wish to join him.

---

71. John Webster, "Perfection and Participation," in *The Analogy of Being: Invention of the Antichrist or the Wisdom of God?* ed. Thomas Joseph White, O.P. (Grand Rapids: Eerdmans, 2011), p. 391.

72. For now, Webster seems hesitant to take this final step. He protests, for example, against philosophers of religion who "are rarely able to extricate themselves from an abstract concept of *deitas,* a preconception of divinity that is not generated from or corrected by God's evangelical self-enactment and self-communication but emerges from the need for a perfect being as a causal explanation of features of the contingent world" (Webster, "Perfection and Participation," p. 381).

III. Christology

Natural Revelation in Creation and Covenant

Keith L. Johnson

The goal of this essay is to show that Thomas Aquinas and Karl Barth do *not* disagree about the existence of natural revelation or its role within Christian theology. In fact, their convergence on this issue is striking: they both believe that God is revealed in and through the created order and that theologians can and should incorporate insights derived from this natural revelation into the church's theology. They also share another important trait: they both build their claims about the existence and role of natural revelation upon the foundation of a presupposed account of God's relationship with creation. It is at this point, however, that the similarities end, because Aquinas and Barth each presuppose a *different* account of God's relationship with creation due to their distinct conceptions of Jesus Christ's saving work relative to creation. This difference leads to a striking divergence in their respective understandings of the *content* of natural revelation, so that while important formal similarities exist in their approach to natural revelation, crucial material differences remain between their views. By providing clarity about these similarities and differences, this essay seeks to make two contributions. First, it hopes to clear away misconceptions about the perceived but largely nonexistent disagreement between Aquinas and Barth on the existence and proper role of this kind of divine revelation in theology. Second, it hopes to clarify the true points of divergence between Aquinas and Barth and thus reframe the conversation between their theological heirs.

Keith L. Johnson

Aquinas and Natural Revelation

Aquinas begins the *Summa theologiae (ST)* with a basic assumption: humans are rational beings created by God for God. He interprets this assumption through the lens of his own biblical adaptation of the neo-Platonic theme of *exitus* and *reditus,* where creatures come forth from God and are ordered to return to him.[1] Since humans are "directed to God as to an end," their most basic need is to acquire authentic knowledge of God so they can "direct their thoughts and actions" to him.[2] Q. 1 explains how sacred doctrine addresses this need. The problem, Aquinas argues, is that even though humans are ordered to God as their true end, God "surpasses the grasp of [human] reason," so that "the truth about God, such as reason can know it, would only be known by a few, and that after a long time, and with the admixture of many errors."[3] This leaves humans in a quandary: they are ordered to an end they cannot achieve under their own power. Sacred doctrine solves this quandary. As a science that "proceeds from the principles made known by the light of a higher science, namely, the science of God and the blessed,"[4] sacred doctrine supplies humans with what they lack: "knowledge of God not only as He is in Himself, but also as He is the beginning of things and their last end, and especially of rational creatures."[5] This supernatural knowledge allows humans to direct their thoughts and actions to God "more fitly and surely" than they could under their natural powers, leading them more certainly to the end for which they were made.[6]

This argument is foundational to Aquinas's entire theology, but it

1. The most influential account of this theme is found in Marie-Dominique Chenu, *Toward Understanding Saint Thomas,* trans. A. M. Landry and D. Hughes (Chicago: Henry Regnery, 1964). For a discussion of this idea and its reception in Thomism, see Jean-Pierre Torrell, O.P., *Saint Thomas Aquinas,* vol. 1: *The Person and His Work,* rev. ed., trans. Robert Royal (Washington, DC: Catholic University of America Press, 2005), pp. 150-56.

2. *ST* I, q. 1, a. 1. Throughout this essay, citations are taken from *Basic Writings of Saint Thomas Aquinas,* 2 vols., ed. Anton C. Pegis (New York: Random House, 1945). For a helpful account of the history of the interpretation of the concept of sacred doctrine in this question, see James A. Weisheipl, "The Meaning of *Sacra Doctrina* in *Summa theologiae* I, Q1," *The Thomist* 38 (1974): 49-80.

3. *ST* I, q. 1, a. 1.

4. *ST* I, q. 1, a. 2.

5. *ST* I, q. 2, prologue.

6. *ST* I, q. 1, a. 1.

raises two immediate questions: *why* and *how?* Specifically, why should humans accept this account, and how does it make sense? If humans really were made *for* God, then why is it the case their natural reason does not suffice to lead them to God? And if the knowledge provided by sacred doctrine really is necessary for humans to reach their true end, then how does this knowledge relate to the knowledge available to humans by use of their natural reason alone? Aquinas knows that, if he is to establish the legitimacy of his claims about the role of sacred doctrine within human life, then he must address these questions in some way. And, in fact, this is precisely what he does in the opening questions of the *ST:* taken together, these questions form a single, coherent argument about the nature of sacred doctrine, its relationship to human reason, and the implications of this relationship for human thought and speech about God. This argument begins with q. 2 and culminates with qq. 12 and 13, where Aquinas establishes the scope and limitations of natural reason and offers a theory for how human concepts that originally arose from reasoned reflection upon creation are rightly applied to God as well. The result is a comprehensive account of the critical yet ongoing relationship between the supernaturally revealed truths of faith and the truths of natural reason, one that allows Aquinas to explain how finite creatures can stand in relationship with, and talk correctly about, the infinite God for whom they were made. This account addresses the "why" and "how" questions and thus provides the foundation upon which the rest of his arguments in the *ST* are built. It also, more relevant to our purposes, helps us see precisely how Aquinas understands the role of natural revelation in Christian theology, which sets the stage for a comparison of his views with those of Karl Barth.

Sacred Doctrine and Natural Reason

When the opening questions of the *ST* are read together as a coherent unit, the logic of Aquinas's argument in them is fairly easy to follow.[7] To establish the claims he made about the necessity and role of sacred

---

7. The argument below concerning the unity and relationship between these questions is drawn from the interpretation found in Anna Bonta Moreland, *Known by Nature: Thomas Aquinas on the Natural Knowledge of God* (New York: Crossroads, 2010), pp. 47-65, 133-34.

doctrine in q. 1, Aquinas needs to provide an account of how sacred doctrine and natural reason relate to one another. Before he can delineate this relationship, however, he has to have a clear account of the difference between the content of the knowledge provided by sacred doctrine and reason respectively. With this goal in mind, Aquinas begins his argument in q. 2 by addressing the question of whether or not God's existence can be demonstrated rationally. Once he has made this case, he then outlines three tasks he must accomplish: "we must consider (1) how [God] is *not;* (2) how He is known by us; and (3) how He is named."[8] These tasks provide a summary of what Aquinas believes he must show in order to explain the relationship between sacred doctrine and human reason. First, he needs to show precisely what humans can know about God by reason alone by describing the positive knowledge of God that can be derived from natural reason alone (qq. 3-11); then he has to explain the scope, nature, and limits of this natural knowledge of God as compared to the knowledge available in and through faith, as well as the relationship between the two types of knowledge (q. 12); and finally, he needs to provide an account of human speech about God in light of his conclusions about the relationship between faith and reason (q. 13). Taken together, these arguments explain how true statements about God made by those both inside and outside of faith relate to one another. Aquinas believes this relationship will confirm the claims about sacred doctrine made in q. 1.

His argument begins with his proofs for God's existence in q. 2. There he establishes that, although God's existence is not self-evident, because humans were made for God, the capacity to know *that* God exists is "in a general and confused way implanted in [humans] by nature."[9] This latent capacity for God needs to be actualized, and this actualization can occur by means of an argument. To this end, Aquinas claims that the existence of any cause can be established by examining the effects it produces, since "from every effect the existence of its proper cause can be demonstrated."[10] Since humans have direct knowledge of the created effects produced by God, it must be possible to "demonstrate the existence of God from His effects."[11] This is precisely

---

8. *ST* I, q. 3, prologue.
9. *ST* I, q. 2, a. 1.
10. *ST* I, q. 2, a. 2.
11. *ST* I, q. 2, a. 2, ad 3.

what his five proofs for God's existence demonstrate: they show that God is the First Cause of everything that exists.[12] Knowledge of God's existence does not rise to the level of sacred doctrine, however, because sacred doctrine discusses God "as He is in Himself."[13] Can humans acquire *this* kind of knowledge from reason alone? Aquinas himself sets up this question: "When the existence of a thing has been ascertained, there remains the further question of the manner of its existence, in order that we may know its essence."[14] He immediately admits that such knowledge cannot be attained directly by humans, because finite humans "have no means for considering how God is" in God's essence.[15] This does not mean that human reason has reached its limits, however. Aquinas believes he can demonstrate that, by using reason to discern what God is *not* and then by reflecting upon the content of this negative knowledge, humans can indirectly arrive at additional, although qualified and limited, *positive* knowledge of God.

Here Aquinas turns to the first part of his threefold outline and to the doctrine of divine simplicity, because he thinks this doctrine can be used to mark off the limits of what humans can know of God's being by natural reason alone. He argues that on the basis of their knowledge that God is the First Cause of everything that exists, humans can also know that "God is His own being." From this point, they can deduce that God's being is *simple* — which is to say that God is *not* composite, his essence and existence are identical, and he does not have his being by participation in anything else.[16] These characteristics distinguish God from every created thing, since essence and existence are not identical in creatures, creatures are composite, and they have their being by participation.[17] For Aquinas, this divine-human distinction, worked out by means of the doctrine of divine simplicity, constitutes the basic limits of what humans can know about God by reason. In qq. 4-11, he simply draws out the implications of this distinction more fully: since humans can know that God's being is simple, they also can deduce that God is

12. *ST* I, q. 2, a. 3.
13. *ST* I, q. 2, prologue.
14. *ST* I, q. 3, prologue.
15. *ST* I, q. 3, prologue.
16. *ST* I, q. 3, a. 4.
17. See *ST* I, q. 44, a. 1: "all beings other than God are not their own being, but are beings by participation. Therefore, it must be that all things . . . are caused by the one First Being, Who possesses being most perfectly."

not imperfect, evil, finite, changeable, limited by time, or composite.[18] Even though these deductions have been derived solely from the negative knowledge of God available by reason alone, Aquinas believes they actually produce *positive* claims about God's being. In other words, as he explains at the end of his examination of these questions, by ruling out characteristics associated with creatures, humans can use their natural reason to know *something* true about God "as He is in Himself."[19] This knowledge of God is not as perfect or full as the knowledge found in sacred doctrine, but it remains true knowledge nonetheless.[20]

This insight brings us back to the original question: What is the relationship between true claims about God derived through the use of natural reason and the true claims about God given to the human in faith? It is here that Aquinas turns to the second of the three tasks he outlined: explaining precisely *how* humans know God both by reason and through faith. This explanation occurs in q. 12, where he proceeds by comparing the content of the knowledge of God that humans will have in the final beatitude — when they will see God "as He is" (1 John 3:2) — to the knowledge of God available to their natural reason in the present that he has just delineated in qq. 2-11. Aquinas thinks this comparison will make the distinction between the two types of knowledge clear and thus set the stage for a discussion of their relationship.

18. This insight comes from Moreland, who argues that, taken together, qq. 3-11 "represent a systematic attempt to reject all idolatrous tendencies to place God into a class with creatures." See Moreland, *Known by Nature,* p. 65.

19. *ST* I, q. 12, prologue. Hence, I disagree with Bruce Marshall's claim that Aquinas "effectively rules out natural theology (unless, of course, it is practiced by Christians)." As we will see, the content of natural theology is certainly qualified on Aquinas's view, but it is not ruled out. See Marshall, *"Quod Scit Una Uetula:* Aquinas on the Nature of Theology," in *The Theology of Thomas Aquinas,* ed. Rik van Nieuwenhove and Joseph Wawrykow (Notre Dame: University of Notre Dame Press, 2005), p. 18.

20. This claim was not new for Aquinas. For example, in his commentary on Boethius's *De Trinitate,* he argued that humans "cannot know *that* a thing is without knowing in some way *what* it is, either perfectly or at least confusedly. . . . For our knowledge of definitions, like that of demonstrations, must begin with some previous knowledge. Similarly, therefore, we cannot know *that* God and other immaterial substances exist unless we know somehow, in some confused way, *what* they are." See Aquinas, *The Division and Method of the Sciences: Questions V and VI of His Commentary on the* De Trinitate *of Boethius,* trans. Armand Maurer (Toronto: Pontifical Institute of Mediaeval Studies, 1986), VI, a. 3. This remark was originally cited by Moreland, who notes that Aquinas "maintains this same vocabulary" in *ST* I, q. 2, a. 1, ad 1. See Moreland, *Known by Nature,* pp. 62, 173.

He begins by arguing that it must be possible for a created intellect to "see the essence of God," since a denial of this possibility would mean that humans could "never attain to beatitude."[21] In light of this claim, five successive questions arise. First, what does it *mean* to "see God" in this way? Aquinas answers that it cannot mean that the human "comprehends" God, since something is comprehended when it is "perfectly known," and an infinite God can never be perfectly known by a finite being.[22] Instead, it means that the beatified "attain" God in the sense that God is always present to them, and they "enjoy Him as the ultimate fulfillment of desire."[23] This answer leads to the second question: *How* can a human "see God" in this way? Aquinas responds by saying that humans cannot do so by nature, because anything that is known always must be known in accord with the nature of the knower. Since God's infinite being exceeds the finite nature of the human knower, knowledge of God's essence is by definition "beyond the natural power of any created intellect." Indeed, only *God* is capable of knowing himself in this way because "to know self-subsistent being is natural to the divine intellect alone." Aquinas thus concludes that humans can "see God" only when "God by His grace unites Himself to the created intellect, as an object made intelligible to it."[24] This union takes the form of a "supernatural disposition" added to the human's natural capacities when God unites himself to her by grace so that she can

---

21. *ST* I, q. 12, a. 1.

22. *ST* I, q. 12, a. 7. He notes that this inability to comprehend God does not mean that God is incomprehensible because "anything of Him is not seen," but because this kind of hiddenness would undermine the very idea of a final beatitude. Rather, God's incomprehensibility means that God is "not seen as perfectly as He is capable of being seen" because only *God* knows himself as fully as he is capable of being known. See *ST* I, q. 12, a. 7, ad 2; also see *ST* I, q. 12, a. 1, ad 3.

23. *ST* I, q. 12, a. 7, ad 1. Aquinas uses this distinction to develop an important point in *ST* I, q. 12, a. 8: in their vision of the divine essence, beatified humans do not see "all that God does or can do" because this would be to comprehend God; rather, even in the beatific vision, God is known "as an effect is seen in its cause," meaning that this knowledge is inexhaustible in the sense that it *always* can be more fully realized. For a more thorough account of this distinction between "comprehend God" *(comprehendere Deum)* and "attain God" *(attingere Deum),* see Moreland, *Known by Nature,* pp. 75-85, 152-53.

24. *ST* I, q. 12, a. 4. Aquinas notes that, in this life, humans are "united to him as to one unknown," because they cannot "see God" until their beatitude. Even so, they can acquire more perfect knowledge than could be obtained by reason, such as the fact that God is triune. See *ST* I, q. 13, a. 13, ad 1.

achieve what otherwise would be impossible.[25] This insight raises the third question: Is the vision of God available to humans through grace *also* available to humans through nature? Aquinas's answer is no. Since the knowledge of a thing always corresponds to the nature of the knower, and since the human is a corporeal being whose "natural knowledge begins from sense," human natural knowledge "can go as far as it can be led by sensible things." Since the human "cannot be led by sense so far as to see the essence of God," the human cannot see God by nature in the same way that God will be seen when he unites himself to the human by grace in the final beatitude.[26] This conclusion leads to the fourth question: If the human cannot see God's essence by nature, what *can* be known of God by nature? In response, Aquinas summarizes the limited content of this natural knowledge:

> But because [the sensible effects of God] are His effects and depend on their cause, we can be led from them so far as to know of God whether He exists, and to know of Him what must necessarily belong to Him as the First Cause of all things, exceeding all things caused by Him. Hence, we know His relationship with creatures, that is, that He is the cause of all things; also that creatures differ from Him inasmuch as He is not in any way part of what is caused by Him; and that His effects are removed from Him, not by reason or any defect on His part, but because He superexceeds them all.[27]

This summary corresponds precisely to the content of the arguments about God that Aquinas had just offered in qq. 2-11. These questions, therefore, stand as his description of what can be known of God by natural reason alone, and Aquinas has now distinguished this knowledge from the knowledge that is available by grace and faith.[28]

With this distinction in hand, Aquinas can now address the fifth and final question: What is the *relationship* between the knowledge of God available through grace and the knowledge of God available to hu-

---

25. *ST* I, q. 12, a. 5. Aquinas calls this disposition a "kind of deiformity." See *ST* I, q. 12, a. 6.

26. *ST* I, q. 12, a. 12.

27. *ST* I, q. 12, a. 12.

28. In line with this claim, Moreland argues this question can be read as a "retrospective analysis" consisting of "a pause and reflection on the methodology of the previous questions." See Moreland, *Known by Nature*, pp. 65-66.

mans by nature? This question marks an important point in Aquinas's argument, because it returns to the questions initially raised in the light of his claims about the purpose and role of sacred doctrine within human life. His answer is to say that the knowledge of God given to humans by grace is "more perfect" than the knowledge of God available by natural reason.[29] The chief reason is that, because it is limited to sensible things, the knowledge of God available to natural reason is partial at best and may be incorrect at worst. This explains why, when reason alone is used, God is "known by a few, and that after a long time, and with the admixture of many errors."[30] Sacred doctrine is necessary, therefore, because it provides humans with the "fuller knowledge" of God they need "to express divine things better" and order their lives rightly.[31]

This conclusion does not mean that human reason has no role to play in the way that humans know God, however. Indeed, Aquinas has just shown that, by using their natural reason alone, humans can and do say *true* things about God. Even though sacred doctrine is "more perfect" than natural knowledge, therefore, it does not replace it altogether. Aquinas explains that, while the knowledge of God available through grace "belongs only to the good," the knowledge of God available through natural reason "can belong to both good and bad."[32] This means that the two types of knowledge stand in an intrinsic and ongoing relationship with one another, with the type that is always good (sacred doctrine) being used to perfect and fulfill the one that may contain errors (natural reason). This conclusion addresses the question lingering after q. 1, and its logic is straightforward. While we must say that the knowledge of God available in sacred doctrine surpasses the limits of human reason, we cannot say this knowledge *contradicts* human reason, because doing so would undermine the claim that humans can naturally know that God exists as the First Cause of creation and that God's being is simple and thus distinct from every created thing. A denial of this claim would contradict the presupposition with which Aquinas started: humans are rational beings naturally ordered to God. Even though sacred doctrine proceeds from higher principles,

29. *ST* I, q. 12, a. 13.
30. *ST* I, q. 1, a. 1.
31. *ST* I, q. 12, a. 13; also see *ST* I, q. 12, a. 13, ad 2.
32. *ST* I, q. 12, a. 12, ad 3.

it is still a *science* that functions according to reason.[33] Natural reason may lead only to limited and partial knowledge of God, but this knowledge is *true* knowledge inasmuch as everything reasonable is intrinsically ordered to the wisdom of God.[34] The knowledge of God available through reason, therefore, must be seen as the preamble and presupposition of the knowledge of God available through sacred doctrine rather than its opposite.[35]

Speaking about God

This account of the relationship between sacred doctrine and natural reason brings Aquinas to the third and final task in his threefold outline: offering a description of human speech about God. He explains that, since "everything is named according to our knowledge of it," human language for God must correspond to the way humans know God through both natural reason and sacred doctrine.[36] Yet the problem facing any such account is that, since God's essence "is above all that we understand about God and signify in words," God is "above being

33. It should be noted that, even though Aquinas affirms that sacred doctrine is a science (*ST* I, q. 1, a. 2), he qualifies this claim by saying that, because it does not proceed from the "vision of the believer, but from the vision of Him Who is believed," it finally "falls short of the nature which knowledge has when it is science." In other words, while sacred doctrine is a science in the sense that it proceeds from first principles, it is a distinct science because it arrives at its first principles, not through reason, but "from the uniting of our intellect with God through grace." See *ST* I, q. 12, a. 13, ad 3.

34. *ST* I, q. 1, a. 6, ad 1. This conclusion rules out Eugene Rogers's argument that, for Aquinas, "'the natural cognition of God' is presented as a misnomer." Overall, Rogers's argument about the convergence between Aquinas and Barth fails to do justice to either figure, since it is derived from both the misplaced idea that Aquinas denies positive natural knowledge of God and an interpretation of Barth that corresponds to his early position on natural revelation rather than the modified, later view that will be discussed below. See Rogers, *Thomas Aquinas and Karl Barth: Sacred Doctrine and the Natural Knowledge of God* (Notre Dame: University of Notre Dame Press, 1995), p. 131.

35. *ST* I, q. 2, a. 2, ad 1. This allows us to conclude, as David Burrell does, that the perfection and fulfillment of reason by faith reveal their fundamentally positive relationship with one another since this perfection "gives direction to reason itself, inviting reason to give expression to its internal orientation to its source and goal." See Burrell, "Analogy, Creation, and Theological Language," in van Nieuwenhove and Wawrykow, eds., *The Theology of Thomas Aquinas,* p. 79.

36. *ST* I, q. 13, prologue.

named."[37] Human speech about God cannot be equivocal, however, because this would leave it empty and nonfunctional, and humans would be unable to reach the end for which they were created.[38] How, then, can words and concepts originally derived from reflection upon finite created things be rightly applied to an infinite God? Aquinas's answer builds upon the foundation of the previous questions. He argues that since words are "signs of ideas," and since "ideas are the similitudes of things" in the human intellect, humans can "give a name to anything in so far as we can *understand* it."[39] As he demonstrated in the previous questions, even though humans cannot see the essence of God in this life, they can, in fact, "know God from creatures as their cause, and also by way of excellence and remotion."[40] This leads to the conclusion that creaturely concepts derived from reflection upon the created order can be rightly applied to God because God can be known, at least in part, through reflection upon that created order.

Once again, the logic behind this conclusion and its implications is straightforward. Since human words and concepts are derived from reflection upon created effects caused by God, any perfection in these created effects can be traced directly back to God, who possesses it "in a more eminent way."[41] This means the words used to signify creaturely perfections also can be used to "signify the divine substance, but in an imperfect manner."[42] This imperfect correspondence stems from the distinction between the thing signified and the mode of signification: even though creaturely words rightly apply to God, they do not apply to him "properly or strictly" because they apply differently to God as the First Cause than they do to the creaturely effects.[43] God thus remains beyond the limits of human language just like knowledge of God's essence always remains beyond the grasp of

37. *ST* I, q. 13, a. 1, ad 1.

38. See *ST* I, q. 13, a. 5.

39. *ST* I, q. 13, a. 1.

40. *ST* I, q. 13, a. 1.

41. *ST* I, q. 13, a. 2, ad 2. Aquinas explains that our concepts for God rightly apply to God first, and only then to creatures, because they exist in God in a more excellent way since he is their cause. See *ST* I, q. 13, a. 6.

42. *ST* I, q. 13, a. 2.

43. *ST* I, q. 13, a. 3. In a certain sense, as Gregory Rocca argues, this distinction can be seen as "an encapsulation of the whole expanse of Aquinas' positive and negative theology." See Gregory Rocca, O.P., *Speaking the Incomprehensible God* (Washington, DC: Catholic University of America Press, 2004), pp. 349-52.

human reason.[44] This limitation does not disqualify creaturely concepts from being applied to God, but simply qualifies them in a similar way to how the knowledge of God available through natural reason is qualified by sacred doctrine. While it is right to say human concepts can be "predicated substantially of God," therefore, we also must say that these concepts "fall short of representing Him."[45] A human employing only natural reason is able to say true things about God because the concepts she uses, derived from her reflection upon the created order, can and sometimes do rightly apply to God. Even so, the picture of God she obtains in this way is not adequate to lead her to her true end, because it is at best partial and may be incorrect. This shows again why sacred doctrine is necessary: the concepts derived from natural reason have a role to play in human speech about God, but they must be refined by the supernatural knowledge found in sacred doctrine. This knowledge unveils the more perfect meaning and content of our concepts about God because it works from a clearer picture of God "as He is in Himself," meaning it works from the basis of a fuller account of the meaning and content of the perfections that the created effects only imperfectly represent. In short, since the concepts humans apply to God were originally derived from reflection upon these created effects, they need to be refined and reinterpreted in the light of the truths provided by sacred doctrine. The true meaning of human language about God thus has to be unveiled to humans, and this unveiling happens by grace.[46]

This account of theological language completes Aquinas's argument and addresses the question of why and how it makes sense to say that, even though humans are rational beings made for God, they still need sacred doctrine in order to reach God as their true end. This establishes the claims made in q. 1 and provides the foundation for the rest of Aquinas's argument in the *ST*. More central to our purposes,

44. See *ST* I, q. 13, a. 1: God "can be named by us from creatures, yet not so that the name which signifies Him expresses the divine essence in itself."

45. *ST* I, q. 13, a. 2. He draws this conclusion more succinctly later on: "In this life, we cannot know the essence of God as it is in himself, but we know it according as it is represented in the perfections of creatures; and it is thus that the names imposed by us signify it." See *ST* I, q. 13, a. 2, ad 3.

46. On this basis, Aquinas argues that "a pagan can take this name 'God' in the same way when he says 'an idol is God' as the Catholic does in saying 'an idol is *not* God.'" See *ST* I, q. 13, a. 10, ad 5.

this argument also supplies a clear account of how Aquinas understands the relationship between natural revelation, human reason, and sacred doctrine. We turn now to Karl Barth's mature account of this same relationship in order to set up a comparison between them.

Karl Barth on Natural Revelation

Just as the opening questions of Aquinas's *ST* can be interpreted correctly only when they are read together as a unit, Barth's view of the relationship between natural revelation, human reason, and Christian theology can be interpreted correctly only when it is seen within the context of his entire theological development. The complicated reality is that some of Barth's early statements about this relationship are qualified in substantive ways by later developments and changes in his theology. A right assessment of Barth's views must account for these developments, and this means that some of his early claims must be reinterpreted in light of his later, more qualified, view.[47] This insight puts us in position to acquire a newfound clarity, because it will help us see that, while Barth and Aquinas share several key theological values and points of convergence in their approach to natural revelation and human reason, key differences remain, although the nature of these differences shifts between the early and later parts of Barth's career.

Developments in Barth's Thought

Like Aquinas, the early Barth holds that every creature is determined by its relationship with God, that God and God's relationship with creation must be described so that God's transcendence is maintained, and that accounts of human reason and language must be carefully formed so as to not constrain God within creaturely limits. Barth, however, adds an additional emphasis to these affirmations: not only is hu-

47. For a full account of these developments as they relate to Barth's dialogue with Roman Catholicism, see Keith L. Johnson, "A Reappraisal of Barth's Theological Development and His Dialogue with Catholicism," *International Journal for Systematic Theology* 14, no. 1 (January 2012): 3-25. The interpretation of Barth offered here presupposes the argument about Barth's development made in that essay.

man reason limited and confused with respect to its ability to know
God apart from grace, it has been so twisted by sin that the human inevitably attempts to transform the revelation she receives into an idol.[48]
Aquinas, of course, accounts for the consequences of sin upon human
reason as well, but he does not allow these consequences to become the
primary lens through which he views the relationship between reason,
faith, and theology. This is precisely what Barth does. He argues that
the person and work of Jesus Christ determine both the human relationship with God *and* all human knowledge of God. Humans cannot
come to accurate knowledge of God through other sources, such as
through reflection upon the created order, because sin has left them
unable to receive or interpret this revelation without distorting it.
While knowledge of God from God's revelation in creation may be "a
possibility in principle," therefore, it is never "a possibility to be realized" because "between what is possible in principle and what is possible in fact there inexorably lies the Fall."[49] Sin has so affected human
reason that insights derived from reasoned reflection upon creation
cannot be put to "positive use in theology either antecedently *or* subsequently ('in faith')."[50] The revelation of the Word of God in Jesus Christ
in Scripture is thus the *only* basis from which humans can know God
or speak accurately about God both before and after faith because this
Word is the only one that accounts for reality and the implications of
human sin.

Barth's construal of this approach, however, contains a fatal flaw:
it proceeds as if *no* intrinsic relationship between God and humans exists after the Fall.[51] Two problems follow from this idea. First, this view
closes the door to the possibility that words and concepts derived from
reflection upon the created order can be rightly applied to God as well,
because if there is no intrinsic connection between their normal use

48. John Calvin's remark that the human heart is a "factory for idols" was forma-
tive for Barth on this point. See Calvin, *Institutes of the Christian Religion* I.11, as well as
Barth's interpretation of Calvin's argument in "No! Answer to Emil Brunner," in *Natural
Theology*, ed. John Baillie (London: The Centenary Press, 1946), pp. 94-109.

49. Barth, "No! Answer to Emil Brunner," p. 106.

50. Barth, "No! Answer to Emil Brunner," p. 108.

51. David Bentley Hart raises this point in his critique of Barth's doctrine of analogy. Although this critique may apply to the early Barth in some form, it most definitely
does not apply to the mature Barth, as will be shown below. See Hart, *The Beauty of the Infinite: The Aesthetics of Christian Truth* (Grand Rapids: Eerdmans, 2003), pp. 241-42.

and their use with respect to God, then there is no way to know what creaturely words and concepts actually *mean* when they are applied to God. In other words, by failing to establish some kind of intrinsic yet analogous connection between everyday human words and the words of divine revelation — as Aquinas does in his account — Barth makes human talk about God functionally equivocal.[52] Barth himself eventually recognized this problem because later he argues that, when humans speak about God, their words cannot "be alienated from their proper and original sense usage" since this would "attribute to our views, concepts, and words a purely fictional capacity, so that the use we make of them is always hedged in by the reservation of an 'as if.'" He thus concludes that "a relationship of analogy, of similarity, of partial correspondence and agreement" must exist between human words and their use with respect to God, but he insists that, due to the reality of sin, this analogy only occurs *in faith*.[53] This leads to the second problem: Barth's claims about the role of faith in divine revelation, salvation, and theology actually *assume* the existence of precisely the kind of intrinsic relationship between God and creation he believes sin has ruled out. For example, in *Church Dogmatics* I/1, Barth concedes that there must be "something common to the speaking God and the hearing person" in order for God's revelation to the human to take place.[54] He insists, however, that this common feature is "real only in faith," because "that which by creation was possible for [the human] in relation to God has been lost by the Fall."[55] This "analogy of faith" thus exists only as an extrinsic capacity made available to humans in and through their participation in Christ by grace.[56] Barth's critics, however, pointed out that this approach assumes that faith and being can be op-

---

52. For a critique of Barth on this point, see Jay Wesley Richard, "Barth on the Divine 'Conscription' of Language," *Heythrop Journal* 38, no. 3 (1997): 247-66.

53. *CD* II/1, pp. 227-28. Throughout, all citations of the *CD* are to Karl Barth, *Church Dogmatics*, 4 vols. in 13 parts, ed. G. W. Bromiley and T. F. Torrance (Edinburgh: T. & T. Clark, 1936-75).

54. Karl Barth, *Kirchliche Dogmatik* I/1 (Zürich: Evangelischer Verlag, 1932), p. 251, translation mine. Cf. *CD* I/1, rev. ed. (Edinburgh: T. & T. Clark, 1975), p. 236.

55. Barth, *CD* I/1, p. 239.

56. Barth's argument here is essentially the epistemological application of the Protestant doctrines of *sola gratia, sola fide, participatio Christi,* and *simul iustus et peccator.* He labels the common feature shared between God and humanity the "capacity of the incapable," a "miracle that cannot be interpreted anthropologically" but one that nevertheless is a "real capacity which is already actualized in faith" (*CD* I/1, p. 241).

posed to one another.[57] Such opposition is false because it contradicts Barth's claims about salvation, given the fact that a participation "in Christ" is a participation in *being* — namely, *God's* being in and through Christ.[58] Barth's claims about revelation and faith are possible, therefore, only because they *presuppose* the existence of an intrinsic and analogous relationship of being between God and humans. Barth later concedes this point by admitting that he "can only observe that there is every justification for the warning that participation in being is grounded in the grace of God and therefore in faith," and he must "take heed to this warning and comply with it."[59] This admission, however, when combined with the first one, fatally undermines his insistence that insights obtained through human reflection upon created realities cannot be used in theology.

The problem is that, by conceding that any account of divine revelation has to explain how the meaning of the words and concepts originally derived from human reflection upon creation relate to the meaning of these same words and concepts as they are applied to God — and by conceding that this relationship, even though it is finally determined by faith and grace, actually presupposes an already-existing, intrinsic relationship of being between God and the human — Barth effectively concedes that his earlier claims that natural revelation can have no positive role in theology are void. After all, if an account of human speech about God *requires* an intrinsic relationship between created human language and divine revelation, and if such an account necessarily presupposes an ongoing relationship of being between God and humans, then one cannot also say that sin fundamentally disrupts this relationship and thus the human ability to think and speak correctly about God on the basis of their created nature, because this would be to deny the very presupposition that makes human speech about God possible. Such speech may be confused or limited in scope because of sin, of course, but it cannot be made *impossible* by it. This means Barth's early claims rejecting any role for natural revelation in theology must be revised to ac-

---

57. On this point, see the critique by Gottlieb Söhngen in "Analogia Fidei. Gottähnlichkeit allein aus Glauben?" *Catholica* 3, no. 3 (1934): 120. This critique was later picked up by Hans Urs von Balthasar in *The Theology of Karl Barth: Exposition and Interpretation,* trans. Edward T. Oakes, S.J. (San Francisco: Ignatius Press, 1992).

58. See Söhngen, "Analogia Fidei," pp. 131-33.

59. Barth, *CD* II/1, p. 82. He thus concludes that "substance and actuality must be brought into this right relationship."

count for this possibility. As Barth considered this fact, he faced a quandary. He could not retreat from his most basic convictions because he still affirmed the depth and reality of human sin and still believed that Jesus Christ is determinative not only for human salvation but for all correct knowledge of God. At the same time, he now recognized that he could not establish these claims on the basis of the idea that sin has fundamentally ruptured the relationship between God and humans; rather, he must establish these claims while *also* affirming that humans stand in an intrinsic relationship with God by virtue of their creation by God, a relationship that is *not* fundamentally disrupted by sin. The problem was how to formulate such an account.

Barth's solution is striking in its simplicity: he says that the created order itself, and thus created human being as such, is a function of God's decision to reconcile sinful humans in and through Jesus Christ. This answer arrives in full form with Barth's doctrine of election in *Church Dogmatics* II/2, where he claims that Jesus Christ is both the subject and object of election and thus the beginning and end of creation. On the ground of this claim, he argues that the entire created order is determined in its inner depths by God's decision to enter into covenant with sinful humans in and through the person and work of Christ. This covenant *is* God's grace, and thus "there is no such thing as a created nature which has its purpose, being or continuance apart from grace, or which may be known in this purpose, being or continuance except through grace."[60] In other words, the created order is intrinsically defined by the covenant, because it exists precisely in order to be the space where the covenant is executed.[61] The same holds true for human being. Every human is intrinsically defined by the covenant because Jesus Christ himself is the ontological ground of human existence, and true human being is found only in him. "It is not that [God] first wills and works the being of the world and [the human], and then ordains [the human] for salvation," he says. "But God creates, preserves and over-rules [the human] for this *prior* end and with this *prior* purpose, that there may be a being distinct from himself ordained for salvation, for perfect being, for participation in his own being."[62] What

60. *CD* II/2, p. 92.

61. The covenant thus serves as creation's "material presupposition." See *CD* III/1, p. 232. For Barth's discussion of the relationship between creation and covenant, see *CD* III/1, pp. 42-329.

62. *CD* IV/1, p. 9.

humans are *intrinsically* is determined at every moment by their relationship to Christ, who as the fully human and fully divine mediator, also remains utterly *distinct* from them in his unique relation to the Father. This means that, while Barth can say that humans have an intrinsic capacity for God, he also can hold that this capacity is established outside of their own being *(extra nos)* because it resides in Jesus Christ himself. A relationship of ongoing continuity between God and humanity exists, therefore, but only because both the created order and human being itself presuppose the *prior* existence of God's covenant of grace. Human sin does not fundamentally alter this covenant because the reconciliation of sin is included within God's eternal covenantal decision, the very divine decision that defines both the being of creation and humanity as such. Sin can thus be acknowledged in its full depth and reality without also making it determinative for the human relationship with or knowledge of God.[63]

This account solves the problem Barth faced in light of his earlier claims, but more significantly for our purposes, it also opens the door for a qualified embrace of natural revelation. Specifically, Barth now can explain how words and concepts originally derived from human reflection upon the created order relate to words and concepts used in God's special revelation: they stand in an analogous relationship to one another because both the created order and human being itself are intrinsically determined by God's covenantal relationship to them. As humans derive words and concepts from their reflection upon created realities, these words and concepts reflect the fact that creation itself is ontologically determined by God's covenant with humanity in Jesus Christ and thus always stands in relationship with God through Christ. Of course, humans cannot understand the nature of their relationship or *how* their words relate to God apart from the specific revelation of the covenant found in Scripture. They are intrinsically capable of receiving this revelation, however, because "something common" exists between God and humanity: Jesus Christ, the fully divine and fully human mediator. This "point of contact" in Christ means that an intrinsic analogy of being exists between God and humans, but this analogy is grounded in God's

---

63. For a fuller discussion of these ideas and their implications in light of Barth's mature theology, see John Webster, *Barth's Ethics of Reconciliation* (Cambridge: Cambridge University Press, 1995), pp. 59-98. Also see Keith L. Johnson, *Karl Barth and the Analogia Entis* (London: T. & T. Clark, 2010), pp. 191-230.

eternal electing decision rather than his act of creation, and ultimately, it is grounded in Christ himself.[64] This allows Barth to say that God's self-revelation in Christ is absolutely determinative for human knowledge of God while *also* affirming that everyday human language can be rightly applied to God. He thus can affirm a role for natural revelation and human reason within the church's theology even though this role always remains qualified by the fact that humans only know the true meaning and purpose of creation or their own being when it is unveiled to them by grace through their reception of the Word of God in Jesus Christ.

Natural Revelation in Covenant

Barth displays his embrace of this qualified role for natural revelation most closely in the opening section of *Church Dogmatics* IV/3.1.[65] There he argues that, since both creation in general and human being in particular are defined by the covenant that takes place in and through Jesus Christ, any account of God's revelation to humans through the created order must begin from a Christological basis and take a Christological form.[66] This basis is the Bible's account of Christ's life, death, and resurrection, and the form corresponds to Christ's prophetic office, which describes the risen Christ's work to make the reconciliation accomplished in him "concretely active and perceptible" within human history through the power of his Holy Spirit.[67] Barth explains that to deal with

64. For more on this claim, see Keith L. Johnson, "Reconsidering Barth's Rejection of Przywara's *analogia entis*," *Modern Theology* 26, no. 4 (October 2010): 642-46.

65. See *CD* IV/3.1, pp. 3-165. Since this volume represents Barth's mature thought on these matters, all of his prior statements about these matters are qualified by what he also says here.

66. See *CD* IV/3.1, p. 38: "As the reconciliation is his work, so is its revelation, in its past and present and future occurrence. As the reconciliation takes place in him, its revelation takes place through him. It does not take place, therefore cannot be understood, apart from him or in any way in itself. For this reason, we have to begin with him." Barth's logic here is straightforward: since the one order of God is the order of reconciliation, everything that occurs within the created order must be understood in the light of this work, meaning that it must be interpreted in light of Jesus Christ. Or, as he puts it later: "As Jesus Christ lives, God and man live in this conjunction. We do not have God here and man there; God is the God of man and man the man of God. This is the epitome of the whole order of creation" (p. 43).

67. *CD* IV/3.1, p. 10.

Jesus Christ is to deal "with the presence and action of God." Wherever God is present and active, there is "not just possibly or secondarily, but definitely and primarily, *declaration,* and therefore light, truth, Word and glory."[68] Since Christ is present and active throughout the entire created order which is intrinsically defined by him, it must be the case that he can and does declare himself in and through this order. It is "perhaps incontestable," Barth says, "that there are real lights of life and words of God in this sphere too, that He alone is the Word of God even here, and that these lights shine only because of the shining of none other light than His [light]."[69] This order cannot directly be identified with Christ, but rather, it is simply the "theater and setting for His being, activity and speech."[70] This adds an important qualification: not *everything* in creation reveals Christ. While Christ can and does take up created realities to declare himself through them, the created order has "its own light and truths and therefore its own speech and words" that are distinct from this revelation.[71] While natural revelation is both possible and actual, therefore, the church must carefully test the truths it receives from nature before it accepts them as truly revelatory of God. The criterion of this testing is "the whole context of the biblical message as centrally determined and characterized by Jesus Christ."[72]

For Barth, three implications immediately follow from this claim. First, since insights drawn from natural revelation can only be critically appropriated by the church, they "cannot be combined" with the revelation of Christ to form "a system superior to both Him and them."[73]

---

68. *CD* IV/3.1, p. 79. He says: "A mute and obscure God would be an idol. The true and living God is eloquent and radiant."

69. *CD* IV/3.1, p. 96.

70. *CD* IV/3.1, p. 137. Barth appeals here to Calvin's formula that the created order is the *theatrum gloriae Dei,* where creation is seen as being "specifically called into being in the beginning and as itself the beginning of all things, to be the theatre and setting, the location and background, of the ordinary and extraordinary mediation of [Christ's] life and work."

71. *CD* IV/3.1, p. 139. This means that creation "shines, speaks, and attests for itself," but this speaking is "its own revelation, i.e., those of the creation or created order itself" (p. 140).

72. *CD* IV/3.1, p. 126.

73. *CD* IV/3.1, p. 101. Here Barth reveals that his early concern about the human tendency toward idolatry lingers: "however illuminating, necessary or successful they may be . . . all these [systems] imply a control over Him to which none of us has any right."

In other words, since creation is intrinsically determined by the covenant, the content of natural revelation must be tested and interpreted by Scripture's account of the covenant rather than the other way around. This ordered relationship leads to the second implication: since any natural revelation is Christ's *own* revelation, it can be seen as a true revelation only when it corresponds to what *already* has been revealed about Christ in Scripture.[74] Any insights about God, humans, or their relationship derived from human reflection upon the created order must be measured by the Bible's account of Christ's life, death, and resurrection before they are deemed to be true.[75] This means that, just like in Barth's early account, God's revelation in Christ still determines the church's knowledge about who God is, what God is like, and the nature of God's relationship with humanity. The shift lies in Barth's new belief that this scriptural revelation may correspond to what humans can know of God through other means, such as through philosophical reflection upon created realities. He holds that such correspondence exists, however, only because Christ himself has "impelled, ordained and fashioned [these realities] for this function of bearing testimony" to himself.[76] Barth compares this action to Jesus' preaching of parables, where common and everyday realities were "likened unto" the kingdom of God for those who had "ears to hear" (Matt. 4:9). The resurrected Christ does the same thing *now* in the service of the same goal: through the power of his Spirit, he uses created realities to testify to the truth about God and God's relationship with humanity. Christ, however, is the one speaking here — not the created realities "likened

---

74. See *CD* IV/3.1, p. 98: "He is not the only word, not even the only good word. But he is the only word which, because it is spoken directly by God himself, is good as God is, has the authority and power of God and is to be heard as God himself. He is the only Word which all human words, even the best, can only directly or indirectly attest but not repeat, replace, or rival, so that their own goodness and authority are to be measured by whether or not, and with what fidelity, they are witnesses of this one Word."

75. See *CD* IV/3.1, p. 107: "Many words might speak of the majesty, goodness, severity and mystery of God. . . . They might say helpful things which in their own way many find illuminating and helpful. But none of them says what the life of Jesus Christ says. . . . What other word speaks of the covenant between God and man?"

76. *CD* IV/3.1, p. 112. On this point, see Webster, *Barth's Ethics of Reconciliation*, p. 92: "Barth is denying that there are two realities, the reality of Christ on the one hand and, on the other hand, the quasi-independent reality of human existence in terms of which Christ's reality has to be made meaningful."

unto" him.[77] This insight leads to the third implication: since Christ is the active agent of the revelation that occurs in and through the created order, the church must be willing to pay attention to this revelation and incorporate the insights it receives from it into the church's own faith and practice. In fact, Barth argues that the church would be "foolish and ungrateful if it closed its ears" to these external insights, since their great benefit is that they proclaim Christ "from a different source and in another tongue."[78] These insights may even serve to "illuminate, accentuate or explain the biblical witness" more clearly for the church within its own particular context, leading it "to preach the one Word of God in its own tongue and manner" better than it could otherwise. A refusal to accept such a gift would be an embrace of the "ossification" of the church, and it would be an effective denial of the reality that the risen Christ works as a living and active agent within the very order that was created *for* him.[79]

In this sense, Barth's acceptance of natural revelation pushes beyond what even Aquinas would endorse: while Aquinas did not believe insights derived from natural reason can or should lead the church to alter its own dogmas, Barth does. He argues that while the insights of natural revelation cannot contradict or supplement Scripture, they may cause the church to rethink its tradition, because the church can "learn something which goes beyond its dogmas and confessions, which is not to be learned directly from them or from its own inner movements, but which it is given by its Lord to learn afresh from without." The church's engagement with the externally derived insights of natural reason may become a powerful force for reform *within* the church, therefore, because they can lead the church, "not to break continuity with the insights of preceding fathers and brethren, but in living obedience to the one Lord of the Church and in the discipleship of the prophets and apostles to take it up and continue it with new responsibility on the basis of better instruction."[80] Barth's rejection of the presuppositions of Aristotelian categories to describe God, as well as his critical embrace of modern philosophical forms within his own

---

77. *CD* IV/3.1, pp. 112-13. Barth puts it succinctly later in his argument: "They are true words only as they refer back to their origin in the one Word, i.e., as the one true Word, Jesus Christ Himself, declares himself in them" (p. 123).

78. *CD* IV/3.1, pp. 115-16.

79. *CD* IV/3.1, p. 115.

80. *CD* IV/3.1, p. 127.

dogmatic theology, find justification here. As he sees it, his account enables him to promote a radical embrace of external insights within the church while simultaneously increasing the church's dependence on Christ, because his description of this embrace takes the form of the church's turning away from itself and turning toward the criterion of its message, Scripture's testimony about Jesus Christ. That is, since the external insights derived from creation are never self-evident but always are revealed by Christ himself, their existence means that the church always has to delve "more deeply into the given word of the Bible as the authentic attestation of the Word of Jesus Christ Himself" in order to locate and test these insights. This leads to the "strengthening, extending and defining of the Christian knowledge which draws from this source and is measured by this norm, to the lending of new seriousness and cheerfulness to the Christian life and new freedom and concentration to the delivery of the Christian message."[81] The church's engagement with the insights of natural revelation and reason, therefore, becomes a life-giving enterprise for the church, one that takes the form of a "history of [the church's] overruling, preservation and continual reformation by the One to whom it belongs."[82] In this way, as Barth sees it, God constantly uses nature to help the church adhere more closely to grace.

This account shows just how much Barth's mature approach to natural revelation has shifted from his early position: he has moved from a posture of hostility to one of "thoughtful inclusion," with his vision for a church that "challenges and relativises" the truths of natural reason as well as "institutes and integrates" them into its faith and practice.[83] The integrity of the created order is maintained because it is viewed as a distinct reality with its own truths. At the same time, since the created order exists "to be the fitting sphere and setting for

81. *CD* IV/3.1, p. 134.

82. *CD* IV/3.1, p. 130. Such a path could be followed on Aquinas's terms, although he himself did not travel it. One would need to begin with Aquinas's argument about human claims about God with respect to the incarnate Christ in *ST* III, q. 16, and then follow out the implications of this argument with respect to Aquinas's doctrine of God. For a discussion of Aquinas's Christological argument in light of his earlier doctrine of analogy, see Bruce D. Marshall, "Christ the End of Analogy," in *The Analogy of Being: Invention of the Antichrist or the Wisdom of God?* ed. Thomas Joseph White, O.P. (Grand Rapids: Eerdmans, 2011), pp. 280-313.

83. *CD* IV/3.1, pp. 152-53.

the great acts in which God expresses and declares himself," it always is seen in the light of God's covenant of grace in the person and work of Christ.[84] This critical posture does not diminish but *elevates* creation, because it allows creation's true status within God's eternal plan to be recognized. This means "the being and existence of creation itself is glorified rather than destroyed by the events of which it is ordained to be the theater, so its words and truths, far from being contradicted or given the lie, acquire in this context and in harmony with God's definitive Word, a similar final force and value and significance."[85] In other words, Barth also holds that grace does not destroy but perfects and fulfills nature, but he understands this idea differently than Aquinas would, because for Barth, nature is "taken, lifted, assumed and integrated into the action of God's self-giving and self-declaring to [humanity] and therefore to the world made by Him."[86] It is in this precise sense that creation can be said to "declare the glory of God" and "proclaim the work of his hands" (Ps. 19:1). It does so as it participates in the ministry of the Word, the proclamation of the gospel of Jesus Christ.

Aquinas and Barth in Dialogue

With the above account in hand, we now are in position to examine points of convergence and divergence between Aquinas and Barth on the issues of natural revelation, human reason, and Christian theology. Both Aquinas and Barth believe that God reveals himself in the created order and that this revelation is a function of God's relationship with creatures in the sense that this natural revelation is not random but ordered to its fulfillment in grace through Christ. They disagree, however, about the nature of this fulfillment and Christ's role within it. Aquinas views God's relationship with creation through the lens of his *exitus* and *reditus* paradigm, where creatures come forth from God and return to him by means of union with God available through Christ. Thus, he understands the saving work of Christ as an element *within* a more basic order of creation and return. In distinction from this view,

84. *CD* IV/3.1, p. 153.
85. *CD* IV/3.1, p. 164.
86. *CD* IV/3.1, p. 164.

Barth sees God's relationship with humanity as the outworking of God's eternal decision to enter into covenant with humans in Christ, and creation is an element within *this* more basic divine order. Aquinas and Barth both affirm the possibility of natural revelation on the basis of an ordered account of creation's relationship with God, therefore, but their accounts work in reverse from one another. For Aquinas, this ordered relationship exists because God's grace in Christ presupposes the order of nature; for Barth, it exists because the order of nature presupposes God's grace in Christ.

This difference plays itself out in the way each theologian describes the content of natural revelation. For Aquinas, the content of natural revelation is God "as He is in Himself," which is something that can be known in a partial way from the created order just as a cause can be known in a partial way from its effects. In other words, as we have seen, since creation testifies to God as its cause, a human can come to limited and qualified knowledge of God's being and perfections by reasonably reflecting upon the created order itself. For Barth, in contrast, the proper content of natural revelation is God's covenant of grace in Jesus Christ, since the created order finds its being and purpose in God's eternal plan to reconcile humanity in the person and work of Christ. Creation as such cannot reveal this plan, since the created order is simply the "theater" in which the plan is executed.[87] Nor can creation reveal God as its Maker, since this could only lead to "abstract impartations concerning God's existence as the Supreme Being and Ruler of all things" rather than the particular revelation of God in God's covenantal relationship with humanity that is the true referent of theology.[88] Instead, the created order simply testifies to itself, revealing "its *own* lights, words and truths."[89] Creation reveals God *only* when it is taken up in Jesus Christ's own self-revelation, and thus the content of this natural revelation is nothing other than Christ's fulfillment of the covenant. This difference regarding content relates to a difference in how Aquinas and Barth conceive its function and role within Christian theology. Aquinas believes that, since the created order always testifies to God as

87. See Barth, *CD* IV/3.1, p. 149: creation, Barth says, can declare "its mystery in its silence at this point."

88. *CD* IV/3.1, p. 117.

89. *CD* IV/3.1, pp. 140-41: "As the words of terrestrial being [creation's] words are only terrestrial words, and as the truths of terrestrial being they are only terrestrial truths. They are not, then, divine disclosures nor eternal truths."

its cause, natural revelation exists as a basic feature of created existence. This means that humans are always capable of discerning at least some truth about God — such as, for example, the fact that God exists — by the use of their natural reason alone. Barth sees things differently, because for him, the created order reveals God *only* as Christ takes it up in a specific act of self-declaration that occurs through the power of his Holy Spirit. Natural revelation occurs as a unique divine act that *is given* to humans but is not "a given" of human existence.

This distinction leads to interesting points of convergence and divergence between the two thinkers. For example, Aquinas and Barth both agree that Christians and non-Christians can say true things about God. For his part, Aquinas believes that a non-Christian can know *that* things about God are true (as Aristotle did when he knew that God existed, for example) without knowing precisely *how* these things are true (Aristotle did not know that God existed *as triune*). This more perfect knowledge must be unveiled to the human knower, and this occurs when the insights of natural reason are perfected by the insights of sacred doctrine. However, since these truths of natural reason converge with the truths of faith on the basis of an always-existing feature of human existence, they are not replaced or abandoned but simply perfected: faith does not destroy but supports and perfects reason. The payoff of this approach is that reasoned human reflection about God can be systematically coordinated with supernaturally given truths in such a way that these reasoned insights are perfected *without* being fundamentally revised with respect to their original referent. The most obvious example of this approach is Aquinas's own joining of the insights of Aristotelian metaphysics with the Catholic faith: the revelation of the triune God does not overturn Aristotle's picture of the "one God" but *perfects* it because Aristotle actually had the one true God in view all along, even if he only had a limited and partial grasp of God's true being and nature.

Barth's approach is quite different. While he agrees that non-Christians can say true things about God, he also holds that they cannot know either *that* or *how* these things are true apart from knowledge of the covenant. In other words, both the fact *that* their reasoned reflection upon natural revelation is true and *how* it is true can only be known retrospectively from the perspective of faith, since a human can know the truth of the created order or her own human being *only* when she knows that both creation and her own being are determined by the life, death, and resurrection of Jesus Christ. This makes it impossible to coordinate the truths of natural reason with the truths of the Christian faith without transforming these natural truths so that they function in a different register than they once did. To illustrate: Barth thinks it is quite possible for a philosopher to say something true about God, and it also is possible for the church to incorporate these insights into its theology. In fact, the church would be foolish to ignore such insights, since they might help it better fulfill its mission in its own time and place. The only way that the philosopher or the church can know *that* this philosophical insight is true or *how* it is true, however, is to turn to Scripture and see if it corresponds to the biblical story that finds its center in Jesus Christ. But once this happens, the primary referent of the philosopher's insight has changed because its truth is determined solely by the covenant to which it corresponds rather than the created order from which it was originally derived. This means that, while both Aquinas and Barth believe that fuller and more perfect knowledge of God is unveiled to humans by grace, Barth thinks this unveiling is a much broader enterprise than Aquinas does because he holds that *everything* true that is said about God finally must be measured by what has been revealed in the person and work of Jesus Christ as attested in Scripture. Indeed, *any* truth about God, even those found in philosophy, finally comes from *Christ himself.*

This distinction carries an important implication. If one holds with Aquinas that reasoned reflection upon natural revelation can be systematically coordinated with the revealed truths of the faith as long as its natural insights are on the same trajectory as the insights of faith and thus have the same referent, then it becomes possible to reify certain philosophical approaches, such as the Platonism of the church fathers or Aquinas's own Aristotelianism, as internal to the faith itself. However, if you hold with Barth that the content, nature, and function of reasoned reflection upon God's natural revelation must be measured by the biblical revelation of Christ and can be coordinated with Christ only because Christ himself takes it up in his own self-declaration, then it becomes impossible to permanently link the insights of the faith to any one philosophical system because no philosophical system derived from natural revelation can ever have the biblical story that finds its center in the life, death, and resurrection of Jesus Christ as its primary referent. Catholic and Protestant distinctions on the relationship between Scripture and tradition, as represented by Aquinas and Barth, have their basis precisely here. Church dogmas and confessions always are spoken within the idiom of the time and place in which they were composed. If a particular idiom can be made internal to the church's faith, then it becomes possible to make the precise formulations of specific dogmas and confessions infallible and nonrevisable. However, if one always and repeatedly measures the church's dogmas and confessions in the light of that to which they ultimately refer — God in God's relationship with humanity as revealed in Scripture — then it becomes possible to revise these dogmas and confessions, not in order to break continuity with previous formulations, but to adhere better to the same referent within a different time and place. This insight concerning Catholic and Protestant approaches in general also applies to Aquinas and Barth in particular since the same logic applies: the possibility of an ongoing tradition of *Thomism* is included in and with Aquinas's approach, while the possibility of a tradition of *Barthianism* is de facto ruled out by Barth's approach.

All of this shows that the key difference between Aquinas and Barth is not whether natural revelation exists, for on this point, they agree. The question is about the proper content of natural revelation, and by extension, the nature of its role within the church's theology. How one answers this question is determined by how one understands the nature of God's relationship with humanity. Are humans defined primarily by the fact that they were created by God and are destined to return to him through Christ, as Aquinas holds? Or are they defined primarily by God's eternal plan for their reconciliation in the person and work of Jesus Christ, as Barth holds? The stories of creation and salvation are always integrally related, of course, but the story one presupposes as basic to the other determines whether one thinks Aquinas or Barth provides a better option for the integration of nature and grace as well as faith and reason. The key factor in this decision is how one understands the saving work of Jesus Christ in its relationship to creation. Are Christ's life, death, and resurrection an integral part of the more basic story of God's creation of humans and their ordering to him? Or are Christ's life, death, and resurrection the presupposition of creation itself, so that the created order exists precisely to be the place where these things are to take place? Future dialogue between the followers of Aquinas and Barth should begin at precisely these questions because Aquinas's and Barth's divergent answers to them determine their respective accounts of the content of the natural revelation they both embrace, as well as their accounts of God, creation, human being, and salvation.

The Crucified Lord: Thomistic Reflections on the Communication of Idioms and the Theology of the Cross

Thomas Joseph White, O.P.

I

"The princes of this world did not know him; for if they had, they would not have crucified the Lord of glory" (1 Cor. 2:8). Christians assuredly worship and announce the truth of a crucified God, or rather a now-risen Lord who was crucified. The implications of this statement of course affect our understanding of the mystery of God himself. As the Second Council of Constantinople in 553 stated succinctly: "If anyone does not confess that Our Lord Jesus Christ who was crucified in the flesh is true God and the Lord of Glory and one of the Holy Trinity: let him be anathema." Reformulated positively, this means that it constitutes a truth about the very Person of the Son of God, and therefore God himself, that he took flesh and suffered for us. Likewise in a more modern idiom, the Second Vatican Council (*Gaudium et Spes* 22) states that the Lord "thought with a human mind . . . and loved with a human heart." He did so, however, while being one in substance with the Father, God from God, light from light, true God from true God.

Based upon this biblical and ecclesiastical confession of the divinity and humanity of the Lord Jesus Christ, classical Christology seeks to offer a plausible understanding of the subject of the communication of idioms: How are we rightly to attribute to Jesus Christ both human and divine properties? If such an ascription implies that the divine and human natures of Christ are united in his Person, how do the deity of God incarnate and his humanity relate to one another? What ontological truths about God and man do such attributions presuppose or make manifest? Not least importantly, what significance do these truths have for our understanding of the character of the crucifixion and the very nature of our redemption?

In what follows I would like to compare the thinking of the later Christology of Karl Barth on this subject with the Christology of Thomas Aquinas. After introducing Barth more succinctly, I will treat Aquinas at greater length, considering each with respect to three interrelated themes: the ontology implied by the communication of idioms, the instrumentality of Christ's human operations, and the nature of the atonement. What emerges from an overview of these two theologies on this key junction of theological reflection is an interesting observation. Barth's theology of the cross event clearly influences a great deal of modern Christological speculation, across a confessionally diverse spectrum of thinkers who have developed his ideas in various ways. Yet simultaneously this innovative theology bears striking points of both comparison and contrast with Aquinas's more classical understanding of the nature of the Incarnation and redemption. A comparison of the two thinkers suggests diverse possible orientations for the future of Catholic-Protestant ecumenism.

II

Karl Barth makes three very original claims about the nature of the redemption of Christ that are interrelated and have widely influenced modern theology across confessional lines. The first relates to his quite innovative interpretation of the communication of idioms, particularly as regards to the so-called *genus tapeinoticum,* by which he attributes properties of the human essence of God the Son to the divine essence, something, as he himself notes, no one before him has ever done.[1] The second has to do with Barth's treatment of the election and reprobation of Christ on behalf of humanity, wherein he reinterprets Calvin's theology so as to understand Christ as the uniquely reprobated subject in substitution for the universal election of creaturely, fallen humanity. The third has to do with the cry of dereliction on the cross as the nadir

---

1. *CD* IV/2, pp. 84-85, 108-15. Throughout, all citations of the *CD* are from Karl Barth, *Church Dogmatics,* 4 vols. in 13 parts, ed. G. W. Bromiley and T. F. Torrance (Edinburgh: T. & T. Clark, 1936-75).

of the Son's "journey into the far country" in obedience to the Father, a point that recapitulates and combines the two previous ones. Allow me briefly to summarize these three ideas.

The notion of a *genus tapeinoticum* was formulated by sixteenth-century Lutheran theologians, most notably Martin Chemnitz, in contradistinction to the notion of a *genus majestaticum*. The two terms were employed by Chemnitz to ascertain how the two natures of Christ interpenetrate, or in what sense the properties of one of the natures of Christ might be attributed to the other. The former genus refers to an idea whereby the human properties of Christ would be attributed to his divine nature, by virtue of the hypostatic union. Chemnitz and the subsequent Lutheran tradition reject such a notion and contrast it with a form of predication whereby the properties of the divine nature are attributed to the human nature: Christ as man, by virtue of the Incarnation and the interpenetration of the natures, can be said to be omnipresent, eternal, omnipotent, etc.: this is the *genus majestaticum*. Such a viewpoint was advocated by a prominent strand of thinking within Lutheran scholasticism. But if the human nature by virtue of its union with the divinity is truly omnipresent, eternal, or omnipotent, then how are we to understand the earthly life of Jesus as a truly human life taking place in a given time and place, under finite creaturely conditions and so on? Two Lutheran schools divided over this question in the seventeenth century, that of Giessen and Tübingen, with one side holding that the Son of God made man simply concealed his divine prerogatives while the other side held that he in some sense suspended their use by way of a kenotic self-abandonment of divine properties.

Meanwhile, the Reformed tradition classically would have none of this, but instead placed the center of gravity of the communication of idioms uniquely in the attribution of both human and divine characteristics to the unique Person of the Son. All that can be said of Jesus as God or as man is only attributable to him in virtue of the hypostatic union and the unity of Person that results therefrom.[2] It is the Lord Jesus Christ who is crucified as man and the Lord Jesus who is the author of creation as God. The distinction and transcendence of the deity

---

2. See, for example, the definition of Amandus Polanus (1561-1610), cited by Barth in *CD* IV/2, pp. 75-76, from *Syntagma theologiae christianae* (1609) VI, 16, col. 2440f.: "Proprietates utriusque naturae Christi personae ipsi communicantur. Quae enim naturis singulis sunt propria, ea personae Christi sunt communia."

of Christ with respect to his humanity is upheld even within the mystery of the Incarnation.

What neither of these traditions considered seriously, and what Barth himself in his early period did not embrace either, is the idea that the Incarnation entails that the human, historical characteristics of Christ should be participated in or assimilated to in some sense the very divine being and life of God.[3] This is, however, precisely the idea that Barth lays out in *Church Dogmatics* IV/1 and IV/2, with his insistence on a unique importance of the *genus tapeinoticum* for understanding not only the mystery of the Son incarnate, but also the very deity of God himself. In essence Barth in this latter period begins from the classical Reformed standpoint that he embraced in his earlier career. The hypostatic union is the ground of attributions of the divine and human properties of Christ to the one subject of the Son.[4] Second, then, Barth rejects two diverse Lutheran considerations. One is the classical notion of the *genus majestaticum:* the idea that the divine characteristics of God are now attributed to the human nature of Christ by virtue of the Incarnation. This viewpoint fails to uphold sufficiently a sense of the distinction of the natures. Furthermore, however, Barth is also critical of the kenotic Lutheran theology of the nineteenth century, particularly as represented by Gottlieb Thomasius and as expressive in some sense of Hegelian ideas of divine alteration. On this model, the Incarnation would require that the divine nature be in some real sense abandoned, at least in some of its distinct prerogatives, as a condition for the Incarnation. Or rather, the free alteration of God as God in becoming man would be expressive of a freedom that is indicative of what God is "prior" to the classical attributes of eternity, immutability, and so forth. Against such ideas, Barth insists that God remains God, in and through the Incarnation, in a certain kind of immutability and constancy representative of his eternal triune identity.[5]

3. See Karl Barth, *Unterricht in der christlichen Religion,* vol. 3: *Die Lehre von der Versöhnung/Die Lehre von der Erlösung, 1925/1926,* ed. Hinrich Stoevesandt (Zürich: Theologischer Verlag Zürich, 2003), p. 41. Here, in this early work, Barth simply follows the Reformed tradition. I am grateful to Bruce L. McCormack for this reference.

4. *CD* IV/2, pp. 47-60.

5. See *CD* IV/1, pp. 180-84, where Barth criticizes this view in some detail, and again, implicitly in *CD* IV/2, p. 86. On this vision of Barth's, see the helpful essay by Bruce L. McCormack, "Karl Barth's Christology as a Resource for a Reformed Version of Kenoticism," *International Journal of Systematic Theology* 8, no. 3 (July 2006): 243-51.

By contrast with these views, however, Barth does argue, quite originally, that the Incarnation implies the decision of God to be God only with humanity and as himself human. This decision touches not only upon the unity of the humanity of Christ with the deity in the person of the Son. It also implies a free self-determination on God's part to be God with humanity *in his very deity*.[6] Consequently, the Incarnation of the Son implies that the nature of God as such is now only intelligible in its very being with reference to the human history of Jesus Christ.[7]

Is this idea consistent with Barth's anti-Hegelian point mentioned above, that God in becoming man does not cease to be what he is eternally as God and that he becomes incarnate only by an entirely free act of God prior to any creaturely need or prerogative? If it is consistent, this can only be for one reason: because there is something that exists "from all eternity" in the life of God himself that is the transcendent condition of possibility for what happens in time. In other words, there is a transcendent analogue to the mystery of the Incarnation and the humanity of Christ in the eternal life of God itself.

This brings us to our second point, one that is well known: Barth reinterprets the significance of Calvin's doctrine of election in ways that are completely innovative with regard to the election and reprobation of Jesus Christ.[8] Here I will be brief: Calvin is understood by Barth to have made a crucial contribution to theology by his decision to place the theology of election and covenant at the heart of Christian doctrine, as its determining thread, so to speak. Election is the fore-determining ground or the structural backbone of the creation. At the same time, influenced by Pierre Maury, Barth reformulated the content of the doctrine: it is Jesus Christ alone who is the eternal object of election, and this in view of all those elected or predestined in

---

6. *CD* IV/2, p. 84: "We must begin with the fact that what takes place in this address is also and primarily a determination of divine essence: not an alteration, but a determination. God does not first elect and determine man but Himself. In His eternal counsel, and then in its execution in time He determines to address Himself to man, and to do so in such a way that He Himself becomes man. God elects and determines Himself to be the God of man. And this undoubtedly means . . . that He elects and determines Himself for humiliation."

7. See, for instance, *CD* IV/2, p. 86.

8. "Innovation" is the word Barth himself employs, with some ambivalence, in *CD* II/2, p. 156.

him.[9] The latter however are not a minority of the human race, as Calvin speculated, but rather in Christ God predetermines to elect all human beings: thus Barth's famous turn away from Calvin in the direction of universalism. Simultaneously, it is Jesus Christ alone who is reprobated for us in the cross event, such that he alone suffers the abandonment by God that is hell, so that the human race is collectively spared this fate by the grace of Christ.[10] This is a form of penal substitutionary atonement doctrine with roots in the Protestant Reformation, but clearly reformulated in a distinctive and novel form.

Lastly, then, Barth sees the nadir of the event of the Son's redemptive mission in the event of the crucifixion, in which he takes upon himself the night of separation from God in the loveless hell of divine abandonment. Following Calvin's powerful but also original formulations (of the *Institutes* II.16), Barth sees the descent into hell of the Apostles' Creed occurring not on Holy Saturday, but on the cross, on Good Friday.[11] Note however, that the uniqueness of Barth's vision, in distinction from that of Calvin, has to be understood in successive measures against the backdrop of our two previous points. First, for Barth, the dereliction of Christ is indicative of his unique reprobation. In other words: he descends into hell alone, so as to be the sole human being that travels into the far country of separation from the Father, in exclusion of and substitution for sinful humanity. He alone is the true prodigal son so that we can be reconciled with the Father.[12] Second, and here is the more radical and most ultimate point, in light of the *ge-*

9. See the treatment of election particularly in *CD* II/2, §32 and §33, sections 1 and 2. In §33.2, on pp. 154-55, Barth mentions the influence of Pierre Maury's essay, "Election et Foi," at the *Congrès international de théologie calviniste* in Geneva in 1936.

10. On universal election and singular reprobation, see, for example, *CD* II/2, pp. 317-18. This viewpoint is programmatic in *CD* IV/1, §59.

11. See *Institutes of the Christian Religion*, trans. F. Battles (Philadelphia: Westminster, 1960), II.16.10-12, with explicit reference to Mark 15:34. Calvin is entirely aware that his interpretation of the Apostles' Creed concerning the "descent into hell" on Good Friday is quite original. In *CD* II/2, p. 164, Barth follows Calvin in affirming that Christ experienced reprobation and hell on the cross.

12. *CD* IV/1, p. 772: "The publican in the temple in Lk. 18:9f. and the prodigal son of Lk. 15:11f. are a likeness of the One who as the Lamb of God took away the sin of the world: no more, but no less. And the man who believes in this One and knows himself in Him can and must and will unreservedly place himself at least alongside the publican and the prodigal — we have in them the minimum — and with them be the likeness, the *analogatum,* of what Jesus Christ has been and done, and is and does, for him."

nus tapeinoticum, the dereliction of the Son upon the cross is itself indicative of something pertaining to the very being and life of God itself. The cross truly reveals God with us, but by that same measure, it also reveals to us God's free self-determination to be with us as one who is obedient, humble, and lowly, even unto this event of personal self-emptying in the night of hell.[13] This requires, then, a transcendent corollary in the life of the triune God himself, and this corollary for Barth is divine obedience.[14] The Son is the eternally, divinely obedient subject in whom or as whom God is eternally subordinate to the Father.[15] The kenosis of Good Friday has its eternal precondition in this eternal kenosis of the Son which takes place in the very life of God. The divine

---

13. *CD* IV/1, p. 215: "We have already said that in this event God allows the world and humanity to take part in the history of the inner life of His Godhead, in the movement in which from and to all eternity He is Father, Son and Holy Spirit, and therefore the one true God. But this participation of the world in the being of God implies necessarily His participating in the being of the world, and therefore that His being, His history, is played out as world-history and therefore under the affliction and peril of all world-history. The self-humiliation of God in His Son would not really lead Him to us, the activity in which we see His true deity and the divine Sonship of Jesus Christ would not be genuine and actual, if there were any reservation in respect of His solidarity with us, of His entry into world-history. He did become . . . the brother of man . . . with him in the stream which hurries downwards to the abyss, . . . to the cessation of being and nothingness. With him He cries . . . 'My God. My God, why have you abandoned me?' (Mk. 15:34). *Deus pro nobis* means simply that God has not abandoned the world . . . that He took it upon Himself, and that He cries with man in this need." See also on Mark 15:34: p. 239 (judgment upon the Son in the cry), p. 264 (on the darkness of the cross expressed by the cry), p. 306 (considered by the Father as the greatest sinner in our stead), p. 308 (subject to divine wrath), p. 458 (helplessness the source of our justification), p. 566 (vindicated in his resurrection), p. 590 (type of Christian discipleship).

14. See Barth's treatment of this theme in *CD* IV/1, §59.2, p. 195: "In this happening we have to do with a divine commission and its divine execution, with a divine order and *divine obedience*. What takes place is the divine fulfillment of a divine decree. . . . But it is clear that once again, and this time in all seriousness, we are confronted with the mystery of *the deity of Christ*" (emphasis added). I have elsewhere offered reflections on this aspect of Barth's thought in "Intra-Trinitarian Obedience and Nicene-Chalcedonian Christology," *Nova et Vetera,* English Edition 6, no. 2 (2008): 377-402.

15. *CD* IV/1, pp. 200-201: "We have not only not to deny but actually to affirm and understand as essential to the being of God the offensive fact that there is in God Himself an above and a below, a *prius* and a *posterius,* a superiority and a subordination. And our present concern is with what is apparently the most offensive fact of all, that there is a below, a *posterius,* a subordination, that it belongs to the inner life of God that there should take place within it obedience."

dereliction of the Son on the cross, then, does not change who God is from all eternity, but it does manifest who the Son is or wills to be eternally, as God in his mode of being as lowliness, as the Son always sent from the Father or subject to the Father.[16] The distinction or "separation" of wills made manifest in the cross event and particularly in the obedience of the Son pertains to the ultimate revelation of who God is.

In stating things this way I am perhaps in part offering a kind of Balthasarian rendering of *CD* IV/1 and IV/2. It is however a defensible interpretation, and even if it is not necessarily textually compelling in all its elements, that is somewhat beside the point. For the main point is this: that whether we look ahead into subsequent Christological thought in Balthasar, Jüngel, Pannenberg, Moltmann, or Kasper, despite their various real differences with Barth and one another, we will find the undeniable legacy of Barth's threefold aforementioned views. Such views have been inscribed in or at least have deeply affected the heart of a great deal of subsequent theological reflection.

---

16. *CD* IV/1, p. 209: "The One who in this obedience is the perfect image of the ruling God is Himself — as distinct from every human and creaturely kind — God by nature, God in His relationship to Himself, that is, God in His mode of being as the Son in relation to God in His mode of being as the Father, One with the Father and of one essence. *In His mode of being as the Son He fulfils the divine subordination,* just as the Father in His mode of being as the Father fulfils the divine superiority. *In humility as the Son who complies, He is the same as is the Father in majesty as the Father who disposes. He is the same in consequence (and obedience) as the Son as is the Father in origin.* He is the same as the Son, that is, as the self-posited God . . . as is the Father as the self-positing God. . . . The Father as the origin is never apart from Him as the consequence, *the obedient One.* The self-positing of God is never apart from Him as the One who is posited as God by God. The One *who eternally begets is never apart from the One who is eternally begotten*" (emphasis added).

Barth connects this eternal self-positing of God as Son to the determination of the divine essence for the mission-unto-dereliction of the Son in *CD* IV/2, p. 86: "No diminution comes to [the divine essence] by the fact that it is wholly directed and addressed to human essence in Jesus Christ, sharing its limitation and weakness and even its lostness in the most radical and consistent way. But again, in this address, direction and participation, it does not acquire the increase of any alien capacity or even incapacity. No difference at all is made. What then is the divine essence? It is the free love, the omnipotent mercy, the holy patience of the Father, Son and Holy Spirit. And it is the God of *this* divine essence who has and maintains the initiative in this event. He is not, therefore, subject to any higher force when He gives Himself up to the lowliness of the human being of the Son of God. . . . The offering is, therefore, elected and determined by His own majesty — the majesty of the divine Subject."

III

In comparison with Barth, I would like to consider three complementary facets of Aquinas's Christology: his hypostatic interpretation of the communication of idioms, his understanding of the grace of Christ as it relates to the instrumentality of the Lord's human knowledge and obedience out of charity, and the way this knowledge and charity are operative in the crucifixion as the principle of human redemption. On all three points, we will find significant grounds upon which to contrast these two great theologians.

Aquinas offers an analysis of the communication of idioms in *Summa theologiae* III, q. 16, after he has treated of the hypostatic union (qq. 2-3), the union in distinction of the divine and human natures of Christ (qq. 4-6), the grace of Jesus (qq. 7-8) and its effects upon his intellect (qq. 9-12), and the finite power and defects of his human body and soul (qq. 13-15). Just after, in q. 17, he treats famously the question of the unitary *esse* of the Person of Christ. The theology of the hypostatic union and that of the existence of Christ form as it were ontological bookends around his treatment of the attribution of properties. The union of God and man occurs in Christ in the Person of the Son, who is both human and divine in such a way that the deity and humanity are united but not confused. Thus the eternal Person of the Son exists as man and subsists in a human nature. This human nature is, therefore, the concrete, existent human nature of God.[17]

Our central observation can be made in this light: for Aquinas all of the properties of deity and humanity that pertain to Christ as God and man, respectively, are properties attributed only and ever to his

---

17. *ST* III, q. 17, a. 2: "Now being pertains both to the nature and to the hypostasis; to the hypostasis as to that which has being — and to the nature as to that whereby it has being. For nature is taken after the manner of a form [a formal determination of the being of the person], which is said to be a being because something is by it; as by whiteness a thing is white and by manhood a thing is man. . . . And thus, since the human nature is united to the Son of God, hypostatically or personally as was said above (q. 2, aa. 5-6), and not accidentally, it follows that by the human nature there accrued to Him no new personal being, but only a new 'possession' [habitudo] of the pre-existing personal being to the human nature, in such a way that the Person is said to subsist not merely in the Divine but also in the human nature" (translation slightly altered). Aquinas posits in the Incarnation a nonreciprocal relativity (the doctrine of "mixed relations"): in the subsistence of the Word made flesh, the human nature is ontologically relative to the divine nature without the divine becoming ontologically relative to the human. See *ST* III, q. 2, a. 7.

Person as the Son. In one sense this can be seen negatively, for how could it be otherwise? If the human properties of the Son were attributed to the ineffable deity of the Godhead as such, then by virtue of the divine unity of God, they would need to be attributed to the Father and the Holy Spirit as well. For all that is proper to God as God (that is, by virtue of the divine essence) is said equally of the Father, Son, and Holy Spirit. Were this not the case, we would have to introduce a bipolar or tripolar distinction of qualities into God, such that the particular Persons would naturally as God possess qualities alien to the others, and this would inevitably obfuscate the revelation and mystery of the divine unity. But since God is ineffably one, there is an impossibility of attributing human characteristics to the deity that would pertain to the Son only, but not to the other Persons or personal modes of being, of the one God. This is something Gregory of Nazianzus and Gregory of Nyssa made clear against Eunomius in distinguishing orthodox Trinitarian theology as such from an Arian theology, in which the personal distinction of Father and Son is achieved at the cost of also proscribing a differentiation of qualities to the Persons.[18] Like them, Aquinas brings in a classical consideration: the distinction of Persons in the triune life of God occurs only by virtue of the relations of origins of the Persons. The Son proceeds from the Father and is therefore distinct from him, but all that is in the Father is in the Son.[19]

Positively restated, however, it is important to note that Aquinas posits a fundamental principle for the communication of idioms that has a broad theological appeal, touching in fact upon a concern of Barth as well. Natures, Aquinas says, never exist in the abstract, as mental objects or realities standing on their own. They only exist in concrete reality as the natural determinations of persons. Consequently, the qualities or properties of deity and humanity are only ever the properties of a singular concrete *person*, in fact, the Person of the Son made man. In *ST* III, q. 16, a. 1 Aquinas makes this clear when he writes:

> Supposing the truth of the Catholic belief, that the true divine nature is united with true human nature not only in person but also in *suppositum* or hypostasis; we say that this proposition is true and proper, "God is man" — not only by the truth of its terms, i.e., be-

18. Cf. Gregory of Nazianzus, *Oratio* 29, n. 2; 31, n. 9; Gregory of Nyssa, *Ad Ablabium quod non sint tres dei*.
19. *ST* I, q. 28, aa. 2-3; q. 29, a. 4.

cause Christ is true God and true man, but by the truth of the predication. For a word *signifying the common nature in the concrete may stand for all contained in the common nature,* as this word "man" may stand for any individual man. And thus this word "God," from its very mode of signification, may stand for the Person of the Son of God. . . . Now of every *suppositum* of any nature we may truly and properly predicate a word signifying that nature in the concrete, as "man" may properly and truly be predicated of Socrates and Plato. Hence, since the Person of the Son of God for whom this word "God" stands, is a *suppositum* of human nature, this word "man" may be truly and properly predicated of this word "God" as it stands for the Person of the Son of God. (Emphasis added)

What is going on here? Basically, Aquinas is saying two things. First, all attributions in the world of existent reality, as opposed to a purely conceptual world, are fundamentally made to hypostases: to concrete entities or subjects, in this case, persons. Second, however, one can attribute natures to a particular person to distinguish him from other persons or entities, so long as the name designating the nature is also used explicitly to indicate a singular hypostatic person. So for instance, "man" can be used in the vocative to indicate Socrates, or "behold the man" can be used to designate Jesus.

What this means for the communication of idioms is the following: when divine or human properties of the Son made man are attributed to him, or are seemingly attributed to one another, they are only ever attributed to the concrete Person of the Word made flesh. He is what Maximus the Confessor calls a composite hypostasis: a Person who is truly naturally God and naturally man; but for this very reason — because only this person is both God and man — therefore all the natural attributes are ascribed to him alone personally. So, for instance, we can say that the Son of God was born of a woman (Gal. 4:4) and suffered death (1 Cor. 2:8) or that the Word of God made man is he who created the world. "All things were made through him" (John 1:3). But simultaneously, we can also refer to the Son in the concrete under the titles of the divine and human natures considered only in reference to the unique Person. We can say, for instance, that the omnipotent One learned obedience (Heb. 5:8), the eternal One was born in time, or that the impassible God suffered, the child born in the cave created the world, or the One killed on the cross is the author of life (Acts 3:15), and so on.

Nevertheless, what such a way of thinking necessarily precludes is that the properties of one nature could ever be predicated directly of another, whether under a *genus majestaticum* or a *genus tapeinoticum*. One problem that exists with either way of thinking is that it confuses abstracted properties with the concrete subject of their inherence by reifying them artificially, thus stepping outside of the proscribed boundaries of biblical revelation into extrabiblical speculations. This of course seems like a Barthian turn of phrase because it is. Barth in his later Christology particularly was concerned with the danger of understanding the "essences" of Christ as "static natures," purposefully introducing instead a doctrine of dynamic, even in some sense historical categories of divine and human acts of self-determination, that participate in one another.[20]

Whatever we may make of this ontological preference for the historicization of ontology on Barth's part, classical Christology still rightly refuses the so-called *genus tapeinoticum* insofar as it risks inevitably undermining a realistic theological account of the personal union of the Word with human nature: that is to say, the hypostatic union as taught by Paul and John, as well as Cyril and the Council of Ephesus. For what should be emphasized is this: that the danger of abstraction with regard to the communication of idioms comes not from a reification of ahistorical, nondynamic, static essences per se, but from a *conceptual reification of essence of any kind* (even the dynamic, historical, actualistic type) *without direct attribution to the Person of the Son* in which alone that essence has its concrete realization, and *through which alone* the person subsists. Nature is only ever the principle *through* which the subject acts, and person is always exclusively the principle *that* or *who* acts. The union-in-distinction of the concepts is inseparable because persons only act naturally and natures are only inherent in concrete subjects.

By attributing human properties of the Son to the divine nature as such, in the so-called *genus tapeinoticum,* this distinction in unity is not observed. Consequently, one of two things will follow: either natures must be understood to act as subjects, or subjects must act without natures. Let us briefly consider these two in turn. The first possibility is that the nature of God must itself serve as an ontological subject of Christ's human natural becoming. The nature *determines it-*

20. *CD* IV/2, pp. 108-12.

self as subject through human historical actions so that the history of man now enters back up into the eternal nature of God. We see this tendency in Barth's thought when he insists on placing the divine essence in eternal ontological relativity (that is, real relation) to the human essence. The *agent* of the action of self-determination of the divine nature in view of the Incarnation is no longer simply the Son, but is now also the *divine nature* as either obeying or commanding, as if the *deity* or *essence* of God were obedient *in se*, and ordered toward or determined in view of the Incarnation *in se, qua* nature. Such language has as a consequence that it turns us away from a history of the Son of God made man toward a *prehistory of the divine nature*, in which diverse states are attributed to that nature across a continuum of becoming, as if that nature were itself a subject of human history.[21] Natures are acting as subjects. The drama of redemption is in a certain sense displaced back up into eternity (a tendency in Barth's thought that becomes more fully developed in Balthasar's *Theo-drama*).

The second possibility is that the Person of the Son must posit for himself the decision to be naturally divine and human in a given way *prior to possessing these natures*. That is to say, there must be a subjective self-determination of nature that is prenatural. (The subject acts without nature or without nature in a given mode.) In this case, the Son of God would posit for himself as subject or determine for himself as subject the divine nature he would come to have as God incarnate, *prior to* or *in distinction from* the possession of the nature or to the possession of the nature in that mode. However, because the Persons are only one if they are one in being and nature, this also means of course that the tri*une* identity of the Father, Son, and Holy Spirit as one in being would in some way come about only in and by a choice, one made prior to or eternally simultaneous with God's eternally preexistent natural identity as the one triune God.[22] It seems from passages cited

---

21. In *CD* IV/2, p. 70, Barth claims quite explicitly that the natures may never be treated as concrete subjects and that it is only ever the Son who acts as God and as man. In practice, however, he frequently transgresses this rule in very interesting ways: *CD* IV/2, p. 85: "it is indeed a part of the divine essence to be free for this decree [to be partaker of the human essence] and its execution, *to be able to elect and determine itself to this form*."

22. For a development of this line of criticism, see Bruce D. Marshall, "The Dereliction of Christ and the Impassibility of God," in *Divine Impassibility and the Mystery of Human Suffering*, ed. James F. Keating and Thomas Joseph White, O.P. (Grand Rapids: Eerdmans, 2009), pp. 246-98.

above that we also do see this tendency in Barth's explicit thought as well. Barth writes, for example: "in the Son of God, and therefore *by the divine Subject,* united in His act, each of the two natures, without being either destroyed or altered, acquires and has its own determination. *By and in Him the divine acquires a determination to the human,* and the human a determination from the divine."[23] But by what nature or in and through what nature does the Son act to bring into determination his two natures? The divine? The human? The free subject is now seemingly elevated in and through at least one act of self-determination, above any nature as a determiner of nature through a happening that precedes either the divine or human mode of being, and determines both simultaneously. Such a view is of a typically modern kind, by which a subject determines his or her own nature freely. It is, however, in real tension with a classical Trinitarian confession of the divine unity of God.[24]

The origins of this difficulty can be traced back to the earliest decisions of Barth's dogmatics, in *CD* I/1. For there, Barth begins from the premise that events in the economy reveal who God truly is (which is a traditional doctrine), but he adds to this a fateful addition: the idea that everything that is revealed in the economy implies some kind of analogous corollary in the life of God himself.[25] In other words, to

23. *CD* IV/2, p. 70 (emphasis added).

24. This anthropomorphism projected onto the deity is reminiscent of Sartre's existential anthropology, wherein the subject determines in freedom his own nature, itself an echo of themes found in Heidegger. It is strange for Catholics therefore to hear from some of Barth's disciples that he is not influenced by the "worldly" ontology in the university around him, that he is busy reading out of the Scriptures what was already present there and which no one had hitherto seen! Speaking realistically, however, Barth's conception certainly does not represent free human agency realistically, which is always the free agency of a determined subject of a given nature (even if the fallen self might wish to be free from the misperceived "constraints" of nature and natural law). Even less appropriately can such a notion be projected upon the eternally wise and good nature of divinity and thus the goodness and wisdom of divine freedom. One might reasonably be concerned on theological grounds that we are looking at an enticing but misguided philosophical concept of freedom (made uniquely in man's image and a fallen image at that) inappropriately projected onto the life of God, against the better judgment of the classical, theocentric Christological tradition.

25. See the two ideas expressed together in *CD* I/1, p. 331: "God's being revealed makes [revelation] a link between God and man, an effective encounter between God and man. But it is *God's own being revealed* that makes it this. In this respect too . . . our statement that God reveals Himself as the Lord is confirmed. The fact that God can do

speak in Rahner's terms: not only does the economy reveal the immanent triune life of God, but in addition, the immanent Trinity is the
economic Trinity. It is a short step from this idea to the affirmation
that the economy is in some way intrinsic to the life of God. Additionally, in *CD* I/1, Barth implicitly adopts a *philosophy* of the modern
human subject (which is simply presupposed but not argued for) in order to articulate the inner mystery of God's developmental freedom as
it is expressed in and through the economy.[26] The inner realization of
the subject who is God, or the eternal event of God's being as a subject,
takes place through his free self-determination as Father, Son, and
Holy Spirit, and *as the one who reveals himself* to man. If we simply combine these two ideas, we stand already on the cusp of the later developments of *CD* II/2, IV/1, and IV/2: the God who reveals himself in Christ
is always, already, a God who determines in himself (in the subject of
his own triune being) to exist only for and in the economy of creation.
God is the subject who determines himself for history in the very event
of his being.[27] But since the being of God now exists in and through a
spectrum of events, its source of unity can only be a shared life of willing, the agreement of the Father and the Son, enacted through the
moral union of decision making.

In writing all this I am of course quoting Barth selectively to denote diverse disequilibria toward which his thought might potentially
be turned. In practice he tends to hold these more experimental and
provocative thoughts together in tension with the more classical Ni-
cene and Chalcedonian ones. However, the point is that such tensions,
for all their creative force, are not sustainable. The humanity of Christ
cannot be the subject of a transcendent history in which it is eternal
or omnipresent. But likewise it is equally problematic to attribute to
the divinity a temporal life replete with properties derived from historical human becoming. In either case there is an abstraction that
turns away from the concrete history of God made man. Of course in

---

what the biblical witnesses ascribe to him, namely, not just take form and not just remain free in this form, but also in this form and freedom of His *become God* to specific
men" (emphasis added).

26. See, for example, *CD* I/1, p. 298: "The question: Who is the self-revealing God?
always receives a full and unrestricted answer also in what we learn about God's self-
revealing as such and about His being revealed among men. God Himself is not just
Himself. He is also His self-revealing."

27. See, for example, *CD* II/2, p. 175.

Thomas Joseph White, O.P.

saying all this, Thomists are at one not only with traditional sources like Leo the Great and the Third Council of Constantinople, but also with the Reformed scholastic tradition which derived much of its thinking from Thomism, from which Barth has taken his departure. For this classical tradition of the communication of idioms, what Barth is undertaking is literally a misnomer. The pure position is either to dissolve the distinction of the natures entirely, like Eutyches or Moltmann (so that the properties of the natures in the end need not be kept distinct), or to observe faithfully the hypostatic referent in all practice of the communication of idioms, such that the abstract predication of the natures to one another apart from the hypostasis is envisaged as a misunderstanding.

IV

A second issue pertains to Aquinas's treatment of the grace of Christ as it relates to the instrumentality of the Lord's human knowledge and his human obedience-in-charity. Let us begin by noting that Barth assuredly maintains a dyotheletist Christology, in which the divine and human operations and wills of Jesus Christ are seen to terminate in one end or effect. However, due to the various conceptual moves referred to above, this classical doctrine, common to the Reformed tradition, undergoes a significant reinterpretation in light of Barth's affirmation of divine obedience in God. For in the classical tradition the human obedience is the obedience of God the Son, and is properly ascribed to his Person, but only by virtue of his human nature. The operations of the human will remain distinguishable from those of the divine will and yet proper to the hypostasis.[28]

28. Following Cyril, Maximus the Confessor, and John Damascene, Aquinas offers a theological analysis of the two wills of Christ in *ST* III, q. 18, the cooperation of the two wills in q. 19, and a consideration of the human obedience of the Son in q. 20. This subordination of the human will to the divine will is the basis for Christ's meritorious mediating prayer (q. 21) and saving priesthood (q. 22). *ST* III, q. 19, a. 1, ad 4 and ad 5: "Being and operation belong to the person by reason of the nature; yet in a different manner. For being belongs to the very constitution of the person, and in this respect it has the nature of a term; consequently, unity of person requires unity of the complete and personal being. But operation is an effect of the person by reason of a form or nature. Hence plurality of operations is not incompatible with personal unity. . . . The proper

Furthermore, Christ's free human activity of will is *instrumentally* subordinated to his divine action as God, who is one with the Father and the Holy Spirit. Consequently, the Son in his human obedience and willing participates as man in the divine power that he possesses as God, and so in turn his human acts refer to and are expressive of the divine will, the will in which the Son as God is one in being and wisdom with the Father, that is to say in their unique divine operation or activity.[29] Following Dionysius, Aquinas will call this action "theandric" or divino-human.[30]

For Barth, however, the human will of man is transposed quasi-univocally into the preexistent life of God as indicative of the very deity of God. But by that same measure, the interrelation in the historical life of Christ of his divine and human operations *as distinct but hierarchically ordered* tends to disappear — or in fact, it no longer appears truly necessary. For now the mission of the Son in his human obedience simply is the direct expression of his eternal will to obey as God. Humanity reveals divinity, but this occurs through a kind of transparent identification of the two natures rather than through an instrumental subordination.

Let us further examine what consequence this difference might make. Aquinas asks the question in *ST* III, q. 7, a. 1: "whether in the soul of Christ there was any habitual grace?" Answering in the affirmative, the first reason Aquinas gives has to do with the hypostatic union: the human nature of Christ is united substantially to the Word of God, as

---

work of the divine operation is different from the proper work of the human operation. Thus to heal a leper is a proper work of the Divine operation, but to touch him is the proper work of the human operation. Now both these operations concur in one work, inasmuch as one nature acts in union with the other."

29. *ST* III, q. 19, a. 1, co. and ad 2.

30. *ST* III, q. 19, a. 1, ad 1: "Dionysius places in Christ a theandric, i.e. God-manlike or divino-human operation, not by any confusion of the operations or power of both natures, but inasmuch as His divine operation employs the human, and His human operation shares in the power of the divine. Hence, as he says in a certain epistle (*Ad Caium* IV), 'what is of man He works beyond man; and this is shown by the Virgin conceiving supernaturally and by the unstable waters bearing up the weight of bodily feet.' Now it is clear that to be begotten belongs to human nature, and likewise to walk; yet both were in Christ supernaturally. So, too He wrought divine things humanly, as when He healed the leper with a touch. Hence in the same epistle he adds: 'He performed Divine works not as God does and human works not as man does, but, God having been made man, by a new operation of God and man.'"

the humanity of God. This is what Aquinas terms the "grace of union" accorded to our humanity in Christ.[31] It is not of course the habitual grace of Christ. However, because of the proximity to the divine nature established by the grace of union, the human nature of Christ should also fittingly partake of the inward graces of divine life to an exalted degree. In other words, because he is God, Christ as man ought to receive the highest or deepest graces of holiness and sanctification. Lest this latter grace seem superfluous, Aquinas notes in response 1 of the article that the irreducible distinction of the natures within the composite Person of the Lord makes it such that the human nature is in need of grace in order fittingly to cooperate with the operations of his deity, operations present and active in him by virtue of his unity with the Father. He writes: "Christ is the true God in divine person and nature. Yet because together with unity of person there remains distinction of natures . . . the soul of Christ is not essentially divine. Hence it behooves it to be divine by participation, which is by grace."

Here we are speaking not about a *genus majestaticum* in which the properties of the natures are attributed to one another, but about something the Reformed scholastic tradition followed Aquinas closely on: the notion of a participation in the life of grace that is proper to the humanity of Christ. Like Aquinas, the Reformed scholastics often distinguished between the grace of union, which is proper to the humanity of Christ as substantially united with the Word hypostatically, and the habitual and operative graces of Christ as man, by which he is able to orient his habitual actions of knowledge and will toward the accomplishment of the divine will. Precisely because of the distinction of the natures even in the Person of the Son, there is a necessity of created grace given by the Holy Spirit in the human life of Christ.[32]

Aquinas goes on to note then (in *ST* III, q. 7, a. 1, ad 2 and 3) that the graces of Christ's soul are given so that he can operate as man in union with the divine activity which he shares in, as God, with the Father and the Holy Spirit. This cooperation is also one of subordination, such that his deliberate and free human agency as man is at the service of his divine life and operation as God. This perspective dovetails with

---

31. *ST* III, q. 2, a. 10; q. 7, a. 11.

32. See also on this the important arguments of *ST* III, q. 7, a. 13. Barth acknowledges these characteristics of the Reformed scholastic tradition in *CD* IV/2, pp. 51, 73, 89-90, 98-99, 104-6, with references to Polanus, Wolleb, Bucanus, and others.

q. 19, a. 1, in which Aquinas appeals to the classical Cyrillian understanding that he received explicitly from John Damascene of the human nature and operations of Christ as the instrument of the Godhead, by which the Son communicates his life of grace to the world.

Thus far we are making a point that, as has been noted, is very
much in harmony with the Reformed scholastic tradition. However,
here we come to a bend in the road. For with Aquinas, this plenitude of
created grace received into the created soul of Christ by virtue of the
hypostatic union and the mission of Christ pertains first and foremost
to the charity that inhabits his human will. It pertains also, however, to
the immediate knowledge of God *(lumen gloriae)* that he possesses in
the heights of his intellect. I am referring to what classical theology
terms the beatific vision of Christ. Christ as man, for Aquinas, has an
exceptional, immediate insight into the identity of the Father, his own
identity as Son, and the Person of the Holy Spirit.[33] (In addition to
this, classical theology holds that he has an infused, prophetic knowledge that grants him insight into the deeper significance of the unfolding situations in the divine economy, as well as into the hearts and
minds of other human beings.)[34] Because Christ's knowledge of God is
immediate and not mediated, two important consequences follow.
First, according to Aquinas, and in contradistinction from Calvin, Jesus
does not have faith in God, since faith acquires knowledge of God only
through the medium of divine revelation, and in dependence on
others.[35] Instead Jesus as man knows God directly and knows of his
own divine identity as God. Consequently, he does receive revelation
from another but is himself the revealer of the Father. He does as man
in his human obedience what he has heard and seen from his Father
(John 5:30; 6:46; 8:38), so as to reveal the identity of the Father and his
will, in his human acts of love and subordination to the divine will.[36]

---

33. *ST* III, q. 9, a. 2; q. 10. I have offered reflections on this doctrine in relation to
contemporary Christology in "The Voluntary Action of the Earthly Christ and the Necessity of the Beatific Vision," *The Thomist* 69 (2005): 497-534, and "Dyotheletism and the
Instrumental Human Consciousness of Jesus," *Pro Ecclesia* 17, no. 4 (2008): 396-422.

34. *ST* III, q. 11. See the helpful treatment of this subject by Jean Pierre Torrell,
O.P., *Le Verbe Incarné* (Paris: Cerf, 2002), vol. 2, pp. 415-39.

35. *ST* III, q. 7, a. 3.

36. Commenting on John 8:38 ("I speak of what I have seen with my Father"), Aquinas writes: "[It is as if he says]: I cannot be accused of speaking things that I have not
heard, for I speak not only what I have heard, but what is more, I speak of what I have

Aquinas's view of the obedience of the Son is not less profound than Barth's but it is quite different: the Son's human obedience is deepened by his vision of the Father, not lessened. The correspondence of his human will with the divine will, engendered by the vision, allows him to act entirely freely as man in such a way that his obedient human acts are the instrumental revelation of the divine life that he shares with the Father as God.

Second, because he has the vision, the man Jesus is not subject to being saved by God. He is, instead, uniquely the Savior.

> Now man is in potentiality to the knowledge of the blessed, which consists in the vision of God; and is ordained to it as to an end; since the rational creature is capable of that blessed knowledge, inasmuch as he is made in the image of God. Now men are brought to the end of beatitude [and therefore saved] *by the humanity of Christ,* according to Heb. 2:10: "For it became Him for whom are all things and by whom are all things, who had brought many children into glory, *to perfect the author* [Greek: *archegon*] of their salvation by his passion." And hence it was necessary that the beatific knowledge, which consists in the vision of God, should belong to Christ pre-eminently, since the cause ought always to be more efficacious than the effect.[37]

This doctrine of Aquinas will affect, to be sure, how we interpret the cry of dereliction, as we will come to in a moment. But more generally we can say that for Aquinas, Christ in his apostolic mission, by virtue of his knowledge of the Father's will, not only has extraordinary insights into the contingencies of the divine will as they unfold in his own historical life (and so the evidences of these in the Gospels to this effect cannot all be considered post-Paschal *theologoumena*). Furthermore, he also cooperates actively in the giving of grace as the Lord incarnate. As Aquinas argues in *ST* III, q. 48, a. 6 (corpus and ad 1), quoting St. Paul:

---

seen. Other prophets spoke the things they heard, whereas I speak the things I have seen: 'No one has ever seen God; the only Son, who is in the bosom of the Father, he has made him known' (1:18); 'That which we have seen and heard we proclaim also to you' (1 John 1:3). This must be understood of a vision which gives the most certain knowledge, because the Son knows the Father as he knows himself: "No one knows the Father except the Son' (Mt 11:27)." *Super Evangelium S. Ioannis Lectura,* VI, lec. 4, 1216, from the translation by J. Weisheipl, *Commentary on the Gospel of St. John,* vol. 1 (Albany: Magi, 1980).

37. *ST* III, q. 9, a. 2 (emphasis added).

"The word of the cross to them that are saved . . . is the power of God" (I Cor. 1:18). But God's power brings about our salvation efficiently. Therefore, Christ's Passion on the cross accomplished our salvation efficiently. [Now] there is a twofold efficient agency, namely, principal and instrumental. The principal efficient cause of man's salvation is God. But since Christ's humanity is the instrument of the Godhead, therefore *all Christ's actions and sufferings operated instrumentally* in virtue of His Godhead for the salvation of men. Consequently, then, Christ's passion accomplishes man's salvation efficiently. (Emphasis added)

This means that when Jesus actively forgives sins, works miracles, teaches with unique authority, founds the Church, and institutes the sacraments, he does so not only as man but also as the Son of God who is one with the Father and the Holy Spirit. The operations of the Spirit do not function as a substitute for the will of the Son as God. Rather, the Spirit's activity in the visible mission of the Son made man is the sign of the presence of Jesus' own divine activity. This is an activity he receives from the Father, and shares in with the Father, and in which he works with the Father, in the power of their shared Holy Spirit. This activity of the Son as God occurs in harmony or synergy with the Son's deliberative action as man, in accord with the Son's human knowledge and willing.[38] This theandric activity of the Lord incarnate is, thus, truly a source of salvation for others (a cause of grace), and his divine-human actions truly express his personal identity as God the Son.

V

This brings us to the topic of the crucifixion as the locus of redemption in Aquinas. In what way are the above-mentioned knowledge and charity of Christ operative in the crucifixion as the principle of human redemption? We have noted that Calvin and Barth, in two different ways, see the cry of dereliction as the locus of Christ's descent into hell on the cross. For Barth this is even a certain inward expression of the

38. *ST* III, q. 8, a. 1, ad 1: "To give grace of the Holy Spirit belongs to Christ as He is God, authoritatively; but instrumentally it belongs to Him as man, inasmuch as His manhood is the instrument of His Godhead. And hence by the power of the Godhead His actions were beneficial, i.e., by causing grace in us, both meritoriously and efficiently."

free and humble descent of God in his deity into the life of man. On this view, however, Christ's dereliction is the expression not primarily of his intrinsic righteousness (though his human innocence is of course maintained) but of his solidarity with us as one coming under the judgment of God. He is condemned in our stead so that we can be forgiven. We witness in Christ an extrinsic attribution of the guilt of humanity onto the Son, one from which we are gratefully excluded.

This is quite different from Aquinas's concept of satisfaction or atonement, which does not attribute such a form of penal substitution to the Son. Christ redeems us, rather, through the merits of his intrinsic righteousness stemming from love. We see this most especially in *ST* III, q. 48, a. 2, where Aquinas asks whether Christ saved us by way of *satisfactio*, alluding to Anselm's *Cur Deus Homo*. He gives three reasons there regarding how Christ atoned for human sin in the crucifixion. The first pertains to the plenitude of charity that inspires the human will of Christ to love and obey the Father and to suffer out of love on behalf of humanity: "by suffering out of love and obedience, Christ gave more to God than was required to compensate for the offense of the whole human race. First of all because of the exceeding charity from which He suffered." According to Aquinas, this charity stems precisely from the plenitude of habitual grace that Christ possesses as man, that which we have discussed above. Christ as man, therefore, loves and obeys God by an intrinsic righteousness and merit that make restitution for the impurity of all human lovelessness and idolatry. Simultaneously, he loves us, even in our waywardness from God.

However, and this is of importance in the context of our discussion: Aquinas underscores that all that Christ does or undergoes out of love, all of his actions and sufferings *(acta et passa)*, he lives out precisely as head of the Church in order to share this new grace of charity with human beings, who receive it unmerited, by grace alone. That is to say, what Christ lives in charity is to become the form of our life in charity by baptism: his love and obedience even unto death and into the life of resurrection are to become by grace the inward form of our lives.

> [G]race was bestowed upon Christ, not only as an individual, but inasmuch as He is Head of the Church, so that it might overflow into His members and therefore Christ's works are referred to Himself and to His members in the same way as the works of any other

man in a state of grace are referred to himself. But it is evident that whosoever suffers for justice's sake, provided that he be in a state of grace, merits his salvation. . . . Consequently Christ by His passion merited salvation, not only for Himself, but likewise for all His members.[39]

Here the form of solidarity stems not from the fact that the man Jesus Christ takes upon himself the burden of our guilt. Rather it derives from the fact that the man Jesus Christ loves and obeys there where we have failed to, and so constitutes humanity anew as rightly ordered toward God. By the graces of redemption, however, we are in turn incorporated into the mystical body of Christ, the Church, in which this life of Jesus' charity is available to us to reorient our hearts toward God by grace.[40]

At the same time, however, Aquinas underscores the infinite qualitative difference between Christ and his members. The second reason he offers (q. 48, a. 2) for the atonement pertains to the divinity of Christ. The man Jesus who makes satisfaction for human sin poses human acts that possess an *infinite dignity* and that are distinct from those of any other person precisely *because of the subject who loves:* the eternal Son of God made man.[41] There is a singular worth associated with the passion of the Son of God, because the reparation made on the cross out of love is that of God himself. Consequently, Christ alone can be said to merit our redemption "condignly" or with the strict merits of justice.[42] By God made man alone can we be saved. It is true that Aquinas does not think that God was bound in his freedom to save us by way of the Incarnation: he could have redeemed us by a sheer act of mercy, without communicating to us a participation in the justice of Christ. Such a decision would not contravene God's intrinsic justice, for he is the source of all that exists and can free us from sin as he pleases without the diminishment of his own goodness

---

39. *ST* III, q. 48, a. 1. Aquinas thinks that Christ merited *for himself* the resurrection of his body. See *ST* III, q. 49, a. 6.

40. *ST* III, q. 49, a. 1, co. and ad 2, 4, and 5.

41. *ST* III, q. 48, a. 2, co. and ad 3; ad 3: "The dignity of Christ's flesh is not to be estimated solely from the nature of flesh, but also from the person assuming it — namely, inasmuch as it was God's flesh, the result of which was that it was of infinite worth."

42. See *ST* III, q. 1, a. 2, ad 2: "for condign satisfaction it was necessary that the act of the one satisfying should have an infinite efficiency, as being of God and man."

and wisdom.[43] But Aquinas does think that only by way of the Incarnation and atonement could God render *us* intrinsically just, and that this form of salvation is itself a greater mercy.[44] So while Jesus is head of the Church as man, in the strictest sense the grace he shares with us justifies us freely (or renders us just for his sake), only because he who suffers on our behalf is also God.[45]

The third reason Aquinas gives (in q. 48, a. 2) for the atoning power of the cross is due to the intensity of the suffering that Christ endured in the crucifixion for our sake. On this last point, it is important to correlate Aquinas's teaching with that which he presents in q. 46, a. 6, especially ad 4. There Aquinas makes clear that he thinks the greatest suffering of Christ on the cross came not from his experience of the absence of God. (Indeed a descent into hell for Jesus is inconceivable for Aquinas, because what he means by "hell" formally speaking is the eternal loss of the vision of God, something that would be ontologically and morally absurd — if not blasphemous — in the life of Christ.) Rather the deepest suffering of the Lord comes from his awareness of human sin, especially insofar as that sin touches upon his own life as the Lord who is crucified:

> Christ grieved not only over the loss of his own bodily life, but also over the sins of all others. And this grief in Christ surpassed all

---

43. *ST* III, q. 1, a. 2; q. 46, a. 2. Barth finds this view particularly offensive (cf. *CD* II/2, pp. 119-20), but it rightly helps to underscore the transcendence and omnipotence of the God revealed in the gospel, against all idolatrous appropriations of the Incarnation as an event binding God to humanity in such a way as to obscure the freedom of the incarnate Lord.

44. *ST* III, q. 46, a. 1, ad 3.

45. We might object at this point with Barth that this vision of the atonement is based upon habitual grace residing in the soul of Christ and so consequently it cannot be indicative of the radical qualitative difference between the Son incarnate and ourselves. Rather, it insinuates merely a difference of degrees such that medieval scholasticism no matter how different from liberal Protestantism contains some essential subterranean point of contact with that tradition that obscures the gratuity of the redemption. Barth's concerns in this respect as expressed in *CD* IV/2 (pp. 55-57) do seem to me accurately to diagnose problems that occur in some modern Catholic Christologies, namely the later Christologies of a Schillebeeckx or a Rahner, which do have commonalities with the thought of a Schleiermacher or a Biedermann. But his views of the classical doctrine of habitual grace are inaccurate (IV/2, p. 90) and his fear of this doctrine being a substitute for the grace of union are unwarranted, at least as regards Thomism, as well as the mainstream teaching of the Catholic Church.

grief of every contrite heart, both because it flowed from a greater wisdom and charity, by which the pang of contrition is intensified, and because he grieved at the one time for all sins, according to Is. 53:4, "Surely he has borne our sorrows." But such was the dignity of Christ's life in the body, especially on account of the Godhead united with it, that its loss, even for one hour, would be a matter of greater grief than the loss of another man's life for howsoever long a time. As the Philosopher says (*Nic. Ethics* III, 9, 1117b10), that the man of virtue loves his life all the more in proportion as he knows it to be better; and yet he exposes it for virtue's sake. And in like fashion Christ laid down His most beloved life for the good of charity, according to Jer. 7:7: "I have given my dear soul into the hands of her enemies."[46]

The beatific vision of Christ plays a central and irreplaceable role here: the Son as man not only knows the Father but he also knows us in light of the divine wisdom. It is precisely his knowledge in wisdom of the depth of human sin, our sin, that is the night into which he peers, and it is the acuity and depth of his charity, of his love for the Father and for us, that grieves his heart with the deepest form of contrition known to man. The cry of dereliction is a cry into the night of our lovelessness. Our darkness is experienced by Christ crucified in his radiant vision and his intensity of love. This is the source of his suffering, endured for our sake in order to atone for our sins out of love.

At the same time, for Aquinas, the Son of God is the crucified Lord. Jesus crucified knows as man the dignity of his own life. On the one hand this enables him as man to offer up to the Father on behalf of humankind the life he uniquely possesses as God. This is the aspect of Christ's merit already alluded to, and which Aquinas rightly notes is a source of greater sorrow for Christ, due to his acute awareness of the evil he endures personally in giving his life. However, this knowledge of his own identity also allows him to act as both God and man, even in his passion. Even in his lowliness, and amidst his cry of dereliction, he can also explain to the good thief, "Today you will be with me in paradise" (Luke 23:43). The promise is made with authority. The gift of divine life here is given not only by the Father or the Spirit, but also by the Son as God and man. He reigns as the crucified Lord from the tree.

46. *ST* III, q. 46, a. 6, ad 4.

The human expression of the gift, in the heart and mind of Christ who contemplates the Father's will as man, is also the instrumental reflection of the saving will of God which he shares in fully with the Father — from him, but also with him, God from God, light from light, true God from true God. It is this same crucified Lord who can send the Holy Spirit out upon the world, and found the Church in water and blood, even as a lifeless cadaver hanging from the cross (John 19:34). That cadaver is the cadaver of the Word. On Holy Saturday God exists even in the Tomb, hypostatically and personally present, in the lifeless corpse of Jesus. Hidden in the being of the corpse is the personal life of God, eternal life, waiting to express itself mysteriously and victoriously in the event of resurrection.

VI

Up to this point, I have argued along distinctly theological lines, in part in order to take account of the presuppositions of my interlocutors, who are Barthian. At the term of these reflections we do not need to come to some kind of adjudicative verdict regarding the theology of the cross in Barth and Aquinas. I have given sufficient indications along the way of why I think the classical theology of St. Thomas bears great promise, and even offers us significant reasons why we might pause for thought regarding trends in contemporary Christology that are largely indebted to Barth.

It is necessary, however, at this juncture, also to say a word about philosophy as it bears upon this subject matter, and the ecumenical consequences of that bearing. Interestingly, when Barth discusses the innovative character of his Christology of the *genus tapeinoticum,* near the end of his treatment of it in *CD* IV/2, he is rather explicit about the motivations behind the changes he has made in the classical Reformed doctrine.[47] These come, he tells us, from his desire to translate the classical orthodoxy of the tradition from ontological terms that are static into the categories of history. Deeming this in his own words an "innovation" that is "radical," he goes on to ask: "How can God . . . in Jesus Christ be understood as history?"[48] Not unimportantly, he then goes on to con-

47. *CD* IV/2, pp. 106-8.
48. *CD* IV/2, p. 108.

cede implicitly in his own original way, on the whole question of the *genus majestaticum,* approaching the Lutheran position by a circuitous route.[49] In other words, he ends up saying that the historical event of the human life of Jesus is in some real sense eternal and omnipresent. And this is only logical, for if the divine essence of Christ is determined for historical existence, then the history of Jesus as man comes in some way to define the very preexistent life and history of God in his eternal deity. The passion of Christ is then omnipresent or indicative as history of something in the very life of God as it always is. We have come back around, then, to attributing divine eternity and omnipresence to the human nature and history of Christ. How could it be otherwise? As Barth says:

> Was He not in the history of that time altogether and once for all the Son of God and Son of Man humiliated and exalted . . . ? Can His being in that accomplished history — *as though it were not His perfect being in that accomplished history* — *as though it were not His perfect being in that "then," that yesterday* — be dissolved or augmented or superseded by any other history? Can it find its continuation in any other history? Can it continue to-day and to-morrow except as His then history, and therefore in such a way that His then history takes place also to-day and will take place also tomorrow? . . . Who is Jesus Christ? Must we not answer: the One who is to-day and will be to-morrow in the then completed *operatio* of His being as God and man, His humiliation and exaltation, the reconciliation of the world with God then accomplished in His death and revealed in His resurrection?[50]

This last phase of Barth's thought suggests a rather radical possibility for revision of divine attributes of God, understanding divine eternity and omnipresence now in light of the historical cross of Christ. Among contemporary inheritors of Barth, perhaps no one so much as Robert Jenson has attempted to undertake the metaphysical reconsideration of eternity and time that such theological principles would seem to evoke.

What is happening here, however, while it stems no doubt in part from specific dogmatic decisions, also has a decidedly philosophical dimension. Barth is purposely setting out to translate the classical Chalcedonian doctrine into categories derived from nineteenth-century Ger-

49. *CD* IV/2, pp. 108-13.
50. *CD* IV/2, pp. 111-12 (emphasis added).

man Idealism, a theological transposition of Schelling and Hegel: God is now denoted in his own life using analogies from human language such as history, act, freedom, decision, self-positing, self-constitution, self-determination, operation, obedience, and a host of other cousin concepts. But why these categories and not others? What was wrong with the so-called static categories? Barth claims that the novelty of his own position stems uniquely from the fact that he alone in the history of Christian thought has read Scripture correctly on this question. Even his Reformed forebears where blinded by pride when they had recourse to static ontology derived from non-Christian, Hellenistic philosophy.[51] We can ignore for the sake of argument that this is a hopelessly narrow mischaracterization of the classical ontology, whether Greek or medieval. (It is Aristotle who derived a notion of *dunamis* in the order of being, precisely against what he considered the ahistoricity of the theory of forms. Aquinas's notion of *esse* as *actus essendi* allowed him to articulate how the Christian God of the Bible was the cause of the concrete existence of dynamic material substances existing in time.)

Returning to Barth, however, the fact of the matter is that we are dealing with an unacknowledged *irreducibly* philosophical decision on his part, which, however, has not been justified philosophically but merely presumed or asserted, based in great part upon philosophical inclinations derived from post-Kantian forms of German idealism. After Kant, it is not that we cease to employ an ontology in the way that we construe the divine essence, but that we may no longer reasonably employ the categories from an age prior to the *Critique of Pure Reason*. Thus the need to transpose the mystery into a distinctly modern key: one of self-determination, life, history, self-positing, decision in freedom, etc.

Surely this is not a particularly absurd suggestion. It might be in

---

51. CD IV/2, pp. 84-85, 108ff.: "It was only the pride of man, making a god in its own image, that will not hear of a determination of divine essence in Jesus Christ. The presupposition of all earlier Christology has suffered from this pride — from the fathers to both Reformed and Lutheran orthodoxy. This presupposition was a Greek conception of God, according to which God was far too exalted for His address to man, His incarnation, and therefore the reconciliation of the world and Himself, to mean anything at all for Himself, or in any way to affect His Godhead." This is a rather unimaginative and noncredibly narrow consideration of the possible theological intentions and values of the entirety of the classical tradition preceding Barth, and is of course, as specious and as lacking in value as any *ad hominem* argument, which by its very nature is unsubstantiated and indemonstrable. Who is projecting here?

fact a warranted decision. However, it seems invariably in part a philosophical question as such. Even to a Thomist in no way wed to the distinctive features of Balthasar's theology, it seems that Balthasar's own project of a Catholic interpretation of Barth has more rational plausibility and internal transparence methodologically speaking: for Balthasar seeks to rearticulate the unity of classical and modern forms of ontology coherently and explicitly, in a distinctively philosophical moment of thinking, yet always with a view toward their Christological application or expression in a theological moment that is superior and ultimately more determining.[52] Of course Barth himself protests in principle against such a project. But it seems to a Thomist that this is arguably a more methodologically pure rendering of what is inherent in Barth's project as such, whether or not this seems admissible to Barthians.

What renders ecumenical discussion awkward, however, is the difficulty for many Barthians of admitting any form of distinctly philosophical *accountability* for the ontological idioms in which Barth chooses to express himself.[53] Ironically, in his desire to forge a post-Enlightenment Christological ontology, Barth has invariably made the use of *philosophy* and not merely theology a Church-dividing issue. Instead of acknowledging, as the Catholic Church has traditionally done, a legitimate plurality of philosophical expressions within theology, de facto, Barth has from the outset excluded the use of philosophies other than those he deems evangelical by a magisterial fiat. In its own odd and indirect way, this is far more extreme a canonization of a particular philosophical tradition than anything undertaken by the Catholic Church at Vatican I, or subsequently.[54]

---

52. I am thinking of the *Theo-Logic,* vol. 1: *The Truth of the World,* and vol. 2, *The Truth of God,* trans. A. J. Walker (San Francisco: Ignatius Press, 2000 and 2004), but also of *The Glory of the Lord: A Theological Aesthetics,* vol. 4: *The Realm of Metaphysics in Antiquity,* and vol. 5: *The Realm of Metaphysics in the Modern Age,* trans. Brian McNeil et al. (San Francisco: Ignatius Press, 1989 and 1991).

53. In his suggestive book *Protestant Metaphysics after Karl Barth and Martin Heidegger* (London: SCM Press, 2010), Timothy Stanley in his own avowedly Barthian way at least vividly acknowledges the problem, p. 241: "Must Protestantism adopt a being-less faith devoid of reason, and be 'deprived of existence,' as Benedict XVI suggests [in his Regensburg address]? Said in another way, must it remain tied to the Heideggerian divide between theology and ontology? I would suggest that the future of ecumenical relations between Roman Catholic and Protestant traditions depends upon our answers to these questions."

54. Cf. *Fides et Ratio,* para. 49: "The Church has no philosophy of her own nor does she canonize any one particular philosophy in preference to others."

It is not that Catholics are unaware that philosophical ideas can derive from the factory of idols in the mind of man, and find their way into the (mis)interpretation of the gospel.[55] On the contrary, the Catholic tradition has a long experience of this problem (in external dialogue and in internal self-clarification), which is why it deems philosophy unavoidable as a dimension of human nature. Consequently, the Catholic tradition has always held that philosophical reflection is an unavoidable dimension of Christian orthodoxy, while simultaneously being concerned that a true philosophical regard on reality be compatible with and ultimately wholly subordinate to the mystery of God revealed in Christ.

The question back to Barthians then is this: Is philosophy like language and human nature — something simply unavoidable and so irreducibly present in theology whether we wish it or not? If so, the question is not whether in Christology all analogies derived from ontological philosophical concepts are idolatrous. For the use of some form of such thinking is necessary and unavoidable, whether our concepts derive originally from a Hellenistic milieu, the scholastic tradition, or German idealism. The real question, rather, is: Why should we adopt one set of such ideas and not another (or perhaps some hitherto unforeseen combination of them)? But this question is the question of philosophical truth, in relation to but also distinct from theological truth. In their own age, the medieval scholastics sought to attempt to discern how to use and not use language correctly to speak of God precisely in this way, ultimately in the service of divine revelation. And one of the strengths of Barth is that he seems to wish to do this for his age as well. That being said, the analysis of his innovative transposition of history into the life God cannot be conducted simply in dogmatic terms, but also invariably entails a philosophical evaluation, or if one refuses such an analysis, then a philosophical presupposition that remains implicit, and unacknowledged but therefore also unjustified, except perhaps unconvincingly through the kind of *ad hominem* arguments that Barth himself employs. After all, it is not only fair, but in fact a duty the Reformed mind should be sympathetic to, to ask whether in his historical and act-centered ontology of the divine nature Barth is himself the one projecting human creation problematically

---

55. *Institutes of the Christian Religion,* I.11.8: "the human mind is, so to speak, a perpetual factory of idols."

and blindly into God, in the place of God, due to a conventional alliance with the intraworldly, passing intellectual spirit of his age. Purity and freedom from idolatry are not only supernatural, but natural, not only dogmatic, but also philosophical. Beware of impure philosophy! The thought of Thomas Aquinas seeks to advance an integral and therefore more self-conscious concept of Christian purity and freedom from worship of false gods, one that reaches right down into our (inalienable) natural capacity for metaphysical reflection. This is in part what is transpiring in his formulation of the metaphysics of *esse*. If a true conversation about *philosophical* ontology in the *Church Dogmatics* were to take place, we might then be able to find places of congruity and convergence in the thought of Aquinas and Barth respectively, and also places of fascinating and creative difference. But so long as this dimension of Barth's thought remains insufficiently acknowledged, a part of the dialogue is inevitably thwarted.

VII

The context of this essay has been ecumenical in character. Let me conclude by posing three ecumenically motivated ideas. First, as I have suggested above, Aquinas has much in common with the classical Reformed scholastic tradition, and pertaining to some particular doctrines, particularly in Christology, the two have more in common with one another than either does with Barth. But this can be said of any two corners of the triangle, since Barth is in many ways the strongest modern Reformed voice, and since modern articulations of Thomism share concerns in common with Barthianism that neither share as perfectly with the premodern Reformed scholastic tradition. So one question to ask is whether or how to define the normative tradition of confessional Reformed theology itself. Barth is clearly its most powerful modern exponent, but perhaps he also should be considered as a sometimes quite experimental advocate of Reformed ideas, reinterpreting them in tantalizing but disputable ways. If this is the case, then perhaps while classical Reformed thinkers have a great deal to learn from Barth's modern orthodoxy, Barthians may yet have much to learn about their own classical heritage, in reference to the scholastic dogmatism of their forebears. If those who are committed to the Reformed confessional tradition were to pursue this line of inquiry, theological dialogue with Catholic Thomism would certainly be not only be possible, but perhaps even fruitful for the discussions within Reformed theological inquiry.

Second, for Catholic thinkers, and perhaps for Thomists in particular, Barth's theology seems habitually to approach true greatness while simultaneously remaining entrenched in an intriguing ambiguity. On the one hand there is his consistent and purposeful condemnation toward all that stems from the Hellenistic-scholastic philosophical tradition, or the autonomy of philosophy generally, as it touches upon the construction of theological doctrine. But this is matched by a self-conscious retrieval over against liberal Protestantism of overtly ontological forms of doctrine reminiscent of premodern thinkers, tangible to Catholic sensibilities, and not without its own appeal to classical scholastic terminology. While Barth criticizes classical uses of notions like pure act, personhood, or the analogy of being, he also mixes revamped uses of these or similarly classical terms with reflections inspired from modern German idealism, and in response to modern theological conundrums, all under the auspices of an overtly theological doctrine. He therefore forges uniquely modern theological amalgamations, so as to rearticulate classical positions in overtly innovative ways. But is that really a way of thinking free of philosophical determinations? Clearly not. The philosophical implications of the theological stances of the *Church Dogmatics* requires more investigation.

Third, Balthasar seems right to observe that in a sense there is not a more Catholic thinker among Protestants than Karl Barth. But this is also ambiguous of course. This "Catholic" Barth is interested in ontological categories and classical sources, and sees in this no inherent conflict with biblical thinking. He is suspiciously anti-Catholic, like someone reacting vigorously to what he considers a temptation to a form of Christianity he must habitually take seriously. He seems as ready to learn something about Scripture from reading Gregory of Nyssa or even Thomas Aquinas as he might from reading Martin Luther. In the name of Reformed freedom, he is recovering Catholic intellectual universalism. Perhaps most impressively, he is willing to engage modern critics of Christianity from all sides, while always intelligently bringing their respective insights and errors back around to a conversation about divine revelation. This marks him off decisively from all who would forfeit the exclusivity of the divine revelation of God in Jesus Christ for the sake of some form of post-Enlightenment adaptationism, and in its own way it gives him a kinship with the simultaneously dogmatic and universal aspirations of classical Catholic thought. Balthasar was right to see all this and underscore its ecumenical possibilities.

Nevertheless, it must be added that Catholic Christians not as Thomists, but only as mere Catholics, cannot really see the history of theology as a foreshadowing and preparation for one man's thought, even that of Thomas Aquinas. It is odd to us to suggest that Barth's theological formulations, not only but especially when they are virtually unique to him, should be considered normative for the whole tradition. Theology is conducted within a larger ecclesial body and no one man can compose a definite "Church Dogmatics" that is normative for the body of Christ. Catholic Christians have much to learn from Barth, and even when they inevitably must disagree with him, they can also learn a great deal about how they might hold their own positions more intelligently by comparing them with the critical engagement of their interlocutor. But whatever the contributions of the great dogmatician from Basel, he remains only one theological voice among others, one that is powerful and insightful, but also experimental and fallible. Those qualifications being in place, his work continues to contribute truly to the discussions regarding constructive theology in the larger life of the Church.

IV. Grace and Justification

Aquinas and Barth on Grace

Joseph P. Wawrykow

These reflections on Aquinas and Barth fall into two sections. In the first, I examine the teaching offered by Aquinas in his *Summa theologiae (ST)*, with particular attention to the treatise on grace with which the first part of the second part (I-II) of that work concludes.[1] Other texts by Aquinas are introduced to clarify, secure, or extend points made in the *Summa*'s treatise on grace. These other texts are taken from the very early *Scriptum* on the *Sentences* of Peter Lombard (to indicate important developments in Thomas's thinking about grace); from his biblical commentaries; and from elsewhere in the *Summa*.[2] The focus in the first section is on Aquinas, although with an eye to engagement with Barth. In the second section, I turn to that engagement, basing my comments about Barth (and Aquinas) on Barth's teaching about rec-

1. The *Summa* has three main parts; the second main part is itself divided into two. The first part is the *Prima pars* (I); the first part of the second part is the *Prima secundae* (I-II), the second part of the second part, the *Secunda secundae* (II-II); and the third part is the *Tertia pars* (III). The final questions of the *Prima secundae* are given over to grace. The treatise on grace in *ST* I-II runs from q. 109 through q. 114. Qq. 106-8, on the New Law that principally is the grace of the Holy Spirit, prepare for the treatise; the questions on the New Law conclude the extensive examination of "law" that begins with I-II, q. 90. I have used the following edition of the *Summa*: *S. Thomae de Aquino Ordinis Praedicatorum Summa theologiae.* Cura et studio Instituti Studiorum Medievalium Ottaviensis (1941), 5 vols.

2. For the writings of Aquinas, with chronological indications, see the catalogue prepared by Gilles Emery, O.P., in Jean-Pierre Torrell, O.P., *Saint Thomas Aquinas,* vol. 1: *The Person and His Work,* trans. Robert Royal (Washington, DC: Catholic University of America Press, 1996), pp. 330-61.

onciliation in *Church Dogmatics* IV/1 and IV/2.[3] My intention through-out is to be fair and accurate in rendering Aquinas and Barth on grace, noting where they differ and where they may agree, without exaggerat-ing either the agreement or the difference.

For Aquinas, salvation means eternal life.[4] The saved are those who live in community with God, who exist in the immediate presence of God, and know and love God face to face. The beatific vision is re-served to the next life. The present life can anticipate it — people can and do now live in community with God, and believe, hope, love, in the way appropriate to this communion — but the present life falls short of the intensity of the full communion of the next. Aquinas insists on the transcendence and gratuity of eternal life. It is God who determines God as human beings' end; God as the beatifying end of human beings is not something due to the human as human, as if that end were owed to the human by virtue of the human's nature. Rather, God freely and in love establishes the triune God as the beatifying end of human being and activity. And, that humans come to know what God does for them, that the triune God has established God as their beatifying end, is itself a mark of God's gracious, loving initiative and due to it. In his discus-sion of sacred doctrine[5] — the body of truths needed for salvation re-vealed by God in Scripture — Aquinas distinguishes between two kinds of truth found in sacred doctrine: articles of faith and preambles of faith. Both are revealed by God and tied to salvation. One set, the pre-ambles, are as a rule held by faith on the basis of revelation. But as Aquinas acknowledges, some have without the benefit of revelation ar-gued to them and demonstrated them, albeit only after a long time and even then with an admixture of error. The other truths, the articles, are revealed and cannot be argued to or demonstrated. Human reason can-

---

3. Karl Barth, *Church Dogmatics* IV/1 (Edinburgh: T. & T. Clark, 1956) and IV/2 (1958), both translated by G. W. Bromiley (hereafter *CD*).

4. For a detailed description of grace in Aquinas, see my *God's Grace and Human Action: "Merit" in the Theology of Thomas* (Notre Dame: University of Notre Dame Press, 1995). For a brisker survey, see my "Grace," in *The Theology of Thomas Aquinas,* ed. R. Van Nieuwenhove and J. Wawrykow (Notre Dame: University of Notre Dame Press, 2005), pp. 192-221.

5. The *Summa* opens (*ST* I, q. 1) with a consideration of sacred doctrine. That opening question sets the tone and provides the context for the theological inquiries that constitute the rest of the *Summa.* What follows in the paragraph is based especially on *ST* I, q. 1, a. 1 (which articulates the necessity of sacred doctrine). For the centrality of Scripture in sacred doctrine, mentioned here, see the final articles of I, q. 1 (aa. 8-10).

not attain to them (although once revealed, one can reflect on them and plumb their meaning). Apart from revelation, one would have no inkling that, for example, God is triune, or that the Son of God has become human. It is not insignificant that in opening the *Summa,* Aquinas gives in the *Summa*'s very first article, as the example of an article of faith, God as transcendent and beatifying end. Without God's revelation in love, humans would not know where they are to go or how they are to get there.

This understanding of salvation shapes the *Summa*'s teaching on grace. Its treatise on grace begins with a consideration of the *need* for grace.[6] Aquinas observes a twofold need. The vision of God, the end of the human person determined by God, transcends human capacity. Acts must be proportioned to their end; the acts that might lead to eternal life thus lie beyond human powers, beyond the human as creature who falls short of the Creator who is end. There is, then, an ontological gap as it were, between the human and the God who is the end of the human, as set by God. There is also a moral gap, established by human sin. By sin, both original and actual, human beings differ radically from the God who is utterly and wholly good; and by sin, humans are most unworthy of eternal life. God addresses human need — both needs — in grace. In God's love for humans, God offers the grace that can bridge both the ontological and the moral gaps. Grace, in Aquinas's account, has thus a twofold function: to elevate, and to forgive and heal.

In the *Summa,* Aquinas asserts two graces, habitual grace and *auxilium,* both rooted in God's love for humans. Each grace performs both functions — of elevating and healing. When infused in the person, habitual grace heals the effects of sin, both original and actual. By that grace, the sinful person is restored to correct order to God, and the disruption in the self is, in principle at least, overcome. Habitual grace also elevates the person to the supernatural order, making the person pleasing to God and orienting the person to God as beatifying end. The other grace, the grace of *auxilium,* is introduced in the first place on metaphysical grounds (*ST* I-II, q. 109, a. 1, co.). Habitual grace pro-

6. *ST* I-II, q. 109, is on the need for grace. Throughout *ST* I-II, q. 109, Aquinas makes adroit use of three pairings, to which I allude in the next few paragraphs: ontological/moral; habitual grace/*auxilium;* and pre-Fall and post-Fall. For a potent statement of the need for grace exploiting these distinctions, see *ST* I-II, q. 109, a. 2, co., where the topic is willing and doing good.

vides new potency, for the natural and for the supernatural good. But potency does not reduce itself to act. What is in potency to act is reduced to act only by what is already in act; and in this telling, for Aquinas, this is God, moving the human person perfected by habitual grace to acts appropriate to that grace and to the virtues infused with it, those of faith, hope, charity, as well as the infused moral virtues. The metaphysical need for an *auxilium* is complemented by an assertion of the healing function of *auxilium*. In the *Summa*'s question on the need for grace, the healing function of *auxilium* is increasingly stressed as the question proceeds. *Auxilium* reduces to act; God through *auxilium* reduces the person to morally correct act.

The second article of q. III of the *Prima secundae* furthers the analysis by incorporating traditional Augustinian language of operation and cooperation *(operans, cooperans)*.[7] Each of Thomas's graces, habitual and *auxilium,* can be further distinguished into operative and cooperative kinds. In terms of habitual grace, "operative" refers to being, to new being. By operative habitual grace, the person is restored to correct order to God and within the self, and is made pleasing to God. By cooperative habitual grace, that person is disposed to acts that are morally good, in compliance with the nature established by God but deformed by sin and so made incapable of the full natural good, and to acts that lead to God and eternal life. As for *auxilium,* "operative" has to do with motion: in operative *auxilium,* God moves the person and the person is simply moved. The great example of this comes in conversion, which is worked by God. But Aquinas knows of other examples of operative *auxilium.* Aquinas earlier in the *Prima secundae* (I-II, qq. 6-17) had distinguished three parts or aspects of a complete human act: intention of the end, choice of the means, and execution of the act. In I-II, q. III, q. 2, co., operative *auxilium* provides good intention, *radically* when the person is turned from sin and toward God and when God as beatifying end is intended by the person (as moved by God), but also any time when the now-reoriented person acts and intends a good that is placed in order, in subordination to the beatifying God. In cooperative *auxilium,* God moves the person but moves the person in such a way that the person also moves herself. While operative *auxilium* has to

7. *ST* I-II, q. III, a. 2 holds pride of place in Bernard Lonergan's brilliant *Grace and Freedom: Operative Grace in the Thought of St. Thomas Aquinas,* ed. J. Patout Burns (London: Darton, Longman & Todd, 1971).

do with good intention (of the end), cooperative *auxilium* has to do with choice of the means to that end and the actual execution of the act. In a complete and good human act, God acts by *auxilium* both operatively and cooperatively, providing good intention and aiding in the realization of that end.

In Aquinas, grace is ordered to glory. Life in this world is conceived in terms of a movement to God as end; the reaching of that end, the attainment of glory, will come only in the next life. The graces posited in this second article (of q. 111) are to be plotted along this journey, in this life. If successful, the human journey involves a conversion followed by actions in the state of grace, ascribed to a person who has been healed and elevated by habitual grace and moved to act, operatively and cooperatively, by God in *auxilium*. In terms of a sequence of graces: an operative *auxilium* moves the person toward God and away from sin; as the term of that moving, habitual grace is infused; that single habitual grace, along with the virtues infused with it, incline the person to good acts that continue the healing of the self and the movement toward God as beatifying end; and subsequent *auxilia* realize the potential provided in habitual grace and the attendant virtues. There will be as many *auxilia* as there are morally good and supernaturally oriented acts of the person in grace. By grace God precedes and accompanies the person every step of the way.

Aquinas continues his explorations into operative and cooperative grace in the final two questions of the *Summa*'s treatise on grace. In q. 113, he presents his teaching on justification — the effect, as he states, of operative grace, concentrating on the beginnings of justification, the movement from the state of sin to the state of grace. In surveys of teachings on justification, it is not uncommon to distinguish between transformational and declarative accounts of justification and to categorize a given teaching as one or the other. In the former (that is, justification as transformational), there will be a real change in the person. Sin removes a person from correct ordering to God, and expresses the person's insubordination. There is also a disordering within the self, with the lower self in rebellion against the higher as it seeks, narrowly, its own goods. From q. 113, it is clear that Aquinas is convinced of the transformation that justification brings, that God achieves by grace. By the infusion of grace, the mind is moved away from sin and toward God in the faith that justifies, and sins are removed. Justification brings a fundamental reconstitution of the person, reordered within the self and toward God. However, in teaching justification, Aquinas can also be attentive to its declarative aspects.[8] Sin is ordered to punishment; the sinner deserves to be punished. In forgiving the person, God waives the punishment. The sin is not reckoned against the person. Aquinas can even refer to the "covering" that justification brings. In regarding the justified, God does not consider that person's sins. As forgiven, those sins are past and do not count against the person (even if that person were to lapse, subsequently, from correct relationship to God). God looks instead at the justice instilled in the justified by God.

The quality of justification as gift is apparent in this particular question, as it is elsewhere in the treatise on grace. Aquinas offers a neat reinterpretation in the treatise of a traditional saying, "facienti quod in se est, Deus non denegat gratiam" (to one who does her best, God will give grace).[9] At first glance, the saying would appear to assert a human initiative in the process of conversion; and that in fact was the conviction of many who affirmed the saying. To get grace, to come into God's favor, all one need do is take the first step to God. And that is how Aquinas presented the saying in his early *Scriptum:* there, taking the first step is due to the decision and activity of a human viewed as a self-mover; when that person does her best, God infuses the grace that is habitual (the only grace, not incidentally, that Aquinas affirms in the *Scriptum*).[10] In the *Summa,* however, Aquinas invokes both of his graces in conversion. Habitual grace is a formal perfection, and matter must be prepared for the induction of form. However, the preparation of the person entailed in the reception of habitual grace is due to *auxilium,* to operative *auxilium.* God moves the person, and the person as moved is open to the habitual grace that follows. There can be no preparation for this *auxilium;* it is simply given by God, in accordance with God's will. Need God give habitual grace to one so prepared, through *auxilium?* God does nothing without purpose; and in moving the per-

8. Especially helpful here is an article by Bruce Marshall, drawing on the biblical commentaries as well as the discussion of the sacrament of penance, in the *ST* III, q. 88. See *"Beatus vir:* Aquinas, Romans 4, and the Role of 'Reckoning' in Justification," in *Reading Romans with St. Thomas Aquinas,* ed. M. Levering and M. Dauphinais (Washington, DC: Catholic University of America Press, 2012), pp. 216-37.

9. See *ST* I-II, q. 112, aa. 2-3.

10. For texts in the *Scriptum* in which Aquinas discusses the *facienti* and conversion, see my *God's Grace and Human Action,* p. 84, n. 47.

son by operative *auxilium* and so preparing the person for the infusion of habitual grace, God intends the giving of habitual grace; and so as prepared by God through operative *auxilium,* the giving of habitual grace follows. In sum, by the time of the *Summa,* Aquinas has stood the traditional saying on its head; the initiative rests squarely with God.

The discussion of merit in the final question (I-II, q. 114) of the *Summa's* treatise on grace displays a certain artistry. In asking about merit, Aquinas is concerned with the biblical teaching about the good actions that will be part of the Christian's life and with biblical comments about reward. For Aquinas, "reward" implies "merit" (I-II, q. 114, a. 1 sc. and co.). Merit is a good act deserving of a reward from another. The *Summa's* teaching on merit conforms to Aquinas's fundamental insights into divine initiative and the sovereignty of God in the salvific process. Merit, he notes at the outset of this question, is the effect of cooperative grace, the grace by which God disposes the human to good actions and moves the person, in choice of means and execution, in such a way that the person moves himself. Talk of merit is to be restricted to those who are in grace; there is no merit prior to or apart from grace (I-II, q. 114, a. 2, co.). Merit, then, is in Aquinas the merit of the elect as they stand and act in the grace of God. God has ordained their actions, as done in and by grace, to be meritorious of the end of the human journey, life with God in heaven. That end, to which they have been lovingly and freely ordered by God, is thus also rendered to them as reward. Aquinas knows of different categories of merit (e.g., I-II, q. 114, a. 3, co.). He refers to both condign and congruent merit. Condignity posits an equality between act and response. Congruent merit acknowledges a gap in value. For Aquinas, one and the same act done in grace can be evaluated from two perspectives; one and the same act is congruently and condignly meritorious. As the free act of a creature viewed as creature, there is no condignity, given the great ontological and moral distance between creature and God. Here, there is a congruent merit: it congrues with and befits God, in God's generous nature, to respond with reward to the strivings of God's creatures. Yet, the same act can and is to be evaluated from the perspective of the divine ordination that grounds merit and especially the grace by which the act is performed. Here, it is the activity of the Holy Spirit that stands to the fore; and since the Spirit is God, what the Spirit does in and with the person has a condignity, an equality to what God gives in response — eternal life, life with God in heaven.

In his version of merit, Aquinas puts the focus on God without losing sight of the human. Aquinas is commenting on the human in relation to God. A meritorious act is that of a concrete human being; but the divine contribution is multiple and indispensable. God elects; God ordains; God gives grace and is active in grace; God summons God's people to action, which God makes possible in God's grace; God responds to the actions that emerge from God's leading and prompting. Merit shows what is possible for God, and for people in correct relation to God, as established in that relationship by God. There is thus a certain credibility to Thomas's comment, in the first article of this question (ad 2), that merit has to do, not with human glory but with God's — proclaiming the goodness of God through the graced good actions of those who belong to God.[11]

The treatise on grace does not stand on its own and is not meant to be read in isolation. That it is to be viewed in connection with the rest of the *Secunda pars* in both of its parts — the *Prima secundae,* on the movement to God as end in general, the *Secunda secundae,* on that movement in particular (with close examinations of each of the principal virtues, good habits that facilitate that movement) — is evident enough. The treatise on grace marks a culmination to the *Prima secundae,* tying together its principal themes while preparing for the more detailed discussions to come in the *Secunda secundae.* The treatise on grace also looks back to the *Prima pars,* on God and the procession of creatures from God, and builds on and reexpresses the teaching there. For our purposes, q. 20 of the *Prima pars* is especially important. That question is on the love of God, the love that God expresses. For Aquinas, love involves willing good with respect to another. There is a crucial difference between God's loving and the love that humans express. Humans will a good that already exists, or is perceived to exist. God's willing of good is on the other hand causal, not responding to a real or apparent good but causal of all good in whatever form it takes. Thus, to take a set scholastic exercise: Does God love the better — that is, something or someone endowed with more good — more (I, q. 20, a. 4)? Once the correct sequence is observed, the answer for Aquinas is yes. God loves the better more, not

---

11. *ST* I-II, q. 114, a. 1, ad 2: "Deus ex bonis nostris non quaerit utilitatem, sed gloriam, idest manifestationem suae bonitatis; quod etiam ex suis operibus quaerit. Ex hoc autem quod eum colimus, nihil ei accrescit, sed nobis. Et ideo meremur aliquid a Deo, non quasi ex nostris operibus aliquid ei accrescit, sed inquantum propter eius gloriam operamur."

that such a one is already good and has more good than another and so evokes God's willing; rather, one's being better is due to God, to God's willing more good to that one. Expressed in conjunction with a teaching about God's wisdom and the wise communication of God's goodness, this teaching about God's causal love weaves its way through the rest of the *Summa* — through the rest of the *Prima pars;* through the *Secunda pars* on human activity in the movement to God; and indeed through the *Tertia pars* of the *Summa,* including in the discussion of the Incarnation. In terms of the first part of the *Summa,* creating is seen as God's communication of God's goodness, in bringing into being what is not God and in bringing into being different sorts of being, with the due ends and activities and passivities proper to each (I, qq. 44ff.). This teaching about God's causal love also stands behind the treatment of predestination in the *Prima pars* (I, q. 23). God loves all things. God loves some beings — rational creatures — more, willing to them the even greater good that is eternal life, a share in what is proper to God. Grace as well is the expression of God's love and shows the causal quality of that loving. That this is so of habitual grace will be obvious, but for Aquinas this holds as well of *auxilium,* of God's direct involvement, whether operatively or cooperatively, in the life and activity of those who will enter eternal life. It applies too to the affirmation of merit, as indicated by the saying earlier quoted,[12] about graced good actions proclaiming the glory of God: God so re-creates the justified that they are able to contribute, according to God's intention for them and as led by God, to their own salvation.

The teaching on grace is continued in the *Tertia pars.* There, Aquinas turns to Christ, who — as Aquinas has stated very early in the *Summa* (in the prologue to q. 2 of the *Prima pars,* where he announces the organization of the entire work) — as human *(secundum quod homo)* is the way to God as end. Christ is not wholly absent from the treatise on grace in the *Prima secundae,* and the mentions are not insignificant. Hence, in q. 112, Aquinas invokes his incarnational Christology in examining the cause of grace. The triune God is the author of grace and so alone the "cause" of grace in a strict sense; but it is through the humanity of Jesus, viewed as the conjoined, personal, animate instrument of the divinity, that grace, taking its origin in God who is the author of grace, is conveyed to those called to God (I-II, q. 112, a. 1, ad 1). In the

12. In the preceding note: *ST* I-II, q. 114, a. 1, ad 2.

discussion of merit in q. 114, Aquinas is attentive to the difference between the merit of Christ and of those who follow Christ's lead, asserting the preeminence as well as prevenience of Christ's meriting (I-II, q. 114, a. 6, co.). In the *Tertia pars*, however, occasional comments give way to more methodical treatment, and in the process Aquinas attests to the Christological shape of his teaching on grace. A few examples will need to suffice here to secure the point. Thus in q. 7 of the *Tertia pars*, Aquinas ascribes Christ's personal holiness to the fullness of the grace and the virtues that he has received, and makes this holiness the basis of his work for others; indeed, that is the purpose of his holiness, to bring others to correct relationship with God and to grow in that relationship. Christ's graced life, death, and resurrection are ordered to the salvation of others. That point is thematized in the following question (8), on Christ as the head of the spiritual body that is Church, and then explored in detail in the later questions of the treatise on Christ (III, qq. 27-59), on Christ's life and doctrine, on his passion and death, on the ways in which Christ's work on the cross can be figured, and on his resurrection. It is in relationship with Christ as their head, through faith and charity and the reception of his justice and holiness, that others can and will come to God as their end. In the *Tertia pars*, Aquinas also revisits predestination, first discussed in the *Summa*'s first part, now (in III, qq. 23-24) restating that teaching in explicitly and insistently Christological terms. Election is in Christ, and the adoption of others to be children of God is patterned on and based in the triune God's election of Jesus as savior. On this basis it is thus also possible (and necessary) to state the Christian life in explicitly Christological terms. The movement to God as beatifying end is a matter of conforming to Jesus. That conforming is made possible and fostered by the grace that comes in Christ; by that conforming, one prepares for entry into eternal life, for coming to share in the inheritance that is proper to the natural Son of God.[13]

Aquinas's teaching about human salvation in the *Summa* is rooted in Scripture and displays his sense of the scriptural teaching about the respective roles of God and the human person in that person's salvation.[14] God's revelation in Scripture is the basis and condition for this

---

13. For a more detailed discussion, see my "Jesus in the Moral Theology of Thomas Aquinas," *Journal of Medieval and Early Modern Studies* 42, no. 1 (2012): 13-33.

14. Lying behind the comments here is *ST* I, q. 1, a. 8, ad 2, in which Aquinas

account of humans in saving relation to God. Philosophy indeed makes its contribution: one can think here of the language of "habit," taken over from ethics, or of the borrowings from physics and metaphysics, in depicting human-divine relations in terms of "motion" and of second-ary and primary causality. Yet the borrowings from philosophy are per-formed critically, and philosophy is bent to Christian ends. Such is in-deed necessary; Aristotle knew nothing of the triune God who is the transcendent end of human beings by God's gracious determination, or of the grace and theological virtues that, as gifts of God, orient a person to the end that far transcends its natural powers, or of the God who, standing outside of the created order, can and does act effectively/effi-ciently in it. Aquinas has especially benefited, in his encounter with God's Word in Scripture, from his reading of St. Augustine. The teach-ing in the *Summa* stands in profound continuity with that of Augustine, especially the Augustine of the final writings, against the Massilians (and others later called "semi-Pelagian").[15] With Augustine, for Aquinas the faith that justifies is formed faith, faith as shaped by charity; this faith is a matter of both intellect and will and of correct orientation of the person to God. In both, the account of the human journey is placed in the context of God's willing and acting, of the expressing of God's love in election and the graces that follow on predestination. Predestina-tion is to eternal life, and God's will for humans is carried out by graces that are operative and cooperative. Operative graces, in the late Augus-tine and in the Aquinas of the *Summa,* work conversion to God and per-severance in grace; conversion and perseverance are simply gift. By coop-erative grace, merit is possible; for both Augustine and Aquinas, merit is

---

outlines a hierarchy of authority in sacred doctrine, and by extension the theology that pertains to it. At the top are the human authors of Scripture, to whom God has infallibly revealed (see *ST* I, q. 1, a. 9, ad 2) the truths needed for salvation. Others men-tioned in this passage from a. 8 are philosophers and the church doctors. The author-ity of the authors of Scripture and the doctors is intrinsic, for they are directly con-cerned with the saving truth that is revealed. That of the philosophers is extrinsic; their ideas, arguments, are of separate origin, originally tailored to other matters, and are brought into sacred doctrine and turned to Christian ends. The authority of the authors of Scripture is greatest, for it is to them that God has revealed saving truth. The authority of the church doctors, like that of the philosophers, is secondary and probable, although as intrinsic to sacred doctrine, their authority is greater than that of the philosophers.

15. I will expand on this point in the second section of this essay; and see n. 17 below.

the merit of the elect as they are in grace, and is of eternal life, which thus stands for both, primarily as gift but also as reward.

With this in mind, we can now turn to Barth and to a Barthian engagement with Aquinas.

In his teaching on reconciliation, Barth affirms both justification and sanctification, takes both seriously, and refuses to reduce the one to the other.[16] Justification is construed in declarative terms, as God's favorable disposition toward the sinner, forgiving her sins. Justification is by faith, which is the acceptance in trust of God's word of forgiveness. Sanctification involves acting, action out of faith and in obedience and love, and in accordance with God's will for people, for God's faithful covenant partner. Barth makes his own the *simul iustus et peccator,* which figures in his presentation of both justification and sanctification; in terms of the latter, there is thus a significant check on claiming too much for the good acts of the Christian. There is a strong Christological flavor to Barth's presentation of both justification and sanctification. Those who are justified and sanctified participate in Christ. Christ alone is truly just and holy. He does what humans of themselves cannot do. His justice and holiness are shared with others by their faith and their obedience, which he evokes. In their sanctification, others look to Christ; in their good actions and in the expression of their Christian freedom, they are responding to the call of God in Christ. Christ would seem to be the form and content of grace.

16. The following is based on *Church Dogmatics* IV/1 and IV/2. I have also consulted the following: Adam Neder, *Participation in Christ: An Entry into Karl Barth's* Church Dogmatics (Louisville: Westminster John Knox, 2009); Paul Dafydd Jones, *The Humanity of Christ: Christology in Karl Barth's* Church Dogmatics (London: T. & T. Clark, 2008); Gerald McKenny, *The Analogy of Grace: Karl Barth's Moral Theology* (Oxford: Oxford University Press, 2010); Bruce L. McCormack, "Grace and Being: The Role of God's Gracious Election in Karl Barth's Theological Ontology," in *The Cambridge Companion to Karl Barth,* ed. John Webster (Cambridge: Cambridge University Press, 2000), pp. 92-110; Bruce L. McCormack, "*Justitia Aliena:* Karl Barth in Conversation with the Evangelical Doctrine of Imputed Righteousness," in *Justification in Perspective: Historical Developments and Contemporary Challenges,* ed. Bruce L. McCormack (Grand Rapids: Baker Academic, 2006), pp. 167-96; George Hunsinger, "A Tale of Two Simultaneities: Justification and Sanctification in Calvin and Barth," in *Conversing with Barth,* ed. John C. McDowell and Mike Higton (Burlington, VT: Ashgate, 2004), pp. 68-89. I have benefited greatly from a vigorous discussion of my conference presentation with my colleague Jerry McKenny prior to the preparation of this essay for publication.

Broad areas of agreement between Barth and Aquinas would appear to exist. With Aquinas, Barth insists on the divine initiative, of God in Christ "going before" any human activity. The initiative in its different moments is indispensable. There will be no human actions apart from or prior to God's outreach to humans in Christ. It is God who opts for humans, determines Godself as the God for others; who establishes, sustains, and fulfills the covenant, in Christ; who offers forgiveness to sinful humans in Christ, and who calls for and makes possible their obedience in Christ. Humans do not take the "first step"; all human acts presuppose and are conditioned and based on God's acting. Correspondingly, Barth shares with Aquinas a resolutely anti-Pelagian stance. Humans do act, in their faith, obedience, and love. It is their action. But it is not only or even primarily theirs. All genuine human action, in sanctification as well as justification, is *response* to all that God does for humans in Christ; the response is itself made possible by and due to God.

There are nonetheless numerous differences between Barth and Aquinas, differences in form, content, tone. The following seem worthy of attention in our "unofficial dialogue." In each case I will indicate a possible criticism from Barth's perspective, and also gesture at a preliminary response from the side of Aquinas.

First, Aquinas lacks the *simul*. Aquinas's version of the Christian's life may at first glance appear too linear and too uncomplicated, imagining a progress along a line that is relatively straightforward. First the person is a sinner, then is justified, and then acts in holiness and grows in that. Another way of putting this is to suggest that in Aquinas the difference between justification and sanctification is blurred, and justification becomes too assimilated to sanctification. Is anyone in this life really just? Even when this just-making is ascribed to God's grace, that seems to be claiming much too much. Christ alone is truly just, and his justice is always needed to cover the sins of those who follow him. Humans remain very much unlike God and Christ while reconciled to God in Christ.

That Aquinas doesn't affirm the *simul* is indeed correct; he tends not to favor the paradoxical statement. Aquinas does assert a transformational view of justification, although not exclusively: he can also acknowledge its declarative aspects. But while he does think that justice is restored, both within the self and in relation to God, there are indications that he does not think that in this life the restoration, the being made just, is complete or total. We can refer here to his talk of the remnants of sin — which although not themselves sin, incline to sin and remain in the person who now stands right with God. Especially significant, I think, is his mature teaching on perseverance, taken over from Augustine.[17] The person healed and elevated by habitual grace remains subject to temptation, from without (we live in a fallen world) and from within; such is the consequence of sin that remains even in the justified. For the Aquinas of the *Summa,* even a person healed by habitual grace cannot overcome each and every temptation, of whatever source. The resisting of temptation requires additional grace — the grace of *auxilium,* of operative *auxilium,* given by God not as a reward but in accordance with God's salvific will for that person. More positively put, the operative grace of perseverance provides good intention anew, keeping the person moving toward God as beatifying end. The teaching about perseverance acknowledges the struggle that will mark the life of the justified; and success in the struggle is very much dependent on God's will and aid.

A second set of possible criticisms is expressed by Barth in a passage in which he addresses what B. Bartmann reports of the Catholic teaching of grace.[18] The passage is lengthy, close to five pages in small print, and is vigorous and self-descriptively polemical. It exhibits the main features of Barth's own understanding in terms of Christ and divine disposition toward humans, working explicitly from that perspective, and aims at exposing the gap that exists (in Barth's opinion) between the Romanist and evangelical doctrines of grace. In his report of Bartmann, Barth notes that Romanists do speak of grace as divine favor, thus locating grace in God as its source, but that they then introduce a series of fine distinctions, on kinds and categories of grace in

---

17. See *ST* I-II, q. 109, aa. 9-10. For the connections between the later Augustine and the Aquinas of the *Summa* when it comes to grace, see in general Henri Bouillard, *Conversion et grâce chez saint Thomas d'Aquin* (Paris: Aubier, 1944). For Aquinas's debt to the later Augustine in developing his own teaching about perseverance as gift, see my "'Perseverance' in 13th-Century Theology: The Augustinian Contribution," *Augustinian Studies* 22 (1991): 125-40. For Augustine's evolution on grace, see J. Patout Burns, *The Development of Augustine's Doctrine of Operative Grace* (Paris: Études Augustiniennes, 1980). As Burns observes, it is in the final writings that Augustine teaches the gratuity of perseverance, grounded in God's predestining will. Aquinas became acquainted with those writings, which had passed out of theological circulation by the end of the Carolingian period, prior to the composition of the *Summa's* treatise on grace.

18. See *CD* IV/1, §58, pp. 84-88.

the world and in humans. Many of the terms mentioned in the first section — habitual grace, grace as operative, grace as cooperative, grace as medicinal or healing, grace as elevating — appear in this rendering of Romanist teaching based on Bartmann, along with a few others that don't (the explicit distinction, in particular between grace as external, aligned with Christ and preaching about Christ, and grace as internal, which in Bartmann does the heavy lifting). There is much that is wrong and distressing in this Romanist teaching. The divisions of grace that Romanist doctrine introduces are abstractions. The doctrine ends up treating grace as something separate from God and Christ, even if Thomists affirm a preliminary unity of grace in God. That unity is dissipated in the multiplication of graces imagined in Roman doctrine. The doctrine ends up shifting the focus from God, from Christ, to humans, grace apparently now made a function of Christian anthropology. Grace becomes something created, something that stands apart from God, something that humans have and so hold as their own and can exploit. Grace is alienated from God and, in a word, domesticated. Here as elsewhere in the *Church Dogmatics,* Barth seems especially allergic to habitual grace, viewed resolutely as the endowment of some human and standing under that person's control. The Catholic teaching alleges a comprehensiveness, including of function, but cannot in the end disguise where the preferences lie: for the human rather than for God; for elevation rather than for forgiving; for the human who accomplishes and excels rather than for the human who acknowledges his/her abiding need.

These pages are stunning and thought-provoking. Is Barth right? In the Romanist teaching, has grace been divorced from God and from Christ, made into a commodity and relegated to a tool for extolling the human at the expense of God?

Whatever may be said of *Bartmann* and his teaching, it is not clear, however, that the criticisms extend to *Aquinas's* teaching on grace, despite the common terminology and the gestures. As reported by Barth, there would seem to be some significant differences between Bartmann and what we meet in Aquinas himself. Aquinas would not isolate the grace of *auxilium* from habitual grace, making it merely preparatory, as Bartmann apparently does; both habitual grace and *auxilium* are involved, in their own ways, in the movement of the Christian to God. Aquinas certainly would not drive a wedge between Christ and grace, marginalizing Christ or denying the Christic form of grace; this is evident from the *Summa*'s *Tertia pars* as well as the biblical commentaries in which Aquinas pursues participation in Christ.[19] In Aquinas, Christ is not a mere occasion of grace, ultimately arbitrary or dispensable, nor is Christ an external husk of what is much more important and decisive, the grace that acts interiorly. And Aquinas would certainly chafe at the language of "product" and "production" that Bartmann apparently uses, not least in discussing habitual grace. Such language does smack of commodification, and at bottom of alienation as well, alienating what God brings about from the God who acts. In Aquinas, habitual grace *is* something created, an accident perfecting the soul in its essence (*ST* I-II, q. 110, a. 2). It *is* granted to an individual, and it heals and elevates the person. But it is imprecise to refer to this grace as that person's possession, as if now it belongs to that person and it is left to that person to do what he or she wills. In this case, at least, the Giver is not separated from what is given. God remains active in habitual grace, just as God is active in the *auxilium* that goes with habitual grace, accomplishing God's will for that person, in disposing that person to the good and moving that person to good intention and good choice and execution. Who is the subject of the graced person's acts? In Aquinas, the answer is plural — the person, to be sure, but primarily God, in God's grace.

Barth's passage is rich and surely deserves more consideration. It calls, for one thing, for a reconsideration of the various graces in their different functions that Catholics imagine. Is this in fact mere abstraction, and all beside the point? Or might there be gains in such a depiction, allowing a more precise accounting, according to the biblical witness, of the different ways in which the God who saves engages and interacts with those who belong to God?

A third difficulty would have to do with what might be called the pedagogy of the text in Thomas's great *Summa,* meaning how he organizes and structures the writing and how he proceeds. At the least, this may be a concern over form, but may also, as suggested by the Bartmann analysis, be a concern about content. A striking feature of Barth's own procedure in discussing reconciliation is the preeminence of Christ throughout. There can be no meaningful talk of covenant, of

---

19. See, e.g., Daniel A. Keating, "Justification, Sanctification and Divinization in Thomas Aquinas," in *Aquinas on Doctrine: A Critical Introduction,* ed. Thomas G. Weinandy, Daniel A. Keating, and John P. Yocum (London: T. & T. Clark, 2004), pp. 139-58.

predestination, of justification, of sanctification, apart from Christ and Christ's acting. None of this occurs in a vacuum; all occurs in Christ. From this perspective, the talk about grace in the *Prima secundae* that largely (although not entirely) brackets Christ, deferring the discussion of Christ to the *Tertia pars,* will appear odd, and probably misdirected. What if someone read only the *Prima secundae,* and didn't read on to the *Tertia pars?* Might one come to think that Christ is to be set apart from grace, that grace has to do only incidentally with Christ, and that all that is crucial about grace can be known apart from Christ? This may be the temptation to which Bartmann, as rendered by Barth, has fallen prey.

The concern is serious and should be taken seriously. In provisional response, one can note that Aquinas doesn't drive a wedge between grace and Christ. We aren't supposed to stop reading, when it comes to grace, at the end of q. 114 of the *Prima secundae.* That discussion has been anticipated by what comes earlier, and should be linked to that, and continues in what follows. It is completed and receives its full form in the reflections on Christ that constitute the *Tertia pars.* It is relevant to observe as well that the *Summa* is not Aquinas's only writing. He has others, not least the biblical commentaries that constitute about a quarter of the extant corpus. There, as led by Scripture, he can write at length on conformity to Christ and participation in Christ, as prompted by the biblical text.

Aquinas is familiar with a distinction: between the order of discovery and the order of the discipline, between coming to know something and conveying that to another.[20] The distinction seems helpful here. It is in Scripture that the truths needed for salvation are revealed, where the triune God who is beginning and end is proclaimed, where one learns of Christ and his grace, and about authentic human exis-

20. For the distinction as it figures in Trinitarian discourse, see Gilles Emery, O.P., "*Theologia* and *Dispensatio:* The Centrality of the Divine Missions in St. Thomas's Trinitarian Theology," *The Thomist* 74 (2010): 546-50. In terms of the Trinity, first one comes to know of the Trinity through the witness of Scripture to the triune God's acts in the world; then there is reflection on that activity, which leads to formulations of the inner life of the Trinity, manifested in those acts in the world; and finally there is a representation of the activities of the triune God in the world, as grounded and based in that inner life. In sum, in Aquinas the immanent and economic Trinity are identical, and comments about the inner life that might at first glance seem abstract and speculative are closely connected to the depiction and apprehension of the triune God in the world.

tence and purpose. In the biblical commentaries the two orders, of discovery and of the discipline, agree, as Aquinas follows in the commentary the biblical ordering, teasing out and restating God's message in Scripture. In a writing such as the *Summa,* the two orders diverge — not that the order of teaching is put at odds with scriptural truth, but in order to re-present it in a way that will contribute to its further understanding. The main truths of revelation are treated discretely, each plumbed for their fuller meaning; these truths are also discussed in their relations to each other, to show how they mutually inform each other. Here, the order of teaching presupposes the order of discovery, and offers an approach that is meant to increase the grasp, intellectually and existentially, of what has been discovered in Scripture and held dear. Again, the doctrine of grace is not restricted to the *Prima secundae.* It is discussed at length there, but the discussion continues into the *Tertia pars.* As in other doctrines pursued in the writing, the discussion is systematic, methodical, and discursive, and each layer of analysis is required for the full account.

For Barth, there likely would be a cognate concern about the use of nonbiblical and originally non-Christian categories in positing Christian truth. Does such use not inevitably distort God-human relations, making God subject to human categories, with all their limitations, quite inappropriate to the God proclaimed in Scripture? The worry might be made more patent by returning to an instance invoked in the first section of this essay — the roles according to Aquinas of *auxilium* and habitual grace in conversion. Does matter (that is, the human person) need to be prepared for the introduction of form (that is, habitual grace)? Such might be the case when water heated to its boiling point eventually begins to steam; but is that really what human-divine relations are about? The use of physical or metaphysical categories can indeed be jarring, but it is, however, important not to miss the main theological point in their application, as in this particular example. To repeat what was stated earlier in this connection: in invoking *auxilium* and habitual grace in this way in stating conversion, Aquinas intends to show that the initiative lies with God, not with the human; that conversion is not a human accomplishment; and that God's acting is intentional, having to do with salvation, with what God intends for humans and acts to bring about.

There is, finally, the idea of *merit,* which Aquinas affirms but Barth denies. Barth offers a thoughtful account of human acting in sanctifica-

tion. He can stress that the Christian life involves more than mortification; it is also a matter of regeneration, of a newness of life that issues in
new, good acts. In looking to Christ, the Christian will do good acts in
obedience and love; such acts of Christian freedom can be genuinely
good, and are obligatory. Barth invokes in this regard the "praise of
works," with praise to be taken in a twofold sense.[21] These acts praise
God, as done to the glory of God; and significantly, they receive God's
praise. But Barth will not allow talk of "merit." Why not? For Barth,
there is a sinful element to the affirmation of merit. Claiming merit, asserting the value of what people do, is to claim too much for people, to
ascribe them too much importance in their salvation, as if what people
do is decisive in achieving salvation. Affirming merit, in this telling, is to
shift the focus away from God and Christ and onto the person, who
imagines that she can manipulate God and put God in her debt. Merit
is thus a matter of human self-aggrandizement.

Barth's concern, of course, has a history; merit was a flashpoint
for Catholic-Protestant polemic in the Reformation. But it is worth
asking whether the concern reaches to the teaching on merit advanced
by Aquinas. *Can* a teaching on merit do what Barth says it does, exalt
the human at the expense of God? Yes, of course; as Aquinas observes
in another context, there is nothing so good that human malice cannot
distort it.[22] *Have* teachings on merit had that effect? Indeed, some undoubtedly have, as history teaches us. *Need* a teaching on merit exalt
the human, ascribe a false righteousness to the human, and make too
much of the human? Perhaps not. In the *Summa*, Aquinas would appear sensitive to Barth's concern, specifying a human contribution to
salvation that is real without making too much of it or in the process
shifting the glory away from God.[23] As described earlier, Aquinas may
have advanced a teaching on merit that is in the end fully compatible
with Barth's praise of works, in the double sense.

---

21. See *CD* IV/2, §66, pp. 584ff.
22. *ST* III, q. 3, a. 8, ad 1.
23. Recall *ST* I-II, q. 114, a. 1, ad 2, cited at n. 11 above.

Reconciliation in Karl Barth and the New Life of the Justified Sinner in Christ

Amy E. Marga

Introduction

Despite the now well-regarded and revolutionary study by Hans Küng pointing to the common ground between the theology of Karl Barth and Roman Catholicism on the doctrine of justification,[1] as well as the ecumenical efforts between Lutherans and Catholics that resulted in the historic *Joint Declaration on the Doctrine of Justification* in 1999, many Protestants still point to justification and grace as a fundamental ground for disagreement between the two church bodies.[2] Indeed on this particular issue, when taken at face value, the deeply Reformed Karl Barth and Thomas Aquinas, the Father of Modern Catholicism, make somewhat strange bedfellows.

However, as this essay will demonstrate, there are some surprising and deep affinities between the theologies of Thomas and Barth regarding grace and justification. Given the presence of convergences,

---

1. Hans Küng, *Justification: The Doctrine of Karl Barth and a Catholic Reflection* (Philadelphia: Westminster, 1964).

2. The literature analyzing the unity and difference between Catholics and Protestants since the *Joint Declaration* is extensive. Some examples of Protestant assessments of and dialogue around the situation include (but are not limited to) Anthony N. S. Lane, *Justification by Faith in Catholic-Protestant Dialogue* (New York: T. & T. Clark, 2002); George Tavard, *Justification: An Ecumenical Study* (Mahwah, NJ: Paulist, 1983); Bruce L. McCormack, ed., *Justification in Perspective: Historical Developments and Contemporary Challenges* (Grand Rapids: Baker Academic, 2006); Wayne C. Stumme, ed., *The Gospel of Justification in Christ: Where Does the Church Stand Today?* (Grand Rapids: Eerdmans, 2006).

this essay will argue that the enduring differences between the Angelic Doctor and the Swiss Reformed theologian do not rest, as is customarily thought, in the way grace operates in the life of the person per se but rather in the way the justified sinner relates to the new history of one's existence, which is found in and mediated through Jesus Christ.

Karl Barth was by no means a despiser of Catholic theology or the theology of Thomas Aquinas. It was Barth himself, decried by leading Protestant thinkers like Georg Wobbermin and Emmanuel Hirsch, who began to pry open the centuries-long locked door between Catholicism and Reformation theology through his ongoing reflection on the paucity of resources within liberal Protestantism for a truly "theological" perspective in the modern world and his serious engagement with Catholic contemporaries such as Erich Przywara, Robert Grosche, and later Hans Urs von Balthasar and Hans Küng. Nor did Barth avoid the "scholastic" theology of Thomas Aquinas. In the winter of 1929 while serving as professor in the Catholic University city of Münster, Westphalia, he conducted a seminar on the theology of Thomas Aquinas and offered further seminars on this towering Catholic figure later in his teaching career. Although the seminar focused its attention on Book I of the *Summa theologiae,* the theology of Thomas was a topic that had interested Barth since at least 1924 when he began reading Thomas Aquinas with Erik Peterson — a practice, continued on his own, in which he read voraciously and eclectically through Thomas's works. Despite the criticisms of Thomas explored by Barth and his students during the 1929 Münster seminar, he wondered out loud whether the "traditional arsenal" of Protestant "weapons" were enough to prevail against this "master" of theology on the Catholic side.[3]

Not only did Barth read Thomas Aquinas with a seriousness and openness that was uncharacteristic for his generation,[4] but later readers of Barth's theology would point out that he conducted his theolog-

---

3. Karl Barth's comments as recorded in student protocols from the "Systematische Seminar im Wintersemester 1928/1929. Thomas von Aquin: *Summa theologiae* (I. Büch)," unpublished typed manuscript (photocopy), Karl Barth Archive, Basel, Switzerland, p. 250.

4. See Barth's remark about watching new developments in the Catholic theology of his day and his comment to Eduard Thurneysen that they ought not to ignore what might possibly be "voices from the real una sancta." Karl Barth and Eduard Thurneysen, *Barth-Thurneysen Briefwechsel,* vol. 2: *1921-1930,* ed. Eduard Thurneysen (Zürich: Theologischer Verlag Zürich, 1974), p. 224.

ical reflection with a kind of freedom and curiosity that characterized the Angelic Doctor himself. Hans Urs von Balthasar, perhaps still regarded as one of the most penetrating analyzers of Barth's theology, remarked that "we would have to go back to Thomas Aquinas to find a similar spirit: free from the constraints of narrowness and tenseness combining intelligence with just the right touch."[5] Barth would engage the medieval master throughout his *Church Dogmatics* and share several fundamental building blocks of the doctrine of reconciliation with him.

Many of the architectural pillars of Barth's understanding of grace and justification share a common concern and a common ordering with Thomas, including aspects of how grace is a movement and action from God and how it is operative in the lives of human beings. A broad survey of Barth's doctrine of reconciliation as he expounds it in the *Church Dogmatics* IV/1, paragraphs 58 and 61, brings some of these compatibilities to light. The first part of this essay will investigate the common ground that lay between Barth and Thomas on reconciliation and grace. The second half of the essay will deal with Barth's major Christological concern when it comes to grace and reconciliation and how this particular concern indicates the significant divergences between the two theologians.

Convergences

Barth's treatment of the doctrine of reconciliation displays three important convergences with that of Thomas. First, both thinkers work in the broad terms of *grace*. The fact that justification is not the dominant aspect or even first principle of Barth's treatment of the doctrine of reconciliation already gives his treatment of the topic an overall shape that is similar to that of Thomas. Second, both Barth and Thomas make distinctions between justification, sanctification, and vocation. That is, both thinkers work with an overall understanding of grace that contains an initial moment of active grace upon the human (justification), a subsequent act of grace that sustains the justified sinner (sanctification), and a further aspect of grace that supports each

---

5. Hans Urs von Balthasar, *The Theology of Karl Barth,* trans. John Drury (New York: Holt, Reinhart & Winston, 1971), p. 23.

individual's journey toward God (vocation in Barth's terms). Moreover, both thinkers tie grace directly to the being of God. Each of these aspects will now be examined in turn.

Barth does not place the doctrine of justification at the top of his treatment of reconciliation, or even at the center, as Lutheran dogmatic theology does.[6] While justification is certainly a primary act of God in reconciliation, it is not a controlling dogmatic locus that determines the treatment of the other areas of reconciliation. Nor is it, as Barth clearly states, *the* decisive doctrine that divides Protestants and Catholics.[7] Rather, the doctrine of reconciliation is determined and controlled by Barth's understanding of grace in the event of Jesus Christ, where reconciliation happens in "three forms," namely justification, sanctification, and vocation. In that Barth chooses to speak in terms of grace to signify the movement and revelation of God in reconciliation rather than in terms of justification, he lays common ground with the theology of Thomas, who also does not discuss reconciliation primarily in terms of justification but in terms of grace as well. The fundamental question regarding grace in Thomas involves questions about its necessity, its cause, and its effect. He only takes up the topic of justification at the conclusion of a long discussion on grace.[8] This parallels Barth's order of thought in the *Church Dogmatics* IV/1. There, Barth too first deals with the topic of the "Justification of Man" (§61) only after he conducts a general survey about reconciliation and grace

6. See Barth's comment on this topic in *Unterricht in der christlichen Religion,* vol. 1: *Prolegomena 1924* (Zürich: Theologischer Verlag Zürich, 1985), §13, pp. 300ff., esp. pp. 362-66; and *Unterricht in der christlichen Religion,* vol. 2: *Die Lehre von Gott/Die Lehre vom Menschen 1924-1925* (Zürich: Theologischer Verlag Zürich, 1990), §19, p. 214; §20, p. 302. In these seminal lectures, Barth points to the basic Lutheran tendency to make one material principle — justification by faith alone — the formal principle of all dogmatic reflection. This dogmatic tradition is still carried on today by Lutheran theologians such as Oswald Bayer. See, for example, his *Theology the Lutheran Way,* trans. Jeffrey G. Silcock and Mark C. Mattes (Grand Rapids: Eerdmans, 2007). For Barth there is no "principle" of dogmatic reflection, only the movement of the Word of God.

7. *CD* IV/1, p. 525 small print. Throughout, all citations of the *CD* refer to *Church Dogmatics,* 4 vols. in 13 parts, ed. G. W. Bromiley and T. F. Torrance (Edinburgh: T. & T. Clark, 1936-75).

8. See *ST* I-II, qq. 109-14, "The Treatise on Grace." Throughout, I have made use of the Blackfriars edition: St. Thomas Aquinas, *Summa theologiae,* 60 vols. (Cambridge: Blackfriars/New York: McGraw-Hill, 2006 [1964-73]). Hereafter abbreviated *ST.* "The Treatise on Grace" is contained in vol. 30 (1a2ae. 106-14), "The Gospel of Grace," trans. Cornelius Ernst, O.P. (New York: Cambridge University Press, 2006 [1971]).

(§58). Clearly, both thinkers conceive of reconciliation in the broader terms of *grace* as the stance and movement of God toward the human.[9]

The clear distinction between justification, sanctification, and vocation constitutes a second, deep affinity with the thought of Thomas. Barth names these categories in terms of the three "forms" of God's grace that come to the human in Christ. The content of reconciliation, thus, is not justification in and of itself but rather the knowledge of Christ, who is none other than God's own being — incarnate, humbled, and at the same time, very man, who is exalted. This divine humiliation and exaltation are wrapped up in one person, the mediator Jesus Christ. Knowledge of Christ means three things. First, it means the knowledge of sin as pride, sloth, and falsehood and how these dimensions of sin are answered by God in Christ through justification, sanctification, and vocation.[10] Second, it means the knowledge of the Holy Spirit as the One who gathers, sends, and builds up the community. Third, reconciliation means the knowledge of the being of the Christian in Christ in faith, love, and hope. Barth outlines the actions of God upon the human in Jesus Christ; then he follows up with a discussion of the ramifications of the event of grace in justification on the life of the community and in the personal existence of the justified individual.

Justification as the first form of grace is a direct answer to the pride of sin. In justification, God pronounces a verdict upon the old, sinful human, a verdict that Jesus Christ receives for us. While Hans Küng has forcefully argued that the doctrine of justification itself is not the divisive shoal upon which the ship of ecumenical connections between Barth's theology and Catholicism might crash, Barth's description of justification's effect on the sinner does lead us into his deeply Christological understanding of grace and the new life of the human; it is this Archimedean point in Jesus Christ that indicates a significant difference between him and Thomas. We will return to this later.

A clear affinity with Thomas lies in the second form of grace, sanctification, which moves the justified sinner into active resistance

---

9. In between these two paragraphs lies a good portion of Barth's Christology. He lays out the details of the work of Jesus Christ as "The Way of the Son into the Far Country" (§59.1); "The Judge Judged in Our Place" (§59.2); and "The Verdict of the Father" (§59.3). After his discussion on "The Justification of Man" in §61, Barth concludes the volume with the work of the Holy Spirit as the One who gathers and is the ontological ground for Christian community.

10. See *CD* IV/1, pp. 145-46, 108-10.

against temptation and concrete acts of love. In Barth's order of thought, it is God's direct and gracious answer to sin as sloth. Sanctification "converts" or places the justified sinner under the divine direction, that is, under God's command, ordinance, and claim. It is a free movement of oneself into God's direction. Barth's description of the grace of sanctification, which could have easily come from the pen of Thomas, allows us to overcome the sin of sloth and continue in our journey in freedom. In the grace of sanctification, "instead of causing himself to fall [the human] can stand and proceed along the way which God has appointed him as the way of true freedom, in this way, rendering obedience."[11] At work here is a sustaining function of grace that aids the justified sinner in one's path in faith, a path that is characterized by Christian acts of love, which "is a being in a co-operation of service with God."[12] It constitutes the basis of all ethics. Such a description converges on many levels with Thomas's understanding of habitual grace that sustains us on our journey. In sanctifying grace, we respond to God through concrete acts of "Christian love," which is "the human response to [God's] direction"[13] and "the active human recognition of [the] proof of the love of God."[14] Sanctification is not a move that compromises the power or authority of justification in Barth's mind. Rather, it is the "necessary consequence" of justification.[15] Barth describes this form of grace as one that gives us direction and strength. In this form of grace, the justified sinner is placed into "the place and kingdom which already surrounds him, in which he is already placed, in which he has only to find himself."[16] Similar language can be seen in Thomas, who states that "the movement of the human mind towards the enjoyment of the good which is God is the act proper to charity."[17] The only caveat to the apparent and deep compatibility with Thomas lies in the fact that Barth will never speak of grace as becoming an inhering *characteristic* of the human soul. He does not use any language to

11. *CD* IV/1, p. 146.

12. *CD* IV/1, p. 113.

13. *CD* IV/1, p. 102. Barth takes this further by claiming that "in general terms Christian love is *the active human recognition* of this proof of the love of God" (*CD* IV/1, p. 103, emphasis mine).

14. *CD* IV/1, p. 103.

15. *CD* IV/1, p. 101.

16. *CD* IV/1, p. 100.

17. *ST* I-II, q. 114, a. 4, co.

suggest a form of infused or habitual grace. However, as with Thomas, Barth does work with a form of grace that sustains us against sloth and *stays with us* in our freedom as human agents and reconciled sinners on our life journeys.[18]

The third form of grace is vocation, or calling, which is a direct answer to the sin of falsehood. The Christian's calling is God's decision to give the human being a teleological direction to his or her life *in time* so that even in *this life span* we can acquire meaning, purpose, and a perspective on our existence based on the activity of God. Barth's description here parallels in a certain sense the Roman Catholic understanding of grace as a healing, exalting, teleological event. However, Barth explicitly roots this in Jesus Christ as the exalted human being. The grace of God that is shown to us in Jesus Christ ushers in a new subject, who is true humanity and a newly created being; God creates a new existence for the reconciled sinner. In this way, Barth's description of the exaltation of the human in Christ communicates a concept similar to the Thomistic concept of healing and elevating grace. We experience healing and new life in Christ, and we can live into the new humanity that Christ has received for us. As with sanctification, the justified sinner gets turned back to God, or "converted" to God, in this instance, through the *calling* of the Christian, when God equips the human to be the bearer of God's promises in the world. This promise of calling is the *preservation* of fellowship in the covenant. This third moment of reconciliation corresponds to what Barth calls earlier the "state of hope."[19]

Again, there are apparent and deep compatibilities with the thought patterns of Thomas here. By self-consciously including the dimension of vocation in his doctrine of reconciliation, Barth sees himself as going above and beyond Reformation theology, which usually relegates the grace of God shown in vocation to an implicit aspect of the larger event of reconciliation rather than naming it as an explicit form and event of grace that sustains the justified sinner and gives life meaning and perspective. Along with his reflections on sanctification, moving above and beyond the Reformation in this case is a step in the

18. Barth writes, "In Jesus Christ, God has created a final and indestructible fellowship between Himself and all men, between all men and Himself, a fellowship which is final and indestructible because it is based upon His own interposition and guaranteed by it" (*CD* I/1, p. 102).

19. *CD* IV/1, p. 601.

direction of Catholic commitments that describe God's act of reconciling grace from the long view of the whole trajectory of human life.

One further way that Barth and Thomas share convergences in their respective doctrines of reconciliation, next to the description of grace as laid out in the above paragraphs, is seen in the way they both tie grace to God's own being. Barth frames this discussion by way of naming the three "Christological aspects" of reconciliation, namely, Christ's divinity, Christ's humanity, and Christ as the Mediator. Grace as grounded in Christ's divinity means it is grounded in God's being as God, namely, grounded in the total and eternal freedom that is God's alone. It is a movement of God that is not necessitated by any external law or event. It operates in the world and upon the human sinner freely and newly and strangely every morning.[20] As grounded in God's uniquely divine freedom, this aspect of grace demonstrates God's glory. It serves God's glory to not let the sinful human creature perish or be punished for breaking the covenant. God has chosen to glorify God's own being precisely by *rescuing* the covenant-breaker, *not* by punishing or abolishing the covenant. In this sense, there is no competition between grace and glory, for grace is a servant and sign of God's glory.

Further, it is a servant and sign of God's *choice* to be boundless in God's faithfulness to the creature. Barth's logic runs as follows: those who understand the act of reconciliation as a consequence of and servant to the constancy and glory of God in the covenant will see that God's act is an act of grace, further that the covenant is a covenant of grace, and therefore, that God's election is an election of grace.[21] This grace and glory of God is a demonstration that God has crossed the abyss from non-sin into the vacuum and annihilating threat of sin. Consequently, when the rebellious human sinner knows this grace of God in Christ's divinity, he or she is *converted* and turned back to God despite himself or herself.[22] From the perspective of Christ's divinity, then, the movement and activity of grace are absolutely consistent with God's eternal act in election. As Barth puts it, God must be understood "as the One who constantly surpasses Himself in His constancy and faithfulness, and yet who never compromises Himself, who does a new

20. *CD* IV/1, p. 84.
21. *CD* IV/1, p. 80.
22. *CD* IV/1, p. 83.

thing and yet does everything in order, who could not be more power-
fully holy and righteous than when by His Word and in His Son He
calls us who are His enemies His children, when He causes us to be His
children, because in His freedom to do that He is truly the Lord."[23]

Similar words could have come from the pen of Thomas. The
constancy of God and the manifestation of God's eternal glory in grace
shown to the sinner constitute the "beginning" and ground of grace in
the theology of Thomas as well. For Thomas, all grace originates in
God's eternal being and action as the One who creates, loves, moves,
has a plan for, and predestines all of creation, especially intelligent beings like humans. As Thomas states, God loves humans with a love that
God has in and for God's own being, "by which [God] draws the rational creature above its natural condition to have a part in the divine
goodness. And it is by this love that [God] is said to love someone simply speaking; because by this love God, simply speaking, wills for the
creature that eternal good which is *himself.*"[24] Further, Thomas gives a
full treatment of grace as a movement of God in which God *chooses* to
bind God's being to the human in order to bring all things into align-
ment with God's own perfection. Thomas states that "[God] intends
only to communicate His perfection, which is His goodness; while every creature intends to acquire its own perfection, which is the likeness
of the divine perfection and goodness. Therefore the divine goodness is
the end of all things."[25]

Grace, then, for both thinkers, is grounded in God's very being, a
being who in a primal, uniquely divine act *elects* to be in relationship
with the creatures whom God loves. The grounding of grace in God's
eternal being by no means compromises God's glory or perfection in
any way. Rather, grace becomes the truest and deepest indicator of
God's eternal character. It reinforces the uniquely divine act of grace
that consists of choosing to live in communion with God's creatures.

Another dimension to grace as the giving of God's own being is
brought to light when God's ongoing presence to the believer is considered. Both Thomas and Barth describe the "giving" of grace as an act in
which God gives God's very self to the beloved creature. This may come
as a surprise, since a popular Protestant argument against the Roman

23. *CD* IV/1, p. 82.
24. *ST* I-II, q. 110, a. 1, co. (emphasis mine).
25. *ST* I, q. 44, a. 4, co.

Catholic understanding of grace is precisely that Thomistic theology seems to conceive of grace as that which is *given* rather than as a *giving of God's being* to the creature. Indeed, on this point, Barth raises this typical Protestant argument against the Catholic teaching in his discussion of inhering grace *(gratia interna)* and habitual grace *(gratia habitualis)*.[26] This polemic turns on two aspects of the question: first, whether or not God's grace is a subjective event that eventually becomes a characteristic of an individual's soul, and second, whether or not God's own presence immediately is and must be with reconciled sinners all along the paths of their lives.

Regarding inhering grace, Protestants typically insist that God's grace is always something that is acted *upon* us externally rather than bestowed so that it grows *within us*. It is always and ever objective and external to the human soul. Indeed, Barth himself will never speak of grace as a characteristic of the human soul nor as something that "inheres" within a human person. But he does argue, as shown above, that there is a form of grace that sustains and calls the justified sinner along life's journey.

Likewise, a close reading of Thomas shows that he holds to a view of grace that is not far from the Protestant view. Thomas argues that grace always remains an objective act of God separate from the human, even as grace has subjective effects on the person's character and life by being at work in the human soul. He lays out the explicit function of grace as an *auxilium* (in the forms of *gratia increata, gratia externa,* and *gratia actualis)*[27] that is basically identical to the external grace that Protestants argue for. This *auxilium* grace is a "conversional" grace that moves us from an existence in sin into new life. The concept of *auxilium* grace in Thomas's theology directly parallels Barth's description of grace in justification as that which moves or transitions us from death to life. Both Barth and Thomas work with an understanding that there is a grace that "converts" and moves us toward God. Likewise, while Thomas maintains a typical "Protestant" concept of grace that is continually external to us, and continually works upon sinners to reconcile us to God, Barth maintains a typical "Catholic" understanding of

26. See *CD* IV/1, pp. 84-88.

27. See Joseph Wawrykow, "Grace," in *The Theology of Thomas Aquinas,* ed. Rik van Nieuwenhove and Joseph Wawrykow (Notre Dame: University of Notre Dame Press, 2005), pp. 192-221.

grace that operates to accompany and sustain the reconciled sinner throughout one's life. Just as Thomas's understanding of perseverance in grace not only depends upon habitual grace but also requires external, or *auxilium* grace, that is, God's continual presence, Barth's understanding of God who gives God's very self includes a divine self-giving that not only justifies externally but sustains and calls with particular subjectivity and internality as well.

The second dimension of the typical Protestant argument against a Catholic notion of "inhering grace" insists that God's own being must be *constantly* and *immediately* present to us as the mover of all that we do in faith. Protestants often see the Catholic concept of "inhering grace" as the giving of a "possession" or a "bestowal" that somehow allows God to relate to the creature in a non-immediate, non-self-giving fashion. The Protestant argument sees the Catholic concept of grace as endowing the creature with a capacity that we simply cannot have, leading to the consequence of no further human need for God to be immediately present to us. Another way to express this divide is to say that Protestants do not let the sinner get beyond the moment of "conversion" to a more stable, integrated understanding of how grace functions in the Christian life. Protestants, including Barth on many occasions, especially in his earlier theology, see the sinner as a constant beggar and beginner who can never move into a place where grace operates within the realm of individual decisions, personalities, character, that is, in our will or our soul. In other words, in a popular version of the Protestant understanding of grace, we are constantly at the conversion "stage."

However, a close reading of Thomas's discussion on grace and justification in the *Summa theologiae* shows that this argument misrepresents Thomas's own view on how God's own being is present within the grace that operates in our wills and souls. Throughout Thomas's work on grace, we see him at every turn insisting that "divine assistance" is necessary for us to act.[28] He shows consistently that it is God's own *being* who continually "moves" us in and within the state of grace.[29] Throughout Thomas's treatment of grace, there is a sense of the immediacy of God to us, a very close presence of God to the human. Therefore, despite the popular Protestant argument against the

28. *ST* I-II, q. 109, a. 1, ad 3; a. 6.
29. See, for example, *ST* I-II, q. 109, a. 6.

Catholic "internal" or "inhering" grace, a close reading of Thomas shows that the two thinkers are not far apart when it comes to understanding the giving of grace as the giving of God's own being to the sinner, which moves the sinner from one way of being to another. Both are committed to the immediate and necessary presence of God's own being to reconciled sinners as they grow in faith and Christian love.

When it comes to certain particulars of how grace operates, there are important concerns and configurations of grace that are common to the understanding of reconciliation in both Barth and Thomas.

The convergences that have been laid out above demonstrate a real and substantial affinity between the thought of Thomas and Barth on reconciliation and grace. Both thinkers conceive of grace as that which is external to the sinner, and which "converts" the sinner from rebel to reconciled. Both argue for a form of grace that sustains the reconciled sinner throughout a deeper movement into grace, even though Barth never speaks of this sustaining grace in terms of inhering, or inhabiting, as it is done in Thomas and Roman Catholic theology. Finally, both argue that the giving of grace is God's giving of God's own being in that grace — a giving that is rooted in God's character as God, and in God's uniquely divine choice to be in relationship with God's creatures. Such unmistakable parallels leave the impression that even though Barth himself never expressed it, he was deeply influenced by the theology of Thomas and the pieces of the *Summa* that he had been reading and revisiting for decades. Perhaps Barth never did let himself sink too deeply into the Protestant ground, as a comment from his early days suggests, but rather allowed himself to be as open as possible to what Catholicism had to offer.[30]

Divergences

At the same time, even though Barth and Thomas share commitments regarding the operation of grace in the life of the sinner, and its expression of the presence of God's own being, there are stubborn differences

---

30. See the remark by Barth to his circle of friends in a letter from February 5, 1924, where he comments that they should guard against planting their feet too deeply in the "ground" of "Protestantism." *Barth-Thurneysen Briefwechsel*, vol. 2: *1921-1930*, ed. Eduard Thurneysen (Zürich: Theologischer Verlag Zürich, 1974), p. 224.

in the ontology of grace that divide the two theologians. Following Barth in his polemic against the numerous categories of grace within Catholic thought leads into the heart of his differences with Thomas.

In and of themselves, Barth's typically Protestant objections to the Roman Catholic understanding of grace do not constitute the divide between his theology and that of Thomas, but they do serve to illuminate the Christological profile of his doctrine of reconciliation.[31] They are objections he consistently waged against Catholicism, even from early in his career, regarding the way it divides up the concept of grace into what appears to be discrete categories. These categories of grace have correspondence to God's own action on the one side and to the natural, creaturely capabilities of humanity on the other. The categories range from God's action *(gratia increata)* with its corresponding grace in human action *(gratia creata),* to the grace of God that heals us *(gratia medicinalis)* and the corresponding grace that elevates the human *(gratia elevans),* from the grace given to humans by God as we need it *(gratia sufficiens)* and the corresponding grace that works with natural human capacities to help the graced individual act in order to do the good *(gratia efficax).* Prompted by the presence of categories of grace and the variety of names for it, Barth's objection has to do with the suggestion that sometimes grace is fully and purely an act of God, and sometimes fully a legitimate characteristic of humanity. The divisions in grace suggest that it is "first of all" God's grace and then "also our grace."[32] Relativizing the unity of grace in this way confuses divine and human actions, which are always to be distinguished.

This objection is in fact one that Barth rehearsed often against Roman Catholic theology. It was an important aspect of the argument that he waged against the Jesuit Erich Przywara, who visited his sem-

---

31. It seems that for whatever reason, for the purposes of the discussion in *CD* IV/1, Barth did not return to the work of Thomas himself but to the work of Catholic dogmatician Bernhard Bartmann and his 1929 *Dogmatisches Handbuch,* vol. 2, as his source for information on Catholic teaching on grace. Indeed, Bartmann's treatment of grace is accurately reflective of Thomas's own work (see *ST* I-II, "The Treatise on Grace"). It is not too surprising that Barth would have leaned heavily on Bartmann for his information here. Bartmann's theological volumes had been part of Barth's library and resources since early in his career and were used in his Göttingen Dogmatic lectures. Bartmann seemed to have been favored by Barth for faithfully and accurately representing Catholic teaching of the time.

32. *CD* IV/1, p. 84.

inar on Thomas, given in Münster in 1929. In those years, Barth polemicized against Przywara's use of the *analogia entis,* claiming that it places the divine and human upon the same plane of "being," thus confusing divine and human action and obscuring the fact that grace is always the initiative and possession of God alone. Such diffusion in grace can end up "domesticating"[33] grace, snatching it from the free hand of God and placing it in the hands of the human creature. In the words from his 1929 lecture on "Fate and Idea in Theology," which can be seen as part of a lengthy response to the earlier theology of Przywara, Barth remarks, "Grace . . . always encounters the human knower as *transforming* grace," for in relation to God, the human is never and nowhere the "already graced."[34] In a question regarding operative and cooperative grace *(gratia operans* and *gratia cooperans),* Barth asks in typical Protestant fashion: How do the work of God and the world of humanity ever come to stand on the same level so that they can mutually limit and condition each other?[35]

If grace truly *is* Jesus Christ, his Person and history, then the division of grace seems, in Barth's eyes, to dispute and obfuscate the simple truth that God's grace comes to the human in unified fashion in Jesus Christ. "The heart and guiding principle of the Romanist doctrine of grace," says Barth, "is the negation of the unity . . . of grace as [God's] grace in Jesus Christ."[36] For example, he asks, is external grace *(gratia externa)* only a "moral" type of grace in which faith forms by way of Christ as an example or moral guide? In another example regarding the subcategory of healing grace *(gratia medicinalis),* Barth asks, once we experience this healing, do we no longer need Christ in an urgent and immediate way?[37] His questions reveal his suspicion that there is a "higher" grace above Christ lurking in the category of the *gratia sanitatis,* which is

---

33. See, for example, *The Epistle to the Romans,* trans. Edwyn C. Hoskyns (New York: Oxford University Press, 1968), pp. 331-32.

34. Karl Barth, "Fate and Idea in Theology," in *The Way of Theology in Karl Barth,* ed. Martin Rumscheidt (Allison Park, PA: Pickwick, 1986), pp. 25-62 (here: translation mine, italics mine). For an analysis of how this particular lecture, along with two others that Barth gave in 1929, constitute a sustained response to Barth's encounter with Erich Przywara, see my volume, *Karl Barth's Dialogue with Catholicism in Göttingen and Münster: Its Significance for His Doctrine of God* (Tübingen: Mohr Siebeck, 2009), esp. pp. 136-52.

35. *CD* IV/1, pp. 85-86.

36. *CD* IV/1, p. 84.

37. *CD* IV/1, pp. 84-85.

defined as the grace given to Adam before the Fall. If such a grace was given, Barth reasons, it must come from another God than the one who elected the *fallen* human being in Christ from eternity.[38] He then goes on to criticize Catholic doctrine for being riddled with several "fatal preferences"[39] for the subjective categories of grace. Even though Catholic doctrine affirms and argues for a unified grace in Christ, it in fact *prefers* the "internal grace," "habitual grace," "cooperating grace," and "elevating grace" within us rather than the actual, external, healing, operating grace of Christ himself that is mediated to us. He perceives that Catholic doctrine makes the subjective side of grace more "real" than the Person and history of Christ himself. Rather than seeing the various forms of internal grace as only having the potential to be present, they seem to be more real and more actual than *Christ's* existence in grace itself.

Barth deepens his argument for the Christological shape of grace by turning specifically to the doctrine of justification. It is actually Christ's *humanity,* not his divinity or his role as mediator, that serves as the foundation for the doctrine of justification. This may come as a surprise given the common Protestant understandings of justification as a deeply *divine* Word or deed that is enacted upon the human on behalf of Christ's actions for humanity on the cross. For Barth, however, it is precisely *as human* that Christ leads the way in regarding how the human gets "converted" or "turned" back to God. This happens, first, through the verdict in justification that is placed upon Christ. In the verdict, the old human is destroyed and denied any kind of future, while the new human in Christ becomes a "suitable partner"[40] for God. In this way, based on Christ's human nature, Barth argues for the creation of a new humanity: humanity exalted and restored in the Person of Christ.

The humanity of Christ leads Barth to the heart of the question of justification, namely, the balance between God's justice and mercy that is to be shown to the fallen human being. Barth asks, "How can it be that peace is concluded between a holy God and sinful man — by grace, but in a way which is completely and adequately right?"[41] In other words, justification has to do with the righteousness and right of God

38. *CD* IV/1, p. 86.
39. *CD* IV/1, p. 86.
40. *CD* IV/1, pp. 94-95.
41. *CD* IV/1, p. 520.

over and against fallen humanity. But can the *right* of God be compatible with the *grace* of God? Naturally, the answer is yes because God employs this right by showing grace and mercy. In other words, it is God's right to be in harmony with God's being.[42] And this harmony is based on grace and mercy. Therefore, God's right in justification is God's right to be faithful to Godself. This in turn means being faithful to the covenant made with humanity despite humanity's breaking the covenant. Justification, then, is about God asserting God's right, that is, mercy, and thus God's very faithfulness and constancy, in the face of human betrayal and wrong.

Barth gets at this reality of God's right and mercy through the use of the two root metaphors for justification as found in Scripture. The first, justification in terms of rights, justice, righteousness, which is brought forth in the imagery of court, judge, defendant, law, and verdict, is otherwise known as the "forensic" model of justification. The second, "ontological" model imagines the event of justification in terms of life and death, dying and rising. Barth takes the imagery of the ontological model quite far by describing justification in terms of the Reformation pattern of the *mortificatio* and *vivicatio* — the killing of the sinner and resurrection of a new subject. Barth even states that in justification, God's verdict is the full destruction of the sinful human being; the sinner becomes a "burnt offering," and a new creation appears.[43] These are indeed radical terms. They are even more radical than the terminology of "conversion" or the "turning back" to God, which Barth also employs.

In both the forensic and the ontological models of justification, Jesus Christ embodies and *receives* something for us. In the forensic terms of law and rights, Jesus Christ sets out to fulfill the law of God. He takes upon himself the verdict of God for the sin that has been committed, for the law that has been broken. But Christ, as the perfectly obedient one and the exalted human, justifies himself in his obedience to God. Likewise, in the ontological terms of life and death, Jesus becomes the "burnt offering" of our sinful selves and *receives* life for us in resurrection.[44] Jesus Christ is the "fulfillment of the covenant,"

---

42. For further discussion on this topic, see Eberhard Jüngel, *Justification: The Heart of the Christian Faith* (New York: T. & T. Clark, 2006), pp. 70ff.

43. *CD* IV/1, p. 542.

44. *CD* IV/1, p. 559.

and "the whole act"[45] of the human conversion to God. And in turn, he is the reality of God remaining faithful to the human. Christ embodies justification, or the verdict we deserve because of human pride. Christ embodies sanctification as the new human subject who lives a life other than that of the sin of sloth. Christ embodies true humanity that is called to place itself under the direction of God's command and ordinance, rather than living a lie and in falsehood. This complex of God's grace is bound up in the singular action and existence of Jesus Christ. Christ is not merely an example or a symbol of this but the reality that grounds everything else. He "corresponds not only to cognition but to being."[46]

The ontological model of justification allows Barth to talk about it in terms of both being *and* history, with history perhaps playing the more dominant role. Barth develops this framework of the ontological model by arguing that with an ontological change, there comes a *new history* for the justified sinner — namely, a new history bound to Jesus Christ's own history. An analysis of this transition becomes the center of gravity of his view on justification.[47] He frames the discussion around the terms of a transition from our old selves and our sinful pasts into the history that belongs to Jesus Christ. What is significant here is how Barth introduces Jesus Christ as *the one, singular* point into which all reality is absorbed, both sinful and reconciled. He describes all human reality — including lived phenomena and experience — as *mediated* in and through Jesus Christ, his person and history. Barth's logic for explaining justification in terms of precisely the *humanity* of Christ thus becomes clear. This perspective and centering on Jesus Christ as Mediator constitutes the heart of the differences between the theologies of Barth and Thomas.

For Barth, the event of justification plunges us into a history that is finally a riddle and a mystery to us[48] because it is, ultimately, the history of Jesus Christ. It is not a history that is "ours" in the sense that

---

45. CD IV/1, p. 122.

46. CD IV/1, p. 123.

47. Barth also describes this transition in the Lutheran terms of *simul iustus et peccator*, but such language will be avoided here so that the common misunderstanding of the *simul* as that which is some kind of double state of being for us can be avoided. The *simul* for Barth, however — as it is for Luther — is truly a movement, a transition, a history, rather than a "state of being."

48. For the imagery of "riddle" see CD IV/1, pp. 546-47.

we've created it with our own hands. As the justified sinners that we are, we no longer belong to ourselves, or often even recognize ourselves as justified sinners. He states, "The justification of man by God belongs neither to the empirical nor to the ideal world but lies beyond this contrast. For God who is at work in it is one God and the Creator of all, even of that which is distinct from himself — visible and invisible reality."[49] This gets carried even further: "there can be no self-experience of this drama" of justification, of *mortificatio* and *vivicatio.*[50] Justification entails a new subject that we do not comprehend — or even perceive empirically.

What Barth describes here is essentially the Reformation concept of God's "alien righteousness" but with a radicalization that reflects his Christological center and a breadth that approaches the theology of Thomas. For Barth, the concept of "alien righteousness" does not just entail righteousness; it is truly an alien *existence* and *history* because it is an existence that is now hidden and wrapped up in the existence and history of Christ. The righteousness that is "ours" is so only by virtue of the righteousness of Christ, who *has received* resurrection and life for us. Our righteousness is the *iustitia Christi* because our existence and history are the existence and history of Jesus Christ. In this sense, Jesus Christ is the most profound and fundamental representative of human individuals.[51] He is not only an example, guide, or even sacrament, but in the fullest and deepest ontological way possible, our mediator and representative. *His* history is our history. He is our past and our future.[52] In Christ, God has *already* achieved God's end with humanity. God has created something *ex contrario.*[53] God has taken our history broken by pride, sloth, and falsehood and has destroyed it so that it has no future. God then gives us a future that is under God's own direction. This is the history of Christ, and it is our history. In this way, justification entails a *claim* upon the human and a *taking possession* of the life of the human, so that we become miracles and puzzles to ourselves.[54] As an illustration of this new, alien existence, Barth gives a lengthy and involved exposition of Romans 7, which lays out

49. *CD* IV/1, p. 545 (translation mine).
50. *CD* IV/1, p. 546.
51. *CD* IV/1, p. 549.
52. *CD* IV/1, pp. 554-55.
53. *CD* IV/1, pp. 574, 581, 593.
54. *CD* IV/1, p. 576.

the Apostle Paul's own reflection on the new life that is being created in him in Christ but which is still an alien part of life that is in a struggle with sin.

The breadth (and common ground with Thomas) that Barth achieves in this description of the new existence is seen in that Barth immediately moves right into a discussion of the "new beginning" of our empirical, subjective lives. Even though reconciled sinners become a mystery to themselves, a new, visible dawn is breaking in the dynamism of Christian love and meaning-making that characterize the reality of sanctification and vocation. Barth is very clear when he points out that "we" here, now, do live and *act* after the event of justification in sanctification and vocation. We live and *have agency* as justified sinners despite the fact that this life is now a riddle and mystery to us. As Barth states, the new beginning is when justification becomes "the demonstration in which the man justified by God shows himself to be real and existent to himself."[55] This is faith. With the faith that is produced in justification, we are stepping into an existence that is a puzzle, riddle, and mystery because it is stepping into a truth that is not always consistently reflected in the reality of our experience. It is the faith of Christ. In this way, our faith, our lives, our hope, our ability to love and to participate in "good" acts are mediated to us through the history of Christ who is our past and our future. When we live into the grace that is justification and the accompanying faith that is mediated to us through the faith of Christ, we are taking on a particular kind of risk.[56] The faith that is produced in justification is a new beginning that we must risk showing to the world. We become pilgrims through the event of justification.[57] Consequently, when we hope, when we love, when we have faith, it is a hope, love, and faith that can only exist from day to day, hour to hour.[58] There is never a smoothly laid-out path along our journey; rather it is constantly mediated to us though Christ and his history, which is our history. His faith is our faith.

Barth's view of the justified sinner's relationship to one's new reconciled reality is the single most important difference between his account of grace and that of Thomas. This difference resides in how each

55. CD IV/1, p. 613.
56. See CD IV/1, p. 583.
57. CD IV/1, pp. 602-4.
58. CD IV/1, p. 602.

thinker conceives of the justified sinner's relationship to his or her new reality. For Karl Barth, this new reality is mediated through Christ in a way that it is not explicitly laid out in Thomas's discussion on grace and reconciliation. The justified sinner in Barth's thought is a foreigner, a pilgrim, a stranger in a new land. He or she may or may not ever experience themselves as justified. As Barth himself says, Scripture shows that even as justified sinners, we present ourselves to God by virtue of our past, that is, through prayers like "Be merciful to me, a sinner," or "Lord, I believe, help my unbelief."[59] We are strangers in a new land because it is a reality, a history that is mediated to us through Jesus Christ alone. *Christ's* faith is our faith. *Christ* is our past, *Christ* is our future, and *Christ* is our "now." Consequently, when Barth speaks of justification as a "transition," he is speaking of a movement into a space that may very well be empirically invisible to the justified sinner; it is an existence and history that dawns anew every moment.

Barth's commitment to the new history and existence of Jesus Christ that is our new existence and history illuminates another important aspect of reconciliation, which is to be distinguished from Thomas. Reconciliation — the event of grace, which is identical to the event of God's giving of God's being to the sinful human — is always an event of *creation*.[60] Barth's deeply Reformational commitments about the ontology of grace are at work in such a polemic. Even though Barth works with different "forms" of grace, which justify, sustain, and exalt, he still maintains that grace is also finally destructive and creative in its nature; grace *destroys* in order to make alive. From this perspective, Barth remains consistent with commitments that he made about how grace operates during some of his most frank and open discussions with Roman Catholicism that took place in the decade of the 1920s.

---

59. *CD* IV/1, p. 616.

60. Thomas actually seems to equivocate on this matter, suggesting that he might have had inclinations to move in this direction as well. In *ST* I-II, "The Treatise on Grace," Thomas weighs whether the justification of the unrighteous or the act of creation out of nothing is the greatest of God's works (q. 113, a. 9). He concludes that the argument depends upon the mode of action, which means that creation is the greatest of God's works. But in a later passage on the question of merit and worthiness, Thomas explicitly states that he can argue that God gives grace to the worthy *precisely because* God "himself *makes* them worthy by grace" (q. 114, a. 5, emphasis mine). Thus, there does seem to be evidence in Thomas's discussion of grace and justification that suggests he understands the reconciling act of God to also be, or at least entail, a creative act of God.

What the Catholic teaching of grace lacks is the sense that God's grace does away with sin in a manner that is fatal, radical, even annihilating, in order to create a completely new subject on a daily basis. Barth calls this act of new creation a work of God that produces something new out of its opposite — *ex oppositio* or *ex contrario*.[61] On this point, he interrogates the Catholic doctrine of grace: Is there then no new creation? No awakening from the dead?[62] Reconciliation is always an event of creation because God meets the *active* sinner, not the one who is already prepared to meet God in grace. This is a point that Barth argued forcefully in a lecture from 1929 titled "The Holy Spirit and the Christian Life," that "grace is our being created . . . towards God."[63] This commitment to a new creation by the force of grace is at the heart of the transition from our old, sinful existence to our new history in Jesus Christ. Reconciliation is creation.

God's act of reconciliation as creation opens the horizon into a final dimension of Barth's Christological reflections on the life of the reconciled sinner. Namely, the life of the reconciled sinner is shown by God's revelation. The "hidden" life of the justified sinner in the life and history of Christ is *revealed* to us through God's creative act of reconciliation. This reconciliation-revelation connection, or what Barth earlier in his career called the *"Versöhnungsoffenbarung,"*[64] ties *knowledge* of God to the *act* of God's reconciliation in grace. Because of this connection, Barth's theology has little room for any explicit divisions of grace. He conceives of the entire event of revelation *and* reconciliation as one single act of God's grace. Everything that is involved in the event of revelation-reconciliation — the Incarnation, judgment, resurrection, the creation of faith in the heart of the believer, the restoration of the covenant and therefore the order of creation, the new life of the individual as saint and sinner — is contained in the *"unum et simul"* of the divine act.[65] The entire

---

61. *CD* IV/1, pp. 574, 581, 593.

62. *CD* IV/1, p. 85.

63. Karl Barth, *The Holy Spirit and the Christian Life,* trans. R. Birch Hoyle (Louisville: Westminster John Knox, 1993), pp. 14-16.

64. Karl Barth, *Die christliche Dogmatik im Entwurf,* in *Karl Barth Gesamtausgabe,* vol. 2: *Akademische Werke,* ed. Gerhard Sauter (Zürich: Theologischer Verlag Zürich, 1982), p. 253.

65. See the unpublished manuscript of the dogmatic lectures given by Barth at the University of Münster between 1927 and 1928, which I have titled the *Münster Dogmatics,* §49, p. 104.

reconciliation-revelation event of the Word is a single, unified, and consolidated act of divine grace. The truth of the sinner's reconciliation with God enters human consciousness only through God's revelation to us about the reality of our lives. Justification is therefore not necessarily an empirical reality, even though Barth does state that our actions in justification and its consequences, sanctification and vocation, *can and do demonstrate* this newly created reality to the world and to ourselves. Therefore, it is not that we do not *have* to act, or that we *cannot* act as justified sinners, but rather that when we *do* act as justified sinners, it is a demonstration of a reality that is actually invisible, a reality, Barth says, to which we can only "witness."[66] We are *witnesses* to our justified selves. It is this definition of our relationship to our own history and our own reality, mediated to us through Jesus Christ, that makes Barth's doctrine of reconciliation quite distinct from that of Thomas.

This analysis of Barth's doctrine of reconciliation and its broader connections to his understanding of creation and revelation is not to suggest that Thomas's doctrine of grace lacks the kind of internal unity that characterizes Barth's theology. Nor does it want to suggest that Thomas offers a guaranteed path or some kind of smooth, problem-free transition from the state of sin into the state of grace in which God plays a hands-off role. The fact that we need the *auxilium* grace to sustain and nourish habitual grace that operates in the details of our lives shows that in Thomas too, the justified sinner is in constant need of God's immediate presence. Likewise, when the details of Barth's highly unified doctrine of reconciliation are scrutinized, as we have laid out above, the similarities to Thomas's own commitments come into view. The central divergence between the two thinkers lies in the way Barth roots the internal unity of reconciliation and grace by locating all aspects of it in the singular divine event of Jesus Christ, who *is* human, *has become* human, and whose history and faith become the history and faith of the sinner who is justified, sanctified, and called in Christ's name.

66. *CD* IV/1, p. 612.

V. Election, Providence, and Natural Law

Barth and Aquinas on Election, Relationship, and Requirement

John R. Bowlin

Understanding, Hegel tells us, is largely a matter of negation. A concept or doctrine becomes more determinate the more precisely we grasp what it is not, what commitments it excludes or prohibits. So, for example, if we don't know what Barth's account of the doctrine of election rules out with respect to human agency, then it's unlikely that his efforts have become sufficiently determinate for us to know what his treatment of the doctrine involves, what it includes and entails.[1] And presumably, the more fine-grained the negation, the more precise the grasp, the more determinate the understanding.[2]

---

1. G. W. F. Hegel, *Phenomenology of Spirit,* trans. A. V. Miller (Oxford: Oxford University Press, 1977), §§114-20. My interpretation of Hegel on these matters follows Robert Brandom's rational reconstruction of the argument embedded in those paragraphs: *Tales of the Mighty Dead: Historical Essays in the Metaphysics of Intentionality* (Cambridge, MA: Harvard University Press, 2002), pp. 178-82. On Brandom's rendering, entailment — what follows from what — is also a matter of negation. "The proposition or property *p* entails *q* just in case everything incompatible with (ruled out or excluded by) *q* is incompatible with (ruled out or excluded by) *p*" (p. 180).

2. According to Brandom, "Hegel embraces the medieval (and Spinozist) principle *omnis determinatio est negatio*" and insists that a defining negation, one that enables us to distinguish this from that, is always "codified in the principle of non-contradiction" (*Tales of the Mighty Dead,* p. 179). Since Aquinas considers that same principle the first and most basic in the order of speculative knowledge (*ST* I-II, q. 94, a. 2), it's no surprise when David Decosimo notes that even Thomists identify and individuate objects and specify concepts by way of negation: "Thomas Aquinas and the Virtue of the Outsider" (Ph.D. diss., Princeton University, 2011), pp. 159-60. He refers to Stephen Brock, *Action and Conduct: Thomas Aquinas and the Theory of Action* (London: T. & T. Clark, 2000), pp. 160-86.

John R. Bowlin

It's this fact about negation and concept mastery that warns us against taking up comparative projects that trade too easily similarities. Aquinas/Barth, Catholic/Protestant, Dominican/Reformed — it's the differences that matter most, that deserve the greater part of our attention, and largely for reasons that Hegel spelled out. If we attend to what a certain rendering of a particular doctrine excludes, what commitments and ways of living it negates, then we will have a better sense of how it stands in relation to other renderings. If, by contrast, we simply point out that this rendering of that doctrine is similar to some other, then we have done next to nothing to specify the concepts involved and grasp their determinate content. As Nelson Goodman pointed out a generation ago, everything is similar to everything else in at least *some* respect, and thus the raw fact of similarity tells us nothing at all about the tokens being compared.[3] Rather, comparison enhances understanding only as negation in some way specifies the raw facts of similarity and identifies the relevant explanatory interests. This is similar to that in this way but not that, and we attend to these *particular* similarities precisely because we have *this* collection of explanatory interests and not some other.

This much is plain. Understanding follows negation and negation specifies the similarities that make useful comparisons possible. Both claims matter, and yet as I said, it's the first that matters most: it's the differences that deserve our attention. At the same time, these Hegelian preliminaries imply that differences must regard something in common, something for them to be about, and thus similarities of some sort must be assumed. They will be the backdrop against which negation proceeds, and every comparative project that attends to differences will have to be explicit about the content of that assumption.

This is where my efforts begin: in the recognition of a shared assumption. Both Aquinas and Barth assume a social theory of obligation. They agree about its basic features, and both use those features to say how it is that divine action creates human obligation, how election becomes demand, how love becomes law, how a relationship graciously established generates requirements willingly received, and not requirements of any just sort, but binding ones. Moreover, for both, it's this latter bit that causes the greatest concern. Neither wants the grace that

3. Nelson Goodman, "Seven Strictures on Similarity," in *Experience and Theory,* ed. L. Foster (Amherst: University of Massachusetts Press, 1970), pp. 19-30.

comes as command to place an alien constraint on the will of the obedient, and neither wants the obedient to regard love's law as the basis
of an illegitimate jurisdiction.

Thus, in the treatise on charity from the *Secunda pars* we find
Thomas insisting that God's loving Spirit orders "all things sweetly"
within *its* jurisdiction *(omnia suaviter)* and that the obligations imposed
by love's requirements "cannot be fulfilled except out of one's very own
will" and thus never in opposition to one's own liberty *(non potest
impleri nisi ex propria voluntate)* *(ST* II-II, q. 23, a. 2; q. 44, a. 1).[4] Read
around in the second part of Barth's account of the doctrine of reconciliation, and we find him expressing roughly the same concern. There
he insists that the command of God never confronts humanity as "an
abstract law — a law without any *locus* in a life fulfilling and embodying
it, but merely advancing the arid claim that it is the law of God, and
that as such it has the right to demand that man should be for God,
and thus fulfill the condition under which God will also be for him.
This abstract law has never yet led a man to conversion, even by killing
him, let alone by making him alive. It has no power to do either. For it
is not the living God, nor His quickening Spirit, who places man under
this law."[5]

Of course, there are also differences. As should be apparent from
this remark, Barth expresses concern with the legitimacy of God's law
and the voluntary character of our obedience in the language of Hegelian discontent with Kantian *Moralität*, and this should give us pause. At
the very least, it should compel us to admit that this shared concern for
coordinating authority and freedom in the relationship between God
and humanity has different sources: for Barth in the modern drama of
self-determination, for Thomas in the vexing relations between things
natural and supernatural. And these different sources generate quite
different replies. For each, God's Spirit quickens the faithful; it
prompts them to recognize the authority of God's command and to

---

4. Throughout, I resort to the translation of Thomas's greater *Summa* made by
the Fathers of the English Dominican Province, *Summa Theologica,* 5 vols. (Westminster,
MD: Christian Classics, 1981), making minor changes without notice.

5. Throughout, all citations of the *CD* are to *Church Dogmatics,* 4 vols. in 13 parts,
ed. G. W. Bromiley and T. F. Torrance (Edinburgh: T. & T. Clark, 1936-75). Here, *CD* IV/2,
pp. 579-80. Gerald McKenny discusses this important remark in his excellent interpretation of Barth's ethics: *The Analogy of Grace: Karl Barth's Moral Theology* (Oxford: Oxford
University Press, 2010), p. 199.

concede the desirability of obedience. Yet, for Thomas, this righteousness comes to humanity, not perfectly, of course, but surely in part, as
nature is re-created and virtue infused, while for Barth this righteousness belongs most basically to Christ, who is the principal subject of
electing grace and the one who responds to its requirements in perfect
freedom, perfect obedience.

Nevertheless, sandwiched between these different sources and replies we find an identical theory of obligation, one that locates the origin and legitimacy of every requirement in a relationship of some kind,
in this instance in the friendship that God's gracious love creates. My
hunch is that this shared theory of obligation, this common account
of friendship, can function as a useful backdrop against which these
different sources and replies come into focus.

In what follows I take up four tasks. First, I spell out the basic
logic of relationship and requirement and the account of authority and
freedom that it assumes; second, I recount Barth's doubts about this
logic as it regards *human* relationships; third, I spell out Barth's response to these doubts, the response we find in his Christological rendering of this same basic logic; and finally, I consider the burdens of
this rendition, burdens that show how Barth's efforts exhibit what
Robert Pippen calls the dialectic of modernity. In large measure, it's
this dialectic that determines Barth's account of the requirements that
accompany God's friendship with humanity, determines both its
Kantian form and its Hegelian content. If we attend to his participation in this dialectic — to the fact that he remains caught up in its concerns — we should be able to identify the differences that distinguish
his account from Aquinas's.

Relationships and Requirements

To say that an action or attitude is obligatory, that it is required of *us,* is
to say that we *have* to act in this way or respond with this attitude, that
failure to do so would be grounds for censure, and that our recognition
of this failure should generate feelings of guilt, for of course, the person who fails to fulfill an obligation is in fact guilty.[6] To say that "obli-

6. Robert Merrihew Adams, *Finite and Infinite Goods: A Framework for Ethics* (Oxford: Oxford University Press, 2002), pp. 232, 239. My account of the relationships and re-

gations are requirements that arise within relationships among persons" is to say that the action or attitude that is required mediates our relations with others and that the character of the relationship specifies the content of the requirement.[7] In many instances, this connection between relationship and requirement is determined by a role. It's the role that one occupies in a relationship that specifies the obligations one has. Parents are obliged to care for the welfare of their children. Batters are obliged to bunt when given that sign. Cashiers are obliged to give correct change. Professors are obliged to return papers in a timely manner. And so on. In other instances, the obligation emerges in a relationship, but not through the offices of a role. So, for example, in any person-to-person relationship I am obliged to refrain from killing the innocent, and this obligation obtains regardless of the ends I intend, the circumstances I find myself in, or the roles I happen to occupy.

Because obligations regard actions or attitudes that mediate our social relations, we tend to refer to them in terms of the expectations of some and the responsibilities of others. A cashier, for example, is obliged to give correct change, and I proceed in our transaction with the expectation that he will. If he fails in this, I'll protest. I'll speak of his responsibility to recognize his status as cashier, to care about his relationship with customers, and to act in accord with the obligations specified by his role. I'll try to hold him accountable by eliciting his recognition of our relationship, of the value of its bonds and the importance of its requirements.

We also tend to speak of these patterns of expectation and requirement in the language of justice, of what is due another by right and what wrong is done when the right is transgressed. So again, the

---

quirements is a variation on Adams's, one that does not assume his distinction between moral and social obligations (pp. 266-67). For doubts about that distinction as Adams deploys it, see Nicholas Wolterstorff, *Justice: Rights and Wrongs* (Princeton: Princeton University Press, 2008), pp. 277-80.

7. Jeffrey Stout, "Adams on the Nature of Obligation," in *Metaphysics and the Good: Themes from the Philosophy of Robert Merrihew Adams*, ed. S. Newlands and L. M. Jorgensen (Oxford: Oxford University Press, 2009), p. 372. A variation on Stout's interpretation of Adams on obligation can also be found in his *Democracy and Tradition* (Princeton: Princeton University Press, 2003), pp. 258-69. Stout praises Adams's resort to a social theory of obligation but doubts that we need an appeal to divine command, as Adams does, in order to guarantee the objectivity of our obligations.

cashier not only fulfills his obligation and my expectation when he returns the correct change, but he also delivers the good that I am due by right. Put another way, by doing what is required he does what *is* right, and, as a result, I am not wronged.

When the goods at stake in these exchanges are substantial, when the requirement to deliver them is easy to ignore, and when the relationship is one that matters, then we might express the obligation in a precept. By doing so, we make explicit that *this* relationship comes packaged with *this* requirement and that this requirement should be honored because the relationship is worth caring about. Some times and places might promulgate this now-explicit obligation in a command to the relevant parties to deliver the relevant goods. Others might accent the receiving end of the relationship and make explicit the expectations one can have of others. Some might even speak of these expectations by referring to a subjective right: the right to be treated in accord with a certain requirement.

Of course, our list of explicit precepts, promulgated commands, and subjective rights is relatively short, even as our obligations and expectations are certainly many. It follows that, for the most part, these remain implicit in our relationships, and we make them explicit only as needed, most commonly as we work to resolve conflicts among roles, requirements, and expectations.[8]

So far so good; but now a difficulty. There are all kinds of relationships that generate all sorts of requirements and surely some of these latter are neither just nor binding. As Jeff Stout points out, if slaves are "to satisfy the requirements of the relationship in which they find themselves," then they are obliged to obey their masters and do what they are told. And yet, "surely these requirements, though generated by a social relationship, are not morally binding."[9] And presumably, it's the moral defect in the underlying relationship that explains the injustice of the requirement. Good relationships generate requirements that are just and genuinely binding. Bad relationships do not. Slavery is plainly unjust, and so too its obligations and expectations. But this implies that the moral validity of any collection of requirements will depend on the reasons for valuing the relationship that gen-

---

8. Here I draw on Jeff Stout's interpretation of Brandom's account of practical reasoning. See *Democracy and Tradition,* pp. 188-89.

9. Stout, "Adams on the Nature of Obligation," p. 373.

erates them, reasons for counting that relationship good if not excellent. And of course, it goes without saying, that counting the relationship good for just any reason is not enough. More than that, the reasons must be right.[10]

Since we have a pretty good handle on the injustice that corrupts the relationship between master and slave, Stout suggests that moral assessment should begin by ruling out those relationships that are, in some relevant way, analogous.[11] After that, and more positively, we will want to make certain that the relationship in question benefits the parties to it, that it is in some important sense good for *them*.[12] Then we will want to pay attention to the character of the person who in some way makes the obligation explicit and expects obedience. We will want to consider their virtues and vices, on the one hand, and their authority to command, on the other.[13] And finally, we will want to assess the merit of the obligation itself: whether it conflicts with other obligations we consider binding; whether it is sufficiently discriminate in object; whether the consequences of obedience are intolerable; and so on.

When the participants in a relationship take up these practices of assessment and criticism they, in effect, hold each other accountable for safekeeping whatever goodness the relationship embodies and for specifying and justifying its requirements. When these practices succeed, they not only identify a just requirement, but by accenting the give-and-take of reasons, they also yoke the authority to command with the willingness to obey. If reasons are offered to "accept as right" (*CD* II/2, p. 579) the legitimacy of a certain requirement, if these reasons attend to the good in the relationship, and if they are assumed to have priority in the order of obligation, then the authority to command obedience to that requirement presupposes a willingness to obey for those reasons. Obedience in cases like these is not simply a matter of fulfilling the demands of a requirement. It is also a matter of acting in accord with one's own reflective endorsement of its demands.[14] In short, it's the give-and-take of reasons within the relationship that pre-

10. Adams, *Finite and Infinite Goods,* p. 244.

11. Stout, "Adams on the Nature of Obligation," p. 383.

12. Stout, "Adams on the Nature of Obligation," p. 373.

13. Adams, *Finite and Infinite Goods,* pp. 244-45.

14. Robert Brandom, "Freedom and Constraint by Norms," in *Hermeneutics and Praxis,* ed. Robert Hollinger (Notre Dame: University of Notre Dame Press, 1985), pp. 182-84.

vents the dynamic of command and obedience from corrupting its goodness and degrading the legitimacy of its requirements. At the very least, this is the hope.

And of course, the person who has been moved to obedience by the relevant reasons will not act in accord with an unfamiliar demand. If she considers the underlying relationship good, and if she identifies with its participants and counts her place among them a blessing, then she can hardly regard its requirements as alien or arbitrary. They emerge from a relationship that she loves and are warranted by reasons she endorses. It follows that her obedience will be an expression of her belonging, of her status as a responsible member of a community that she values, of her love and respect for its society.[15]

To be sure, the requirement that she recognizes and endorses does *oblige* her to act in certain ways, and it may turn out that these ways conflict with her other obligations and interests. In this respect, the requirement may confront her as a constraint, not something alien, but a constraint nevertheless. Still, when she attends to the reasons that justify obedience, and when those reasons win out, she will indeed find herself bound to act in those ways, but not because she is compelled *contra voluntas*. Rather, she will be *bound* to act because this is precisely how she *will* act given her acceptance of this claim upon her, given the content of her judgments and the shape of her loves.

Of course, life in a relationship is not all obedience to its requirements, but obedience to its requirements does make that life possible, and thus there is a sense in which a just demand generates positive freedom, the freedom to participate in the relationship and enjoy its benefits, above all the common good that is the relationship itself. And if this is right, then it is hardly a stretch to say that the requirements of a just and good relationship arrive as gifts. Like the relationship itself, they come as grace. They permit the person subject to them to participate in the relationship, to enjoy her status as a responsible member, and to recognize herself as a recipient of its benefits. We might say that in her obedience, she embodies that status, embraces that permission, and expresses that recognition. We might say that she is reconciled with its norms.

Relationship and requirement, goodness and authority, grace and freedom — these features of our social life are displayed most promi-

---

15. Adams, *Finite and Infinite Goods,* p. 244.

nently in our friendships. The point is not that I'm obliged to bestow friendship's grace willy-nilly, to offer my love and well-wishing to whomever asks. Rather the point is that once I make this choice – this election, we might say – and receive the love and well-wishing of another in return, a relationship is created, a fellowship of mutual love and care, with its own requirements, its own tacit expectations and explicit demands. I am, after all, obliged to make a return on the love and well-wishing my friends provide, to care for them as they care for me, and to sustain the friendship we share. I am also obliged to extend my care and concern to those who belong to my friends, to *their* friends and relations, whom I must love in some measure for *their* sake.

At times, these obligations come easily, more a permission to love our friend than a demand to make good on her love. But at times, it doesn't. At times, we find it difficult to provide the act of love our friend deserves. Repeated failure here will likely elicit her disappointment, if not her protest, and justly so. A true friendship is a good relationship, and its requirements and expectations are obviously just. Less obvious is the fact that the principal good that friends wish for each other is precisely the friendship itself. This also falls under requirement, indeed the most basic. To my friends, I am obliged to be a friend – to recognize that this is precisely who I am, to live freely in accord with this normative status, and to accept as right the expectation to love in return, to love as I am loved.

This obligation to recognize myself as beloved of another and to respond as one who has received this grace is made explicit, indeed vividly so, when my friend incurs a loss on my behalf. The obligation is brought into sharp relief by her willingness to sacrifice some good for my sake. And of course, that obligation becomes even more vivid when her sacrifice is made against a backdrop of wrong. If I have somehow wronged her and yet she is nevertheless willing to forgive me and suffer loss for my sake, then I am ever more obliged to acknowledge what she has done, to accept who I have become as a result of that doing and act in accord with this new reality.

If it happens that our friendship is already up and running, then this sacrifice not only expresses the quality of love that binds but it also deepens our union and further specifies its requirements. If, however, there is no antecedent relationship, and if the sacrifice is both offered as grace and received as love, then the sacrifice *creates* that union, it establishes the friendship, and thus generates its requirements. In formal terms, the good that is done sacrificially creates the relationship within which the right is in fact due, and the person who recognizes that good and acknowledges that relationship must concede that right.

Sociologist Nancy Jay has argued, convincingly I think, that sacrifice is the means through which the most powerful and meaningful relationships are created and sustained — above all friendships and spiritual lineages.[16] The loss that another willingly incurs on my behalf expresses her love for me, and, as an agent, her portion of the friendship is nothing but that expression. My portion is to recognize that sacrifice for what it is, to receive it as an act of friendship, and to live freely in accord with my new status as one beloved of another. That response will presumably include love in kind, but also gratitude, and presumably both responses are requirements of the relationship established by the sacrifice.

Goodness and Doubts

So goes my basic account of how social relationships generate binding obligations. Anyone familiar with Aquinas's treatment of charity will recognize that he assumes roughly this account. He begins in *ST* II-II, q. 23, a. 1 by insisting that charity, considered in itself, is a relationship of mutual love, a friendship between God and humanity established graciously by the Holy Spirit. The person who has been re-created by that Spirit is, according to Thomas, treated faithfully by God and "called into the fellowship of his Son" (1 Cor. 1:9; *ST* II-II, q. 23, a. 1). Since the Holy Spirit is precisely "the love of the Father and the Son," the person chosen by God and called into this fellowship is re-created by that love in the image of that love and is thus able to respond with love for God in return (*ST* II-II, q. 24, a. 2). Twenty-one questions later, Thomas spells out the obligations that come packaged with this fellowship of mutual love, obligations specified in the precepts of charity, precepts that come in the command of the gospel "as stated in Matthew 22:36-40" (*ST* II-II, q. 44, a. 1): you shall love the Lord your God with all your heart, soul, and mind, and your neighbor as yourself.

Look around with the eyes of faith, Thomas seems to say, and we

---

16. See Nancy Jay, *Throughout Your Generations Forever: Sacrifice, Religion, and Paternity* (Chicago: University of Chicago Press, 1992).

find that certain human beings simply love this God. Created and then re-created, this is just what they do. Look again and we find that everywhere and always, those who love the triune God also love their neighbors. Thomas admits that these loves are commanded, that their content takes the form of an explicit requirement, and yet it is a command that re-creates those who hear, that generates their virtue, and that allows them to regard themselves as they are, as God's beloved. To the re-created, God's command comes *suaviter* because it enables what it commands (*ST* II-II, q. 23, a. 2). So enabled, the people of God do not so much receive the command as external constraint or alien demand but more as permission and gift. It follows that, for the most part, those who love God will conclude, after very little consideration, that they ought to love their neighbor as well. Some, of course, will stumble here. Some will fail to derive the second precept of charity from the first, and it is for this reason, says Thomas, that "it behooved us to receive precepts not only of the love of God but also of the love of our neighbor" (*ST* II-II, q. 44, a. 2). And yet, the facts on the ground speak for the ease and immediacy of the derivation. For the most part, "He who loves God, loves also his neighbor" (*ST* II-II, q. 44, a. 2 sc.).[17] And thus he who consistently fails to love his neighbor or repeatedly refuses to extend that love to sinners and enemies cannot be said to love God.

Notice the relationship that Thomas assumes among our ordinary talk of friendship, the reality it picks out, and the work of grace. He assumes that the discourse of friendship and demand, of love that generates relationships and relationships that generate requirements, can be used to explicate the work of grace, that it can be gathered up into the purposes of *sacra doctrina* and used to speak of love's precepts precisely because some of our friendships are, well, friendships. He assumes that they are good human relationships, not perfect of course, but good nevertheless, that they can be known as such, again imperfectly, and that our discourses of friendship not only pick out that goodness but also presuppose that knowledge.

The point here regards basic concept mastery. We cannot understand a concept, apply it with simple competence, or grasp its relations with the other concepts we care about without simultaneously assuming the truth content of certain claims. We cannot use the concept "friendship," for example, without, at the same time, knowing how to

17. 1 John 4:21.

set apart, more or less, those relationships that count as friendships from those that do not. We will have to be able to distinguish paradigmatically good friendships from the obviously bad, the plainly real from the merely apparent, and so on. Judgments like these, distinctions of this kind — judgments and distinctions that more or less track the truth about the matters they regard — must be assumed by the person who makes use of the concept and speaks of friendship.[18] The same applies to the conceptual connection between a true friendship and a just demand. Some demands are plainly unjust. No friendship, no matter how dear, can warrant them. Fail to note this exclusion across a number of paradigmatic cases and it's likely that we'll doubt your mastery of the concepts involved.[19]

So, for example, the person who insists that he understands the concept well enough but nevertheless contends that the relationship between master and slave is in fact a friendship, that its demands are in fact just, either has failed to acquire basic mastery, despite his avowals to the contrary, or has confused this concept with some other.[20]

But this means that knowledge of the most basic distinction between good and bad relationships, true and false friendships, just and unjust requirements, comes packaged with the concepts themselves. We can't make the simplest use of these concepts or apply them intelligibly in most ordinary circumstances without assuming that knowledge and deploying these distinctions. No doubt, our sin will frequently distort the enterprise, both the knowledge we assume and the applications we make, and yet sin's distortions cannot go all the way down without undoing altogether our grip on these concepts.

If this is right, if this tight packaging of concept, normative content, and authoritative assumption can neither be bypassed nor es-

18. Put in Hegel's terms, a concept becomes determinate through the medium of negation, and negation proceeds against a backdrop of authoritative assumption.

19. Thomas doesn't put the point in quite this way, but this way of putting it is, I think, a faithful, if somewhat modern, rendering of his claim that being and goodness regard the same matter but under different formalities. Knowing what friendship *is* necessarily entails knowing, at least in broad strokes, which relationships in fact embody its goodness.

20. It might also be that the difference here regards application not mastery, that the person knows what the concept involves and yet under the influence of passion or self-deception has simply failed to apply it well. Still, repeated failure of basic application will indeed cast doubt upon basic mastery.

caped, then at least two implications follow, one that regards the work of the Holy Spirit as Thomas describes it, the other that regards the obligations that the theologian must bear.

On the one hand, this tight packaging implies that the gracious transformation of our loves that Thomas describes in the treatise on charity includes the gracious transformation of our concepts, of the normative content assumed in our discourse of friendship and requirement. Thomas makes this point explicit in his account of befriending enemies. Most of us begin with doubts about these relationships. When confronted by an example, we tend to speak of folly, self-deception, or injustice, not friendship, and not without reason.[21] Those who have done us harm and who wish us ill hardly provide us with a reason to do them good and wish them well. It's not that those reasons are unimaginable, but rather that they are hard to find without first casting the enemy under some other description, one that complicates his status as enemy. For Thomas, grace provides precisely this complication. The person whose loves have been transformed by the Holy Spirit and who befriends an enemy out of supernatural charity does so for *God's* sake. "Dilectionis inimici solus Deus est ratio" — for loving one's enemy, God alone is the reason (*ST* II-II, q. 27, a. 7). The exclusive character of the claim — *solus Deus* — ignores the imaginative possibilities here, but the point is that grace specifies one such possibility. It enables the re-created to regard the enemy as one beloved of God and the enemy can now be befriended because of this graciously complicated status. The friendship proceeds under this reason, and this reason loads new normative content into the concept, into our understanding of friendship.

On the other hand, this tight packaging of concept and normative content obliges the theologian who speaks of friendship in order to specify how divine action generates human obligation to say something about the source of the normative content that comes loaded with the concept and something about the prospects of that content after sin and under grace.

For Thomas, that source is God's eternal law, our participation in which according to our created nature provides both knowledge of the basic outlines of the human good and inclination toward that outline (*ST* I-II, q. 93, a. 6). That inclination forms the seedbed of acquired vir-

21. Brock, *Action and Conduct*, p. 238.

tue, and, given the power of sin, Thomas admits that this seedbed will not come to full flower (*ST* I-II, q. 85, a. 2). Yet he also assumes that some of us can, "even in the state of corrupted nature," cultivate some variety of scraggly virtue and that nearly all of us can "work some particular good" (*ST* I-II, q. 109, a. 2). He mentions building dwellings, planting vineyards, and the like, and presumably the person who takes up these tasks will usually do so in the company of others, and presumably this social character of the work will demand rudimentary judgments about the goodness of the relationships involved, friendships among others. When these judgments more or less hit the mark with the regularity of habit, it is likely that the cause is our scraggly virtue. When, through the gracious work of the Holy Spirit, our participation in God's eternal law becomes ever more substantial and our subjection to it ever more complete, Thomas contends that those same tasks, friendships, and virtues will be graciously gathered up into the love of God. They will be referred by God's grace to the ends of charity (*ST* II-II, q. 26, a. 7). He contends, in other words, that whatever good that remains after sin in those tasks, friendships, and virtues, and whatever truth about that good is embedded in our application of these concepts, can be perfected by grace only as they are assumed by grace.

It's here, in *this* assumption, that we find the *real* object of Barth's doubts about the logic of relationship and requirement as Thomas deploys it. But before we consider that object, we need to dismiss an apparent one. Barth, of course, expresses many doubts about what he calls the "Roman Catholic view of the matter" (*CD* II/2, p. 528), but not all of them stick to Aquinas, certainly not the claim that our knowledge of the good, whatever it amounts to, has its source in the light of human reason, with "its independent, if limited illumination" (*CD* II/2, p. 533), a light that stands "inflexible and inviolate" and thus apart from "the grace and command of God" (*CD* II/2, p. 522).

The work that has been done on Aquinas's treatment of the natural law over the last generation shows, conclusively I think, that he regards this knowledge as ours only as we receive it from the God who creates and governs all things by ordering them to their proper ends. In our case, that ordering is mediated through our participation in God's wisdom about our good, God's knowledge of the ends characteristic of our kind. This ordering comes to be and this participation happens only as God's knowledge of our good is expressed by God's Word as law, as a dictate of practical reason that we can grasp (*ST* I-II, q. 93, a. 1, ad 2).[22] Apart from that gift, expression, and grasp, and without that participation in divine wisdom, we would have no such knowledge, no access to the human good.

So Barth's objection to *Thomas's* account of friendship and obligation cannot be that it assumes knowledge of the good that is somehow independent of God in Jesus Christ, somehow a "man-made ethics" (*CD* II/2, p. 517). No, as I said, the objection regards Thomas's insistence that a portion of that knowledge remains after sin (*ST* I-II, q. 85, a. 2), that this portion can be used to speak intelligibly (although fallibly) of friendships and their requirements, and that grace both assumes and perfects these moral realities.

To this, Barth offers his own emphatic no![23] It's an objection that comes in two parts, and we might say that it begins in Kantian commitment and ends in Nietzschean suspicion. First, Barth insists that the good we claim to know, whether it comes by created nature or re-creating grace, cannot be used to identify the obligations that we actually have. Or rather, if you make use of that knowledge to assess the goodness of a relationship and the rightness of its requirements, then you won't get a genuine obligation, just a semblance. You will not have, as Barth puts it, a "real order of obligation" (*CD* II/2, p. 532). If the identity and legitimacy of some supposed requirement assumes our antecedent knowledge of the good, then it cannot really oblige, it cannot really bind. To use Kant's language, if an obligation assumes our grasp of the good for its identity and substance, then it cannot be unconditional, its imperative cannot command us categorically, indeed it cannot "be a 'calling,' something that [makes] a claim on us independently of our own situation in life."[24] Or in Barth's words, how can such an obligation "be and become imperative except with the assistance and co-operation of man, except on the presupposition of his agreement?

---

22. Many thanks to Professor Coolman for bringing this remark to my attention. She discusses it in her contribution to this volume.

23. This conclusion confirms Keith Johnson's argument that Barth's resistance to the *analogia entis* follows from his desire to preserve traditional Protestant claims about justification. Or rather, Barth's resistance follows from his desire to secure traditional Protestant claims against a backdrop of neo-Kantian assumption about knowledge and subjectivity. See Keith L. Johnson, *Karl Barth and the Analogia Entis* (London: T. & T. Clark, 2010).

24. Terry Pinkard, *German Philosophy 1760-1860: The Legacy of Idealism* (Cambridge: Cambridge University Press, 2002), p. 51.

. . . On this presupposition it is quite impossible that it should confront him, his being and existence as an absolute challenge; that it should dominate him and claim him with absolute sovereignty; . . . [that it should] affect him personally and bind him unconditionally" (*CD* II/2, pp. 532-33).

Assume human judgments about the good in the specification of the right and you do not get the predetermination of God's command, but rather the self-determination of our broken humanity (*CD* II/2, p. 516), the spurious directives of our own "arbitrary ethic" (p. 515). And our humanity is indeed broken, and the effect is indeed dire.[25] If we cannot know the obligatory, if our claim to that knowledge is always polluted by our own subjectivity, by our own faulty grasp of the good, then it follows that every such claim will simply express our own selfish wants and twisted desires.

Barth puts the point in terms of master and slave (*CD* II/2, p. 594), of freedom and authority (pp. 602-3). Suppose we share a friendship, and I conclude that certain requirements follow. Given the goodness of that relationship, you are obliged to act in certain ways, or so I say. And suppose that you are in fact convinced by the reasons I provide and now feel bound by the requirements that I have specified. Well, then, by Barth's lights I have captured you with this talk and enslaved you to my will. The obligation that I have identified is conditioned by my sinful, self-interested grasp of the good, and thus it arrives, not with real authority, but as duty's semblance. Its imperative is not in any way categorical, but comes instead as an expression of my will to power, of my desire to dominate dressed up in obligation's drag.

Of course, I might be unaware of this swindle. Indeed, given the fact that I couch this will to power and this desire to dominate in the language of the good and the right, it's likely that I offer my assessment of our relationship and my specification of its requirements with heartfelt conviction. I might even believe my own words when I say that obedience to these demands makes possible your participation in this good relationship, that it liberates and permits even as it binds and requires. But no matter. Self-deception is sin's faithful servant. More to

25. About the "misplaced optimism" in the Roman Catholic view of the Fall's effects, Barth writes that "we cannot accept that merely relative and quantitative scope and significance of the fall, that doctrine of the nature of man as merely sick, deranged, and impotent, that talk of a remnant of the original divine image and likeness which remains in spite of the fall" (*CD* II/2, p. 532).

the point, sincere belief in the authority of a requirement and in the freedom that obedience yields cannot erase the fact that my talk of obligation is false, the freedom it promises an illusion. Tit for tat, Barth insists that the freedom I appear to have in the mastery I exercise over you is just that, an appearance. You are obviously bound by this semblance of an obligation that I have fabricated, and unjustly so, but I am enslaved to the sin that does the fabricating. I might experience this mastery over you as freedom, but in truth that experience regards the lawlessness of sin, not the true liberty that only genuine authority can provide (*CD* II/2, p. 603).

Specify the right on appeal to our grasp of the good, and you get nothing but a semblance of an obligation. Do this under the conditions of radical sinfulness, and the obligations you specify will be nothing but an expression of your will to dominate. Put the matter in these terms, as Barth does, and you drive your reader toward a choice. You can begin with the claim that human beings have some sense of what is good, but if you do, then your ability to answer "the ethical question, the question of the moral law" vanishes altogether, and you land instead on Nietzsche's doorstep (*CD* II/2, p. 515). As it is with Alasdair MacIntyre, so it was with Karl Barth. Both contend that the modern drama of self-determination leaves us on that doorstep and confronts us with a choice. Do we stay and enjoy its bracing air, its view of the wild orchids, or do we leave, and if we leave, how do we go? For MacIntyre, departure comes through a return to the tradition of the virtues and the norms of natural law theory. For Barth it comes through the doctrine of election.

Election as Friendship

What's striking about Barth's rendering of the moral effects of election is how closely he follows the logic of relationship and requirement. If you apply that logic in human affairs, then you end up with unjust requirements posing as legitimate obligations, with morality as a medium of lawlessness and domination, or so Barth assumes. You won't end up with requirements that bind categorically, but rather with sin that asserts the right without knowing the good. But if you find something like that same logic animating intertriune relations, and if you use that logic to explicate the gospel of grace, as Barth does in *CD* II/2, chapter VIII, then you get precisely what Barth contends: you get Law as the form of Love.[26]

Stripped to the bone, the argument is familiar. Begin with an act that creates a relationship, count that relationship good precisely because it is a friendship, take note of the fact that this friendship comes into being against a backdrop of wrong, and what follows by way of requirement is the obligation to accept this gift, acknowledge this relationship, and reproduce this act, to be this friend, and to participate in this new relationship with a grateful heart.

Add some Christological flesh to this bone, and the argument, in brief outline, goes roughly like this. In Jesus Christ "God elects Himself to be gracious toward man" (*CD* II/2, p. 510). Since Jesus is both subject and object of this act, both "the electing God and the elected man in One," all of humanity exists as predicate to this divine Subject (*CD* II/2, p. 539) and thus all enjoy the effects of Christ's perfect obedience to this call.

And these effects are desperately needed. This call finds us in the condition of Adam, a creature determined by God to live as God's image, but now a "sinner who has perverted this determination" (*CD* II/2, p. 560). And yet, because "this God is He who in Jesus Christ became man, . . . it follows that the relationship between Him and man consists in the event in which God accepted man out of pure, free compassion, in which He drew him to Himself out of [this same] pure kindness" (*CD* II/2, p. 531). In *this* event, in this kind and gracious call of God, in this free and humble obedience of Jesus, "the good is done," the real good, as Barth says, "beyond all that merely pretends to be . . . good" (*CD* II/2, p. 517).

Make no mistake, this good is done on *our* behalf. It expresses God's good will for *us*. Insofar as we are predicates of Christ who is the Subject of this gracious election, we too are called, elected, and loved; we too participate in his righteousness, and in this call and response we are judged and restored to his image (*CD* II/2, pp. 539-40). While we were still sinners, God "assumed our humanity into His deity," subjected "Himself to the judgment and punishment that must be executed if we are to be raised up to Him," and in that resurrection he "ac-

---

26. Barth denies that he is borrowing an abstract account of social obligation and then just applying it in order to spell out the gospel's unity of authority and freedom. About this he is explicit. See *CD* II/2, p. 602.

complished both His own and our justification and glorification" (*CD* II/2, p. 558). All this, God has done for "His own good pleasure, His incomprehensible compassion"; all this, so that "our human existence is no longer alone" (*CD* II/2, p. 558).

Incomprehensible in origin but not necessarily in purpose. At the very least, we find Barth unwilling to say that God acts on our behalf for no good reason, for no identifiable end. Rather, he thinks that God's grace has "teleological power," that it intends to restore man "to divine likeness" for the sake of "fellowship with God in eternal life" (*CD* II/2, p. 566). The aim of election, in other words, is friendship or at least the promise of friendship. So Barth writes: "The revealed truth of the living God in His quickening Spirit has its content and force in the fact that it is He first who is for man, and then and for that reason man is for Him. God precedes therefore, and sets man in the movement in which he follows. He says Yes to him when man says No, and thus silences the No of man and lays a Yes in his heart and on his lips. He loves man even though he is an enemy (Rom. 5:10), and thus makes him the friend who loves Him in return" (*CD* IV/2, pp. 579-80).

Like every offer of friendship, this one comes with requirements that find their substance and warrant in the grace that initiates the relationship and delivers its goodness to the beloved. And like every friendship, this one requires friendship's love in return. To hear God's call and respond with obedience, we can do nothing "higher and deeper than to love Jesus" and keep his commandment to love all others (*CD* II/2, p. 569). And to do this, we must simply recognize that "in Him the realization of the good corresponding to divine election has already taken place — and so completely that we, for our part have nothing to add, but have only to endorse this event by our action" (*CD* II/2, p. 540). Actions that endorse this event will do nothing higher and deeper than express our recognition of the fact that we have been so loved and befriended. They will do nothing more than exhibit our acceptance of the good that God has done, our acquiescence in this new social status as God's beloved (CD II/2, p. 579).[27]

And of course, the justice of this divine claim and the real basis of

27. It is in this sense that "grace is the answer to the ethical problem," for it is grace that creates the indicative, the new social reality, from which the imperative follows. In this respect, "man will himself in some way be the answer" to the ethical question, for he is obliged to do nothing more than live in accord with his new social status (*CD* II/2, p. 516).

this obligation are consequences of this same election and obedience of Jesus Christ (*CD* II/2, pp. 556, 567). In that call and obedience, God wishes us well and does us good, and thus initiates a friendship, and it is the goodness of this relationship that justifies the requirements that follow and that gives us reason to respond as we should. The original covenant establishes the norm. God can justly bind Israel with the law precisely because God has graciously delivered Israel from unjust bondage (*CD* II/2, p. 572). And Israel can obey God's law and become God's people precisely because in the redemption that God has effected and in the relationship God has established, Israel has reason to "accept the gracious action of God as right" (*CD* II/2, p. 579). We must do the same, but this time, by accepting as right that our sole access to the good is through what God has done for us in Jesus Christ and that the sole content of our obligation is derived from this same good, this same grace and mercy (*CD* II/2, pp. 580-81). We must, in other words, have faith (*CD* II/2, p. 583).

The fallout of this faithful response to God's offer of friendship is the perfect union of authority and freedom, a union that finds its source and fulfillment in the person of Jesus Christ. As both the subject and object of election, Christ both commands and obeys, and his rightful authority is justified by his willing obedience (*CD* II/2, p. 606). For us, the promise of this union becomes a reality only as we have faith; only as we hear the Word of God, acknowledge the good that God has done for us, accept the friendship that has been extended to us, and respond in accord with this new social status. We experience this union, in other words, precisely when the requirement that emerges from this relationship comes as permission, when it amounts to nothing more than the obligation to be who we are, forgiven and befriended in Jesus Christ (*CD* II/2, p. 602), and to respond to this new reality with gratitude (*CD* II/2, p. 413).

Alien Obligation and Deferred Reconciliation

It is, without a doubt, a brilliant solution to "the ethical problem" that Barth takes up (*CD* II/2, p. 513). If you begin, as he does, with Kant's refusal of every heteronomous demand, of every obligation conditioned by some speculative given, and if you endorse the progression of nineteenth-century idealism from these Kantian commitments to

Hegel's anxieties about the alien character of unconditional require-ments to Nietzsche's suspicion that every *human* requirement expresses resentment's will to dominate, then finding something like Hegel's so-cial theory of obligation in the life of the Trinity is, as I said, brilliant. Through Christ's election and obedience, God establishes a relation-ship, a covenant of grace whose requirements are both categorical, be-cause they arise from the good that God has done, and yet not alien, because that good is done on our behalf by One who shares our hu-manity and because its yield is a friendship in which we can freely abide.

Of course, every theological account asks us to bear burdens of some sort, even the brilliant ones. Barth's is no exception and its bur-dens are well known, but they are given a new twist when put in terms of relationship and requirement, authority and freedom. An obligation that arises from a relationship will be neither illegitimate nor alien when the parties to it know the relationship to be good and its de-mands to be just. This, we said, requires practices of assessment, criti-cism, and mutual accountability, and this accent on reason-giving con-nects the authority to command with the willingness to obey. Since Jesus is both the electing God and the elected man in One, this connec-tion between authority and obedience is, in a sense, assumed in the cov-enant of grace. It is established and determined in divine action, not in critical practice. This much is plain.

But when we turn to our own action, to the temporal relations we find ourselves in and to the obligations that bind us all around, we have no choice but to take up these critical practices. The hope here is to separate wheat from chaff, to distinguish those relationships and at-tendant requirements that correspond to the friendship with human-ity created by Christ's election and to the obligation to love that ac-companies this friendship. In his excellent treatment of Barth's ethics, Gerry McKenny calls this correspondence "an analogy of grace,"[28] and he notes that Barth regards discernment of this analogy as an exercise of ordinary moral criticism, "albeit under the power of the Holy Spirit."[29] What the Spirit provides is direction, which bestows both the ability to hear God's command and do what it demands.[30]

---

28. McKenny, *Analogy of Grace,* p. 207.
29. McKenny, *Analogy of Grace,* p. 217.
30. McKenny, *Analogy of Grace,* p. 215.

But now the burdens. Barth insists that God's command comes in concrete circumstances, that it regards particular matters of choice, and that its formal character can never be known in advance (*CD* II/2, p. 663). But this means that whatever constancies we distill from the history of God's people as they hear that command can only be regarded as uncertain guidelines.[31] As McKenny puts it, the course of action that God actually commands can always go "against the balance of reasons" embedded in those constancies.[32] This uncertainty would be trouble enough, but things get worse. Barth expresses little, if any, confidence in our ability to grasp the normative content of those constancies, to know the good they embody or do the good they direct.[33] Our sanctification, like our justification, remains ever alien, which means that our retrospective accounting of past commands falls under the same hyper-Augustinian skepticism about our access to the good that Barth assumes throughout. The good is done in Jesus Christ, the good *for* us, and yet on the horizontal plane, *quoad nos,* that good remains opaque. Without access to that good, it's not at all clear how an analogy of grace can be discerned. Indeed, without a backdrop of normative assumption, of the ability to distinguish paradigmatic examples of good and bad relationships, good and bad requirements, it's not at all clear how we can deploy these concepts to speak of what God has done and what we must do.

Taken together, these two burdens — the actualist and the hyper-Augustinian — not only generate uncertainty about the concrete content of God's command, but they also make criticism and assessment of temporal obligations and their underlying relationships subject to this same uncertainty, this same troubling voluntarism.[34] It also means that critical practice within those relationships can never hope to unite authority and freedom in any reliable way. When God's command runs afoul of prior constancies exhibited in past commands, those who hear can only *assert* its content and *proclaim* its authority. They cannot appeal to reasons that refer to past constancies; they cannot engage in critical give-and-take. And of course, when this happens, their partners in a relationship who do not hear under the direction of the Spirit are

---

31. As my boys say, inspired by a recent movie, they come as pirate code: "The code is more what you'd call 'guidelines' than actual rules."

32. McKenny, *Analogy of Grace,* p. 269.

33. McKenny, *Analogy of Grace,* pp. 220-23.

34. I am grateful for Adam Eitel's excellent commentary on these matters.

likely to regard that command as alien. Indeed, they are likely to receive it as either lawlessness or domination.

Barth concedes as much. He writes: "the unity of authority and freedom which characterises the form of the divine command as opposed to all others is revealed and present to us as a promise and only as such, and therefore only in faith" (*CD* II/2, p. 603). It is a unity that the faithful can believe by acknowledging its source and substance in Christ's election, but it is a reality that they will experience in their temporal relationships only sporadically, if at all. More often than not, it will come as eschatological promise, not imperfect foretaste.

Aquinas's account of obligation has other troubles but not this one, and the reason is simple. The grace that creates a relationship and comes as command generates virtue and the Spirit's gifts. It re-creates judgments and loves. It forms them into habits, habits that have a certain fragility, no doubt, that need to be activated by the continual work of Holy Spirit, yes, and yet it is precisely this imperfect and dependent constancy of habit that the faithful use in their assessment and criticism of temporal affairs.[35] Since these virtues are infused by the Holy Spirit and enhance our participation in God's eternal law, we might say that these affairs are assessed only as God's law is brought to bear.

And of course, it is precisely the habitual character of this participation and the relative constancy of these re-created judgments and loves that enable the virtuous to engage in these critical practices in a way that is neither arbitrary, nor, for the most part, received as such. No doubt, their critical assessments of the good and the right will frequently run off the rails, and even when they stay on track, they will not always be *received* as true by those with whom they share a relationship. In this respect Thomas must also regard the perfect union of freedom and authority as a matter of faith's hope. Still, charity's accent on fraternal correction and mutual forbearance is designed to address disagreements of precisely this sort (*ST* II-II. q. 33). When these disagreements cannot be resolved, when correction has no purchase, the charitable are willing to bear the burden of these differences for the sake of the relationship they share with those they endure.

Forbearance across difference is plainly not the same as mutual endorsement of a valid requirement; it is not a union of authority and

---

35. Eugene Rogers, "How the Virtues of the Interpreter Presuppose and Perfect Hermeneutics," *Journal of Religion* (January 1996): 64-81.

freedom. But it does create the time and space for that union to come, and not only by eschatological anticipation, but also, in some measure, by faint foretaste also.

Modern Virtue

The social theory of obligation that Barth and Aquinas share brings these theological differences into focus. They are differences that are, in many ways, determined by distinct starting points. If you begin with Kant's insistence that only a spontaneous command can bind categorically and with Nietzsche's suspicion of every human attempt to locate categorical commands, then your account of sin and justification, of grace and election, of virtue and norm, can only take certain forms. Your appeal to a social theory of obligation will come with these same constraints. Begin elsewhere and those doctrines and that appeal will not be so constrained.

Whether by direct influence or tacit inspiration, Barth's social theory of obligation is Hegelian in form, if not in substance, and Hegel developed that theory, in part, to liberate himself from precisely these constraints.[36] This is the mystery in Barth's appeal to that theory. Liberation never came.

Those of us who admire this line of inspiration and like to imagine what might have been had Barth taken the next step down this Hegelian path could do no better than to develop a thoroughly modern account of the virtues, both acquired and infused. Such an account would take the critical turn seriously and distrust every speculative appeal, every arbitrary assertion of some abstract given. It would hold fast to traditional claims about justification, but without hyper-Augustinian exaggerations. And it would follow Barth's lead on the moral consequences of election, but without being compelled to satisfy Kant's commitment to the unconditional and without fear of Nietzsche's nihilism.

It would do all this, and nevertheless find a way to retain the tra-

---

36. Hegel borrowed it from Aristotle. That Barth, in some way, borrows it from Hegel implies that his account of divine command and human obligation is Aristotelian. For an account of Barth's ethics that spells out its connections to the traditions of *eudaimonia,* see Matthew Rose, *Ethics with Barth: God, Metaphysics and Morals* (Farnham, UK: Ashgate, 2010).

ditional pieces — action ordered to ends and perfected by habits, habits informing the soul, the soul habituated by imitation, imitation mediated by communal norm, and communal norm as a medium of God's grace.[37] This is a lot to ask, I know, and happily, we can defer an answer to another day.

37. This work has already begun. See Thomas Lewis, *Freedom and Tradition in Hegel: Reconsidering Anthropology, Ethics, and Religion* (Notre Dame: University of Notre Dame Press, 2005).

Divine Action and Human Action in St. Thomas Aquinas: An *Analogia Legis*

Holly Taylor Coolman

In this work of bringing Aquinas and Barth into dialogue, we have considered a number of important themes: (1) the nature of God; (2) Trinity, in particular; (3) Christology; and (4) under the designation of "grace and justification," the salvific union of the human person with Christ. Here in this essay, our focus broadens from "grace and justification" to consider the larger matter of "divine and human action." In a sense, then, the very logic of this volume sets the agenda for this essay. It invites reflection on the topic of divine and human action in a way that is other than — or broader than — grace and justification, or salvific union with Christ. This is, in fact, a salutary task, as it reveals important dimensions of Aquinas's thought, and highlights both differences with Barth, as well as, perhaps, ground for convergence.

The Surprising Scope of *Lex*

I would like to address the question of divine and human action by focusing on a particular section from St. Thomas's *Summa theologiae*. This essay will, in fact, proceed as a kind of exegesis of this section. In the *Prima secundae*, qq. 98-108, Aquinas offers a remarkably rich and coherent account in what is called the "treatise on the law."[1] Taking for its

---

1. It is important to note that this designation is not original to Aquinas himself. Mark Jordan puts it thus: "There is no 'treatise' on the law. The *Summa* is not built out of treatises, but from clusters of Questions caught up into larger and larger dialectical

conceptual center *lex,* or law, this section of the *Summa* deals with divine and human action in a unique way, and attention to it can assist us not only in understanding Aquinas, but also in understanding Aquinas vis-à-vis Barth.

Interestingly enough, students of Aquinas have tended not to read this "treatise on the law" — or at least not to read it as a whole. Although the section is clearly unified by this single term, *lex,* it has been almost invariably dismembered, and isolated sections carried off to be studied without any reference to the others.[2] Particularly the long battles over nature and grace in the modern period have tempted scholars to wrest a single question, 94, from its context, in an attempt to understand Aquinas on "nature."

It is worth noting, however, if we are to speak precisely, that q. 94 does not deal with "nature," nor is there any treatise on "nature" in the *Summa.* Aquinas does, of course, speak of nature; well known is his claim that "gratia non tollit naturam, sed perficit" ("grace does not destroy nature, but rather perfects it"). What he is treating here in this much-discussed section, however, is natural *law.* If we are to understand his claims, we must keep this second term, the term being qualified, in mind. In fact, "natural law" is an integral part of a larger discussion; it is just one of five forms of this larger reality that Aquinas calls *"lex."* As we focus our attention on that larger reality, certain crucial emphases appear.

In fact, *lex,* as it is presented here, is a surprisingly large reality. Although this treatise has a very specific focus, which is clearly spelled out, its scope extends much further than readers might initially guess. In order first to explore its more specific ambit, we must step back even further in order to see the treatise on the law in the context of the

rhythms. Within *Summa* I-II, . . . the reader begins with the end, with the goal toward which human life tends. The reader ends with law and grace, which Thomas counts as exterior principles of human acts leading toward the good and given by God. The entire structural unit moves forward in response to the pull of the highest human end." Mark Jordan, *Rewritten Theology: Aquinas After His Readers* (Malden, MA: Wiley-Blackwell, 2006), p. 139.

2. The practice of "dismembering" the *Summa* is almost as old as the *Summa* itself. Cf. Leonard E. Boyle, O.P., "The Setting of the *Summa Theologiae* of St. Thomas — Revisited," in *The Ethics of Aquinas,* ed. Stephen J. Pope (Washington, DC: Georgetown University Press, 2002), pp. 17-29. In this case, however, the antiquity of the practice does not render it salutary.

whole of the second part of the *Summa*. Aquinas describes very explicitly his purpose: the subject matter of the *Secunda pars,* he says, is human happiness. Aquinas understands the proper end *(telos)* of humanity to be happiness, but he believes that ultimate happiness is achieved only as human persons "surpass their own nature,"[3] attaining by the power of God to the perfect good. The perfect good is God alone,[4] or, to speak more precisely with respect to human beings, this happiness consists in the vision of God's own essence.[5] This elevation beyond humanity's natural power, Aquinas names "grace" — or, from another perspective — friendship with God. It is, in other words, through friendship with God that God shapes human beings for the vision of the divine essence itself. This is not, it is important to note, an instantaneous achievement, or one simply accomplished by divine fiat. It is rather a concrete, gradual process in which God moves humans toward the goodness that allows for happiness,[6] and Aquinas says that preparation will be characterized, above all, by right ordering of the will. We might say, then, that the specific question addressed by the whole *Secunda pars* is how this process works, how, that is, human beings are drawn into friendship with God, and fitted for the vision of God.

Now, the first part of the *Secunda pars,* the *Prima secundae,* attends to the process by which human beings are fitted for the vision of God in two large sections: (1) human action and (2) the principles of this human action. The second section, on principles of human action, is then further divided into two parts: "intrinsic" principles and "extrinsic" principles. Under intrinsic principles, Aquinas treats the "habits," good and bad, in which human persons are formed. These habits are healthy and elevate fundamental inclinations toward the good that are inscribed within human nature itself by God. Under "extrinsic principles," he treats that which inclines humans "from without," either to evil — which Aquinas also describes in its personal form, as Satan — or

---

3. "Alia autem est beatitudo naturam hominis excedens, ad quam homo solo divina virtute pervenire potest. . . ." *ST* I-II, q. 62, a. 1, co. All citations of the *Summa* in Latin are taken from the Corpus Thomisticum S. Thomas de Aquino Opera Omnia (Universitatis Studiorum Navarrensis, 2009), available online at: www.corpusthomisticum.org/iopera.html. Hereafter, *ST.* English translations are taken from the Blackfriars edition (London: Blackfriars, 1964-80).

4. *ST* I-II, q. 2, a. 8, co.

5. *ST* I-II, q. 2, a. 8, co.

6. *ST* I-II, q. 5, a. 1, co.

to good, which is God. In this last category, the extrinsic principles that lead human beings toward good, Aquinas delineates even further. God "inclines us to good," he says, in two ways: he "both instructs us by His Law, and assists us by His Grace." We can now say more specifically what the placement of the treatise on the law indicates, according to Aquinas's own claims: the law is one of the two primary things outside of human beings that move them toward ultimate happiness in seeing God.

As it turns out, however, there is more than that involved. In this treatise — as I will try to spell out here briefly — under this single term, *lex,* Aquinas in fact describes the whole sweep of God's wise work in and with humanity, as well as God's own wisdom. *Everything,* he says, can be understood as ordered according to the eternal law, which is a name for God's own reason,[7] and which, indeed, "is not distinct from Himself."[8] *All* truth, he goes on, consists in participation in this eternal law, and *all* created things gain their inclinations to certain acts and ends — their identity, we might say — by this participation. *Lex* includes all of God's action for creation, but also all human actions that imitate and participate in God's work. It's a sweeping statement, but it is true to say: Aquinas describes *all of reality* here not in terms of, say, being, but in terms of *lex.*

As a way of summing up this introduction and laying out clearly what I hope to argue here, I would first briefly note two more specific things about this reality of *lex* in Aquinas's thought. First — as one might begin to guess from the scope just described — the term *lex* is here unfolded in a complex and analogical way. For Aquinas, to offer any term as describing both God and creation means that the term in question must be deployed analogically.[9] Second, this analogy that encompasses everything that exists deserves more attention than it gets. This *analogia legis,* if we may speak of it as such, can serve to specify and nuance Aquinas's larger claims.

Specifically, for our purposes here, I would argue that in the way Aquinas employs the single, unifying concept of *lex,* we are able to see the relationship between human and divine action with coherence and, within that coherence, with a kind of nuanced complexity that does

---

7. "Et ideo ipsa ratio gubernationis rerum in Deo sicut in principe universitatis existens, legis habet rationem." *ST* I-II, q. 91, a. 1, sc.
8. ". . . eius lex est aliud ab ipso." *ST* I-II, q. 91, a. 1, ad 3.
9. *ST* I, q. 13, a. 5.

not appear in any other single section of his writing — and this nuance is helpful when considering Aquinas vis-à-vis Barth.[10]

With this in mind, we can turn to consider *lex* in the five forms in which Aquinas describes it: (1) eternal, (2) natural, (3) human, and (4) Divine, with its dual forms of (4a) Old and (4b) New.

Eternal Law

First and most foundational is the eternal law. The eternal law, we might say, is simply *lex* itself. Aquinas quotes Augustine to describe it as "the Supreme Reason,"[11] and argues that we must posit this fundamental sense of *lex* as a logical correlate of Providence: "Now it is evident, granted that the world is ruled by Divine Providence, as was stated in the First Part (q. 22, aa. 1-2), that the whole community of the universe is governed by Divine Reason. Wherefore the very idea of the government of things in God the Ruler of the universe, has the nature of a law."[12]

The eternal law, we might say in the context of this section, is for Aquinas the most fundamental principle of divine action. For Aquinas, of course, this principle, this divine reason, exists in God in complete simplicity, and so Aquinas is able to say that the eternal law is so closely related to God that, in fact, it "is not distinct from Himself."[13] The eternal law is the source of every other kind of law; every other law is derived from it.

Immediately, though, a question confronts us, if we note a definition that Aquinas has already given of *"lex."* Aquinas begins the treatise on the law by introducing three crucial characteristics. *Lex* is (1) an ordinance of reason (2) directed to the common good and (3) promulgated by one who has the authority to do so. The first two of these are ones we can perhaps affirm of the eternal law, but the third and final

---

10. Teachers of Aquinas's thought may want to consider this section of the *Summa theologiae* as perhaps the best candidate for a single excerpt — with original integrity preserved — to use as an introductory text for students.

11. "Summa ratio," *ST* I-II, q. 91, a. 1, sc.

12. "Manifestum est autem, supposito quod mundus divina providentia regatur, ut in Primo habitum est, quod tota communitas universi gubernatur ratione divina. Et ideo ipsa ratio gubernationis rerum in Deo sicut in principe universitatis existens, legis habet rationem." *ST,* I-II, q. 91, a. 1, co.

13. ". . . nec eius lex est aliud ab ipso." *ST* I-II, q. 91, a. 1, ad 3.

raises a more serious question. What could it possibly mean to say that the eternal law, the "very idea of the government of things in God," is promulgated? Is the eternal law *imposed* upon God?

The notion of promulgation "in" God is, of course, odd, and Aquinas wrestles with the issue elsewhere: "Since good as perceived by intellect is the object of the will, it is impossible for God to will anything but what His wisdom approves. This is, as it were, His law of justice, in accordance with which His will is right and just. Hence, what He does according to His will He does justly: as we do justly what we do according to law. But whereas law comes to us from some higher power, God is a law unto Himself."[14] In other words, we can understand promulgation in the eternal law in a certain sense: this is timeless promulgation, not between a subject and object, but existing in the perfect expression of God's will, which always simply is just.

In this difference between eternal law and the everyday forms of law with which we are more familiar, we see what must be a sort of analogy, although Aquinas does not here use the word. *Lex*, as it exists in God, is both like and unlike the other forms of *lex* we know more immediately. Without advancing an elaborate theory of analogy or dealing carefully with various sorts of analogy, we should begin by saying: what this first form of *lex*, the eternal law, makes clear is that *lex* is treated by Aquinas analogically, that we are dealing with what we might call an *analogia legis*.[15]

Were we dealing with that more famous *analogia*, the *analogia entis*,

14. "Ad secundum dicendum quod, cum bonum intellectum sit obiectum voluntatis, impossibile est Deum velle nisi quod ratio suae sapientiae habet. Quae quidem est sicut lex iustitiae, secundum quam eius voluntas recta et iusta est. Unde quod secundum suam voluntatem facit, iuste facit, sicut et nos quod secundum legem facimus, iuste facimus. Sed nos quidem secundum legem alicuius superioris, Deus autem sibi ipsi est lex . . . ." *ST* I, q. 21, a. 1, ad 2.

15. It is certainly valuable to keep in mind the variety of ways in which "analogy" can be, and has been, deployed. Cf., e.g., Wolfhart Pannenberg, *Analogie und Offenbarung. Eine kritische Untersuchung zur Geschichte des Analogiebegriffes in der Lehre von der Gotteserkenntnis* (Göttingen: Vandenhoeck & Ruprecht, 2007), as well as treatments that have Aquinas, in particular, in view: Reinhard Hütter, "Attending to the Wisdom of God — From Effect to Cause, from Creation to God: A Contemporary *relecture* of the Doctrine of the Analogy of Being according to Thomas Aquinas," in *The Analogy of Being: Invention of the Antichrist or the Wisdom of God?* ed. Thomas Joseph White, O.P. (Grand Rapids: Eerdmans, 2011), pp. 209-45; and Gregory P. Rocca, O.P., *Speaking the Incomprehensible God* (Washington, DC: Catholic University of America Press, 2004).

which must be faced in any dialogue between Aquinas and Barth, we would face the crucial questions that arise in relation to that *analogia*. What is this category *ens*? From where does it arise? Finally, and most important of all, what has it to do with Christ? In the context of an *analogia legis,* however, Aquinas answers this final and most important question explicitly and decisively.

Aquinas describes the eternal law, this founding component of *lex,* in *explicitly Christological terms.* In *ST* I-II, q. 93, a. 1, Aquinas begins to establish this important characterization as he discusses whether the eternal law is a [*ratio*] "sovereign type" existing in God. In the form of an objection, he suggests that perhaps the law should not be called a *ratio,* but rather a personal name for God; after all, "it is essential to a law that it be promulgated by word [*verbum*]. . . . But Word is a personal name for God."[16] In his response, he rejects this suggestion (he argues, in other words, that "eternal law" should be understood as a *ratio,* and not as a personal name), but he does so in a way that clearly asserts Christological connections to the eternal law:

> in God the Word conceived by the intellect of the Father is the name of a Person: but all things that are in the Father's knowledge, whether they refer to the Essence or to the Persons, or to the works of God, are expressed by this Word, as Augustine declares (De Trin. XV. 14). And among other things expressed by the Word, the eternal law is expressed thereby. Nor does it follow that the eternal law is a personal name in God: yet it is appropriated to the Son, on account of the kinship between type and word.[17]

The eternal law, along with all things that are "in the Father's knowledge," then, is specifically expressed by Christ and is "appropriated" to him. (Here, Aquinas makes use of the traditional Trinitarian doctrine of appropriations to the individual Persons.)

16. ". . . de ratione legis est quod verbo promulgetur. . . . Sed Verbum in divinis dicitur personaliter. . . ." *ST* I-II, q. 93, a. 1, obj. 2.
17. "Sic igitur in divinis ipsum Verbum, quod est conceptio paterni intellectus, personaliter, dicitur: sed omnia quaecumque sunt in scientia Patris, sive essentialia sive personalia, sive etiam Dei opera exprimuntur hoc Verbo, ut patet per Augustinum, in XV de Trin. Et inter cetera quae hoc Verbo exprimuntur, etiam ipsa lex aeterna Verbo ipso exprimitur. Nec tamen propter hoc sequitur quod lex aeterna personaliter in divinis dicatur. Appropriatur tamen filio, propter convenientiam quam habet ratio ad verbum." *ST* I-II, q. 93, a. 1, ad 2.

And yet the appropriation of the eternal law to Christ is not the end of its Christological connections. Just a little later, Aquinas argues in a way that makes clear that there is, from another perspective, an even closer connection between Christ and the eternal law specifically. In *ST* I-II, q. 93, a. 4, Aquinas — continuing to explore issues of God's nature and Christology — argues that it is not appropriate to describe the Son as subject to the eternal law, since "God the Son was not made by God, but was naturally born of God. Consequently He is not subject to Divine Providence or to the eternal law: but rather is Himself the eternal law by a kind of appropriation."[18] Here, then, we have even more than the law being expressed by Christ. Although the law does not serve as a personal name for God, nevertheless it can be said, if we keep in mind the doctrine of appropriations, that Christ "*is* himself the eternal law" [emphasis added].

Here, then, at the foundation of his discussion of *"lex,"* Aquinas makes clear that all *lex* has its ground in the eternal law, the wisdom of God, and — we can now say more specifically — in Christ himself.

So, as we explore Aquinas on divine and human action via this category of *lex*, we must remember that all forms of *lex* are what they are by virtue of participation in the eternal law, a law that by appropriation *is Christ himself.* At this point, we see the full implication of Aquinas's Christological focus. At the deepest level, when we ask of Aquinas, "What is *lex*? What is this foundational category in which all of reality can be understood?" he could respond by saying: "By way of appropriation, Christ himself, or else a relation to him."

With an engagement of Aquinas and Barth in view, this is a very important point. Keith Johnson has noted that, in the end, the difference between Barth and Aquinas on the analogical relationship between God and creation might best be thought of as the difference between an analogy rooted in creation and an analogy rooted in redemption.[19] This direction of thinking is profoundly promising. Perhaps, though, we could more accurately describe Aquinas by saying that here, in this *analogia legis,* in the way that he describes the eternal

<hr>

18. ". . . Filus Dei non est a Deo factus, sed naturaliter ab ipso genitus. Et ideo non subditur divinae providentiae aut legi aeternae: sed magis ipse est lex aeterna per quondam appropriationem. . . ." *ST* I-II, q. 93, a. 4, ad 2.

19. Keith L. Johnson, "A Reappraisal of Barth's Theological Development and His Dialogue with Catholicism," *International Journal for Systematic Theology* 14, no. 1 (January 2012): 3-25.

law, he posits Christ as the term of the analogy in a way that precedes and encompasses both creation and redemption. This *analogia legis,* in other words, is an *analogia Christi.*

If we are seeking common ground, we might do well to begin with an *analogia Christi.* We might agree together that Christ is, fundamentally, the common term of the analogy, that Christ is always the way in which humanity is related to God, and then go on to address the relationship between creation and redemption in the way that humans beings know, and are related to, God.

Natural Law

Already, however, our *analogia legis,* an *analogia Christi,* begins to be complicated as we go on to the natural law. In a section much studied and debated, Aquinas describes this second form of law.[20] With the topic of divine and human action in mind, we might say that human action per se begins here, with the natural law.

Unfortunately — and perhaps especially because of the way it is read in isolation, as mentioned above, the natural law is sometimes thought of (1) primarily in reference to the human beings who are governed by it, or (2) in reference to the precepts that are contained within it. Aquinas is clear, however, that natural law precedes both of these

---

20. This has certainly been the most studied section of the treatise on the law. Unfortunately, the natural law is often treated as relevant strictly for questions of moral theology and is often abstracted from the treatise as a whole. Pamela Hall's excellent work in *Narrative and the Natural Law* is a welcome counterexample; her focus is the natural law, but her study is conducted within the context of the whole treatise (Notre Dame: University of Notre Dame Press, 1994). Another example: "Thomas Aquinas's *Treatise on Law* (hereafter '*Treatise*') is enjoying a resurgence of interest among legal scholars. It is excerpted in leading legal philosophy texts, assigned in jurisprudence courses and even cited in law journal articles and legal monographs on a wide range of subjects. Although the *Treatise* consists of nineteen chapters ('questions'), the average student of legal philosophy is likely to have been exposed only to portions of the first eight and little, if any, of the last eleven. The *Treatise* is not a short work, and most of the editorial decisions are both practically necessary and pedagogically understandable. Nevertheless, omitting the 'rest' of the *Treatise* has had some unfortunate consequences." From "The Bible as a Law Book? Thomas Aquinas on the Juridical Uses of Scripture," William S. Brewbaker III, http://www.lawandreligion.com/sites/lawandreligion.com/files/Vol%2012%20F10-2%20Brewbaker_0.pdf.

things: it is present, in fact, even in those who might never act by it. It is important at this point to note the most basic definition of natural law. It is above all the participation of rational creatures in the eternal law and, more precisely, the participation of humanity's practical reason in the good.[21] This participation does yield concrete precepts as human reason follows the first principle of practical reason: "good is to be done and pursued, and evil is to be avoided."[22]

Now natural law, of course, operates in human beings, and so, unlike eternal law, it becomes at the Fall, subject to the effects of sin. It is not, however, completely erased by it. The continued reality of natural law in the face of sin makes sense, though, if we consider that natural law is what constitutes human action as human. This is a second, crucially important point. Whereas the positing of an *analogia legis* may set the stage for a new rapprochement between Aquinas and Barth, Aquinas's positing of the natural law reminds us how complicated any such rapprochement must be.

We can make best sense of Aquinas's position if we recall that the natural law springs, in the first place, from God. God, of course, creates human beings as good and sinless, and Aquinas simply does not see human beings as capable of their own basic un-creation. Their sin can mar, but it cannot undo, God's work. Human beings can weaken and distort the essential relation to Christ that makes them to be human beings — and here we could say more specifically, human *agents* — but they cannot break it completely. Or, we could say this: although human beings exercise the capacities inherent in the natural law, they do not, in the end, wield ultimate power over it. Something must come into one's control in order for one to destroy it. Rather than describing the natural law fundamentally as a capacity that human beings control, for Aquinas, we should rather describe it as a capacity by which they are constituted by God. Here, of course, is a serious disagreement between Aquinas and Barth. For Barth, human beings are tremendously powerful in their sin: by their action, they have revoked any access at all to

21. "Now among all others, the rational creature is subject to Divine providence in the most excellent way, in so far as it partakes of a share of providence, by being provident both for itself and for others. Wherefore it has a share of the Eternal Reason, whereby it has a natural inclination to its proper act and end: and this participation of the eternal law in the rational creature is called the natural law." *ST* I-II, q. 91, a. 2, co.

22. "Hoc est ergo primum praeceptum legis, quod bonum est faciendum et prosequendum, et malum vitandum." *ST* I-II, q. 94, a. 2, co.

creation as such. For Aquinas, on the other hand, natural law is the name of this unbreakable form of the participation in Christ.

There is, of course, also the greater reality of salvific union with Christ, so that we could say, in positing natural law, Aquinas allows for differing intensities of participation in this *analogia legis*. There are, he would say, individual human beings who exercise the capacity of natural law, but do not (yet) come into this union with Christ. There are human beings who are only related to Christ in the sense that they are constituted by their participation in the eternal law — and, on the other hand, there are human beings who are united to Christ by faith, who trust in God and believe in him through grace (or, as we shall shortly delineate, those who are constituted by their participation in the new form of the divine law).

Here, then, seems to be an impasse as far as Aquinas and Barth are concerned. Perhaps, given the practical theme at hand — divine and human action — we might simply pose a very practical point. One advantage, we could say, of Aquinas's position, is that it allows him to delineate a way in which human actions apart from salvific union with Christ can be seen as truly human, and indeed, truly good, although only in a limited sense. With the focus here on *lex,* we could say that the natural law allows for genuine appreciation of human attempts, quite apart from faith in Christ, to govern the affairs of human beings, to work for peace. What possibility exists for this, if we insist that our *analogia Christi* has only to do with redemption? This issue may be even clearer as we consider human law.

Human Law

Closely related, then, to the natural law is the third form of law, human law, a flexible form of law, in which particular precepts governing a particular community are derived from natural law. Now again, Aquinas here is claiming that human law, as a derivation of natural law, is orderly and good because it is the expression of a relation to God's own wisdom, a divine attribute, that is especially appropriated to the Second Person.

Indeed, Aquinas argues that laws bind the conscience, that is, obligate when, and only when, they conform to the eternal law.[23] Insofar

---

23. *ST* I-II, q. 96, a. 4.

as any law does not do this, insofar as it is not ordered to the common good (including the requirement that it not place disproportionate burdens on any of the subjects involved), or insofar it is not promulgated by one who has authority to do so, then Aquinas argues it is not a law at all. Although it seems to be a law, it is really more like an act of violence. Thus he approvingly quotes Augustine as saying that it seems that an unjust law is no law at all.[24]

Now, I would argue that there are two salutary elements in this deceptively simple section on human law. First, it clearly involves the everyday exercise of practical human reason in a way that is radically ennobling in our context. As the concrete, specific making of law and submission to human law and enforcement of law are seen as part of *lex*, these actions come to be seen as an integral way in which God is drawing humanity to himself. To think in this way is to accord a remarkable level of dignity to everything from the deliberations of a town council to the deliberations of the Supreme Court, and to everything from a stop sign to the Magna Carta.

Second, the category of human law presses even more sharply the question about the account Christians give about non-Christians. In this practical light, with the question of human law at hand, we see even more clearly a question emerging. In pluralistic settings, those who are living by faith in Christ must collaborate in various ways with those who are not. If Christians, however, are unable to give any account of the actions of their collaborators as truly human, and, in some sense, truly good, it is unclear how any form of collaboration can go forward.

And this appears as a challenge to Barth. If there is no category such as the one proposed by Aquinas in the natural law — a category in which human action is understood in connection to Christ and yet outside of the redemptive encounter with Christ through the Spirit — then what could Christians think of non-Christians? We simply do not have much to say to those who do not have this encounter. Even as he demonstrated what it would look like to resist an evil political structure during the Nazi regime, Barth himself did not found a commune. He continued to live in the *polis,* as we do. In his description of human law within the wider context of *lex,* Aquinas gives a coherent account of what it means to be not of the world, but yet in it.

24. *De lib. arbit.* I, 5. PL 32, p. 1227.

Divine: Old and New

Finally, we come to the two most closely related forms of law, the Old Law and the New Law. Indeed, these two are described by Aquinas under a single term, Divine Law, so called because it is a law given directly to humanity by God. This single entity, says Aquinas, is the form by which humanity is moved beyond natural faculties — expressed in the natural and human laws — and is directed toward its final end, the vision of God, or "friendship with God."[25] The Divine Law also exceeds previous forms of human law in at least two other respects. First, it forbids all sins, a task too great for natural or human law. Second, it is able to treat not only "exterior acts," which human beings are competent to regulate, but also "interior movements" that are seen by God alone.[26]

Aquinas begins the discussion of the relationship of the Old Law and New Law by focusing on this unity. Both forms of the Divine Law, he reminds us, possess crucial characteristics. Especially important for our purposes is that they are both (1) directed toward making human beings righteous, and (2) imposed upon those who are subject to them, or, we might say, promulgated. In these twin forms of the Divine Law, the specific form of righteousness engendered is subjection to God.[27]

Aquinas further insists that as it is defined by these ends, the New Law adds nothing to the Old. This is true, for example, in regard to practice. It is not possible, for example, to say that the Old Law is distinguished by "works," since, in the case of the moral precepts, the observance required by the Old Law continues under the New Law.[28] Aquinas's surprising claim that "the letter, even of the Gospel, would kill, unless there were the inward presence of the healing grace of faith,"[29] makes clear his assumption that the New Law, too, involves works.[30] Perhaps even more startling, Aquinas claims that in regard to belief, the New adds nothing to the Old. Anything revealed in the New

---

25. ". . . amicitiam hominis ad Deum. . . ." *ST* I-II, q. 99, a. 2, co.

26. *ST* I-II, q. 91, a. 4, co.

27. *ST* I-II, q. 107, a. 1, co.

28. *ST* I-II, q. 107, a. 2, ad 1.

29. "Unde etiam littera Evangelii occideret, nisi adesset interius gratia fidei sanans." *ST* I-II, q. 106, a. 2, co.

30. Elsewhere, he expands on a twofold relationship between grace and external acts in the New Law: some external acts, i.e., the sacraments, lead to grace; others "ensue from the promptings of grace." *ST* I-II, q. 108, a. 1, co.

Law, he says, is also present in the Old. Indeed, at every point, Aquinas insists that the "substance" of the New Law is not new at all, but is entirely "in" the Old.[31]

At this point, we might ask how any differentiation can be made at all between Old and New Law. In explaining his position, Aquinas himself turns several times to a quotation from the epistle to the Hebrews: "The priesthood being translated, it is necessary that a translation also be made of the Law."[32] The New Law is, in other words, the Old Law *in translation*. The question, then, is: What is the nature of this translation?

There are at least three elements involved. In the first two, perfection and fulfillment, it becomes clear: the move from Old Law to New Law is one of teleological development, and the substance that the two share is precisely a relatedness to *Christ*. While the Old Law primarily looks forward to Christ, the New Law offers him as fully present; now New Law brings [quoting Aquinas] "a power flowing from Christ already incarnate and crucified."[33]

Stepping back then, to consider again this larger reality of *lex*, we must say that Christ is not only the foundation of the law, but also its *telos*. Just as all law begins in the eternal law, which is Christ, so law reaches its fullest form for humanity in the New Law, which is characterized by Christological fulfillment. Furthermore, in this unfolding of *lex*, we see the way in which the historical work of God, in Israel and in Christ, is paramount. *Lex* is not simply related to the second person of the Trinity in the ways described with connection to the eternal law. Moving on to the Divine Law reminds readers of Aquinas that *lex* — this category that describes all things — is a reality firmly and explicitly rooted in the concrete realities of unfolding salvation history.

The New Law, however, has further claims to make. Another crucial difference between the two forms of Divine Law appears in the most basic respective *forms* of the Old and of the New Law. The Old Law — not surprisingly — consists most essentially in the written pre-

31. "Sed quantum ad ipsam substantiam praeceptorum Novi Testamenti, monia continentur in Veteri Testamento. . . ." *ST* I-II, q. 107, a. 3, ad 2.

32. "Translato sacerdotio, necesse est ut legis translatio fiat." Cf. Hebrews 7:12. See, for example, *ST* I-II, q. 104, a. 3 and q. 107, a. 1.

33. "Et quiam mysterium incarnationis et passionis Christi nondum erat realiter in se continere realiter virtutem profluentem a Christo incarnate et passo. . . ." *ST* I-II, q. 103, a. 2, co.

cepts that constitute it. The New Law, on the other hand, although it can also be described as "written," has a profoundly different form. The New Law, says Aquinas, "is chiefly the grace itself of the Holy Ghost, which is given to those who believe in Christ."[34] Here again, Aquinas quotes Augustine: "as the law of deeds was written on tables of stone, so is the law of faith inscribed on the hearts of the faithful" and "What else are the Divine laws written by God Himself on our hearts, but the very presence of His Holy Spirit?"[35]

The relationship between Old and New, then, involves a radical translation in form, as radical as the difference between words engraved on stone and the grace of the Holy Spirit itself. This characterization makes clear, as it is added to those above, that in the movement toward teleological perfection and fulfillment, there is also surprising disjunction.[36] This work of the Spirit *is* something new. It is *not*, however, something that undermines or overruns Aquinas's category of law. Indeed, if we return to Aquinas's foundational definition of law, we can see this work of the Spirit in the New Law as finally making law itself fully and perfectly law. This comes about as the Spirit becomes the crucial agent of law's fourth essential characteristic, promulgation.

We recall Aquinas's argument that "in order that a law obtain the binding force which is proper to a law, it must needs be applied to the men who have to be ruled by it."[37] He makes clear that for law to be present in a full sense, those under the law must not only be made aware of the law; they must also be bound to obey it. We might note

34. "Id autem quod est potissimum in lege novi testamenti, et in quo tota virtus eius consistit, est gratia Spiritus Sancti, quae datur per fidem Christi." *ST* I-II, q. 106, a. 1, co.

35. ". . . sicut lex factorum scripta fuit in tabulis lapideis, ital ex fidei scripta est in cordibus fidelum. . . . Quae sunt leges Dei ab ipso Deo scripta in cordibus, nisi ipsa praesentia Spiritus Sancti?" *ST* I-II q. 106, a. 1, co., quoting *De Spiritu et Littera* 24, PL 44, p. 225 and 21, p. 222.

36. To speak of the relationship between Old and New *solely* in terms of "analogy" is ill-advised, since this term used alone could obscure dimensions of profound relatedness between the two. Specifically, the use of the term "analogy" here must be distinguished from its most common referent, Aquinas's discussion of the Divine Names in *ST* I, q. 13. The analogical relationship outlined there is clearly one of more profound disjunction than this one.

37. "Unde ad hoc quod lex virtutem obligandi obtineat, quod est proprium legis, oportet quod applicetur homnibus qui secundum eam regulari debent." *ST* I-II, q. 90, a. 4, co.

here Aquinas's insistence on the impossibility of a private person making law: "A private person cannot lead another to virtue efficaciously; for he can only advise, and if his advice be not taken, it has no coercive power, such as law should have, in order to prove an efficacious inducement to virtue."[38] Law, then, is not fully law without coercive power. But it is also the case that one forced against her will to obey does not have the law "in" her, at least not in a "perfect way," as Aquinas describes one component of promulgation; a law is "in" a person "by participation as in one that is ruled. In the latter way each one is a law to himself, in so far as he shares the direction that he receives from one who rules him."[39] Perfect *lex*, then, will not only advise, but induce efficaciously to virtue, and yet this in perfect accord with, rather than in opposition to, the will of the one ruled.

Thus, we can see the Spirit's work of writing the law on hearts as perfect promulgation. The New Law is "instilled into man, not only by indicating to him what he should do, but also by helping him to accomplish it."[40] This help, in fact, consists in bringing those under the law to obey the law *precisely in compliance with their own will;* because their hearts have been changed, obedience is at the same time the law's demand and their own free choice. Thus, he says, the New Law is called "the law of liberty," because it "makes us comply freely with these precepts and prohibitions."[41] The Spirit, far from overcoming or undermining the law, rather makes the law perfect.

Strengthening the sense that the Spirit's work should be understood as "promulgation" is Aquinas's argument regarding the natural law and promulgation. In his objection, he asks whether promulgation really is essential to law, after all, and cites the example of natural law. Natural law isn't really *promulgated,* is it?[42] It is, says Aquinas: "The nat-

---

38. ". . . persona privata non potest inducere efficaciter ad virtutem. Potest enim solum monere, sed si sua monitio non recipiatur, non habet vim coactivam; quam debet habere lex, ad hoc quod efficaciter inducat ad virtutem. . . ." *ST* I-II, q. 90, a. 3, ad 2.

39. ". . . lex est in aliquot non solum sicut in regulante, sed etiam participative sicut in regulato. Et hoc modo unusquisque sibi est lex, inquantum participat ordinem alicuius regulantis." *ST* I-II, q. 90, a. 3, ad 1.

40. "Et hoc modo lex nova est indita homini, non solum indicans quid sit faciendum, sed etiam adiuvans ad implendum." *ST* I-II, q. 106, a. 1, ad 2.

41. ". . . huiusmodi etiam praecepta vel prohibitions facit nos libere implore, inquantum ex interiori instinctu gratiae ea implemus." *ST* I-II, q. 108, a. 1, ad 2.

42. *ST* I-II, q. 90, a. 4, obj. 1.

ural law is promulgated by the very fact that God instilled it into man's mind so as to be known by him naturally."[43] For Aquinas, then, we might say that the New Law involves God's making the Christological substance of the Divine Law to be promulgated in a way similar to that of the natural law. This form of law then — promulgated perfectly through pneumatological power — constitutes not the law's distortion or disruption, but rather its perfection.

Just as importantly, we see here a culmination of *lex* not only in Christ, but also in the work of the Spirit. As we are trying to parse carefully the differences between Aquinas and Barth, it may be that, ultimately, the need to describe the nature of the Spirit's work in this analogy is even more important than the recognition of Christological common ground. So it is important to note here that the term of this analogy, *lex,* which can be said to *be* Christ, can also, in its culminating form, be said to *be* the grace of the Holy Spirit. So, we have an *analogia legis,* which is also an *analogia Christi,* and perhaps also an *analogia spiritus.* By the power of the Holy Spirit, the human spirit can participate to varying degrees in the knowledge of the eternal law, itself identical in some real sense to God himself.

But a full consideration of an *analogia spiritus* must await further investigation. For now, I propose that we can see in Aquinas's treatise on the law an *analogia legis,* which is established in the eternal law as an *analogia Christi.* In comparison with an *analogia entis,* the *analogia legis* makes clear that both Aquinas and Barth begin in a world in which Christ is the form of the relation between humanity and God.

The natural and human law, on the one hand, and the Divine Law, on the other, remind us, nevertheless, that Aquinas does create distinctions foreign to Barth. Aquinas clearly outlines the possibility for different intensities of participation in this *analogia legis:* some human persons will participate only in the natural and human law; others will participate in the fullness of law, the New Law.[44] One practical strength of Aquinas's position is that, in the context of a pluralistic so-

43. ". . . dicendum promulgation legis naturae est ex hoc ipso quod Deus eam mentibus hominum inseruit naturaliter cognoscendam." *ST* I-II, q. 90, a. 4, ad 1.

44. The group omitted from this taxonomy is that whose members participate in natural law, human law, and the Old Law, but not the New: the Jewish people. For more on that matter, cf. Holly Taylor Coolman, "Christological Torah," *Studies in Jewish-Christian Relations* 5 (2010): CP1-12. http://ejournals.bc.edu/ojs/index.php/scjr/article/view/1557/1410.

ciety, in which Christians work together with others for political good, it allows for some account of the work of non-Christians as being, in a relative and limited sense, good. The ability to give such an account seems closely linked to the possibility of real collaboration and not simply cynical maneuvering.

Finally, in the Divine Law, we have the reminder that not only *lex*'s foundation, but also its *telos,* is Christological — and that this Christological reality is ultimately also pneumatological. While this reading of Aquinas does note important differences between him and Barth, perhaps it also offers us assistance in better understanding Aquinas in such a way as to indicate genuine points of convergence between the two.

Epilogue: Musings on the Role Played by Philosophy in Ecumenical Dialogue

Bruce L. McCormack

Confronted by the Roman Catholic commitment to the irreformability of dogma, it is all too easy for modern Protestant theologians to doubt whether common ground for the kind of ecumenical dialogue that leads to real convergence at a fundamental level could ever take place. After all, "irreformability" might well suggest that the teachings of the church are somehow "finished products" — requiring only repetition (with a bit of explanation) to be fully honored. And yet, most of the Catholic theologians I know (including even some traditional Thomists among them) do not function in this way. Many believe that the Holy Spirit is still leading their church into greater depths of understanding of the truths embodied in officially proclaimed dogma and that Catholic "orthodoxy" is, therefore, a living and vibrant tradition rather than a "dead" one. Doctrinal development is indeed possible even in the area of authoritative teaching, however true it may be that any legitimate development will necessarily be governed by that teaching. On the face of it, such an understanding of the irreformability of dogma need not be an impediment to modern Protestant engagement in a search for common understanding and shared belief.

But to say only this much is to operate at a much too formal level. Catholics and Protestants may both affirm in theory that the experimental work of individual theologians can contribute to advances in a church's understanding of its own teachings. In practice, however, fundamental differences may still remain with regard to what constitutes fidelity to authoritative teaching, differences that have their root — in part, at least — in conflicting answers given to the question of whether fidelity requires unreserved adoption of the linguistic categories employed in authoritative teaching. Modern Protestants will inevitably point out that the concepts employed in the dogmas (concepts like essence, Persons, natures, and hypostases) were borrowed from philosophies that were available to the bishops attending those councils — and to the theologians whose writings were most influential upon their deliberations. The question then becomes pressing: Are we bound to employ these categories *and these alone* (thereby also granting a certain degree of authority to the philosophies to which appeal was made by the ancients)? Or are we free to identify the theological values that the fathers sought to clarify and to translate the categories employed to bring those values to expression in a more modern philosophical idiom? Modern Protestants will tend to opt for the latter possibility; traditional Catholics will, in all likelihood, incline themselves to the former. But that is not the end of the story.

Most modern Protestant theologians (including a good many "Barthians") would agree that philosophies perform a much-needed service in relation to Christian theology. Philosophies provide a language with whose help one can come to a better understanding of theological subject-matters. In doing so, they also provide important aids in communicating those subject-matters to thoughtful people in one's own day. But no one philosophy can lay claim to being binding upon Christian reflection. The answers given by philosophers to the questions with which they deal can at most be a *parable* of the answers Christian theologians must give to the theological questions with which they are concerned — and a parable is never the thing itself. To put it that way is to suggest that no philosophy, no matter how good it is or how influential it has been, can be granted control of the conditions under which theology is done. Certainly, that was the conviction of Karl Barth — which helps us to understand why the influence of Kant on his early theology or of Hegel on his later theology could never become *principled*. Theology, for Barth, is critical reflection upon the church's talk of God, an attempt to measure the adequacy of that talk to its "object" (God's self-revelation in Jesus Christ). Given the nature of this "object" (its non-givenness precisely in its givenness as a Christological state-of-affairs), no language — not even biblical language — can be *completely* responsible to its object. It follows that theology consists in large measure in a critical testing of its borrowed language (recognizing that even the language of Scripture is "borrowed" in the sense of being culturally embedded). And no philosophy can be exempted from such critical scrutiny, not even if done by Kant or Hegel.[1]

But, then, a fair number of Catholics will be quick to point out that Thomas was no slave to the thinking of Aristotle either. He made use of Aristotle's thought in his efforts to explain theological subject-matters but at no point did he allow the Philosopher to dominate or control his thinking about theological questions. But if all of this be true, then the philosophies drawn upon in the articulation of orthodox Christian opinion ought to be open to negotiation — and with that, the terms employed in the creeds themselves. It should be permissible to ask: Can we say the same thing that was said by authoritative teaching in different words? Even more importantly, perhaps, may we say something different, something new, so long as we do not make ourselves guilty of the historical errors that were identified by the great ecumenical councils?

I quite deliberately lay emphasis here on "historical errors." For all too many of today's self-described "orthodox" theologians (both Catholic and Protestant), it is proving very hard to resist the temptation to turn an ancient heresy into a "type" and to assign to it an expansive meaning that allows it to be applied to theologies not envisioned by the bishops. New proposals have been rejected as "Arian" or "modalist" or "Nestorian" that have, in truth, little or nothing in common with that which the church actually opposed under these headings. Where this happens, the meaning of "orthodoxy" is also cut loose from its historical moorings, making it an answer to questions that were not being asked when first formulated.

Be that as it may, it is clear from the essays contained in this volume that even in areas of ecumenically approved teaching like the doctrines of the Trinity and Christology, the different philosophical resources employed in the attempt to bring theological subject-matters to expression do give rise to theological differences as well. We have also seen that some of these theological differences are not as great as the differences in

---

1. Neither the assumption that the old is better because it is older nor the assumption that the new is better because it is newer is valid. Barth put it this way: "Our one concern must be with the truth itself. . . . The truth itself demands complete openness. From the standpoint of the truth itself, thoroughgoing conservatives are as useless as thoroughgoing modernists. The old will persist and the new will come if they are worthy to do so. And the old will pass and the new will be excluded if they are not." Karl Barth, *Church Dogmatics,* II/2, ed. Geoffrey W. Bromiley and T. F. Torrance (Edinburgh: T. & T. Clark, 1957), p. 648.

philosophical commitments might have led one to expect. Given the negotiable character of the latter commitments, should we not expect and allow room for differing interpretations of shared teachings? And rather than seeking a premature ecumenical agreement that would likely entail the assimilation of the teachings of one's own church to those found in another, should we not enter dialogue with the expectation that the theology that will enable us to confess a common faith does not exist yet — and can only come into existence where representatives of both great communions seek to further develop their own theologies with the questions and concerns of the conversation-partners firmly in mind? What I am suggesting is that what we should be seeking is not ways to adapt ourselves to or simply to adopt the teachings of another church in relation to questions whose form gave rise to the divisions that now exist; we should be asking instead whether it is necessary to continue to put the old questions in precisely the same way. We should allow shared dogmas to continue to provide authoritative answers to old questions, but we must also be open to the possibility that new questions may assume a greater importance today — for both sides participating in a dialogue.

The conference that gave birth to these essays was the third in which I have worked with my co-editor, Thomas Joseph White, O.P. The first took place at Providence College in 2007; the second at the John Paul II Cultural Center in 2008.[2] I have learned to value highly my friend's erudition, his keen mind and servant's heart, and, above all, his willingness to engage experimental projects like my own in a spirit of charity and friendship. I have also learned (through engagement with the range of Catholic theologians who have contributed to these projects) that the best way in which I can be "pro-Catholic" is not by ceasing to be Protestant or by asking Catholics to be less Catholic but by committing myself to join with them in shared witness to the gospel of Jesus Christ and by praying for them regularly — and praying not only that God would bless their work as individual theologians but that he would richly bless the Catholic Church they represent, making it stronger spiritually, morally, and theologically for the sake of our shared witness. I am confident that they do the same.

2. See James F. Keating and Thomas Joseph White, O.P., eds., *Divine Impassibility and the Mystery of Human Suffering* (Grand Rapids: Eerdmans, 2009); Thomas Joseph White, O.P., ed., *The Analogy of Being: Invention of the Antichrist or the Wisdom of God?* (Grand Rapids: Eerdmans, 2011).

Bibliography

Works Cited of Thomas Aquinas

Aquinas Against the Averroists: On There Being Only One Intellect. Translated by Ralph McInerny. West Lafayette, IN: Purdue University Press, 1993.

Corpus Thomisticum S. Thomas de Aquino Opera Omnia (Universitatis Studiorum Navarrensis, 2009), available online at: www.corpusthomis ticum.org/iopera.html.

The Division and Methods of the Sciences. Questions V and VI of His Commentary on the De Trinitate of Boethius. Edited by Armand Maurer. Toronto: Pontifical Institute of Mediaeval Studies, 1963.

In duodecim libros Metaphysicorum Aristotelis expositio. Edited by M. R. Cathala and R. M. Spiazzi. Turin and Rome: Marietti, 1964.

In librum Beati Dionysii de divinis nominibus expositio. Edited by C. Pera, P. Caramello, and C. Mazzantini. Taurini-Rome: Marietti, 1950.

Quaestiones disputatae de anima. Edited by B. C. Bazán. Rome and Paris: Commissio Leonina-Éditions Du Cerf, 1996.

Quaestiones disputatae de veritate, Vol. 22, pts. 1-3, of *Sancti Thomae de Aquino opera omnia.* Leonine Edition. Rome: Editori di San Tommaso, 1970-76.

Sancti Thomae Aquinatis Tractatus de unitate intellectus contra Averroistas. Edited by Leo Keeler. Rome: Pontifical Gregorian University, 1946.

Summa contra gentiles, 4 vols. Translated by Anton C. Pegis, James F. Anderson, Vernon J. Bourke, and Charles J. O'Neil. Notre Dame and London: University of Notre Dame Press, 1975 [1955-57].

Summa contra gentiles, Editio Leonina Manualis. Rome: Marietti, 1934.

Summa Theologica, 5 vols. Translated by English Dominican Province. New York: Benziger, 1947 [1920].

Summa Theologica, 60 vols. Edited by Thomas Gilby. London: Eyre & Spottis-woode/New York: McGraw-Hill, 1964-73.

Super Epistolam ad Philippenses Lectura, in *Super Epistolas S. Pauli Lectura* II. Edited by Raphael Cai. Rome: Marietti, 1953.

Super Evangelium S. Matthaei Lectura. Edited by Raphael Cai. Rome: Marietti, 1951.

Super Evangelium S. Ioannis Lectura. Edited by Raphael Cai. Rome: Marietti, 1952.

Works Cited of Karl Barth

Ad Limina Apostolorum: An Appraisal of Vatican II. Translated by Keith R. Crim. Richmond, VA: John Knox, 1968.

Die christliche Dogmatik im Entwurf. Edited by Gerhard Sauter. Zürich: Theologischer Verlag Zürich, 1982.

Church Dogmatics, 4 vols. in 13 parts. Translated by G. W. Bromiley and T. F. Torrance. London: T. & T. Clark/New York: Continuum, 2004 [1936-75].

Dogmatics in Outline. Translated by G. T. Thomson. New York: Harper & Row, 1959.

The Epistle to the Romans, 6th ed. Translated by Edwyn C. Hoskins. Oxford: Oxford University Press, 1968.

"Fate and Idea in Theology." In *The Way of Theology in Karl Barth,* edited by Martin Rumscheidt, pp. 25-62. Allison Park, PA: Pickwick, 1986.

The Holy Spirit and the Christian Life. Translated by R. Birch Hoyle. Louisville: Westminster John Knox, 1993.

Kirchliche Dogmatik, 4 vols. in 13 parts. München: C. Kaiser/Zürich: Theologischer Verlag Zürich, 1932-67.

"No! Answer to Emil Brunner." In *Natural Theology: Comprising "Nature and Grace"* by Professor Dr. Emil Brunner and the Reply "No!" by Dr. Karl Barth, translated by Peter Fraenkel. Eugene, OR: Wipf & Stock, 2002.

Unterricht in der christlichen Religion, vol. 1: *Prolegomena,* 1924. Edited by Hannelotte Reiffen. Zürich: Theologischer Verlag Zürich, 1985.

Unterricht in der christlichen Religion, vol. 2: *Die Lehre von Gott/Die Lehre vom Menschen,* 1924-25. Edited by Hinrich Stoevesandt. Zürich: Theologischer Verlag Zürich, 1990.

Unterricht in der christlichen Religion, vol. 3: *Die Lehre von der Versöhnung/Die Lehre von der Erlösung,* 1925/1926. Edited by Hinrich Stoevesandt. Zürich: Theologischer Verlag Zürich, 2003.

Barth, Karl, as recorded in student protocols. "Systematische Seminar im Wintersemester 1928/1929. Thomas von Aquin: *Summa theologiae* (I. Büch)." Unpublished typed manuscript (photocopy). Karl Barth Archive, Basel, Switzerland.

Barth, Karl, and Eduard Thurneysen. *Barth-Thurneysen Briefwechsel,* vol. 2: *1921-1930.* Edited by Eduard Thurneysen. Karl Barth Gesamtausgabe, vol. 5: Briefe. Zürich: Theologischer Verlag Zürich, 1974.

Select Other Works Cited

Adams, Robert Merrihew. *Finite and Infinite Goods: A Framework for Ethics.* Oxford: Oxford University Press, 2002.

Antweiler, Anton. *Die Anfangslosigkeit der Welt nach Thomas von Aquin und Kant.* Trier: Paulinus-Verlag, 1961.

Ashley, Benedict. *The Way toward Wisdom: An Interdisciplinary and Intercultural Introduction to Metaphysics.* Notre Dame: Notre Dame University Press, 2006.

Ayres, Lewis. *Nicaea and Its Legacy: An Approach to Fourth-Century Trinitarian Theology.* Oxford: Oxford University Press, 2004.

Balthasar, Hans Urs von. *The Glory of the Lord: A Theological Aesthetics.* 7 vols. Translated by Erasmo Leiva-Merikakis, Oliver Davies, et al. San Francisco: Ignatius Press, 1983-91.

———. *The Moment of Christian Witness.* Translated by R. Beckley. San Francisco: Ignatius Press, 1994.

———. *Mysterium Paschale.* Edinburgh: T. & T. Clark, 1990.

———. *Theo-Drama: Theological Dramatic Theory.* 5 vols. Translated by Graham Harrison. San Francisco: Ignatius Press, 1988-98.

———. *Theo-Logic.* 3 vols. Translated by A. J. Walker. San Francisco: Ignatius Press, 2000-2005.

———. *The Theology of Karl Barth.* Translated by Edward Oakes. San Francisco: Ignatius Press, 1992.

———. *The Theology of Karl Barth.* Translated by John Drury. New York: Holt, Reinhart & Winston, 1971.

Balthasar, Hans Urs von, and Adrienne von Speyr. *To the Heart of the Mystery of Redemption.* San Francisco: Ignatius Press, 2010.

Bayer, Oswald. *Theology the Lutheran Way.* Translated by Jeffrey G. Silcock and Mark C. Mattes. Grand Rapids: Eerdmans, 2007.

Berger, David. "Die letzte Schrift des heiligen Thomas von Aquin." *Forum Katholische Theologie* 14 (1998): 221-330.

Boethius of Dacia. *On the Supreme Good. On the Eternity of the World. On Dreams.* Edited and translated by John F. Wippel. Toronto: Pontifical Institute of Mediaeval Studies, 1987.

Boulnois, Olivier. *Être et representation. Une généalogie de la métaphysique modern à l'èpoche de Duns Scot (XIIIe-XIVe siècle).* Paris: Presses Universitaires de France, 1999.

————. "Quand commence l'ontothéologie? Aristote, Thomas d'Aquin et Duns Scot." *Revue Thomiste* 95 (1995): 85-105.

Boyle, Leonard E., O.P. "The Setting of the *Summa Theologiae* of St. Thomas — Revisited." In *The Ethics of Aquinas,* edited by Stephen J. Pope, pp. 1-16. Washington, DC: Georgetown University Press, 2002.

Brady, Ignatius. "John Pecham and the Background of Aquinas's *De Aeternitate Mundi.*" In *St. Thomas Aquinas 1274-1974: Commemorative Studies,* 2 vols., edited by Armand Maurer et al., vol. 2, pp. 141-78. Toronto: Pontifical Institute of Mediaeval Studies, 1974.

Brague, Rémi. "Inklusion und Verdauung. Zwei Modelle kultureller Aneignung." In *Hermeneutische Wege: Hans-Georg Gadamer zum Hundertsten,* edited by G. Figal et al. Tübingen: Mohr, 2000.

————. *The Legend of the Middle Ages: Philosophical Explorations of Medieval Christianity, Judaism, and Islam.* Translated by Lydia G. Cochrane. Chicago: University of Chicago Press, 2011.

Brandom, Robert. "Freedom and Constraint by Norms." In *Hermeneutics and Praxis,* edited by Robert Hollinger, pp. 173-91. Notre Dame: University of Notre Dame Press, 1985.

————. *Tales of the Mighty Dead: Historical Essays in the Metaphysics of Intentionality.* Cambridge, MA: Harvard University Press, 2002.

Brewbaker, William S., III. "The Bible as a Law Book? Thomas Aquinas on the Juridical Uses of Scripture." http://www.lawandreligion.com/sites/lawandreligion.com/files/Vol%2012%20F10-2%20Brewbaker_0.pdf.

Brock, Stephen. *Action and Conduct: Thomas Aquinas and the Theory of Action.* London: T. & T. Clark, 2000.

Bouillard, Henri. *Conversion et grâce chez saint Thomas d'Aquin.* Paris: Aubier, 1944.

Buber, Martin. *Die Erzählungen der Chassidim.* Zürich: Manesse, 1949.

Burns, J. Patout. *The Development of Augustine's Doctrine of Operative Grace.* Paris: Études Augustiennes, 1980.

Burrell, David. "Analogy, Creation, and Theological Language." In *The Theology of Thomas Aquinas,* edited by Rik van Nieuwenhove and Joseph Wawrykow, pp. 77-98. Notre Dame: University of Notre Dame Press, 2005.

————. *Aquinas: God and Action.* Notre Dame: University of Notre Dame Press/ London: Routledge & Kegan Paul, 1979.

Busch, Eberhard. *Karl Barth und die Pietisten. Die Pietismuskritik des jungen Karl Barth und ihre Erwiderung.* München: Chr. Kaiser Verlag, 1978.

Calvin, John. *Institutes of the Christian Religion,* 2 vols. Translated by Ford Lewis Battles. Philadelphia: Westminster, 1960.

Cassian, John. *The Conferences,* Ancient Christian Writers 57. Translated and annotated by Boniface Ramsey, O.P. New York: Newman Press, 1997.

Chenu, Marie-Dominique. *Toward Understanding Saint Thomas*. Translated by A.-M. Landry, O.P., and D. Hughes, O.P. Chicago: Henry Regnery, 1964.

Cohen, Jeremy. *Living Letters of the Law: Ideas of the Jew in Medieval Christianity*. Berkeley: University of California Press, 1999.

Coolman, Holly Taylor. "Christological Torah." *Studies in Jewish-Christian Relations* 5 (2010): CP1-12. http://ejournals.bc.edu/ojs/index.php/scjr/article/view/1557/1410.

Courtenay, William J. *Covenant and Causality in Medieval Thought*. London: Variorum Reprints, 1984.

Courtine, Jean François. "Métaphysique et ontothéologie." In *La Métaphysique,* edited by J. M. Narbonne and L. Langlois, pp. 137-58. Paris and Quebec: J. Vrin and Les Presses de l'Université de Laval, 1999.

Daguet, Francois. *Finis Omnium Ecclesia. Théologie du dessein divin chez Thomas d'Aquin* Paris: Vrin, 2003.

Dales, Richard C. *Medieval Discussions of the Eternity of the World*. Leiden: E. J. Brill, 1990.

Dales, Richard C., and Omar Argerami, eds. *Medieval Latin Texts on the Eternity of the World*. Leiden: E. J. Brill, 1991.

Daniélou, Jean. *Why the Church?* Translated by M. de Lange. Chicago: Franciscan Herald Press, 1975.

Dewan, Lawrence. *Form and Being: Studies in Thomistic Metaphysics*. Washington, DC: Catholic University of America Press, 2006.

Di Noia, J. A. *The Diversity of Religion: A Christian Perspective*. Washington, DC: Catholic University of America Press, 1992.

Dondaine, Antoine. "La Lettre de Saint Thomas à l'Abbé du Montcassin." In *St. Thomas Aquinas 1274-1974: Commemorative Studies*, 2 vols., edited by Armand Maurer et al., vol. 1, pp. 87-108. Toronto: Pontifical Institute of Mediaeval Studies, 1974.

Ebeling, Gerhard. "Existenz zwischen Gott und Gott. Ein Beitrag zur Frage nach der Existenz Gottes." In *Wort und Glaube,* vol. 2: *Beiträge zur Fundamentaltheologie und zur Lehre von Gott,* pp. 257-86. Tübingen: Mohr Siebeck, 1969.

————. "Über den hermeneutischen Ort der Gotteslehre bei Petrus Lombardus und Thomas von Aquin." In *Wort und Glaube,* vol. 2: *Beiträge zur Fundamentaltheologie und zur Lehre von Gott,* pp. 209-56. Tübingen: Mohr Siebeck, 1969.

Eliot, T. S. "Dante." In *Selected Essays, 1917-1932*. Boston: Houghton Mifflin, 1950.

Emery, Gilles, O.P. "*Theologia* and *Dispensatio:* The Centrality of the Divine Missions in Teaching St. Thomas's Trinitarian Theology." *The Thomist* 74 (2010): 515-61.

————. *The Trinitarian Theology of Saint Thomas Aquinas*. Translated by Francesca Murphy. Oxford: Oxford University Press, 2007.

————. *Trinity, Church, and the Human Person: Thomistic Essays*. Naples, FL: Ave Maria Press, 2007.

————. *Trinity in Aquinas*. Ann Arbor, MI: Sapientia Press, 2003.

Fabro, Cornelio. *Participation et causalité selon saint Thomas d'Aquin*. Paris and Louvain: Publications Universitaires de Louvain, 1961.

Feingold, Lawrence. *The Natural Desire to See God according to St. Thomas Aquinas and His Interpreters*. Naples, FL: Sapientia Press, 2010.

Feser, Edward. *Aquinas*. Oxford: Oneworld, 2009.

Gilson, Étienne. *Being and Some Philosophers*. Toronto: Pontifical Institute of Mediaeval Studies, 1952.

————. *Elements of Christian Philosophy*. Garden City, NY: Doubleday, 1960.

Goodman, Nelson. "Seven Strictures on Similarity." In *Experience and Theory*, edited by L. Foster, pp. 19-29. Amherst: University of Massachusetts Press, 1970.

Gregory of Nyssa. *An Answer to Ablabius: That We Should Not Think of Saying There Are Three Gods*. Translated by Cyril Richardson. In *Christology of the Later Fathers*, edited by Edward R. Hardy. Philadelphia: Westminster, 1954.

Gundlach, Theis. *Selbstbegrenzung Gottes und die Autonomie des Menschen*. Frankfurt am Main: Peter Lang, 1992.

Gustav, Siewerth. *Der Thomismus als Identitätssystem*. Frankfurt: Verlag Schulte-Bulmke, 1939.

Hall, Pamela. *Narrative and the Natural Law*. Notre Dame: University of Notre Dame Press, 1994.

Hamm, Berndt. *Promissio, Pactum, Ordinatio. Freiheit und Selbstbindung Gottes in der scholastischen Gnadenlehre*. Tübingen: Mohr Siebeck, 1977.

Harnack, Adolf von. *Das Evangelium vom fremden Gott. Eine Monographie zur Geschichte der Grundlegung der katholischen Kirche. Neue Studien zu Marcion*. Darmstadt: Wissenschaftliche Buchgesellschaft, 1985.

————. *Marcion. Der moderne Gläubige des 2. Jahrhunderts, der erste Reformator*. Berlin: W. de Gruyter, 2003.

Hart, David Bentley. *The Beauty of the Infinite: The Aesthetics of Christian Truth*. Grand Rapids: Eerdmans, 2003.

Hector, Kevin. *Theology without Metaphysics: God, Language, and the Spirit of Recognition*. Cambridge: Cambridge University Press, 2011.

Hegel, G. W. F. *Lectures on the Philosophy of Religion*, vol. 3. Edited by Peter C. Hodgson. Translated by R. F. Brown, P. C. Hodgson, and J. M. Steward. Berkeley: University of California Press, 1985.

————. *Phenomenology of Mind*. Translated by J. B. Baillie. New York: Harper, 1967.

————. *Phenomenology of Spirit*. Translated by A. V. Miller. Oxford: Oxford University Press, 1977.

Hildebrand, Dietrich von. *Ethics*. Chicago: Franciscan Herald Press, 1953.

————. *Transformation in Christ*. Manchester, NH: Sophia Institute Press, 1990.

Hunsinger, George. *Disruptive Grace: Studies in the Theology of Karl Barth*. Grand Rapids: Eerdmans, 2002.

————. "A Tale of Two Simultaneities: Justification and Sanctification in Calvin and Barth." In *Conversing with Barth,* edited by John C. McDowell and Mike Higton, pp. 68-89. Burlington, VT: Ashgate, 2004.

Hütter, Reinhard. "Attending to the Wisdom of God — From Effect to Cause, from Creation to God: A Contemporary *relecture* of the Doctrine of the Analogy of Being according to Thomas Aquinas." In *The Analogy of Being: Invention of the Antichrist or the Wisdom of God?* edited by Thomas Joseph White, O.P., pp. 209-45. Grand Rapids: Eerdmans, 2011.

————. *Dust Bound for Glory: Explorations in the Theology of Thomas Aquinas.* Grand Rapids: Eerdmans, 2012.

Jay, Nancy. *Throughout Your Generations Forever: Sacrifice, Religion, and Paternity.* Chicago: University of Chicago Press, 1992.

Jenson, Robert. "Ipse Pater Non Est Impassibilis." In *Divine Impassibility and the Mystery of Human Suffering,* edited by James F. Keating and Thomas Joseph White, O.P., pp. 117-26. Grand Rapids: Eerdmans, 2009.

————. "Once More the Logos *asarkos.*" *International Journal of Systematic Theology* 13 (2011): 130-33.

————. *Systematic Theology,* vol. 1. Oxford: Oxford University Press, 1997.

Johnson, Keith L. *Karl Barth and the Analogia Entis.* London: T. & T. Clark, 2010.

————. "A Reappraisal of Barth's Theological Development and His Dialogue with Catholicism." *International Journal for Systematic Theology* 14, no. 1 (2012): 3-25.

————. "Reconsidering Barth's Rejection of Przywara's *analogia entis.*" *Modern Theology* 26, no. 4 (2010): 632-50.

Jones, Paul Dafydd. *The Humanity of Christ: Christology in Karl Barth's* Church Dogmatics. London: T. & T. Clark, 2008.

Jordan, Mark. *Rewritten Theology: Aquinas After His Readers.* Malden, MA: Wiley-Blackwell, 2006.

Jüngel, Eberhard. *God as the Mystery of the World.* Translated by Daniel Guder. Grand Rapids: Eerdmans, 1983.

————. *God's Being Is in Becoming: The Trinitarian Being of God in the Theology of Karl Barth.* Translated by John Webster. London: T. & T. Clark, 2004.

————. *Justification: The Heart of the Christian Faith.* Translated by Jeffery F. Cayzer. London: T. & T. Clark, 2006.

Kant, Immanuel. *Critique of Pure Reason.* Translated by N. K. Smith. New York: Macmillan, 1965.

————. *Prolegomena to Any Future Metaphysics.* Translated by P. Carus and J. Ellington. Indianapolis and Cambridge: Hackett, 1977.

Kasper, Walter. *The God of Jesus Christ.* Translated by Matthew J. O'Connell. New York: Crossroad, 1989.

———. *Jesus the Christ.* Translated by V. Green. London: Burns & Oates, 1976.

Keating, Daniel A. "Justification, Sanctification and Divinization in Thomas Aquinas." In *Aquinas on Doctrine: A Critical Introduction,* edited by Thomas G. Weinandy, Daniel A. Keating, and John P. Yocum, pp. 139-58. London: T. & T. Clark, 2004.

Kerr, Fergus. *After Aquinas: Versions of Thomism.* Oxford: Blackwell, 2002.

Küng, Hans. *Christianity: Essence, History and Future.* Translated by J. Bowden. New York: Continuum, 1995.

———. *The Church.* Translated by Ray and Rosaleen Ockenden. New York: Sheed & Ward, 1968.

———. *Infallible? An Inquiry.* Translated by E. Quinn. Garden City, NY: Doubleday, 1971.

———. *Justification: The Doctrine of Karl Barth and a Catholic Reflection.* Translated by Thomas Collins, Edumund E. Tolk, and David Granskou. Philadelphia: Westminster, 1964.

Lane, Anthony N. S. *Justification by Faith in Catholic-Protestant Dialogue.* New York: T. & T. Clark, 2002.

Le Guillou, M.-J. *Christ and Church: A Theology of the Mystery.* Translated by C. Schaldenbrand. New York: Desclée, 1966.

———. *Le mystère du Père. Foi des apôtres, Gnoses actuelles.* Paris: Fayard, 1973.

Leinsle, Ulrich G. *Introduction to Scholastic Theology.* Translated by M. J. Miller. Washington, DC: Catholic University of America Press, 2010.

Levering, Matthew. "Christ, the Trinity, and Predestination: McCormack and Aquinas." In *Trinity and Election in Contemporary Theology,* edited by Michael Dempsey, pp. 244-73. Grand Rapids: Eerdmans, 2011.

———. *Scripture and Metaphysics: Aquinas and the Renewal of Trinitarian Theology.* Oxford: Blackwell, 2004.

Lewis, Thomas. *Freedom and Tradition in Hegel: Reconsidering Anthropology, Ethics, and Religion.* Notre Dame: University of Notre Dame Press, 2005.

Lindbeck, George. *The Nature of Doctrine: Religion and Theology in a Postliberal Age.* Louisville and London: Westminster John Knox, 1984.

Lonergan, Bernard. *De Deo Trino,* vol. 2: *Pars Systematica.* Rome: Pontifical Gregorian University, 1964.

———. *Grace and Freedom: Operative Grace in the Thought of St. Thomas Aquinas.* Edited by J. Patout Burns. London: Darton, Longman & Todd, 1971.

Luther, Martin. *Heidelberg Disputation.* In *Luther's Works,* American Edition, vol. 31, edited by Harold J. Grim. Philadelphia: Fortress Press, 1957.

MacIntyre, Alasdair. *Three Rival Versions of Moral Enquiry: Encyclopaedia, Genealogy, and Tradition.* Notre Dame: Notre Dame University Press, 1991.

Marga, Amy. *Karl Barth's Dialogue with Catholicism in Göttingen and Münster: Its Significance for His Doctrine of God.* Tübingen: Mohr Siebeck, 2009.

Marion, Jean-Luc. "Saint Thomas d'Aquin et l'onto-théo-logie." *Revue Thomiste* 95 (1995): 31-66.

Marius, Jan, and J. Lange van Ravenswaay. *Augustinus totus noster. Das Augustin-verständnis bei Johannes Calvin.* Forschungen zur Kirchen- und Dogmengeschichte, vol. 45. Göttingen: Vandenhoeck & Ruprecht, 1990.

Marshall, Bruce. "Christ the End of Analogy." In *The Analogy of Being: Invention of the Antichrist or the Wisdom of God?* edited by Thomas Joseph White, O.P., pp. 280-313. Grand Rapids: Eerdmans, 2011.

———. "The Dereliction of Christ and the Impassibility of God." In *Divine Impassibility and the Mystery of Human Suffering,* edited by James F. Keating and Thomas Joseph White, O.P., pp. 246-98. Grand Rapids: Eerdmans, 2009.

———. *"Quod Scit Una Uetula:* Aquinas on the Nature of Theology." In *The Theology of Thomas Aquinas,* edited by Rik van Nieuwenhove and Joseph Wawrykow, pp. 1-36. Notre Dame: University of Notre Dame Press, 2005.

———. *Trinity and Truth.* Cambridge: Cambridge University Press, 1999.

———. "The Unity of the Triune God: Reviving an Ancient Question." *The Thomist* 74 (2010): 1-32.

Maspero, Giulio. *Trinity and Man: Gregory of Nyssa's* Ad Ablabium. Leiden: E. J. Brill, 2007.

Maury, Pierre. "Election et foi." *Foi et Vie* 37 (1936): 203-23.

McCormack, Bruce L. "*Beatus vir:* Aquinas, Romans 4, and the Role of 'Reckoning' in Justification." In *Reading Romans with St. Thomas Aquinas,* ed. M. Levering and M. Dauphinais, pp. 216-37. Washington, DC: The Catholic University of America Press, 2012.

———. "Divine Impassibility or Simply Divine Constancy? Implications of Karl Barth's Later Christology for Debates over Impassibility." In *Divine Impassibility and the Mystery of Human Suffering,* edited by James F. Keating and Thomas Joseph White, O.P., pp. 150-86. Grand Rapids: Eerdmans, 2009.

———. "The Doctrine of the Trinity after Barth: An Attempt to Reconstruct Barth's Doctrine in the Light of His Later Christology." In *Trinitarian Theology After Barth,* edited by Myk Habets and Phillip Tolliday, pp. 87-118. Eugene, OR: Pickwick, 2011.

———. "God *Is* His Decision: The Jüngel-Gollwitzer 'Debate' Revisited." In *Theology as Conversation: The Significance of Dialogue in Historical and Contemporary Theology (A Festschrift for Daniel L. Migliore),* edited by Bruce L. McCormack and Kimlyn J. Bender, pp. 48-66. Grand Rapids: Eerdmans, 2009.

———. "Grace and Being: The Role of God's Gracious Election in Karl Barth's

Theological Ontology." In *The Cambridge Companion to Karl Barth,* edited by John Webster, pp. 92-110. Cambridge: Cambridge University Press, 2000.

——. *"Justitia Aliena:* Karl Barth in Conversation with the Evangelical Doctrine of Imputed Righteousness." In *Justification in Perspective: Historical Developments and Contemporary Challenges,* edited by Bruce L. McCormack, pp. 167-96. Grand Rapids: Baker Academic, 2006.

——. "Karl Barth's Christology as a Resource for a Reformed Version of Kenoticism." *International Journal of Systematic Theology* 8 (2006): 243-51.

——. *Karl Barth's Critically Realistic Dialectical Theology: Its Genesis and Development, 1909-1936.* New York: Oxford University Press, 1995.

——. "Karl Barth's Version of an 'Analogy of Being': A Dialectical No and Yes to Roman Catholicism." In *Analogy of Being: Invention of the Antichrist or the Wisdom of God?* edited by Thomas Joseph White, O.P., pp. 88-144. Grand Rapids: Eerdmans, 2011.

——. "The Lord and Giver of Life: A 'Barthian' Defense of the *Filioque."* In *Rethinking Trinitarian Theology: Disputed Questions and Contemporary Issues in Trinitarian Theology,* edited by Giulio Maspero and Robert J. Wozniak, pp. 105-45. London: T. & T. Clark, 2012.

——. *Orthodox and Modern: Studies in the Theology of Karl Barth.* Grand Rapids: Baker Academic, 2008.

——. "Seek God Where He May Be Found: A Response to Edwin Chr. van Driel." *Scottish Journal of Theology* 60 (2007): 62-79.

——. "Trinity and Election: A Progress Report." In *Ontmoetingen — Tijdgenoten en Getuigen. Studies aangeboden aan Gerrit Neven,* edited by Rinse Reeling Brouwer, Akke van der Kooi, and Volker Küster, pp. 14-35. Kampen: Kok, 2009.

McInerny, Ralph. *Praeambula Fidei: Thomism and the God of the Philosophers.* Washington, DC: Catholic University of America Press, 2006.

McKenny, Gerald. *The Analogy of Grace: Karl Barth's Moral Theology.* Oxford: Oxford University Press, 2010.

Milbank, John. *The Word Made Strange: Theology, Language, Culture.* Oxford: Blackwell, 1997.

Milbank, John, and Catherine Pickstock, *Truth in Aquinas.* London: Routledge, 2000.

Moltmann, Jürgen. *The Crucified God.* Translated by R. A. Wilson and John Bowden. New York: Harper & Row, 1974.

Moreland, Anna Bonta. *Known by Nature: Thomas Aquinas on Natural Knowledge of God.* New York: Crossroad, 2010.

Morerod, Charles. *Ecumenism and Philosophy: Philosophical Questions for a Renewal of Dialogue.* Translated by Therese C. Scarpelli. Ann Arbor, MI: Sapientia Press, 2006.

Mostert, Walter. "Glaube und Trauer: Zur Frage der Wahrheitserkenntnis bei Thomas von Aquin und Martin Luther." In Walter Mostert, *Glaube und Hermeneutik. Gesammelte Aufsätze,* edited by Pierre Bühler and Gerhard Ebeling, pp. 69-79. Tübingen: Mohr Siebeck, 1998.

———. *Menschwerdung. Eine historische und dogmatische Untersuchung über das Motiv der Inkarnation des Gottessohnes bei Thomas von Aquin.* Tübingen: Mohr, 1978.

Neder, Adam. *Participation in Christ: An Entry into Karl Barth's* Church Dogmatics. Louisville: Westminster John Knox, 2009.

Nietzsche, Friedrich. *The Genealogy of Morals.* Translated by Walter Kaufmann. New York: Vintage, 1967.

Nimmo, Paul. *Being in Action: The Theological Shape of Barth's Ethical Vision.* London: T. & T. Clark, 2011 [2007].

Oliva, Adriano. *Les débuts de l'enseignement de Thomas d'Aquin et sa conception de la Sacra Doctrina.* Paris: Vrin, 2006.

O'Rourke, Fran. *Pseudo-Dionysius and the Metaphysics of Aquinas.* Leiden and New York: E. J. Brill, 1992.

Pannenberg, Wolfhart. *Analogie und Offenbarung. Eine kritische Untersuchung zur Geschichte des Analogiebegriffes in der Lehre von der Gotteserkenntnis.* Göttingen: Vandenhoeck & Ruprecht, 2007.

———. *Systematic Theology,* vol. 2. Translated by Geoffrey W. Bromiley. Grand Rapid: Eerdmans, 1994.

Pinkard, Terry. *German Philosophy 1760-1860: The Legacy of Idealism.* Cambridge: Cambridge University Press, 2002.

Rahner, Karl. *The Trinity.* Translated by Joseph Donceel. London: Herder & Herder, 1970.

Ratzinger, Joseph. *Eschatology, Death and Eternal Life.* Translated by Michael Waldstein and Aiden Nichols, O.P. Washington, DC: Catholic University of America Press, 1988.

———. *The God of Jesus Christ: Meditations on the Triune God.* Translated by Brian McNeil. San Francisco: Ignatius Press, 2008.

———. *Principles of Catholic Theology: Building Stones for a Fundamental Theology.* Translated by Mary Frances McCarthy, S.N.D. San Francisco: Ignatius Press, 1987.

RB 1980: The Rule of St. Benedict in Latin and English with Notes. Edited by Timothy Fry, O.S.B. Translated by Timothy Horner, Marian Larmann, et al. Collegeville, MN: Liturgical Press, 1981.

Richard, Jay Wesley. "Barth on the Divine 'Conscription' of Language." *Heythrop Journal* 38, no. 3 (1997): 247-66.

Ricoeur, Paul. "Welches neue Ethos für Europa?" In *Europa imaginieren,* edited by Peter Koslowski, pp. 108-22. Berlin: Springer, 1992.

Rocca, Gregory P., O.P. *Speaking the Incomprehensible God.* Washington, DC: Catholic University of America Press, 2004.

Rogers, Eugene F. "How the Virtues of the Interpreter Presuppose and Perfect Hermeneutics." *Journal of Religion* (1996): 64-81.

—————. *Thomas Aquinas and Karl Barth: Sacred Doctrine and the Natural Knowledge of God.* Notre Dame: University of Notre Dame Press, 1995.

Rose, Matthew. *Ethics with Barth: God, Metaphysics, and Morals.* Farnham, UK: Ashgate, 2010.

Schelling, F. W. J. *Philosophie der Offenbarung.* Edited by Manfred Frank. Frankfurt am Main: Suhrkamp Verlag, 1977.

Schenk, Richard, O.P. "From Providence to Grace: Thomas Aquinas and the Platonisms of the Mid-Thirteenth Century." *Nova et Vetera,* English Edition, 3 (2005): 307-20.

Schillebeeckx, Edward. *Christ: The Experience of Jesus as Lord.* Translated by J. Bowden. New York: Crossroad, 1981.

—————. *God and the Future of Man.* Translated by N. Smith. New York: Sheed & Ward, 1968.

—————. *Jesus: An Experiment in Christology.* Translated by H. Hoskins. New York: Crossroad, 1979.

—————. *Ministry: Leadership in the Community of Jesus Christ.* Translated by J. Bowden. New York: Crossroad, 1981.

Schönberger, Rolf. "Der Disput über die Ewigkeit der Welt." In *Über die Ewigkeit der Welt. Bonaventura, Thomas von Aquin, Boethius von Dacien,* edited by Peter Nickl. Frankfurt am Main: Klostermann, 2000.

Schweitzer, Albert. *The Quest of the Historical Jesus: A Critical Study of Its Progress from Reimarus to Wrede.* Translated by William Montgomery. London: A. & C. Black, 1910.

Sherwin, Michael. *By Knowledge and by Love: Charity and Knowledge in the Moral Theology of St. Thomas Aquinas.* Washington, DC: Catholic University of America Press, 2005.

Söhngen, Gottlieb. "Analogia Fidei: Gottähnlichkeit allein aus Glauben?" *Catholica* 3, no. 3 (1934): 113-36.

Sokolowski, Robert. *Eucharistic Presence: A Study in the Theology of Disclosure.* Washington, DC: Catholic University of America Press, 1994.

—————. "Formal and Material Causality in Science." *American Catholic Philosophical Quarterly* 69 (1995): 57-67.

—————. *Phenomenology of the Human Person.* Cambridge: Cambridge University Press, 2008.

Stanley, Timothy. *Protestant Metaphysics after Karl Barth and Martin Heidegger.* London: SCM Press, 2010.

Stout, Jeffrey. "Adams on the Nature of Obligation." In *Metaphysics and the Good: Themes from the Philosophy of Robert Merrihew Adams,* edited by

S. Newlands and L. M. Jorgensen, pp. 368-87. Oxford: Oxford University Press, 2009.

————. *Democracy and Tradition*. Princeton: Princeton University Press, 2003.

Strawson, Peter. *Freedom and Resentment and Other Essays*. London and New York: Routledge, 2008.

Stumme, Wayne C., ed. *The Gospel of Justification in Christ: Where Does the Church Stand Today?* Grand Rapids: Eerdmans, 2006.

Tavard, George. *Justification: An Ecumenical Study*. Mahwah, NJ: Paulist, 1983.

Torrell, Jean-Pierre, O.P. *Initiation à saint Thomas d'Aquin*. Paris: Cerf, 1993.

————. *Le Verbe Incarné*. Paris: Cerf, 2002.

————. *Saint Thomas Aquinas*, vol. 1: *The Person and His Work*, revised edition. Edited and translated by Robert Royal. Washington, DC: Catholic University of America Press, 2005.

Wawrykow, Joseph. *God's Grace and Human Action: "Merit" in the Theology of Thomas Aquinas*. Notre Dame: University of Notre Dame Press, 1996.

————. "Grace." In *The Theology of Thomas Aquinas*, edited by Rik van Nieuwenhove and Joseph Wawrykow, pp. 192-221. Notre Dame: University of Notre Dame Press, 2005.

————. "Jesus in the Moral Theology of Thomas Aquinas." *Journal of Medieval and Early Modern Studies* 42, no. 1 (2012): 13-33.

————. "'Perseverance' in 13th-Century Theology: The Augustinian Contribution." *Augustinian Studies* 22 (1991): 125-40.

Webster, John. "Article Review: Webster's Response to Alyssa Lyra Pitstick, *Light in Darkness*." *Scottish Journal of Theology* 62 (2009): 204.

————. *Barth's Ethics of Reconciliation*. Cambridge: Cambridge University Press, 1995.

————. "The Church and the Perfection of God." In *The Community of the Word: Toward an Evangelical Ecclesiology*, edited by Mark Husbands and Daniel J. Treier, pp. 75-95. Downers Grove, IL: InterVarsity, 2005.

————. "Perfection and Participation." In *The Analogy of Being: Invention of the Antichrist or the Wisdom of God?* edited by Thomas Joseph White, pp. 379-94. Grand Rapids: Eerdmans, 2011.

————. *Word and Church: Essays in Church Dogmatics*. London: T. & T. Clark, 2006.

Weisheipl, James A. "The Date and Context of Thomas's *De aeternitate mundi*." In *Graceful Reason: Essays Presented to Joseph Owens*, edited by Lloyd Gerson, pp. 239-71. Toronto: Pontifical Institute of Mediaeval Studies, 1983.

————. *Friar Thomas D'Aquino: His Life, Thought, and Work*. Garden City, NY: Doubleday, 1974.

————. "The Meaning of *Sacra Doctrina* in *Summa theologiae* I, q. 1." *The Thomist* 38 (1974): 49-80.

Wengst, Klaus. *Humility: Solidarity of the Humiliated.* Philadelphia: Fortress Press, 1988.

White, Thomas Joseph, O.P. "Dyotheletism and the Instrumental Human Consciousness of Jesus." *Pro Ecclesia* 17, no. 4 (2008): 396-422.

———. "Intra-Trinitarian Obedience and Nicene-Chalcedonian Christology." *Nova et Vetera,* English Edition 6 (2008): 377-402.

———. "The Voluntary Action of the Earthly Christ and the Necessity of the Beatific Vision." *The Thomist* 69 (2005): 497-534.

———. *Wisdom in the Face of Modernity: A Study in Modern Thomistic Natural Theology.* Naples, FL: Sapientia Press, 2009.

Wissink, J. M. B., ed. *The Eternity of the World in the Thought of Thomas Aquinas and His Contemporaries.* Leiden: E. J. Brill, 1990.

Wolterstorff, Nicholas. *Justice: Rights and Wrongs.* Princeton: Princeton University Press, 2008.

Young, Julian. *Heidegger's Later Philosophy.* Cambridge: Cambridge University Press, 2002.

Contributors

JOHN R. BOWLIN is the Rimmer and Ruth de Vries Associate Professor of Reformed Theology and Public Life at Princeton Theological Seminary, Princeton, New Jersey. He is the author of *Contingency and Fortune in Aquinas's Ethics* (Cambridge: Cambridge University Press, 1999) and *On Tolerance and Forbearance: Moral Inquiries Natural and Supernatural* (2012).

HOLLY TAYLOR COOLMAN is Assistant Professor of Theology at Providence College, Providence, Rhode Island. Her doctoral work at Duke University compared the Christological readings of Mosaic law offered by Thomas Aquinas and John Calvin. She has published several articles on the relationship between the Old and New Covenants in the theology of Thomas Aquinas.

ROBERT W. JENSON is senior research fellow at the Center of Theological Inquiry in Princeton, New Jersey. He has been the associate director of the Center for Catholic and Evangelical Theology and the co-editor of its journal *Pro Ecclesia*. He has published numerous books and articles, including his two-volume *Systematic Theology:* volume 1, *The Triune God,* and volume 2, *The Works of God* (Oxford: Oxford University Press, 1997 and 1999).

KEITH L. JOHNSON is Assistant Professor of Theology at Wheaton College, Wheaton, Illinois, where he teaches courses on the thought of Karl Barth and Thomas Aquinas. He is the author of *Karl Barth and the*

Analogia Entis (London: T. & T. Clark, 2010) and of *Thinking After God: The Method and Practice of Theology* (Downers Grove, IL: InterVarsity, 2012).

GUY MANSINI, O.S.B., is a monk of Saint Meinrad Archabbey, Saint Meinrad, Indiana, and Associate Professor of Systematic Theology at the Saint Meinrad School of Theology. He has published numerous articles on Christology and ecclesiology, particularly in *The Thomist* and *Nova et Vetera*. He is the author of *The Word Has Dwelt Among Us: Explorations in Theology* (Naples, FL: Sapientia Press, 2008).

AMY E. MARGA is Associate Professor of Systematic Theology at Luther Seminary, St. Paul, Minnesota. She is the author of *Karl Barth's Dialogue with Catholicism in Göttingen and Münster: Its Significance for His Doctrine of God* (Tübingen: Mohr Siebeck, 2010). She has published several articles on Barth's theology of justification as it relates to both the Lutheran and Catholic theological traditions.

BRUCE L. MCCORMACK is Charles Hodge Professor of Systematic Theology at Princeton Theological Seminary, Princeton, New Jersey. He is the author of *Karl Barth's Critically Realistic Dialectical Theology: Its Genesis and Development, 1909-1936* (New York: Oxford University Press, 1995) and *Orthodox and Modern: Studies in the Theology of Karl Barth* (Grand Rapids: Baker Academic, 2008).

RICHARD SCHENK, O.P., is President of Katholische Universität Eichstätt-Ingolstadt in Eichstätt, Germany. He is author and editor of numerous books in English and German, including *Der Gnade vollendeter Endlichkeit. Zur transzendental-theologischen Auslegung der thomanischen Anthropologie* (Freiburg: Herder, 1989). He has also written numerous articles, many pertaining to contemporary Lutheran-Catholic debates on justification. He was the 2007-8 president of the Academy of Catholic Theology.

JOSEPH P. WAWRYKOW is Associate Professor of Theology at Notre Dame University. He is the author of *God's Grace and Human Action: "Merit" in the Theology of Thomas Aquinas* (Notre Dame: University of Notre Dame Press, 1996) and *The Westminster Handbook to Thomas Aquinas* (Philadelphia: Westminster, 2005). He is the co-editor, with Rik van

Nieuwenhove, of *The Theology of Thomas Aquinas* (Notre Dame: University of Notre Dame Press, 2010).

THOMAS JOSEPH WHITE, O.P., is Director of the Thomistic Institute at the Pontifical Faculty of the Immaculate Conception, Dominican House of Studies, Washington, D.C. He is the author of *Wisdom in the Face of Modernity: A Study in Modern Thomistic Natural Theology* (Naples, FL: Sapientia Press, 2009) and a member of the Pontifical Academy of St. Thomas Aquinas.

Index of Names

Anselm, 71, 178
Aristotle, 7-9, 46, 79, 87, 154, 184, 282
Augustine, 15, 24, 56, 203, 206, 266, 268, 273, 276

Balthasar, Hans Urs von, 3, 17, 22, 32, 96, 164, 169, 185, 188-89, 213-14
Bartmann, Bernhard, 206-9
Brague, Rémi, 53-54
Burrell, David, 15

Calvin, John, 3, 56, 158, 161-62, 175, 177
Chemnitz, Martin, 159
Chenu, Marie-Dominique, 23-24, 31
Congar, Yves, 31

Daniélou, Jean, 32
Dilthey, Wilhelm, 18
Di Noia, Augustine, 14
Dionysius the Areopagite, 3, 15, 56, 60, 173

Ebeling, Gerhard, 57-63
Emery, Gilles, 27, 101-2, 104-5, 111, 124-25

Gadamer, Hans-Georg, 18
Gilson, Étienne, 31-32
Gregory of Nyssa, 89-91, 166, 188

Hegel, G. W. F., 14, 18-20, 37, 48, 160-61, 184, 237-40, 257, 260, 281-82
Heidegger, Martin, 13, 31, 34, 45
Hildebrand, Dietrich von, 82-84
Hunsinger, George, 14

Jay, Nancy, 246
Jüngel, Eberhard, 3, 16, 34, 164

Kant, Immanuel, 13, 31, 59, 62, 112, 184, 239-40, 251, 256, 260, 282
Kasper, Walter, 4, 22, 164, 184
Kerr, Fergus, 15
Küng, Hans, 32, 212-13

Levering, Matthew, 101-3, 106-8, 110, 116, 124
Lewis, C. S., 71-73, 97
Lindbeck, George, 14
Lonergan, Bernard, 96
Luther, Martin, 3, 26, 52, 55-57, 60, 188

MacIntyre, Alasdair, 2, 253
Marshall, Bruce, 14, 72-73, 120n58, 122n61, 123n63
McKenny, Gerry, 257-58
Melanchthon, Philipp, 43
Milbank, John, 15
Moltmann, Jürgen, 22, 164, 172

Index of Names

Newman, John Henry, 54
Nietzsche, Friedrich, 13, 223, 251, 257, 260

Pannenberg, Wolfhart, 3, 22, 164
Przywara, Erich, 34, 213, 224-25

Rahner, Karl, 17, 22, 171
Ratzinger, Joseph, 22, 31, 32-33
Ricoeur, Paul, 55

Schelling, Friedrich W. H., 18, 20, 184
Schillebeeckx, Eduard, 31, 32
Schweitzer, Albert, 19
Sokolowski, Robert, 93, 95-96
Stout, Jeffrey, 242
Strawson, Peter, 93

Thurneysen, Eduard, 99

Webster, John, 125-26
Weiss, Johannes, 19

Index of Subjects